YEAR B ■ 2000

workbook

FOR LECTORS AND GOSPEL READERS

Susan E. Myers

Liturgy Training Publications
1800 North Hermitage Avenue
Chicago, IL 60622-1101
1-800-933-1800
fax 1-800-933-7094
orders@ltp.org

Visit our website at www.ltp.org.

Editor: David A. Lysik
Production editor: Bryan Cones
Cover art: Barbara Simcoe
Interior art: Steve Erspamer, SM
Original book design: Jill Smith
Revised design: Anna Manhart and Jim Mellody-Pizzato
Typesetting: Jim Mellody-Pizzato

Printed in the United States of America by Bawden Printing of Eldridge, Iowa.

ISBN 1-56854-290-9
WL00

CONTENTS

The Author

Susan E. Myers is a doctoral candidate in New Testament and Early Christianity at the University of Notre Dame. She has degrees in theology and biblical studies, as well as experience in parish ministry and teaching. Susan's academic interests lie in all aspects of the beliefs, practices and prayer life of early Christians; her current research in early Christianity is concentrated in the region of eastern Syria. Her previous work with Liturgy Training Publications includes *At Home with the Word* (1997, 1998) and *Pronunciation Guide for the Sunday Lectionary* (1998). Susan brings to the *Workbook for Lectors and Gospel Readers* a knowledge of biblical languages and exegesis, as well as knowledge of and participation in the pastoral and liturgical life of the Christian church.

Dedication

To the women of Saint Benedict's Monastery, Saint Joseph, Minnesota.

INTRODUCTION

The Ministry of Proclaiming the Word of God

You were probably encouraged to become a lector in your parish or community by someone who knows you well and appreciates your love of God, or by someone who has witnessed your skills at public speaking. Or perhaps you volunteered for this ministry, moved by God's Spirit to share your gifts with others. Whatever brought you here, you are now part of the team of those who minister at liturgy. Some ministers have visible positions, such as the music director, the presider or the choir members, while others labor quietly behind the scenes: the members of the liturgy committee and its director, those responsible for the decor and presentation of the worship space, bread bakers, ushers and church maintenance crew members. Even the work of the pastoral ministers—RCIA catechists, religious education instructors, counselors, youth ministers, those involved in sacramental preparation—all comes together in the liturgy, the central event of our life as a church. It is through gathering for prayer and praise that we celebrate who we are as God's people. When we come together for liturgy, we encounter God—in one another, in the sacramental actions (such as baptism or eucharist), and in the proclamation of the word of God.

You have the task of making God present in the liturgy of the word for your community. God has been among us in the past, especially in the person of Jesus. The prologue to the Gospel of John says it best: "In the beginning was the Word, and the Word was with God, and the Word was God. . . . And the Word became flesh and lived among us." The Greek for "word" in this passage is *logos,* which can mean "reason"; it is what goes on in God's "head" and "heart." *Logos* can also mean "word," and that is how it is usually translated in this passage. It is the communication of the thoughts of God.

Jesus is God's word incarnate, but God's word is also spoken through others. God has spoken in the past through leaders and prophets, evangelists, apostles and many others. Today God speaks also through you as you proclaim in the assembly God's word as communicated through the individuals who composed the scriptures.

When the word of God is proclaimed in the assembly, it challenges and comforts, encourages and admonishes. Your task is to proclaim a living Word, not simply words on a page. When we read or hear the scriptures, we become part of the story they tell. We are part of the chosen people of God, struggling to understand God and ourselves, striving to be faithful, repenting when we fail. We are disciples of Jesus, following him and learning from his teachings. We are members of the Christian communities served by the evangelists and letter-writers of the New Testament. The word of God shapes our lives, teaching us, changing us, bringing us into an encounter with God.

In the liturgy, the Christian community depends on you, the lector or gospel reader, to mediate an encounter with God. In order to do this effectively, you must make the text come alive for your listeners. The job of making God present is an awesome responsibility, one that requires commitment and time. But do not worry. The Spirit of God will guide you in your ministry. You have been chosen.

Preparing to Proclaim

You can begin to bring God into your assembly by experiencing God's presence yourself, communicated through the words you are asked to read. Spend time with the selection you will proclaim. Read it several times. Pray about it. Allow God to speak to you through it.

Learn about the reading. The commentaries in this *Workbook* are intended to help you understand something about the purpose of the author who wrote the passage, as well as the historical setting out of which the passage arises. You might wish also to turn to your Bible and read the verses that precede and follow your selection, so that you can better understand its context. It might be helpful as well to read any introductory material in your Bible about the book

from which the selection is taken, or consult a Bible commentary. The more you know about the reading, the more effectively you can share it with others.

Do not worry if the text does not completely make sense to you. Biblical scholars have long argued about the precise meanings of some passages and continue to find new information that adds to our understanding of the text. In addition, do not be alarmed if you find the reading confusing or bothersome. "There is nothing comfortable about the Bible" if we are truly engaged with it, as Thomas Merton has said. Remember that God has communicated this word to fallible human beings who sometimes inserted some of their own interests and biases into the text. Trust that God is bigger than any uncertainty or difficulty you have with the reading. If you are open to the movement of the Spirit of God in your life, you will enable the Spirit to move in your listeners in ways beyond your imaginings.

Preparation to proclaim the word of God ideally takes place in a group setting. Participants, usually other lectors and gospel readers, gather to discuss and summarize the readings, to practice together and to provide practical tips for one another. The sessions are most effective if a skilled leader directs them. If group meetings of lectors are not the norm in your parish, you might want to suggest that a group be formed or offer to organize one yourself. If you are unable to prepare with others, practice individually, but always try to have another person listen to you and offer suggestions at least once.

When you practice, it can be especially enlightening to have yourself videotaped or, if that is not possible, to create an audio tape of the reading. You will learn a great deal about your posture and vocal inflection, your phrasing and your pace by hearing and seeing yourself on tape. Always prepare with the microphone in the church and, if possible, with the same lectionary from which you will be reading. This *Workbook* is not suitable for use in the assembly; an elegantly bound lectionary, carried in procession, is the appropriate choice. Check also with your liturgy director or the presider for any special instructions, such as a choral refrain or other interlude, especially if you are preparing to read on a special feast day.

A microphone amplifies your every sound. It must clearly project your whispers, but not be too loud for forceful proclamation. Know how to adjust the microphone, how far away to stand from it and when to lean forward slightly or back away. Some microphones are very sensitive and should not be approached too closely. Especially avoid the popping of "p" and "b" sounds, or the hissing of "s" and "z" that microphones tend to produce. Practice making these sounds subtly but clearly, so that your congregation will understand you but not be distracted by unwelcome noises. It is important that someone else listen to you and give you feedback when you are practicing with the microphone.

The Proclamation of God's Word

It is natural to approach the task of reading before an assembly with a bit of trepidation. Such nervousness, if controlled, can be to your advantage. God's word is powerful and active, and your energy can be channeled into a more effective proclamation. You are not giving a history lesson or telling a story but proclaiming the movement of God throughout history for the benefit of your listeners. The process of reading the scriptures does include some teaching, but you stand in the dual role of teacher and disciple. Most of all, you stand before your community as a believer. Proclaiming the word involves an active sharing of faith between the reader and the assembly; your community will sense your energy and will communicate back to you its trust in God's fidelity and love.

Despite the power of God's word, many of us adopt a monotone whenever we read before an assembly. Reading the word of God is unlike any other public proclamation, but it requires some of the same skills that are necessary for effective speeches, oral interpretation or debate. For many of us, the time we are most likely to put great expression into our oral reading is when reading children's books to a captive audience. Try adopting some (but not too much) of the inflection and exaggeration of reading to a child in your public proclamation. Although you may feel you are adding too much emphasis and inflection, it probably sounds quite differently to your listeners.

A small minority of people tend to exaggerate when reading in public. Although most of us need to "ham it up" more than might make us comfortable at first, we all need to remember that we are not entertaining. Proclaiming the word of God is a formal task, one requiring dignity and restraint. Avoid anything that might draw attention to you and away from the word you proclaim. This is not a performance but a noble ministry, entrusted to you by God and by your community.

Be careful, then, how you communicate through your body language. Stand erect and hold your head high. Move slowly and deliberately.

Plan your phrasing and know when you will pause. Be certain that you can pronounce all of the words you will read. Enunciate clearly; this is especially important in a church with a great deal of reverberation. If you do stumble while reading, correct yourself and then continue without drawing undue attention to your error. Your composure will allow the dignity of God's word to be retained.

When you approach the microphone, pause and wait for any activity in the assembly to die down. Take a moment to compose yourself. Be sure that you have the attention of your entire congregation before you begin. Proclaim in a strong voice, "A reading from . . ." and then pause. At the end of the reading, be sure you do not swallow "The word [or gospel] of the Lord." Instead, pause before the phrase and then proclaim it as something in which you take great pride. Your community will remind you through their response that they are as involved in this proclamation as you. If returning to your seat, move slowly and with dignity.

Eye contact is essential in a reading before an assembly. If you have practiced the reading well, you will be able to address your congregation directly during important phrases, and glance back at your text during pauses. You might want to keep your finger at the spot from which you are reading so that you do not lose your place, if you can do this without drawing attention to your movements. But remember that this is a reading of God's word, not a speech; there is no need for constant eye contact.

Trying to establish some eye contact can aid in achieving another objective of most readers: slowing down. In order for the members of your community to reflect on what you are proclaiming, they need time to digest the message, not simply to hear the words. Many of us, in our nervousness, rush through a reading and return to our seats hurriedly. In everything you do, act slowly and deliberately, as is fitting for a proclamation of the majestic word of God. Your goal is to capture your congregation's attention so completely that your listeners will be transfixed by your words, experiencing God in their midst. Those who have the habit of reading along in a missalette or worship aid will leave the printed word behind and truly listen, with ears attentive to God's voice speaking through yours.

Your physical appearance should convey your respect for your ministry. Dress comfortably but nicely. Remember that you are not trying to draw attention to yourself, either by dressing shabbily or by trying to turn the liturgy into a fashion show. Before the liturgy begins, check your appearance in a mirror one last time so that you do not have to worry about how you look prior to or during the reading. And know that it is very difficult for your community to concentrate on your words if you have a tuft of hair sticking straight up during your proclamation.

Throughout everything, be confident. Know that you are not only capable of the task before you but have the guidance of the Spirit of God to assist you. If you are focused on God's word and have prepared well, you will be the vehicle through whom God speaks to your community.

The *Workbook for Lectors and Gospel Readers*

This *Workbook* includes the scripture readings for Masses on Sundays and feast days. It does not include the psalm selection, since that is properly sung, not proclaimed in the same manner as the readings.

Be sure that you know if you are to read a shorter version of the passage than that provided here. Shorter options are available for especially long readings, but this *Workbook* always gives the longer form.

The commentaries provided for each reading are intended to provide background information for the minister of the word. Historical and literary information is stressed, as well as suggestions for making your proclamation of the reading most effective. Understanding the reading is a first step toward proclaiming it.

Included to the left of the readings are margin notes with specific suggestions for your proclamation, as well as occasional information that will explain certain words and phrases or ancient practices. Pronunciations of difficult words are provided as well; refer to the pronunciation key that follows this section. Consult the *Pronunciation Guide for the Sunday Lectionary,* available from Liturgy Training Publications, for additional terms that are unfamiliar to you.

The italics evident in the text are intended to indicate an appropriate emphasis on certain words.

Not all of the italicized words are to be stressed to the same degree. Instead, the italics provide a guide to the rhythm of the passage; truly significant words will need to be given added emphasis. The italics are provided as a service to readers, but there are other legitimate ways to convey the meaning of the text. If after careful preparation you find that another pattern of stress seems to communicate more effectively God's word as you understand it, feel free to adopt that pattern.

Since you will be reading from a lectionary and not from this *Workbook,* lectionary numbers are provided for each Sunday or other day in order to facilitate the location of the readings in the lectionary. You may wish to practice with the lectionary from which you will read as well as from this *Workbook,* since the layout of the reading might differ from that printed here. Anything you can do in order to be more confident and self-assured in proclaiming the word will allow you to communicate God's presence more effectively.

Pronunciation Key

Most consonants in the pronunciation key are straightforward: The letter B always represents the sound B and D is always D, and so on. Vowels are more complicated. Note that the long I sound (as in kite or ice) is represented by *ī,* while long A (skate, pray) is represented by *ay.* Long E (beam, marine) is represented by *ee;* long O (boat, coat) is represented by *oh;* long U (sure, secure) is represented by *oo* or *yoo.* Short A (cat), E (bed), I (slim) and O (dot) are represented by *a, e, i* and *o* except in an unstressed syllable, when E and I are signified by *eh* and *ih.* Short U (cup) is represented by *uh.* An asterisk (*) indicates the schwa sound, as in the last syllable of the word "stable." The letters OO and TH can each be pronounced in two ways (as in cool or book; thin or they); underlining differentiates between them. Stress is indicated by the capitalization of the stressed syllable in words of more than one syllable.

bait = bayt
cat = kat
sang = sang
father = FAH-ther
care = kayr
paw = paw
jar = jahr
easy = EE-zee
her = her
let = let
queen = kween
delude = deh-LOOD
when = hwen
ice = īs
if = if
finesse = fih-NES
thin = thin
vision = VIZH-*n
ship = ship
sir = ser
gloat = gloht
cot = kot
noise = noyz
poison = POY-z*n
plow = plow
although = awl-THOH
church = church
fun = fuhn
fur = fer
flute = floot
foot = foot

Bibliography of Recommended Works

Guides for Proclaiming God's Word

Connell, Martin. *Guide to the Revised Lectionary.* Chicago: Liturgy Training Publications, 1998.

Lector Training Program: This is the Word of the Lord. Audio tapes and booklet. Chicago: Liturgy Training Publications, 1988.

The Lector's Ministry: Your Guide to Proclaiming the Word. Mineola, New York: Resurrection Press, 1990.

Lee, Charlotte I., and Frank Galati. *Oral Interpretation,* 9th ed. Boston: Houghton Mifflin, 1997.

Myers, Susan E. *Pronunciation Guide for the Sunday Lectionary.* Chicago: Liturgy Training Publications, 1998.

Proclaiming the Word: Formation for Readers in the Liturgy. Video. Chicago: Liturgy Training Publications, 1994.

Rosser, Aelred R. *A Well-Trained Tongue: Formation in the Ministry of Reader.* Chicago: Liturgy Training Publications, 1996.

———. *A Word That Will Rouse Them: Reflections on the Ministry of Reader.* Chicago: Liturgy Training Publications, 1995.

———. *Guide for Lectors.* Chicago: Liturgy Training Publications, 1998.

General Introductions to the Bible

Brown, Raymond E. *The Critical Meaning of the Bible.* New York: Paulist Press, 1981.

Boadt, Lawrence. *Reading the Old Testament: An Introduction.* New York: Paulist Press, 1984.

Charpentier, Etienne. *How to Read the Old Testament.* New York: Crossroad, 1982.

———. *How to Read the New Testament.* New York: Crossroad, 1982.

Perkins, Pheme. *Reading the New Testament.* New York: Paulist Press, 1988.

Introductions to the Gospel of Mark

Achtemeier, Paul J. *Mark.* Philadelphia: Fortress Press, 1975.

Harrington, Daniel J. *The Gospel according to Mark.* New York: William H. Sadlier, 1983.

Harrington, Wilfrid J. *Mark.* Wilmington, Delaware: Michael Glazier, 1979.

Van Linden, Philip. *The Gospel according to Mark.* Collegeville, Minnesota: The Liturgical Press, 1983.

There is, in a word, nothing
comfortable about the Bible—
until we manage to get so used to it
that we make it comfortable for ourselves.
But then we are perhaps too used to it
and too at home in it.
Let us not be too sure we know the Bible
just because we have learned
not to be astonished at it,
just because we have learned
not to have any problems with it.
Have we perhaps learned at the same time
not really to pay attention to it?
Have we ceased to question the book
and be questioned by it?
Have we ceased to fight it?
Then perhaps our reading is no longer serious.

Thomas Merton

1st SUNDAY OF ADVENT

Lectionary #2

READING I Isaiah 63:16b–17, 19b; 64:2b–7

A reading from the book of the prophet Isaiah.

You, LORD, are our *father*,
our *redeemer* you are named *forever*.
Why do you let us *wander*, O LORD, from your ways,
and *harden* our *hearts* so that we fear you *not*?
Return for the sake of your servants,
the *tribes* of your heritage.

The question is mournful, sad. The pleading of the following verse must be spoken sincerely, as one who yearns for a former time.

Oh, that you would *rend* the heavens and come *down*,
with the *mountains quaking* before you,
while you wrought *awesome* deeds we could not *hope* for,
such as they had not *heard* of from of *old*.
No *ear* has ever *heard*, no *eye* ever *seen*, *any* God but *you*
doing *such deeds* for those who *wait* for him.

There is excitement in these words; speak them with vigor.

Would that you might meet us doing *right*,
that we were *mindful* of you in our ways!

Behold, you are *angry*, and we are *sinful*;
all of us have become like *unclean* people,
all our *good deeds* are like polluted *rags*;
we have all *withered* like leaves,
and our *guilt* carries us away like the *wind*.
There is *none* who calls upon your *name*,
who *rouses* himself to *cling* to you;

Again, there is yearning as the speaker confesses the unfaithfulness of the people.

READING I Although the historical prophet Isaiah was active during the eighth century BCE, chapters 40–66 of the book of Isaiah are from a later date. Someone who admired the prophet wrote in his name during a time of great change, when the Hebrew people were returning from exile in Babylon.

The final chapters of Isaiah are essentially a celebration of the return of the people to their beloved Jerusalem. But today's passage is a lament, a mournful cry raised after seeing the destruction of the city and its Temple.

The reading opens with a reminder that God has chosen this people, and continues with an appeal for God to return after an apparent absence that allowed the devastation of the city and humiliation of the exile to occur. While the author acknowledges that the sinfulness of the people has caused the present state of affairs, God is chastised for appearing not to offer divine protection.

God is presented here as all-powerful, as the master of everything — even of the ability of the people to sin. The present state of the people, resulting from that sinfulness, is clear: They are withered and dying, polluted, in need of forgiveness. The passage closes with a beautiful description of the relationship between these chosen people and their God: They are malleable clay in the hands of the potter.

We too know that we turn from God and bring destruction upon ourselves. We too wonder how God could allow us to make destructive choices. Your task today is to lead your assembly in this prayer, a prayer that changes its mood several times. It opens with confusion and pleading, moves to a recollection of God's wondrous deeds, seems to blame God as it reflects on the

for you have *hidden* your *face* from us
and have *delivered* us up to our *guilt.*

Read the final verse as a statement of hope and peacefulness. The author has declared the present reality — the people have sinned — but concludes with the declaration that God can form them into a vessel of beauty.

Yet, O LORD, you are our *father*;
we are the *clay* and *you* the *potter:*
we are all the *work* of your *hands.*

READING II 1 Corinthians 1:3–9

A reading from the first letter of Saint Paul to the Corinthians.

Open with a peaceful, confident tone. Say "Lord Jesus Christ" slowly and with emphasis on each word.

Brothers and sisters:
Grace to you and *peace* from *God* our Father
and the *Lord Jesus Christ.*

Speak warmly.

I give *thanks* to my God *always* on your account
for the *grace* of God *bestowed* on you in Christ Jesus,
that in him you were *enriched* in *every* way,

Pause, then speak the next line a little more quickly, then pause again.

with *all discourse* and *all knowledge,*
as the *testimony* to Christ was *confirmed* among you,
so that you are *not lacking* in any *spiritual gift*
as you *wait* for the *revelation* of our *Lord Jesus Christ.*

He will keep you *firm* to the end,
irreproachable on the day of our *Lord Jesus Christ.*

Speak these final lines with confidence.

God is *faithful,*
and by *him* you were called to *fellowship* with his *Son,*
Jesus Christ our *Lord.*

present, and closes with an acknowledgment of God's authority and creative power. Allow your voice to shift with the mood, as you offer this lament to God.

READING II In the ancient world there was a standard form of letter-writing, similar to the conventions of a modern business letter. After an introduction that mentioned the author's name and the recipients, the author included a thanksgiving. Paul prefaces his thanksgiving with a blessing ("grace to you and peace"), and adds a Christian character to the letter-writing conventions he adopts.

Although he spends much of this letter to the Corinthian community chastising them for favoring some gifts of the Spirit over others, here Paul points out that God has bestowed on the community a wealth of blessings and gifts. He recognizes that all knowledge, all gifts, come from God, who is the source of all strength.

This beautiful prayer can easily be addressed to your own community. As you read Paul's words of blessing and thanks, reflect on the members of your congregation and speak with a sincere heart. Acknowledge the riches bestowed on individuals and on the community as a whole, and encourage your listeners by reminding them of the strength God provides, a font of power that will keep them pure and blameless and will draw them into unity with Jesus Christ.

GOSPEL During Advent we concentrate on waiting. Just as the world around us seems to speed up and become busier than ever, our liturgies urge

GOSPEL Mark 13:33–37

A reading from the holy gospel according to Mark.

There is urgency in this command. It is central to the reading.

Jesus said to his disciples:
"Be *watchful!* Be *alert!*
You do *not know* when the time will *come.*

"It is like a man traveling *abroad.*
He *leaves* home and places his *servants* in charge,
each with his own work,
and orders the *gatekeeper* to be on the *watch.*
Watch, therefore;
you do not know when the Lord of the house is *coming,*
whether in the *evening,* or at *midnight,*
or at *cockcrow,* or in the *morning.*
May he not come *suddenly* and find you *sleeping.*
What I say to *you,* I say to *all: 'Watch!'"*

Through all the divisions of the night, the disciple is to be ready.

us to slow down and wait. The season of Advent developed out of a genuine eschatological fervor: the hope that Jesus would soon return to inaugurate a new age. Today's gospel reminds us how urgent that hope was for the earliest Christian community. On Jesus' lips is placed an exhortation to watchfulness.

Jesus' words in today's gospel could easily have been spoken to us, approaching the dawn of a new millennium. We depend on predictions — of the weather, of the significance of current events, of economic "indicators" — in order to make decisions about our daily actions, our careers, our plans. Some people even attempt to predict the end of the world. But Jesus says that day cannot be known, any more than we can predict with absolute certainty the day of our own deaths. Only God knows when we will be called to judgment.

And so Jesus warns us to be prepared always, to live as though each day might be the last. That does not require sitting on a mountaintop or irresponsibly dropping everything to focus on the approaching end. It does mean living expectantly, always aware that time is a gift over which humans have no real control. We cannot know when the end will come — whether the end of the world or the end of our individual lives — so we wait and hope, living active lives, but lives characterized by expectant watching, waiting and listening.

Proclaim this gospel as a call to be an Advent people, a people longing for the Christ to come and preparing for that reality, whatever form it may take.

2ND SUNDAY OF ADVENT

Lectionary #5

READING I Isaiah 40:1–5, 9–11

A reading from the book of the prophet Isaiah.

Speak with warmth and tenderness.

Comfort, give *comfort* to my people,
says your God.
Speak *tenderly* to Jerusalem, and *proclaim* to her
that her *service* is at an *end*,
her *guilt* is *expiated*;
indeed, she has *received* from the hand of the LORD
double for all her *sins*.

expiated = EK-spee-ay-t*d

The speaker and mood shift. Pause before beginning this section.

A voice cries *out:*
In the *desert prepare* the *way* of the *LORD!*
Make *straight* in the *wasteland* a highway for our *God!*
Every *valley* shall be filled *in*,
every *mountain* and *hill* shall be made *low*;
the *rugged* land shall be made a *plain*,
the *rough* country, a broad *valley*.
Then the *glory* of the *LORD* shall be *revealed*,
and *all* people shall see it *together*;
for the *mouth* of the *LORD* has *spoken*.

Pause again. Continue with enthusiasm. Zion is another name for Jerusalem.

Go *up* on to a high *mountain*,
Zion, herald of *glad tidings*;
cry out at the *top* of your *voice*,
Jerusalem, herald of *good news!*

READING I The beautiful message of comfort and hope in today's reading is taken from a section of the book of Isaiah called Second Isaiah. This second part was written approximately 150 years after the first 39 chapters, which carry the message of the historical prophet Isaiah himself. The Hebrew people have been in exile in Babylon, an exile that will soon end and allow them to return to their beloved Jerusalem. Captivity is presented as a punishment for wrongdoing, but the penalty has been paid and the promises of God abound.

The passage depicts the anticipated return as another Exodus through the desert, in which God will lead the people through the wasteland to the mountain of God in Jerusalem. Just as a red carpet is laid out for a person of honor, so also is a path prepared through the desert for God, whose journey will provide a display of divine glory for all the world to witness.

Not only will all people recognize God's greatness, but the very city of Jerusalem will sing God's praises. God is both a powerful ruler and a gentle shepherd, gathering the lambs and holding them closely.

This reading is both a joy and a challenge to proclaim. The mood shifts from comfort and gentleness, to joyful proclamation of God's glory and might, and back again to profound tenderness. Just as often, the speaker shifts from God in the heavenly assembly to a herald proclaiming God's coming. The herald calls on Jerusalem to alert the other cities of Judah to God's presence. Finally, Jerusalem itself describes the divine shepherd, who tenderly cares for the city and the "flock" that inhabits it.

Allow your voice to shift from warmth to conviction to tenderness. Challenge your

Fear *not* to *cry out*
and say to the cities of *Judah:*
Here is your *God!*

Pause before proceeding.

Here comes with *power*
the *Lord* GOD,
who *rules* by his *strong arm;*
here is his reward *with* him,
his *recompense before* him.

Again the mood shifts. Let your voice become quiet and gentle.

Like a *shepherd* he *feeds* his *flock;*
in his *arms* he gathers the *lambs,*
carrying them in his *bosom,*
and leading the *ewes* with *care.*

READING II 2 Peter 3:8–14

A reading from the second letter of Saint Peter.

Do *not ignore* this one fact, beloved,
that with the *Lord one day* is like a *thousand years*
and a *thousand years* like *one day.*
The Lord does not *delay* his promise, as *some* regard "delay,"
but he is *patient* with you,
not wishing that any should *perish*
but that *all* should come to *repentance.*

Speak these words with urgency and a bit of terror.

But the *day* of the *Lord* will come like a *thief,*
and then the *heavens* will pass *away* with a mighty *roar*
and the *elements* will be *dissolved* by *fire,*
and the *earth* and everything *done* on it will be found *out.*

community to recognize both the glory of God and the tender care God lavishes upon them. The message is indeed comforting: God is great, protecting the chosen people; God is good, loving and providing for all who trust in the care of the Lord.

READING II **When Jesus did not immediately return as the early Christian community expected, some began to claim that there was no validity to the expectation. The second letter of Peter refutes this attitude and associates it with those who lead lives of debauchery and licentiousness. The opening lines of today's passage address the reason for the apparent delay of Jesus' second coming: Time, which may appear to pass slowly or quickly for humans, is understood in a totally different way by God. In fact, God is hoping that an increase in the available time before the end will allow more people to recognize their sinfulness and repent, and thus be included in the welcome judgment of the world.**

Using many of the spectacular images of apocalyptic literature (a loud noise and blazing heavens), the author indicates much the same message spoken by Jesus in last Sunday's gospel: No one can know when the day of the Lord will come, so be prepared. In contrast to the ungodly lives of the author's opponents, the members of the community are to live lives of holiness and peace. The second coming of Jesus, denied by those under criticism, is to be eagerly welcomed by the recipients of the letter. Although they

Pause briefly before continuing. The sentence is long; read each phrase as a unit, but be careful not to break up the unity of the sentence. Raise your voice with the words "to be" (as though a question ends here), and read the rest of the sentence as an answer to the question.

Proceed with a voice filled with hope and increasing gentleness.

Since *everything* is to be *dissolved* in this way,
what sort of *persons* ought you to *be*,
conducting yourselves in *holiness* and *devotion*,
waiting for and *hastening* the *coming* of the *day* of *God*,
because of which the *heavens* will be *dissolved* in *flames*
and the *elements* melted by *fire.*
But according to *his promise*
we await *new* heavens and a *new* earth
in which *righteousness* dwells.

Therefore, beloved, since you *await* these things,
be *eager* to be found without *spot* or *blemish* before him, at *peace.*

GOSPEL Mark 1:1–8

A reading from the holy gospel according to Mark.

This sounds much like the introduction that precedes it ("A reading from . . ."). Pause more than usual before beginning this line. Pause again before proceeding.

The beginning of the *gospel* of Jesus *Christ*, the Son of *God.*

As it is written in *Isaiah* the prophet:
"*Behold*, I am sending my *messenger ahead* of you;
he will *prepare* your *way.*
A *voice* of one crying out in the *desert:*
'*Prepare* the *way* of the LORD,
make *straight* his *paths.*'"

This is the sound of a herald calling out over a great distance; project your voice, pause and continue in a more subdued tone. John is clearly that voice, and his baptism is the preparation for the Lord.

John the Baptist appeared in the desert
proclaiming a baptism of *repentance* for the forgiveness of *sins.*

cannot know when it will occur, they can hasten it by righteous behavior.

Some of the specific images sound foreign to our ears (and were not understood literally even by the first readers of this letter), but the author's point is well worth taking by modern Christians. In fact, it is an appropriate Advent message. Encourage your assembly to reflect on what it means to be an Advent people: to wait expectantly for Christ to come, always ready and eager, while acknowledging that the time and manner of his coming cannot be predicted.

GOSPEL The gospel of Mark, the earliest of the four gospels, opens with a bold claim that it tells the good news of the anointed one of God—and then proceeds to preface any further reference to Jesus with an introduction to the person of John the Baptist. John was a popular preacher of repentance, and his disciples formed an early rival group to the followers of Jesus. Today's gospel makes it clear that John's mission was to prepare for and point to Jesus.

The passage from the first reading is quoted and supplemented, slightly altering the thrust of the message from Isaiah. It fits well the career of John, however, whose preaching was conducted in the desert areas, and it adapts his message to the Christian proclamation that he foretold the coming of Jesus. Much of our knowledge of John comes from these verses, which depict him preparing the way for the Lord, just as Second Isaiah proclaimed, and calling the people to repentance, as was expected of Elijah.

Convey excitement of the people.

People of the *whole* Judean *countryside*
and *all* the inhabitants of *Jerusalem*
were going *out* to him
and were being *baptized* by him in the Jordan *River*
as they *acknowledged* their sins.

John's appearance is that of a desert wanderer; his clothing recalls the dress of some prophets, including Elijah.

John was clothed in *camel's* hair,
with a leather *belt* around his *waist*.
He fed on *locusts* and *wild honey*.

And this is what he proclaimed:
"One *mightier* than I is coming *after* me.
I am not *worthy* to stoop and *loosen* the *thongs* of his *sandals*.
I have baptized you with *water*;
he will baptize you with the *Holy Spirit*."

Just as the herald in the first reading told of preparing a wide and level path through the desert for the sovereign God's passage, so also John here prepares the path for the Lord. But his role as prophet is not confined to that of Second Isaiah, who joyfully anticipated the return of the Babylonian exiles to their homeland; he is also Elijah, in both demeanor and message. His dress and food reflect that of the wandering Elijah, while his message that there is a greater one following him reflects the Jewish expectation that Elijah would return and call the people to repentance prior to the great Day of the Lord.

The theme of preparation is apt for this season. Just as the road must be leveled and cleared of stones before the monarch arrives with great fanfare, so too our hearts must be cleared in order to embrace the ruler of our lives. The repentance advocated by John is necessary for us as well. Through this passage, call upon your community to prepare for God's coming by reflecting on John's message. Be sure to convey the same joyful urgency that fills the text of Isaiah: God is coming! Get ready! Rejoice!

IMMACULATE CONCEPTION

Lectionary #689

READING I Genesis 3:9–15, 20

A reading from the book of Genesis.

After the man, *Adam*, had eaten of the *tree*,
the LORD God *called* to the man and *asked* him,
"Where *are* you?"

Allow God's question to sound genuine, rather than like a trap for the man.

He answered, "I *heard* you in the *garden*;
but I was *afraid*, because I was *naked*,
so I *hid* myself."

Let the man's embarrassment be heard.

Then he asked, "Who *told* you that you were naked?
You have *eaten*, then,
from the tree of which I had *forbidden* you to eat!"

God understands the situation now; a bit of indignation can be heard.

The man replied, "The *woman* whom you *put* here with me—
she gave me fruit from the tree, and so I *ate* it."

Speak the man's words in a tone resembling a child trying to pass blame.

The LORD God then asked the *woman*,
"*Why* did you *do* such a thing?"
The woman answered, "The *serpent tricked* me into it,
so I *ate* it."

The woman's words also sound childish.

Then the LORD God said to the *serpent:*
"Because you have *done* this, you shall be *banned*
from *all* the animals
and from *all* the wild creatures;
on your *belly* shall you crawl,
and *dirt* shall you *eat*
all the *days* of your *life.*
I will put *enmity* between *you* and the *woman*,

Speak God's words firmly but without overemphasis.

READING I The myths in the early part of Genesis are stories that tell great truths about life. Today's reading gives an account of how sin entered the world and explains why human life can be difficult. Although God creates humans to dwell in paradise, this story indicates that we often overstep the boundaries of what is good for us, with dire results.

The story opens with a discussion between God and the man. When confronted with the truth of what he has done, the man instantly tries to blame the woman. The woman points to someone else as well—namely, the serpent. The sin was a social action; it was something the pair chose to do together. But they are embarrassed when it becomes known and want to deny it.

The punishment recounted here is directed at the snake. An attempt is made to explain natural phenomena: Because of what happened in the garden, snakes crawl, and humans and snakes seem to have a natural aversion to one another. In fact, the whole story suggests that everything wrong in the world is the result of the choice of humans to reach beyond themselves, to act in ways that are reserved for the divine. The Greeks called it *hubris*, which we usually translate as "pride." It means trying to be bigger than one actually is.

Although it is not part of today's reading, the account in Genesis also explains the punishment of the man and the woman:

and between *your* offspring and *hers*;
he will *strike* at your *head*,
while *you* strike at his *heel*."

The tone changes here. Pause and read this last verse with warmth and hope.

The man called his wife *Eve*,
because she became the *mother* of *all* the *living*.

READING II Ephesians 1:3–6, 11–12

A reading from the letter of Saint Paul to the Ephesians.

Open with a resounding word of praise. Read this as a joyous statement of honor to God.

Brothers and sisters:
Blessed be the *God* and *Father* of our *Lord Jesus Christ*,
who has *blessed* us in Christ
with every *spiritual blessing* in the *heavens*,
as he *chose* us in *him*, before the foundation of the *world*,
to be *holy* and *without blemish* before him.

The tone changes with the second paragraph, becoming more explanatory.

In *love* he *destined* us for *adoption* to himself
through Jesus Christ,
in accord with the *favor* of his *will*,
for the *praise* of the *glory* of his *grace*
that he *granted* us in the *beloved*.

Our response to God is to offer praise and thanksgiving.

In *him* we were also *chosen*,
destined in accord with the purpose of the *One*
who accomplishes *all things* according to the intention
of his *will*,
so that we might *exist* for the praise of his *glory*,
we who *first hoped* in Christ.

Men are doomed to a life of struggle, while women suffer in childbirth and in their husbands' "rule" over them. This is hardly a prescription for proper behavior, but describes life as it was known to the ancients. Far from being the will of God, such suffering and degradation are instead the result of sin.

The final verse of the reading accords the woman great honor and is the reason this passage is chosen for today's feast. In a play on words (Eve means "life"), the woman is said to be the mother of all the living. This is somewhat similar to the promise of descendants given to Abraham; having many children was considered a great blessing to the Hebrews. Mary, the new Eve, chooses right instead of wrong, and restores life where there is death; she reverses the downward spiral begun in Genesis by bearing the one who offers life to all.

This passage is read most effectively when the emotions of the speakers are heard through their words. Avoid speaking in a deep, booming voice for God, however, and close with a tone of hope.

READING II In a tone of praise and thanksgiving, the author of the letter to the Ephesians reflects on the many blessings bestowed on humanity in Christ. These are not mere physical blessings but are of a heavenly cast, and they have been intended from the beginning. Even before creation, God chose us to be adopted children. The human choice to thwart God's plan for us, recounted in the first reading, was undone even before it occurred. God chose us to inherit all the blessings that rightfully belong to Christ.

GOSPEL Luke 1:26–38

A reading from the holy gospel according to Luke.

The angel *Gabriel* was sent from *God*
to a town of Galilee called *Nazareth*,
to a *virgin* betrothed to a man named *Joseph*,
of the house of *David*,
and the virgin's name was *Mary*.
And *coming* to her, he *said*,
"*Hail*, full of grace! The *Lord* is with *you*."

Pause slightly after "name" to give emphasis to Mary's name.

The angel's words are joyful but weighty. Speak them accordingly.

But she was greatly *troubled* at what was said
and *pondered* what sort of *greeting* this might be.
Then the angel said to her,
"Do *not* be *afraid*, Mary,
for you have found *favor* with God.
Behold, you will *conceive* in your womb and bear a *son*,
and you shall name him *Jesus*.
He will be *great* and will be called *Son* of the *Most High*,
and the *Lord God* will give him the throne of *David* his father,
and he will *rule* over the house of *Jacob forever*,
and of his *kingdom* there will be *no end*."

Mary is confused. Read the angel's words with a tone of comfort and reassurance.

Jesus' name is significant.

But Mary said to the angel,
"*How* can this *be*,
since I have no relations with a *man*?"

Mary is puzzled.

And the angel *said* to her in reply,
"The *Holy Spirit* will come *upon* you,
and the *power* of the *Most High* will *overshadow* you.
Therefore the *child* to be *born*
will be called holy, the *Son* of *God*.

Pause before concluding. Then continue with solemn conviction.

The goal of all this—indeed the goal of all creation—is to offer praise to God, who has made all this possible. Because of God's tremendous love for us, we are given blessings of such abundance that we could never claim to deserve them. The only response possible is praise and gratitude.

Speak these words with a tone of great sincerity. Urge your listeners to reflect on the wondrous way in which God has chosen us even before creation, despite our sin, to be adopted children, heirs of all goodness. Lift your voice in praise and give glory to God!

GOSPEL Although today's feast celebrates the conception of Mary, the gospel reading is an account of the conception of Jesus. Stories about Mary's own origins are relatively late, but she is remembered for her important role in giving life to the true life-giver. As we prepare our hearts for receiving Christ this season, this reading is appropriate and honors Mary for her trusting "Yes!" to God.

The story is familiar (and is also used on the Fourth Sunday of Advent, where there is a fuller discussion), but deserves all the attention and fresh presentation of any other text. It is the story of a young girl who experiences a most extraordinary event—the appearance of an angel—and is given an even more extraordinary promise. She is confused, perhaps frightened, but in the end her response is firm: Yes, Lord, whatever you will.

And behold, *Elizabeth*, your relative,
has also *conceived* a son in her *old age*,
and this is the *sixth* month for *her* who was called *barren*;
for *nothing* will be impossible for *God*."

Mary said, "Behold, *I* am the *handmaid* of the *Lord*.
May it be *done* to me according to your *word*."
Then the angel departed from her.

As we honor Mary today, it is appropriate to remember her for her strength and conviction, the characteristics attributed to her in the gospel of Luke, from which most of our knowledge of Mary comes. Only a few verses after the conclusion of this story is Mary's Magnificat, a song of praise to God for turning the world on its head. Not only has God chosen a young Jewish girl to bear the hope of the world, but God has brought down the wealthy and powerful, giving honor to the lowly and disenfranchised. God is to be found not in palaces or splendid abodes, but in the humble hearts of those who have nothing.

This gospel brings full circle the story begun in the first reading. Mary turns her face in trust toward God, reversing the cowardly flight of the sinful couple in Genesis. Whereas Adam and Eve refused to do God's will, Mary's "Yes!" resounds.

Offer this reading to your congregation as though they are hearing it for the first time. Inspire all to trust in God's goodness, even when it does not seem to make sense. And honor Mary by presenting her as the quietly forceful woman of conviction that she was.

3RD SUNDAY OF ADVENT

Lectionary #8

READING I Isaiah 61:1–2a, 10–11

A reading from the book of the prophet Isaiah.

Speak these and the following words with great conviction.

The *spirit* of the *Lord GOD* is *upon* me,
because the LORD has *anointed* me;
he has sent me to bring *glad tidings* to the *poor*,
to *heal* the *brokenhearted*,
to proclaim *liberty* to the *captives*
and *release* to the *prisoners*,
to announce a *year* of *favor* from the *LORD*
and a *day* of *vindication* by our *God*.

Pause and change your tone to one of wonder and joy.

I *rejoice heartily* in the *LORD*,
in my God is the *joy* of my *soul*;
for he has *clothed* me with a robe of *salvation*
and *wrapped* me in a mantle of *justice*,
like a *bridegroom* adorned with a *diadem*,
like a *bride* bedecked with her *jewels*.

diadem = DĪ-uh-dem

This final phrase unites the passage. Again, speak with conviction.

As the *earth* brings *forth* its *plants*,
and a *garden* makes its growth *spring up*,
so will the *Lord GOD* make *justice* and *praise*
spring up before *all* the *nations*.

READING I The title "Third Isaiah" is often given to the final chapters of the prophet's book. Today's passage is one that promises great things for the oppressed; it includes the section read by Jesus in the synagogue at the beginning of his ministry, a passage fulfilled in him.

In this passage, God's "spirit," present at creation and active in history, gives rise to the prophet's proclamation. The prophet also claims to have been anointed, an action usually reserved for royalty. Although the terminology may be used here figuratively, it brings to mind the belief of Christians that baptism confers the Holy Spirit and makes us a royal people.

Interestingly, the prophet then proceeds to speak, not for the elite, but for those who are suffering or in prison. The outcasts and lowly have reason to rejoice, for God's favor rests on them. The prophet declares that all slates are wiped clean and that all people are vindicated.

The final verses of the passage seem to be spoken by Israel, here adorned as a priestly people. Israel rejoices in the favor shown by God, and all the nations will recognize the people's righteousness.

Read this passage joyfully and with awe at the promises of God. At the same time, challenge your community to enact the social justice proclaimed in the first half of the reading, that it may be genuinely thankful to be honored in the second half. Close with the conviction that God does indeed bring about justice for all peoples.

READING II The Third Sunday of Advent takes the name "Gaudete Sunday" from this reading from Paul's first letter to the Thessalonians; the word for

READING II 1 Thessalonians 5:16 – 24

A reading from the first letter of Saint Paul to the Thessalonians.

Brothers and sisters:
Rejoice *always.* Pray without *ceasing.*
In *all* circumstances give *thanks,*
for *this* is the will of God for you in *Christ Jesus.*

Let your voice ring with quiet joy.

Do *not* quench the *Spirit.*
Do not *despise* prophetic *utterances.*
Test everything; *retain* what is *good.*
Refrain from every kind of *evil.*

These are gentle instructions, not harsh commands.

May the God of *peace* make you *perfectly holy*
and may you *entirely*, spirit, soul and body,
be preserved *blameless* for the *coming* of our *Lord Jesus Christ.*
The one who *calls* you is *faithful,*
and he will also *accomplish* it.

Speak this blessing of your assembly warmly.

There is a finality to these words. Speak them firmly.

GOSPEL John 1:6 – 8, 19 – 28

A reading from the holy gospel according to John.

A *man* named *John* was sent from *God.*
He came for *testimony*, to testify to the *light,*
so that *all* might *believe* through him.
He was *not* the light,
but came to *testify* to the light.

The key image here is that of light, which illumines the world.

And *this* is the *testimony* of *John.*

"rejoice" in Latin is *gaudete.* The passage sings with joy as it exhorts its hearers, then and now, to be holy in everything.

Paul's first letter to the Thessalonians is the earliest Christian writing we possess. It reveals Paul's love for the Thessalonian community and his fervent belief that Jesus would return to earth soon. This passage describes the joy that Paul derived from his belief in God, the same joy he tried to instill in the communities he visited.

There is a threefold command given at the outset: Rejoice, pray, give thanks. All are to be done continually. These are the hallmarks of the Christian life, and a fitting way to remain vigilant and to prepare for Christ during Advent.

In addition, Paul advocates openness to the movement of the Spirit, while at the same time recognizing that all claims of spiritual inspiration must be tested to ensure their genuineness. In everything, the Christian is to strive for holiness in order to be prepared for the coming of Jesus Christ.

In keeping with the theme of joyful expectation during Advent, offer this reading to your listeners as an exhortation to be ready to meet the Lord, whatever form that encounter might take.

GOSPEL All of the gospel writers agree that John was a precursor of and witness to Jesus. The gospel of John is particularly emphatic concerning this point, as well as poetic in its presentation. The early Christians found it necessary to account for John's role, especially since Jesus himself had received John's baptism of repentance. It is especially effective for the evangelist to have John himself deny that

When the Jews from *Jerusalem* sent *priests* and *Levites* to him
to ask him, "Who *are* you?"
He *admitted* and did not deny it,
but admitted, "I am *not* the *Christ.*"

John is firm in his denials.

So they asked him,
"What *are* you then? Are you *Elijah?*"
And he said, "I am *not.*"
"Are you the *Prophet?*"
He answered, "*No.*"

So they said to him,
"Who *are* you, so we can give an *answer* to those who *sent* us?
What do you have to *say* for yourself?"
He said:
"I am 'the *voice* of one *crying out* in the *desert,*
make *straight* the *way* of the *Lord,*'
as *Isaiah* the *prophet* said."

Express the frustration or impatience of the questioners.

Be conscious that these words echo Isaiah. The selection began on a quiet note, but let John's words here and below resound forcefully in the assembly.

Some Pharisees were *also* sent.
They asked him,
"*Why* then do you *baptize*
if you are *not* the *Christ* or *Elijah* or the *Prophet?*"
John answered them,
"I baptize with *water;*
but there is one *among* you whom you do not *recognize,*
the one who is coming *after* me,
whose *sandal* strap I am *not worthy* to *untie.*"

This happened in *Bethany* across the Jordan,
where John was *baptizing.*

The precise location is unclear and may be an error. There is no known Bethany near the Jordan.

he is the Messiah and to point to Jesus as the one for whom he was preparing the way. The story is creatively told as a conversation between John and the Jewish authorities in charge of the Temple in Jerusalem.

When the Temple authorities ask who he is, John immediately replies that he is not the Messiah. As Roman rule became more heavy-handed, there was active expectation of a Messiah (or Messiahs) in the Judaism of the day. "Messiah" originally meant simply "anointed one" (such as a ruler). The term later came to be associated with a heavenly figure who would inaugurate a new age of autonomy and prosperity for the Jewish people.

John also denies that he is either Elijah or "the prophet," reflecting the tradition that other figures in addition to the Messiah were to arrive on the scene to prepare for the Day of the Lord. In every way, John is portrayed as denying any special role for himself. He is instead the voice crying in the wilderness, preparing a path for the Lord's travel.

The final question, posed to John by the Pharisees, involves the nature of John's baptism. John indicates that his baptism is of water only; it does not result in spirit-possession. The early Christians contrasted baptism in the Spirit and the spectacular actions it inspired with baptism only "in the name of the Lord Jesus" (Acts 8:14). Perhaps the evangelist's community also knew of different levels of initiation.

Encourage your listeners to see John's testimony as a challenge to them to live lives that herald God's presence in the world, to be prepared to acknowledge their faith in Jesus as the Christ, and to allow themselves to recede and not to be too concerned about their own importance.

4TH SUNDAY OF ADVENT

Lectionary #11

READING I 2 Samuel 7:1–5, 8b–12, 14a, 16

A reading from the second book of Samuel.

When King *David* was settled in his *palace,*
and the LORD had given him *rest* from his *enemies* on every *side,*
he said to *Nathan* the *prophet,*
"Here *I* am living in a house of *cedar,*
while the ark of *God* dwells in a *tent!"*
Nathan answered the king,
"Go, do *whatever* you have in *mind,*
for the *LORD* is *with* you."

Make the contrast between David's dwelling and that of the ark abundantly clear. Emphasize especially the idea of David's "house."

Nathan initially approves, apparently thinking that David's plan is appropriate. Only later does he realize that God has other things in mind.

But that *night* the LORD spoke to Nathan and *said:*
"Go, tell my servant *David, Thus* says the *LORD:*
Should *you* build *me* a *house* to *dwell* in?

It is not David's role to decide where the ark is to reside; God is to be in charge of everything. Read it with appropriate authority.

"It was *I* who took you from the *pasture*
and from the *care* of the *flock*
to be *commander* of my people *Israel.*
I have been *with* you wherever you *went,*
and I have *destroyed* all your enemies *before* you.
And I will make you *famous* like the *great* ones of the *earth.*

"I will fix a *place* for my people *Israel;*
I will *plant* them so that they may *dwell* in their *place*
without further *disturbance.*

READING I **The reign of David was characterized by prosperity and triumph. David successfully conquered Israel's enemies, joined the tribes of Israel together into a harmonious kingdom, and brought the ark of the covenant, the dwelling place of God, into the capital city of Jerusalem. David himself dwelt in splendor and comfort, but he soon questioned his noble surroundings, knowing that the ark remained housed in humble quarters.**

Today's passage recounts David's desire to build a temple for the ark and the subsequent message from God. God's message is a promise of favor for David and his descendants, a promise that gives hope to Israel through the ages and to which Christians have also laid claim.

The point of today's reading centers on a play on words. David's concern is to build a "house" for God, but God speaks of a different kind of a house, promising to establish David's lineage forever. Through the court prophet Nathan, God pledges faithfulness to David and favor to his descendants.

Most of the passage is in God's words, which Nathan is to relay to David. God recounts the ways in which David has been given divine aid. But instead of requiring some sign of gratitude, God further promises that David's kingdom will not cease with David's death but will be ruled by his immediate heir. Familial language beautifully expresses the closeness of the relationship that will exist between God and David's son; and God's commitment to David's line will never end.

Neither shall the *wicked* continue to *afflict* them as they did of *old*,
since the time I *first* appointed *judges* over my people *Israel.*
I will give you *rest* from all your *enemies.*

"The LORD also *reveals* to you
that he will establish a *house* for you.
And when your *time* comes and you *rest* with your *ancestors*,
I will *raise up* your *heir* after you, sprung from your *loins*,
and I will make his kingdom *firm.*

The belief that Jesus was descended from David, as claimed in today's gospel, indicates to Christians that God's promises were fulfilled. Read this prophecy with confidence.

This promise to David has sustained the Jewish people through foreign occupation, destruction of the Jerusalem Temples, revolutions and widespread dispersion; it continues to inspire the state of Israel today.

"I will be a *father* to him,
and he shall be a *son* to me.
Your *house* and your *kingdom* shall endure *forever* before me;
your *throne* shall stand *firm forever."*

READING II Romans 16:25–27

A reading from the letter of Saint Paul to the Romans.

Read "To him" slowly and strongly, then pause. Do not rush through the verses from here until "faith," but let your tone convey the fact that they interrupt the main point of the sentence.

Take a breath after "faith" before continuing.

Brothers and sisters:
To *him* who can *strengthen* you,
according to my *gospel* and the *proclamation* of Jesus *Christ*,
according to the *revelation* of the *mystery* kept *secret* for long *ages*
but now *manifested* through the prophetic *writings* and,
according to the *command* of the eternal *God*,
made known to *all nations* to bring about the *obedience* of *faith*,
to the *only* wise *God*, through Jesus *Christ*
be *glory* forever and *ever.* Amen.

This promise to David provided assurance to subsequent rulers of Israel, and especially to the rulers of Judah after the kingdom was divided, offering hope even during exile. After the dissolution of the Davidic monarchy, the promise of God to David was understood by some to refer to a Messiah from the line of David, a savior who would restore Israel to its glory. This perspective was adopted by Christians, but with an otherworldly interpretation of the reign of that Messiah.

The key to proclaiming this passage well is to emphasize the play on the word "house." The rest of God's pledge can be proclaimed as a judgment of favor upon God's people. Encourage your listeners to take comfort in these words, knowing that the promises are fulfilled in Jesus and that God's promises are forever.

READING II This doxology—a prayer of praise to God—closes the letter to the Romans in most modern Bibles.

Paul was proud of the gospel he preached, the proclamation of the works of God in the person of Jesus Christ, the fulfillment of the hopes that were spoken by the prophets. Mysteries formerly known only to God are revealed, not only to the Jewish people but to all the nations as well, in order that all the earth's peoples may come to faith in and obedience to God.

Although the content of today's reading complicates a simple prayer of praise, it also enriches it. God is glorified for making known the meaning of the prophetic word

GOSPEL Luke 1:26–38

A reading from the holy gospel according to Luke.

The angel *Gabriel* was sent from *God*
to a town of *Galilee* called *Nazareth,*
to a *virgin* betrothed to a man named *Joseph,*
of the house of *David,*
and the virgin's *name* was *Mary.*

And coming to *her,* he said,
"*Hail, full of grace!* The *Lord* is *with* you."
But she was greatly *troubled* at what was said
and *pondered* what sort of *greeting* this might *be.*

The appearance of an angel in biblical stories often results in fear and awe. Proclaim Mary's response appropriately.

Then the angel *said* to her,
"Do *not* be *afraid,* Mary,
for you have found *favor* with God.
Behold, you will *conceive* in your womb and bear a *son,*
and you shall *name* him *Jesus.*

"He will be *great* and will be called *Son* of the *Most High,*
and the Lord *God* will give him the *throne* of *David* his *father,*
and he will *rule* over the house of *Jacob forever,*
and of his *kingdom* there will be no *end.*"

Pause before proceeding with Mary's practical question. Let the angel's response resonate and inspire your listeners with the same awe and wonder that Mary must have experienced.

But *Mary* said to the *angel,*
"*How* can this *be,*
since I have no *relations* with a *man?*"
And the angel said to her in *reply,*
"The Holy *Spirit* will come *upon* you,
and the *power* of the *Most High* will *overshadow* you.

through Jesus. Paul's mission of preaching to the Gentiles, while not a central theme of the letter to the Romans, is suggested as well; the culmination of the revelation in Jesus is the inclusion of all people in the promises of God. This is truly a reason to praise God!

Because this passage is one long sentence or phrase, it is extremely difficult to read. The key is to emphasize strongly the first two words ("To him") and then the material after "faith." Everything before "faith" is parenthetical and can be read as such, but be careful not to rush through it. Instead, speak it in a lower tone that conveys its secondary status in the sentence, but read slowly and deliberately in order to communicate its important message.

Finally, attempt to draw your listeners into honoring God, letting excitement fill your voice. Allow this prayer to be a word of blessing from you and your community to God through Jesus the Christ.

GOSPEL Only the gospel of Luke records Gabriel's announcement to Mary. Mary's conception of Jesus by the power of God's Spirit was familiar to early Christians as a way of acknowledging Jesus' divine origins. But only here is the encounter between the mother of Jesus and God's messenger imaginatively told and the promises of God to this humble Jewish girl spelled out.

Gabriel begins by telling Mary of God's favor for her, a greeting that confuses her. Gabriel proceeds to explain to Mary what his statement means: Her child will be given

The angel's words affirm a Christian belief formulated more fully later regarding the person of Jesus: Descendant of David and son of Mary, he is fully human; son of God and conceived by the Holy Spirit, he is fully divine.

Mary speaks with simple faith. Speak her words quietly but sincerely.

Therefore the *child* to be born
will be called *holy*, the *Son* of *God*.

"And behold, *Elizabeth*, your *relative*,
has also conceived a *son* in her old *age*,
and this is the *sixth* month for her who was called *barren*;
for *nothing* will be impossible for *God*."
Mary said, "*Behold*, I am the *handmaid* of the *Lord*.
May it be *done* to me according to your *word*."
Then the angel *departed* from her.

both honor and a mission. The name for this child—Jesus—bears special import; the name means "he will save" in Hebrew. What is involved in Jesus' saving actions is not revealed to Mary; she is told only of the glory due him. The pain Mary would come to know remains shrouded in the dark silence of her womb.

Mary's question brings us back to the situation at hand. The author wants to clarify that this child of hers is no ordinary child, but sent directly from God. Her child will be the Davidic ruler for whom Israel longed. Writing long after Jesus' humiliating death and triumphant resurrection, the evangelist knows that the reign of this child will not be an earthly one. But in this child the hopes of Israel find true and lasting fulfillment; his reign will be eternal.

Mary's humble response to this awesome message is an inspiration for all times. She simply and quietly opens her heart to God's word and accepts her role in birthing the savior. Her trust in God's goodness leads her down paths she could never have imagined.

Read this story as if you are reading it for the first time. Allow the characters to come to life for you and for the members of your assembly. Offer Mary's trusting response to God as a model for your community's own reaction to God's communication to it.

CHRISTMAS VIGIL

Lectionary #13

READING I Isaiah 62:1–5

A reading from the book of the prophet Isaiah.

Let your voice be heard loud and clear; you are the prophet's mouthpiece.

For *Zion's* sake I will *not* be *silent,*
for *Jerusalem's* sake I will *not* be *quiet,*
until her *vindication* shines *forth* like the *dawn*
and her *victory* like a burning *torch.*

Jerusalem will shine forth in splendor for all to see. Proclaim these words with great joy.

Nations shall behold your *vindication,*
and *all* the kings your *glory;*
you shall be called by a *new* name
pronounced by the mouth of the LORD.
You shall be a *glorious crown* in the hand of the LORD,
a royal *diadem* held by your God.

diadem = DĪ-uh-dem

Pause briefly before and after the words in quotation marks so that they can be heard as names.

No more shall people call you "*Forsaken,*"
or your land "*Desolate,*"
but you shall be called "*My Delight,*"
and your land "*Espoused.*"

Let tenderness fill your voice.

For the LORD *delights* in you
and makes your land his *spouse.*

As a *young man* marries a *virgin,*
your *Builder* shall marry *you;*
and as a *bridegroom* rejoices in his *bride*
so shall your *God* rejoice in *you.*

READING I **Written at the end of the exile in Babylon, this passage declares the importance of the holy city Jerusalem for the Hebrew people and the renewed blessings God will bestow on it. The exile was understood as a punishment for wrongdoing; the destruction of Jerusalem and the Temple gave witness to the barrenness of its former inhabitants. But all that is over; what matters now is that God has forgiven the sins of the people and Jerusalem is to be restored to glory. The vindication of the city and its inhabitants is for all the world to know and see.**

Jerusalem's "new name" is significant; the name of something indicates its very essence. Jacob's name was changed to Israel as a sign of the change in his life; Jerusalem's new titles indicate that the status of the city (and of the people who reside within it) has changed. Perhaps the most famous instance of assigning names of particular significance occurs in the story of the prophet Hosea, whose children bear names that reflect their mother's faithlessness (and by implication the faithlessness of Israel). However, their names are altered in the end to represent the conversion of Israel after God woos the people into a new committed relationship of love.

The former names of Israel in today's passage are reflected also in an earlier passage of the book of Isaiah (54:1–8). There, exiled Judah is called barren and is compared with a desolate woman. Although the terms can also be applied to agricultural devastation, the introduction of a woman into

READING II Acts 13:16–17, 22–25

A reading from the Acts of the Apostles.

Antioch = AN-tee-ahk
Pisidia = pih-SID-ee-uh

When *Paul* reached *Antioch* in *Pisidia* and entered
the *synagogue,*
he stood *up, motioned* with his hand, and said,

Raise your voice over the crowd, just as Paul must have done.

"Fellow *Israelites* and you *others* who are God-fearing, *listen.*
The *God* of this people *Israel* chose our *ancestors*
and *exalted* the people during their *sojourn*
in the land of *Egypt.*
With *uplifted arm* he led them *out* of *it.*

Paul gives a brief history of Israel, concentrating especially on David and God's favor to him.

"*Then* he removed Saul and *raised* up *David* as *king;*
of *him* he *testified,*
'I have found *David,* son of *Jesse,* a *man* after my own *heart;*
he will carry out my every *wish.*'

Although the Davidic dynasty no longer rules Israel, God's promises to David are realized in the person of Jesus.

"From *this* man's descendants *God,* according to his *promise,*
has *brought* to Israel a *savior, Jesus.*
John heralded his *coming* by proclaiming a *baptism* of *repentance*
to all the *people* of *Israel;*
and as John was *completing* his course, he would say,

Speak with humility and conviction.

'*What* do you suppose that I *am?* I am not *he.*
Behold, one is coming *after* me;
I am not *worthy* to unfasten the *sandals* of his *feet.*'"

the imagery and the play on the word for "married" reflect the status of women in Hebrew society. Marriage and children were seen as the greatest blessings a woman could receive, and the lack of them could be understood as punishment. But the use of terms related to commitment and the close bond of family ties is especially appropriate when applied to God's relationship of love and commitment with the chosen people.

Today's passage affirms the honor that will be given Jerusalem. It will be crowned and revered as royalty, espoused to God. The wedding of a monarch was always cause for great celebration in antiquity (as it often is today) and the passage reflects that joy. The desolation of old is left behind, and the bridegroom (God) professes delight with the bride. The restored Jerusalem will enter into a new and deeper relationship with God, a marriage marked by the passion of newlyweds.

Allow the joy of this passage to ring out in your words. Just as Christians joyfully celebrate the union of divine and human in the person of Jesus, so also the Hebrew people knew that they were to be intimately united with God. Let the newness of the marriage you announce remind your hearers of the renewed relationship possible with God, based as it is on the new covenant inaugurated by Jesus.

READING II The author of the Acts of the Apostles always depicts Paul proclaiming the gospel first in the Jewish synagogue, turning to the Gentiles only after being rejected there. Paul himself

Take a deep breath before beginning this long list of Jesus' ancestors. Take your time as you read, and convey the importance of family in what could otherwise be a wearying selection.

Perez = PAYR-ez
Zerah = ZEE-rah
Tamar = TAY-mahr
Hezron = HEZ-ruhn
Ram = ram
Amminadab = uh-MIN-uh-dab
Nahshon = NAH-shuhn
Salmon = SAL-muhn
Boaz = BOH-az
Rahab = RAY-hab
Obed = OH-bed

Pause briefly before beginning the next section.

Uriah = yoo-RĪ-uh
Rehoboam = ree-huh-BOH-uhm
Abijah = uh-BĪ-juh
Asaph = AY-saf
Jehoshaphat = jeh-HOH-shuh-fat
Joram = JOHR-uhm
Uzziah = uh-ZĪ-uh

GOSPEL Matthew 1:1–25

A reading from the holy gospel according to Matthew.

The book of the *genealogy* of Jesus *Christ*,
the son of *David*, the son of *Abraham*.

Abraham became the father of *Isaac*,
Isaac the father of *Jacob*,
Jacob the father of *Judah* and his *brothers*.
Judah became the father of *Perez* and *Zerah*,
whose mother was *Tamar*.
Perez became the father of *Hezron*,
Hezron the father of *Ram*,
Ram the father of *Amminadab*.
Amminadab became the father of *Nahshon*,
Nahshon the father of *Salmon*,
Salmon the father of *Boaz*,
whose mother was *Rahab*.
Boaz became the father of *Obed*,
whose mother was *Ruth*.
Obed became the father of *Jesse*,
Jesse the father of *David* the *king*.

David became the father of *Solomon*,
whose *mother* had been the wife of *Uriah*.
Solomon became the father of *Rehoboam*,
Rehoboam the father of *Abijah*,
Abijah the father of *Asaph*.
Asaph became the father of *Jehoshaphat*,
Jehoshaphat the father of *Joram*,
Joram the father of *Uzziah*.

gives us a quite different picture of his mission. Whatever the historical reality, the speech in today's reading provides Paul with the opportunity to indicate that the new revelation in Jesus is the fulfillment of God's promises to David. Jesus does not simply arrive in the world from nowhere, but was born into a people chosen by God and given protection and guidance through many travails. God promised eternal favor to the descendants of David.

Although the Davidic monarchy suffered through exile, foreign occupation and defeat, the Jews continued to hope that a descendant of David would arise and restore the people to right relationship with God. In today's speech, Paul indicates that Jesus is that descendant, the savior of Israel. And it was John, the revered preacher of repentance, who declared Jesus to be the one for whom Israel was waiting.

Read this passage as a claim that God's promises are always kept. Allow John's humble words to inspire you and your listeners, so that you may celebrate the manifestation of God in the world in humility and joy.

GOSPEL **The evangelist today offers a message similar to that of Paul in Acts. Jesus came into the world as part of a particular people and a particular family. It is this particularity that is often baffling to non-Christians: How could God be present in such ordinariness? But that is what Christians claim, as we acknowledge**

Jotham = JOH-thuhm
Ahaz = AY-haz
Hezekiah = hez-eh-KĪ-uh
Manasseh = muh-NAS-uh
Amos = AY-m*s
Josiah = joh-SĪ-uh
Jechoniah = jek-oh-NĪ-uh

Uzziah became the father of *Jotham*,
Jotham the father of *Ahaz*,
Ahaz the father of *Hezekiah*.
Hezekiah became the father of *Manasseh*,
Manasseh the father of *Amos*,
Amos the father of *Josiah*.
Josiah became the father of *Jechoniah* and his *brothers*
at the time of the Babylonian *exile*.

Pause briefly before beginning the next section.

Shealtiel = shee-AL-tee-uhl
Zerubbabel = zuh-ROOB-uh-b*l
Abiud = uh-BĪ-uhd
Eliakim = ee-LĪ-uh-kim
Azor = AY-zohr
Zadok = ZAY-dok
Achim = AH-kim
Eliud = ee-LĪ-uhd
Eleazar = el-ee-AY-zer
Matthan = MATH-uhn

After the Babylonian exile,
Jechoniah became the father of *Shealtiel*,
Shealtiel the father of *Zerubbabel*,
Zerubbabel the father of *Abiud*.
Abiud became the father of *Eliakim*,
Eliakim the father of *Azor*,
Azor the father of *Zadok*.
Zadok became the father of *Achim*,
Achim the father of *Eliud*,
Eliud the father of *Eleazar*.
Eleazar became the father of *Matthan*,
Matthan the father of Jacob,
Jacob the father of *Joseph*, the husband of *Mary*.
Of *her* was born *Jesus* who is called the *Christ*.

This is the announcement for which your congregation has been waiting. Slow down and proclaim it solemnly.

Thus the *total* number of generations
from *Abraham* to *David*
is *fourteen* generations;
from *David* to the Babylonian *exile*,
fourteen generations;
from the Babylonian *exile* to the *Christ*,
fourteen generations.

Jesus' human ancestry and proclaim that he truly is one of us.

The long genealogical list establishes Jesus as one who inherited both the blessings and the struggles of the Hebrew people. His lineage is traced back to Abraham, the original recipient of God's promises of favor and protection. He is the descendant of David as well, whose royal house was to endure forever. Jesus' ancestors survived the exile in Babylon, the humiliation of being deported to a foreign land, and the joy of returning home again. Jesus received all the hopes and dreams of his people at his birth: the covenant established with Abraham; the Davidic dynasty; the struggles for independence from foreign powers. Jesus was fully human and profoundly Jewish.

While Luke emphasizes the role of Mary in the story of Jesus' conception and birth, the gospel of Matthew focuses on Joseph. Joseph is the noble one, unwilling to embarrass Mary, found pregnant before their marriage, and willing to accept God's will without fully understanding it. The divine messenger who appeared to Mary in Luke appears instead to Joseph in Matthew with the astonishing news of an unusual conception. To Joseph is given the command to name the child Jesus, which means "he will save" in Hebrew.

Just as in the gospel of Luke, the purpose of the story of Jesus' conception and the angel's message is to assert Jesus' otherworldly origin. He is, as later Christians would articulate, fully human, descended from Abraham and David, and at the same time fully divine, conceived of the Holy Spirit. The author adds a final note, claiming that these events fulfill the scriptures, and quotes

Pause again before beginning the story about Joseph. Proceed with an animated voice.

Now *this* is how the *birth* of Jesus *Christ* came *about.*
When his mother *Mary* was betrothed to *Joseph,*
but *before* they lived *together,*
she was found with *child* through the *Holy Spirit.*

The Jewish Law suggests that infidelity on the part of a betrothed woman is to be punished by stoning. Joseph, although he believes that Mary has been unfaithful, does not seek to disgrace her or hold her subject to such a penalty.

Joseph her *husband,* since he was a *righteous* man,
yet unwilling to *expose* her to *shame,*
decided to divorce her *quietly.*
Such was his *intention* when, *behold,*
the *angel* of the Lord *appeared* to him in a *dream* and said,
"*Joseph,* son of *David,*
do *not* be afraid to take *Mary* your *wife* into your *home.*
For it is through the *Holy Spirit*
that this *child* has been *conceived* in her.
She will bear a *son* and you are to *name* him *Jesus,*
because he will *save* his people from their *sins.*"

All this took place to *fulfill*
what the Lord had said through the *prophet:*
"*Behold,* the virgin shall *conceive* and bear a *son,*
and they shall *name* him *Emmanuel,*"
which means "*God* is with *us.*"

When Joseph *awoke,*
he *did* as the angel of the Lord had *commanded* him
and took his *wife* into his *home.*
He had *no relations* with her until she *bore* a *son,*
and he named him *Jesus.*

[Shorter: Matthew 1:18–25]

from the prophet Isaiah. This child is the very manifestation of God on earth: Emmanuel.

Because of the long list of obscure names, this passage can be difficult to read. It is important to learn the pronunciations well and to practice them carefully. However, it is always more important to be confident in your proclamation than to do it without error. If you stumble or forget a pronunciation, try not to draw attention to your error, but continue as though nothing had happened. It is better to keep your congregation's attention focused on the gospel than to distract it by your efforts to correct your mistakes.

The list of names is divided into three sets. Pause between the sets in order to provide a break for your listeners and to emphasize the structure of the passage. There is also a natural rhythm to the genealogical list; be sure that you do not allow your voice to become sing-song. This can happen when a reader becomes bored and does not focus on communicating the intent of the passage: to demonstrate Jesus' origins.

The account of Joseph can be told as a tender story of commitment and honor, as well as an indication of the special character of this young child. As we celebrate this Christmas the Incarnation of the divine Son of God, this story draws us into the events of 2000 years ago. Offer it as a meditation on trust in God and a proclamation of the fact that, in Jesus, God is truly with us as never before.

CHRISTMAS MIDNIGHT

Lectionary #14

READING I Isaiah 9:1–6

A reading from the book of the prophet Isaiah.

Speak these words warmly and joyfully.

The *people* who walked in *darkness*
have seen a great *light*;
upon *those* who dwelt in the land of *gloom*
a *light* has *shone*.
You have brought them abundant *joy*
and great *rejoicing*,
as they rejoice *before* you as at the *harvest*,
as people make *merry* when dividing *spoils*.

Midian = MID-ee-uhn

For the *yoke* that *burdened* them,
the *pole* on their *shoulder*,
and the *rod* of their *taskmaster*
you have *smashed*, as on the day of *Midian*.

Begin anew, quietly but joyfully, then increase in volume and intensity until you fairly shout with joy the titles given to the ruler.

Continue with confidence and conviction.

For every *boot* that tramped in *battle*,
every *cloak* rolled in *blood*,
will be *burned* as fuel for *flames*.
For a *child* is *born* to us, a *son* is *given* us;
upon his *shoulder dominion* rests.
They name him *Wonder-Counselor, God-Hero,*
Father-Forever, Prince of Peace.
His dominion is *vast*
and forever *peaceful*,
from David's *throne*, and over his *kingdom*,
which he *confirms* and *sustains*

READING I Coming soon after Isaiah's promise that a child would be born who would be the answer to threats of doom, this passage seems to rejoice in the birth of that child. Isaiah was deeply committed to the promise made to David that his royal line would last forever. Despite adversity, he placed his hope in God's commitment to the Davidic monarch. He assured the king that God would never forsake Judah.

Today's passage came to represent the Jewish hope in a messianic savior. It enlivened the thought of subsequent generations and provided fertile ground for the establishment of Christianity.

Christians have long held this passage as a favorite text, a hymn celebrating the qualities of Jesus the Christ. Indeed, as we gather during the darkest days of the year, we proclaim that it is precisely through the birth of a child that a piercing light, one that can never be extinguished, has shone through the darkness. The burdens placed on our shoulders are removed through the actions of this one sent by God. He fulfills all hopes for a royal Messiah. Even Solomon's wisdom cannot compare with his; David's victories pale next to the heroic activity of God through him; he has inspired the patriarchs, the "fathers" of Israel, from the beginning; and his rule is marked by peace and justice. But his dominion is not that of any human king; he will rule forever in glory.

This familiar text is a joy to read in the assembly. Recall the exuberant majesty of Handel's *Messiah* as you share the source of Handel's inspiration. Let your words echo with joy and hope as you proclaim the fulfillment of God's promises in the God-child born in Bethlehem.

by *judgment* and *justice*,
both *now* and *forever*.
The *zeal* of the LORD of *hosts* will *do* this!

READING II Titus 2:11–14

A reading from the letter of Saint Paul to Titus.

Beloved:
The *grace* of *God* has *appeared*, saving *all*
and *training* us to reject godless *ways* and worldly *desires*
and to live *temperately*, *justly*, and *devoutly* in this age,
as we await the blessed *hope*,
the *appearance* of the *glory* of our great *God*
and *savior* Jesus *Christ*,
who *gave* himself for *us* to *deliver* us from all *lawlessness*
and to *cleanse* for himself a people as his *own*,
eager to do what is *good*.

The meaning of Christmas is that God's graciousness is evident on earth.

That is, for Jesus to come again.

This is why he came to earth.

GOSPEL Luke 2:1–14

A reading from the holy gospel according to Luke.

In *those* days a decree went out from Caesar *Augustus*
that the *whole world* should be *enrolled*.
This was the *first* enrollment,
when *Quirinius* was governor of *Syria*.

Caesar Augustus = SEE-zer aw-GUHS-tuhs

Quirinius = kwih-RIN-ee-uhs

READING II We celebrate today not simply the babe in the manger but the entry of God into human history in the person of Jesus. We know that Jesus' willingness to suffer and die, and his defeat of death, are the central salvific events in history. But today's passage suggests that salvation becomes a reality because of God's willingness to become human, to share in our struggles and our joys, our hopes and our dreams.

The gift God gives in being willing to become one of us also provides moral instruction. The passage suggests ways in which to live upright lives, adopting values that are instilled when we accept and give thanks for the gift of Jesus and look forward to his return. The gift of salvation comes first; righteous deeds follow.

This short passage can be difficult to read because of the long sentence in the opening section. There are three parts to the sentence: a statement about the "grace of God," an exhortation to holy living, and a closing declaration of praise (following the statement about waiting). Practice dividing the sentence according to parts, but do not rush the intervening material. Close with a sincere hope that your congregation will eagerly choose the good deeds desired by God.

GOSPEL As one of the best-loved passages in the New Testament, today's gospel has the ability to inspire children and adults alike. It is far more than a story about a cute baby, although the birth of this child is central to its proclamation. But the implications of the birth are far-reaching.

The text begins on a historical note, since the birth of this lowly child, wearing

Because Jesus was raised as Joseph's adopted child, he was considered of the same ancestral line as Joseph. Thus, he was of the royal line of David.

So *all* went to be *enrolled*, *each* to his own *town*.
And Joseph *too* went up from *Galilee* from the town of *Nazareth*
to *Judea*, to the city of *David* that is called *Bethlehem*,
because he was of the *house* and *family* of *David*,
to be enrolled with *Mary*, his *betrothed*, who was with *child*.

While they were *there*,
the time came for *her* to have her *child*,
and she gave *birth* to her firstborn *son*.

Jesus was born in abject poverty.

She *wrapped* him in swaddling *clothes* and laid him in a *manger*,
because there was no *room* for them in the *inn*.

Now there were *shepherds* in that region living in the *fields*
and keeping the night *watch* over their *flock*.

The appearance of an angel and a bright light must have been terrifying. Try to convey some of that fear in your voice.

The *angel* of the Lord *appeared* to them
and the *glory* of the Lord shone *around* them,
and they were *struck* with great *fear*.
The *angel* said to *them*,

Speak reassuringly.

"Do *not* be *afraid*;
for *behold*, I proclaim to you *good news* of great *joy*
that will be for *all* the *people*.

Slow down and proclaim this announcement with great solemnity.

For *today* in the city of *David*
a *savior* has been born for you who is *Christ* and *Lord*.
And *this* will be a *sign* for you:
you will find an *infant* wrapped in swaddling *clothes*
and lying in a *manger*."

And *suddenly* there was a *multitude* of the heavenly *host*
with the *angel*,
praising God and *saying*:

Raise your voice in joyful song.

"*Glory* to *God* in the *highest*
and on *earth peace* to *those* on whom his favor *rests*."

rags and sleeping in an animal's food trough, changes all of human history. The claims made about him are not about some fictitious figure, but about a real person, born at a particular time and place. The unattended birth of a baby in a stable inaugurates a new age in God's dealings with humans and a new era of world history.

The journey of Joseph and Mary to Bethlehem, home of King David, is another way of claiming Jesus' royal ancestry and identifying him as the fulfillment of God's promises God to David. This child will change human history, but he was sent precisely to answer the hopes of a particular people, the Jews.

A host of angels appears at Jesus' birth, offering praise to God for the wondrous event. But, as the rest of the gospel of Luke will make clear, the earth-shattering, life-changing, heart-warming event is one quite contrary to all expectations. The great Davidic ruler for whom Israel was waiting is born poor and unknown in a stable. No palace welcomes the Davidic ruler, no precious ointment caresses the skin of the anointed one of God. The announcement of his birth by a heavenly host, proclaimed as good news of joy for all people, is heard only by lowly, illiterate shepherds. The first visitors to the Messiah, the Savior and royal child, are not wealthy rulers or powerful elite, but unassuming guardians of sheep.

This is an exciting gospel to share with your congregation. Try to read it as though for the first time. Share the quiet joy of the baby's birth, the exultation of the angels and the excitement of the shepherds. On this day is born a Savior, Christ the Lord.

CHRISTMAS DAWN

Lectionary #15

READING I Isaiah 62:11–12

A reading from the book of the prophet Isaiah.

The whole world will know the salvation given to Jerusalem. (Zion is another name for Jerusalem.)

See, the LORD *proclaims*
to the *ends* of the *earth:*
say to daughter *Zion,*
your *savior* comes!
Here is his *reward* with him,
his *recompense before* him.

Your voice may become slightly quieter here, but still joyfully reassuring.

They shall be called the *holy people,*
the *redeemed* of the LORD,
and you shall be called *"Frequented,"*
a city that is *not forsaken.*

READING II Titus 3:4–7

A reading from the letter of Saint Paul to Titus.

Beloved:
When the *kindness* and generous *love*
of *God* our *savior appeared,*

Pause briefly. The next line can be spoken a little faster; it is parenthetical.

not because of any righteous *deeds* we had done
but because of his *mercy,*

READING I The end of the exile in Babylon brought about the joyous return of the Hebrew people to their beloved Jerusalem. The renewed city, rebuilt and restored, was the fulfillment of the people's hopes and the sign of God's favor bestowed on them. Although the exile was often understood as punishment for lack of faithfulness, the restoration of Jerusalem was proof of God's favor and Israel's vindication.

The song of joy in today's reading proclaims God's delight in the holy city, here called Zion, and in the people returning to dwell there. A name formerly appropriate for the city is changed: Zion is no longer "forsaken" but is now once again the dwelling place of many. These are the holy people, the redeemed of God. They have paid their price and now can rejoice to return to their beautiful homeland.

Christians see the salvation of God offered most fully in the person of Jesus. It is he who makes us a holy people. Share this brief selection with your community as a song of praise and thanksgiving for what God has done for us in Jesus the Christ.

READING II This passage from the letter to Titus addresses the question of salvation in a uniquely Christian manner. It clarifies that salvation is a gift and does not result from any human actions. Instead, it is something God offers purely out of love for us, and it is effected through baptism. It is appropriate on this feast of the birth of the Savior that we reflect as well on our own rebirth in the waters of baptism.

Through baptism the Spirit of God is offered, a Spirit who gives us the strength to call out to God, not as a foreigner or a guest, but as a member of the household of God.

Slow down as you describe baptism, through which the Spirit is given. Pause briefly after "Holy Spirit."

he *saved* us through the bath of *rebirth*
and *renewal* by the Holy *Spirit*,
whom he *richly* poured *out* on us
through Jesus *Christ* our *savior*,
so that we might be *justified* by his *grace*
and become *heirs* in hope of *eternal life*.

GOSPEL Luke 2:15–20

A reading from the holy gospel according to Luke.

When the angels went *away* from them to *heaven*,
the shepherds *said* to one another,
"Let us *go*, then, to *Bethlehem*
to *see* this thing that has taken *place*,
which the *Lord* has made *known* to us."

The shepherds are eager and curious.

So they went in *haste* and found *Mary* and *Joseph*,
and the *infant* lying in the *manger*.
When they *saw* this,
they made *known* the *message*
that had been *told* them about this *child*.
All who *heard* it were *amazed*
by what had been *told* them by the *shepherds*.

Be careful of your phrasing here; pause after "Joseph" (so that Mary and Joseph do not appear to be lying in the manger!).

Convey amazement in your voice.

And *Mary* kept *all* these things,
reflecting on them in her *heart*.
Then the shepherds *returned*,
glorifying and *praising God*
for all they had *heard* and *seen*,
just as it had been *told* to them.

Speak quietly and warmly about Mary, then enthusiastically as you describe the shepherds again.

We are heirs, recipients of the gift of life willed to us as children of God.

Offer this passage to your assembly as a confirmation that it is chosen by God. Read it with confidence and conviction. Because the passage is one long sentence, practice your phrasing so that you do not rush or run out of breath.

GOSPEL This morning's gospel passage picks up and continues where the passage for the midnight Mass left off. The shepherds have received from the angels the joyous announcement of the birth of a child, a child who is proclaimed as the anointed one of God, Savior and Lord. In eagerness, they visit the child and share the angels' announcement with those they meet, including Mary and Joseph. The words of the angels are greeted with astonishment and awe. The earlier scene, with splendid light and a chorus of angels' voices, continues to inspire. For the evangelist, everything about this event is amazing.

It is unlikely that Mary would find something new in the words of the shepherds; what is more interesting is what she does with the good news: She ponders it in her heart. The shepherds, on the other hand, praise God and continue to proclaim the glad tidings.

Inspire your congregation to join with the shepherds in going forth filled with wonder at the goodness of God, who did not deem it undignified to be born in a stable, to walk the earth as a human, to live among the poor and downtrodden. Convey as well the priceless treasure we celebrate today, so that the entire assembly might join with Mary as she ponders the good news in her heart.

CHRISTMAS DAY

Lectionary #16

READING I Isaiah 52:7–10

A reading from the book of the prophet Isaiah.

Speak in a gentle, peaceful tone, building as you approach the end of the sentence.

How *beautiful* upon the *mountains*
are the *feet* of him who brings glad *tidings*,
announcing *peace*, bearing *good news*,
announcing *salvation*, and saying to *Zion*,
"Your *God* is *King!*"

The guards on the towers are awaiting the coming of God to Jerusalem (here called Zion).

Hark! Your *sentinels* raise a *cry*,
together they shout for *joy*,
for they see *directly*, before their *eyes*,
the *LORD* restoring *Zion*.

Even the fallen walls of Jerusalem break forth in song.

Break *out* together in *song*,
O *ruins* of *Jerusalem!*
For the LORD *comforts* his *people*,
he *redeems* Jerusalem.
The LORD has *bared* his holy *arm*
in the *sight* of all the *nations*;
all the *ends* of the earth will *behold*
the *salvation* of our *God*.

READING I Announcing the end of the exile in Babylon and the restoration of Jerusalem, a messenger runs along the mountaintops, shouting out the good news that God rules over all the earth. During the Babylonian exile, it must sometimes have seemed that God was no longer in power and could not save the people of Judah, living in captivity. But the Persians under King Cyrus defeated the Babylonians, confirming the hopes of those who trusted in God.

The beautiful passage that forms today's reading also announces the end of the exile through the words of the guards in the towers above the city, and even through the stones of the ruined city of Jerusalem. God was understood to be with the people as they returned to their beloved homeland. Throughout the exile, God remained with the people and now joins them in coming home, restored as well to the proper divine dwelling. It is time for rejoicing.

As Christians, we too rejoice that God is present in the birth of a child, which we celebrate today. We cry out in joy as we sing the good news that God reigns, confident that all the earth can come to know the salvation offered by our God.

Allow the joy of the speakers in the passage to fill your heart and your voice, so that the community may see and proclaim the wonders of God. Encourage the members of your assembly to see God's activity not only in Jesus, but also in the story of the Hebrew people and in their lives today. God is active throughout all of human history.

READING II Hebrews 1:1–6

A reading from the letter to the Hebrews.

Brothers and sisters:
In times *past*, God *spoke* in *partial* and *various* ways
to our ancestors through the *prophets*;
in these *last* days, he has spoken to *us* through the *Son*,
whom he made *heir* of all *things*
and *through* whom he created the *universe*,
who is the *refulgence* of his *glory*,
the very *imprint* of his *being*,
and who *sustains* all things by his mighty *word*.

These terms and images were once applied to Wisdom, and the preexistent Son is presented in much the same way that Wisdom is elsewhere.

When he had *accomplished purification* from *sins*,
he took his *seat* at the right *hand* of the Majesty on *high*,
as far *superior* to the *angels*
as the *name* he has inherited is more *excellent* than *theirs*.

The terminology recalls the actions of the Jewish high priests in the Temple, offering expiation for the sins of the people.

For to *which* of the angels did God ever *say*:
"*You* are my *son*; this *day* I have *begotten* you"?
Or again:
"I will be a *father* to him, and *he* shall be a *son* to me"?
And again, when he leads the firstborn into the *world*, he says:
"Let *all* the *angels* of God *worship* him."

Hebrews quotes several Old Testament passages; three are included here. The first (Psalm 2:7) was originally applied to a king, seen as God's son; the second (2 Samuel 7:14) designated the descendant of David; and the third (Deuteronomy 32:43 in the Greek version) comes from a song of Moses.

READING II The opening verses of the letter to the Hebrews lay out the principal themes that will be addressed in the work. In terms similar to those in today's gospel, this passage declares that Christ the exalted Son reflects God's glory and was present at creation, referring to his salvific actions and his enthronement in heaven. This is one of the strongest statements in the entire New Testament regarding the preexistence of the Son, and it paves the way for development of the doctrine of the Trinity.

Initially, a contrast is made between the way in which God formerly communicated, through the prophets, and God's communication in the final age, through God's Son. With amazing succinctness, the passage declares the special status of this Son, the one who is declared "heir of all things," and is above even the angels; he is, in fact, an imprint of the very essence of God.

Reference to the Son's role in cleansing humans from sin draws the reader from reflecting on the Son's preexistent state to the concrete historical actions of Jesus. From the earthly existence of Jesus, the author moves on to discuss his exaltation at the right hand of God. Here his superiority to the angels is revealed. He, unlike the angels, is called "Son."

The richness of this passage could make it difficult to proclaim. Be sure to read it slowly and deliberately, pausing briefly after each phrase so that the complexity of the passage will be clear to your listeners. Read the quotations as expressions of God's word and, as the author intends, proclamations of the greatness of Christ.

GOSPEL John 1:1–18

A reading from the holy gospel according to John.

Speak very slowly, so that your listeners can follow the progression of thought.

In the *beginning* was the *Word,*
and the *Word* was with *God,*
and the Word *was* God.
He *was* in the beginning with *God.*
All things came to be through *him,*
and *without* him *nothing* came to be.
What came to be through him was *life,*

The image shifts here: The one through whom the world was created is also light for all people.

and this *life* was the *light* of the human *race;*
the light *shines* in the *darkness,*
and the *darkness* has not *overcome* it.

Change your tone and tempo to indicate the shift in subject. The present text interrupts the hymn at this point with a discussion of John.

A *man* named *John* was sent from God.
He came for *testimony,* to *testify* to the *light,*
so that *all* might *believe* through him.
He was *not* the *light,*
but came to *testify* to the *light.*

The *true* light, which enlightens *everyone,*
was coming into the *world.*

Slow down again, and speak with regret in your voice.

He was *in* the *world,*
and the *world* came to be *through* him,
but the *world* did not *know* him.
He came to what was his *own,*
but his own *people* did not *accept* him.
But to those who *did* accept him

Speak with hope and wonder.

he gave *power* to become *children* of *God,*
to those who *believe* in his *name,*

GOSPEL **The beautiful hymn that forms the prologue to the Fourth Gospel is a complex literary work. It is at once a hymn of creation, perhaps originally celebrating Wisdom as the co-creator of the world and at the same time a proclamation of the Incarnation. In its present state, it declares that the Word *(logos)* presided at the creation of the world, bringing life and light to all people. The light is then personified and identified with Jesus, the Word made flesh, who is the only Son of God. Within this broad framework are inserted two digressive statements about John the Baptist, the one who gives witness to the coming of the light.**

"In the beginning" recalls the creation story of Genesis, but the creation story is more complex than it appears at first, for with God at the beginning was the Logos, through whom God fashioned the world. The Greek term, usually translated "word," means a single word or story, or communication itself. It also signifies reason and intellectual capacity. To declare that the "Word was with God and the Word was God," then, is to speak of the communication of God's thought processes; the Word is divine, as intimately connected with God as a person's thought and speech are with that person.

After the digression concerning John the Baptist, the author resumes the discussion of the light. To explain to the original readers of the prologue (and to us today) why not everyone became a disciple of Jesus, the author claims that "his own" did not recognize or accept him. Surely this is

who were born not by *natural* generation
nor by human choice nor by a man's *decision*
but of *God.*

And the *Word* became *flesh*
and made his *dwelling among* us,
and we saw his *glory,*
the *glory* as of the Father's *only Son,*
full of *grace* and *truth.*

Communicate the awe of witnessing the glory of Christ.

John *testified* to him and cried *out,* saying,
"*This* was he of whom I *said,*
'The one who is coming *after* me ranks *ahead* of me
because he existed *before* me.'"

Again there is a digression, as John is said to declare the superiority of the Word made flesh. When the hymn begins again, it continues with the same awe as before.

From his *fullness* we have *all* received,
grace in place of *grace,*
because while the *law* was given through *Moses,*
grace and *truth* came through *Jesus Christ.*
No one has ever seen *God.*
The only *Son, God,* who is at the Father's *side,*
has *revealed him.*

The passage closes with a statement of the closeness of the Son to God; the revealer knows intimately who it is that he reveals.

[Shorter: John 1:1–5, 9–14]

an argument by the Jewish-Christian evangelist against the other Jews who did not follow Jesus. But, says the author, those who do follow Jesus become children of God, a relationship made possible because of the Word's special role as the very Son of God.

The claim that the divine could become flesh defies all human reason. The chasm between divine and human, especially evident to one unaccustomed to Christian claims, is great. But as Christians, we believe that this *Logos* of God, active in creation and the bearer of life, was born as a human and lived on earth. A God who may at times appear remote has become one of us. The awesome wonder of the Incarnation is ultimately beyond our understanding; we proclaim this with faith and gratitude, and with amazement at the tremendous love of a God who would share fully in our human life.

What a wonderful celebration of the Incarnation you offer to your community as you read this awe-inspiring and poetic passage. Allow the sections about John to stand as the parenthetical statements they are; lower your voice a bit and increase your speed slightly in order to convey this. Meditate upon this gospel reading, so that the wonder it evokes in you can be heard as you proclaim it in the assembly.

HOLY FAMILY

Lectionary #17

READING I Genesis 15:1–6; 21:1–3

A reading from the book of Genesis.

Abram = AY-br*m

The word of the LORD came to *Abram* in a *vision*, saying:
"Fear *not*, Abram!
I am your *shield*;
I will make your *reward* very *great.*"
But Abram said,
"O Lord *GOD*, what *good* will your gifts be,
if I keep on being *childless*
and have as my *heir* the steward of my house, *Eliezer?*"
Abram continued,
"*See*, you have given me *no offspring*,
and so one of my *servants* will be my *heir.*"
Then the *word* of the LORD *came* to him:
"No, *that* one shall *not* be your heir;
your *own issue* shall be your *heir.*"

It is only natural for Abram to question how he could be great, since he was already old and had no direct heirs who could carry his name. In fact, all his land and possessions were to be claimed by another family.

The LORD took Abram *outside* and said,
"*Look* up at the *sky* and count the *stars*, if you *can*.
Just *so*," he added, "shall your *descendants* be."
Abram put his *faith* in the LORD,
who *credited* it to him as an act of *righteousness.*

The promise is far-reaching; convey its magnitude in your voice.

Abram's willingness to trust God's promise, despite all evidence to the contrary, demonstrates his faithfulness.

The LORD took note of *Sarah* as he had *said* he would;
he *did* for her as he had *promised.*

There are two choices for the first and second readings today. Speak with the liturgy coordinator or pastor to find out which readings will be used.

READING I **GENESIS.** The promises God made to Abraham have given hope to the Hebrew people throughout the ages. God chose a man who responded with trust and obedience. God then promised that Abraham's descendants would be numerous and blessed by God.

In an age in which there was no recognition of an afterlife, the promise of descendants was equivalent to immortality. For this reason, children were of great importance in ancient Hebrew thought. In addition, children carried on the traditions and name of the family, and could inherit the land and possessions of their parents.

Since Abram was quite old when he received God's word that his reward would be great, he naturally questioned God. In a memorable section, God declares that Abram's descendants will be as numerous as the stars of the sky. But the most significant part of this section is Abram's belief and his righteousness in God's eyes.

The covenant God made with Abram and Sarai was signified in the new name each received. Names were of great significance in antiquity; the name change indicates a new destiny for the characters and gives evidence of the authority God has over them. Abraham's name also has particular meaning: Abram, "exalted father," becomes Abraham, "father of a multitude"; both Sarai and Sarah mean "princess." The name given to their child, Isaac, is especially significant: The name Isaac comes from the Hebrew

The promise to Sarah is astounding, given the fact that she was 90 and Abraham was 100.

Sarah became *pregnant* and bore Abraham a *son* in his old *age*,
at the set *time* that God had *stated.*
Abraham gave the name *Isaac* to this *son* of his
whom Sarah *bore* him.

Or:

READING I Sirach 3:2–6, 12–14

Sirach = SEER-ak

A reading from the book of Sirach.

Both father and mother have authority and should be honored.

Respecting one's parents is not a burden but brings blessings.

God sets a *father* in *honor* over his *children;*
a mother's *authority* he confirms over her *sons.*
Whoever *honors* his father atones for *sins,*
and *preserves* himself from them.
When he *prays,* he is *heard;*
he stores up *riches* who reveres his *mother.*
Whoever honors his *father* is gladdened by *children,*
and, when he *prays,* is *heard.*
Whoever *reveres* his father will live a *long* life;
he who *obeys* his father brings *comfort* to his *mother.*

The aged are to be given special consideration. Speak here in a gentle and encouraging tone.

My son, take *care* of your father when he is *old;*
grieve him *not* as long as he *lives.*
Even if his mind *fail,* be *considerate* of him;
revile him *not* all the *days* of his *life;*
kindness to a father will not be *forgotten,*
firmly *planted* against the debt of your *sins*
—a *house* raised in *justice* to you.

word for "laughter," and laughter figures prominently in accounts of his conception and birth. Sarah laughs with joy at his birth.

Today's passage is both a joy and a challenge to read. Because the entire selection includes material from several different chapters of Genesis, and much intervening material has been removed, it is a challenge to read this selection as a coherent story. If you are able to see the progression of the story, you will be able to convey its continuity to your listeners. It is also a challenge because the promises made to Abraham and Sarah have long been understood by Christians to apply not only to the Hebrew people but also to Jesus, and consequently to his followers. Both Isaac and Jesus were conceived and born by the direct intervention of God; both are seen as answers to promises made to God's people; and both are involved in the ratification of covenants made with God — the covenant with Isaac's parents, and the new covenant, established by Jesus.

Read this story as an account of the blessings of family life and children, but also as a recollection of why we call one ancient Jewish family "holy." Recall the trust and obedience of Jesus' parents. Remember also the promises God has made, promises fulfilled in Jesus. Inspire your listeners to see in Isaac's birth a foreshadowing of the birth of Jesus.

SIRACH. The book of Sirach is part of the wisdom tradition of Israel; it seeks to instruct people on how to live good and holy lives. Today's passage offers guidance for putting into practice the commandment to honor one's parents.

The authority of parents over their children is established by God. In keeping with a standard belief of Hebrew thought, good deeds are believed to result in blessings,

READING II Hebrews 11:8, 11–12, 17–19

A reading from the letter to the Hebrews.

Brothers and sisters:
By *faith* Abraham *obeyed* when he was called to go *out* to a place
that he was to *receive* as an *inheritance*;
he went *out*, not *knowing* where he was to *go*.

Emphasize the repeated phrase "by faith," which is the principal theme of the passage.

By *faith* he received *power* to *generate*,
even though he was past the *normal* age
—and Sarah *herself* was *sterile*—
for he thought that the one who had *made* the promise was
trustworthy.

This refers to Abraham's advanced age.

So it was that there came forth from *one* man,
himself as good as *dead*,

The promise made to Abraham and Sarah is summarized here.

descendants as *numerous* as the *stars* in the *sky*
and as *countless* as the sands on the *seashore*.

By *faith Abraham*, when put to the *test*, offered up *Isaac*,
and he who had received the *promises* was ready to offer
his *only son*,

Speak with amazement that someone would be so trusting as to do what Abraham did.

of whom it was said,
"Through *Isaac descendants* shall bear your *name*."
He reasoned that God was able to *raise* even from the *dead*,
and he received Isaac *back* as a *symbol*.

Or:

including forgiveness of sins, riches, children and a long life. However, to honor one's father and mother is not only prudent behavior designed to ensure prosperity for oneself; it demonstrates recognition of a higher, divine authority.

It is important to note that the passage does not advocate blind acceptance of parental demands. Instead, it talks about giving honor and reverence to those who have given us life. For some, that may best be offered from afar. However, for most of us, honoring and revering our parents involves an active concern and willingness to provide for their needs, while continuing to respect their privacy and independence whenever possible.

The passage closes with reference to a parent who may be reaching old age and becoming increasingly vulnerable. This is an especially pertinent message in our day of longer life spans. Our age has also seen the public acknowledgment of the abuse of the elderly, often by their own children.

Offer this passage both as a tribute to legitimate parental authority and as a challenge to the modern tendency to reject anything that is "old," including other human beings. Encourage all the members of your congregation to reflect on what they have learned from their parents and to resolve to give respect and honor in return.

READING II **HEBREWS. The story of Abraham, Sarah and Isaac is treated here by a Christian concerned especially that faith be demonstrated by action. It is set in the context of an exhortation to faith and a list of numerous examples from the Hebrew tradition of faithful people. As we reflect on what it means to be a holy**

READING II Colossians 3:12–21

A reading from the letter of Saint Paul to the Colossians.

Speak warmly as you encourage your listeners to live virtuous lives.

Pause after each term, in order to let each one stand on its own.

Brothers and sisters:
Put on, as God's *chosen* ones, holy and beloved,
heartfelt *compassion*, *kindness*, *humility*, *gentleness*,
and *patience*,
bearing with one another and *forgiving* one another,
if one has a *grievance* against another;
as the *Lord* has forgiven *you*, so must you *also* do.

Pause, then raise your voice a little as you reach the crowning virtue, love.

And over *all* these put on *love*,
that is, the bond of *perfection*.

These lines require a delivery characterized by firm gentleness.

And let the *peace* of *Christ* control your *hearts*,
the *peace* into which you were also *called* in one *body*.
And be *thankful*.

Reflect the richness of the message you proclaim. Speak with enthusiasm and conviction.

Let the *word* of Christ *dwell* in you *richly*,
as in all *wisdom* you *teach* and *admonish* one another,
singing *psalms*, *hymns*, and spiritual *songs*
with *gratitude* in your hearts to *God*.

Once again, your voice can be warm and encouraging.

And *whatever* you do, in *word* or in *deed*,
do *everything* in the name of the Lord *Jesus*,
giving *thanks* to God the Father *through* him.

Try to emphasize the parallel structure of the passage, although the content is not parallel.

Wives, be subordinate to your *husbands*,
as is *proper* in the *Lord*.
Husbands, love your *wives*,
and avoid any *bitterness* toward them.
Children, obey your parents in *everything*,
for this is *pleasing* to the *Lord*.

family, the members of this family are singled out today as exemplars of faithfulness.

The passage begins with the story of Abraham. When he left his homeland he trusted God, although he did not know what to expect. The example of Sarah is that told in the first reading, when she conceived Isaac because she believed in God's word. Her faith resulted in the fulfillment of God's promise that Abraham and Sarah's descendants would be numerous. Finally, Abraham's willingness to sacrifice his only son demonstrates his tremendous trust in God. Christians have long connected the story of the sacrifice of Isaac to the crucifixion of Jesus. It also prefigures the resurrection of Christ, the author of Hebrews asserts, since Isaac was given back to his father.

Emphasizing the word "faith" is the key to reading this passage well. The stories are told in order to encourage Christians to maintain faith at all times, both in the midst of sufferings and during peaceful times. Inspire the members of your community to hold fast to the faith that has given them understanding and strength in the past, and that will sustain them in the future.

COLOSSIANS. In today's passage, after telling the Colossian community what not to do in the previous verses, the author provides a list of virtues appropriate to the lives of Christians. The attributes are to be embraced not only because they are good advice, but because they are offered to people who are to respond as God's chosen ones. They are a holy people, beloved of God, and should live as such.

Stress each virtue in a way that will convey its importance, even when it is only one word. But give special attention to those

Fathers, do not *provoke* your children,
so they may not become *discouraged*.

[Shorter: Colossians 3:12–17]

GOSPEL Luke 2:22–40

A reading from the holy gospel according to Luke.

Note the importance of the Mosaic Law; five times this section declares that Mary and Joseph were fulfilling divine precepts.

When the days were *completed* for their *purification*
according to the law of *Moses*,
they took him up to *Jerusalem*
to *present* him to the *Lord*,
just as it is written in the *law* of the Lord,
"*Every* male that opens the *womb* shall be *consecrated*
to the *Lord*,"
and to offer the *sacrifice* of
"a pair of *turtledoves* or two young *pigeons*,"
in accordance with the *dictate* in the law of the *Lord*.

Raise your voice a bit for the quotations so that your hearers know that you are quoting.

Two separate rituals are combined: the dedication of a firstborn male to God, and the sacrifice by a mother following the birth of a child.

Simeon = SIM-ee-uhn

Now there was a *man* in Jerusalem whose name was *Simeon*.
This man was *righteous* and *devout*,
awaiting the *consolation* of *Israel*,
and the Holy *Spirit* was *upon* him.
It had been *revealed* to him by the Holy *Spirit*
that he should *not* see *death*
before he had seen the *Christ* of the *Lord*.

He came in the *Spirit* into the *temple*;
and when the *parents* brought in the child *Jesus*
to perform the custom of the *law* in *regard* to him,
he took him into his *arms* and *blessed* God, saying:
"*Now*, Master, you may let your servant *go*

that form the core of the passage: forgiveness and love. These are central to living as Christians, for they have been offered freely to us by God. When these virtues are present and all are bound together by love, genuine peacefulness can be known.

In addition to the virtues already mentioned, the author encourages a life grounded in prayer. It is a natural outgrowth of allowing the word of Christ to take root in one's heart.

After offering poetic encouragement to holiness, the passage closes with a very specific admonition to members of a household: husbands and wives, children and parents, and (although not quoted here) slaves and masters. The importance of this section is to note the reciprocity involved in all these relationships. Although the specifics of what is required may seem foreign to us, there is always a balance between what each member of a family has to offer. At no time is it appropriate to read this to demonstrate the superiority of some people over others; the scriptures are never to be used to dominate other people.

Your task is to encourage your listeners to put into practice the admonition to live holy lives in love. Offer the reading as an example of one Christian's attempts to encourage others to live correctly. Do not shrink from the final section, but proclaim it simply as the author's example of how to put holy lives into practice.

GOSPEL The story of Jesus' presentation in the Temple introduces several key themes from the gospel of Luke, including the importance of the Jewish Law and the centrality of Jerusalem and the Temple. As with the account of Jesus' birth, today's reading makes clear that this baby is

Speak these words slowly and deliberately; let them resonate throughout the church.

in *peace*, according to your *word*,
for my *eyes* have seen your *salvation*,
which you prepared in sight of *all* the peoples,
a light for *revelation* to the *Gentiles*,
and *glory* for your people *Israel*."

The child's *father* and *mother* were *amazed* at what was said about him;
and Simeon *blessed* them and said to *Mary* his *mother*,

Simeon's words to Mary are powerful and painful. Read them with a quiet forcefulness.

"*Behold*, this *child* is destined
for the *fall* and *rise* of *many* in Israel,
and to be a *sign* that will be *contradicted*
—and you *yourself* a *sword* will pierce—
so that the thoughts of many *hearts* may be *revealed*."

Pause before beginning this new scene.
Phanuel = FAN-yoo-el
Asher = ASH-er
Read the information about Anna's age relatively quickly; it is not as central as her response to encountering Jesus.

There was also a *prophetess*, *Anna*,
the daughter of *Phanuel*, of the tribe of *Asher*.
She was *advanced* in years,
having lived *seven* years with her husband after her *marriage*,
and then as a *widow* until she was *eighty-four*.
She never *left* the *temple*,
but worshiped *night* and *day* with *fasting* and *prayer*.
And coming *forward* at that very time,
she gave *thanks* to God and *spoke* about the child
to *all* who were awaiting the *redemption* of *Jerusalem*.

Pause again, then continue with a tone of finality. Slow down for the final sentence, and speak it with a bit of wonder in your voice.

When they had fulfilled *all* the prescriptions
of the *law* of the *Lord*,
they returned to *Galilee*,
to their *own* town of *Nazareth*.
The child *grew* and became *strong*, filled with *wisdom*;
and the *favor* of God was *upon* him.

[Shorter: Luke 2:22, 39–40]

no ordinary child, but has been long awaited and will be greeted with joy by those of insight and piety.

The entire story revolves around the actions of Mary and Joseph in fulfilling requirements of the Law of Moses. Since the Jewish people attributed great holiness to blood, anything that involved blood, including childbirth, required special rituals. The author emphasizes that Jesus' parents revered the Law and followed the Mosaic prescriptions to the letter; this holy family was Jewish to the core.

The gospel of Luke begins and ends in the Temple in Jerusalem. Jerusalem is the goal of Jesus throughout his ministry in Luke's gospel, and it is the center of Christian evangelization in its sequel, the Acts of the Apostles. Jesus is revealed in Jerusalem, whether as a baby in the Temple precincts or as an adult on the cross.

Through Simeon's words Jesus is proclaimed here as Messiah. But Jesus' ministry will involve rejection as well, and pain for his mother. Anna prophetically announces the significance of Jesus not only to his parents but to anyone who will listen. In the end, Jesus is like any other child, growing and learning, yet also especially favored by God's love.

Proclaim this beautiful story as the author intended it: as a proclamation of the truth given in the commands to Israel, and in the promises that God would always care for the chosen people; as a statement about the uniqueness of this child; and as a reflection on the piety and love which inspired Jesus' family.

MARY, MOTHER OF GOD

Lectionary #18

READING I Number 6:22–27

A reading from the book of Numbers.

The family of Aaron had priestly responsibilities in ancient Israel.

The LORD said to *Moses:*
"Speak to *Aaron* and his sons and *tell* them:
This is how you shall bless the *Israelites.*

Speak this blessing over your assembly with warmth and encouragement.

"*Say* to them:
The LORD *bless* you and *keep* you!
The LORD let his *face* shine *upon* you,
and be *gracious* to you!
The LORD look upon you *kindly*
and give you *peace!*

"So shall they invoke my *name* upon the *Israelites,*
and I will *bless* them."

READING II Galatians 4:4–7

A reading from the letter of Saint Paul to the Galatians.

Brothers and sisters:
When the *fullness* of time had *come,* God sent his *Son,*
born of a *woman,* born under the *law,*
to *ransom* those under the law,
so that we might receive *adoption* as sons.

God's Son was born of a woman, subject to the Law of Moses.

READING I Today we celebrate Mary, the mother of Jesus, but we also gather as a people beginning a new calendar year. Offer the blessing in this reading over your community as it begins a new year in the hope that God will indeed look with kindness on this people.

This blessing is extremely ancient and is still being used today in many Jewish and Christian congregations. The blessing itself consists of three parts. The first asks God to provide for and protect the people; the second refers to God's "face" and asks that it be turned toward God's chosen ones, a way of asking for God's benevolence and graciousness. God's face shines like the sun, giving warmth and attention to the beloved of the Lord. The third line asks that all of God's acts result in peacefulness.

Speak the introductory words and conclusion with firmness; this is God's command. But look upon your assembly with gentle fondness as you warmly pray the words of the blessing for their sake.

READING II Paul wrote these words to remind the Galatians of their newfound status as Christians. He claims in an earlier passage that the Galatians were like slaves to sin prior to their reception of faith, lacking the freedom to act rightly. But when the Son came into the world, he freed people and allowed us all to be called children of God.

For Paul, slavery was a fact of life. He freely refers to it to make his point. Because of the history of our nation, however, the mention of slavery brings to mind painful memories and unresolved tensions. Read this passage with sensitivity to the feelings of your listeners. At the same time, remind

As proof of their new status, Paul appeals to the Galatians' own prayer: They call upon God as "Abba," the address of a child to its father.

As *proof* that you are *sons,*
God sent the Spirit of his *Son* into our *hearts,*
crying out, *"Abba, Father!"*
So you are no longer a *slave* but a *son,*
and if a *son* then also an *heir,* through *God.*

GOSPEL Luke 2:16–21

A reading from the holy gospel according to Luke.

Pause after Joseph, so that it does not seem that Mary and Joseph are lying with the baby in the manger!

The shepherds went in *haste* to *Bethlehem*
and found *Mary* and *Joseph,*
and the *infant* lying in the *manger.*
When they *saw* this,
they made *known* the message
that had been *told* them about this *child.*

Raise your voice to convey the excitement of all who heard the message.

All who *heard* it were *amazed*
by what had been *told* them by the *shepherds.*

Speak quietly and reflectively.

And *Mary* kept *all* these things,
reflecting on them in her *heart.*
Then the shepherds *returned,*
glorifying and *praising* God
for all they had *heard* and *seen,*
just as it had been *told* to them.

Again, raise your voice in joy and wonder.

When eight *days* were completed for his *circumcision,*
he was named *Jesus,* the name given him by the *angel*
before he was *conceived* in the *womb.*

them of their status as Christians; they are truly God's children, free to approach God in intimacy and trust.

GOSPEL This selection was also used as the gospel reading for Christmas Mass at dawn. See that commentary for a fuller discussion.

Today's gospel reminds us of the wondrous event of the Incarnation. It recalls the birth of a child who will inspire countless people to change their lives and acknowledge God's goodness. This child will grow to be a preacher and teacher, and will live his life in total obedience to God. This child will become a symbol of the overturning of the old order and a completely new offer of life from God. Finally, this child will one day be proclaimed as so intimately united with God that the child himself is divine.

The central mood of this passage is one of wonder. The shepherds are transformed, inspired to sing God's praises. More importantly, Mary quietly reflects on the events of the day and the words of the visitors.

The gospel closes with the account of Jesus' circumcision, a detail that reveals the importance of the Jewish Law for his parents. The account of the circumcision also reminds us of the words of the angel to Mary at Jesus' conception. He is given the name that indicates what he will do: In Hebrew, the name Joshua (in Greek, Jesus) means "he will save."

Although this passage was used only a few days ago on Christmas, many in your assembly might not have heard it yet. Read it as though for the first time, emphasizing the awe of all involved, and especially concentrating on the tender trust of Mary as she ponders the significance of her son.

EPIPHANY OF THE LORD

Lectionary #20

READING I Isaiah 60:1–6

Sing out with joy and wonder at the splendors the author describes.

Lower your voice just a bit, then build to the end of the line.

Let your voice be filled with joy.

A reading from the book of the prophet Isaiah.

Rise up in *splendor*, Jerusalem! Your *light* has *come*,
the *glory* of the *LORD* shines *upon* you.
See, *darkness* covers the *earth*,
and thick *clouds* cover the *peoples*;
but upon *you* the LORD *shines*,
and *over* you appears his *glory*.

Nations shall walk by your *light*,
and *kings* by your shining *radiance*.
Raise your *eyes* and look *about*;
they all *gather* and *come* to you:
your *sons* come from *afar*,
and your *daughters* in the arms of their *nurses*.

Then you shall be *radiant* at what you see,
your *heart* shall *throb* and *overflow*,
for the *riches* of the *sea* shall be *emptied out* before you,
the *wealth* of *nations* shall be *brought* to you.
Caravans of *camels* shall *fill* you,
dromedaries from *Midian* and *Ephah*;
all from *Sheba* shall come
bearing *gold* and *frankincense*,
and proclaiming the *praises* of the *LORD*.

READING I The early Christians kept the feast of the Epiphany as the celebration of the Incarnation and the manifestation of God to the world in the person of Jesus. The celebration of Christmas came later and is still secondary for many of the world's Christians. At today's feast we proclaim that God's glory is made known to all. This brings with it a responsibility to ensure that all peoples are welcome, that all needs are met.

The first reading is a joyous proclamation about the splendor of the holy city of Jerusalem. It is a beacon of light in a world of darkness, splendid and radiant as the sun. Its brightness guides not only its own sons and daughters (the people of Israel returning from exile) but even provides light for foreigners, who stream to the city, praising God and bearing riches from their own lands.

This selection also recognizes the responsibility Israel had to be a light to the nations, telling others of both the expectations and the blessings of God. Christians believe that the promises made to Israel are fulfilled in Jesus and that he is most fully the light for the nations. Jesus is like Jerusalem, radiant in glory, guiding all peoples and receiving gifts of wealth and honor.

Cry out with joy and excitement as you share this passage with your community. Let it inspire your listeners to rejoice in the splendors of God, now revealed in Jesus. Encourage them to be welcoming to all people, friend and foreigner, in order to become a new Jerusalem, shining for all to see.

READING II Paul's ministry was marked by controversy. Among the earliest followers of Jesus (all conscientious Jews, as was Jesus himself), there

READING II Ephesians 3:2–3a, 5–6

A reading from the letter of Saint Paul to the Ephesians.

The author claims that Paul's ministry to the Gentiles was undertaken in response to a revelation.

Brothers and sisters:
You have heard of the *stewardship* of God's *grace*
that was given to me for your *benefit,*
namely, that the *mystery* was made *known* to me
by *revelation.*

To describe the relationship of the Gentiles to Judaism, the author speaks in terms of inheritance; Gentiles are adopted into the same family as Jews.

It was not made known to people in *other* generations
as it has *now* been revealed
to his holy *apostles* and *prophets* by the *Spirit:*
that the *Gentiles* are *coheirs,* members of the *same body,*
and *copartners* in the promise in Christ *Jesus*
through the *gospel.*

GOSPEL Matthew 2:1–12

A reading from the holy gospel according to Matthew.

There were people in the ancient Middle East who were known for their knowledge of the movement of stars. The evangelist has them in mind here.

When Jesus was born in *Bethlehem* of *Judea,*
in the days of King *Herod,*
behold, magi from the *east* arrived in *Jerusalem,* saying,
"Where is the newborn *king* of the *Jews?*
We saw his *star* at its *rising*
and have come to do him *homage."*

arose a dispute about who could be saved. Paul and others argued that the salvation offered in Christ was available to all, regardless of race or religious heritage. The original view held that Jesus had come to his own people, the Jewish nation, and that it was necessary to be Jewish in order to be his follower. The letter to the Ephesians, written by an admirer of Paul, insists that God's blessings are for all; Gentiles together with Jews are recipients of the promises made to Israel and fulfilled in Jesus.

Today's passage recalls the ministry of Paul in establishing and serving churches composed primarily of non-Jews. The author uses the Pauline image of the body. Gentiles are pictured as a limb of the body of Israel. By being part of the same body, Gentiles are able to inherit all that belongs to the Israel, all that has been promised by God to the chosen people.

Since most of us are non-Jewish followers of Christ, we are the direct recipients of this Epiphany message. But just as the Jewish followers of Jesus were challenged to accept Gentiles, so also we cannot truly claim to follow Jesus unless we proclaim him to all the world without regard to race or class or appearance.

Your task is to present this challenge to your listeners by reading the concluding lines of the passage with special forcefulness. Encourage them to appreciate both the abiding nature of God's promises to the Jewish people and the inclusiveness that we must offer to others.

GOSPEL **High drama now greets us as we turn from the adorable child in the manger and the choirs of angels celebrating his birth to the scheming of the**

Herod the Great was a ruthless, greatly disliked puppet king. He jealously guarded his power and was sincerely afraid that he would be ousted from his throne.

When King Herod *heard* this,
he was greatly *troubled,*
and all Jerusalem *with* him.
Assembling all the *chief priests* and the *scribes* of the *people,*
he *inquired* of them where the *Christ* was to be *born.*
They said to him, "In *Bethlehem* of *Judea,*
for *thus* it has been written through the *prophet:*
'And *you, Bethlehem,* land of *Judah,*
are by *no* means *least* among the *rulers* of Judah;
since from *you* shall come a *ruler,*
who is to *shepherd* my people *Israel.'"*

Then Herod *called* the magi *secretly*
and *ascertained* from them the time of the star's *appearance.*
He sent them to *Bethlehem* and said,
"Go and search *diligently* for the child.
When you have *found* him, bring me *word,*
that I *too* may go and do him *homage."*

They begin to "follow" the star at this point. Convey the wonder and joy the wise men felt.

After their audience with the *king* they set *out.*
And *behold,* the *star* that they had seen at its *rising*
preceded them,
until it came and *stopped* over the place where the *child* was.
They were *overjoyed* at seeing the star,
and on *entering* the *house*
they saw the *child* with *Mary* his *mother.*

They *prostrated* themselves and did him *homage.*
Then they *opened* their *treasures*
and offered him gifts of *gold, frankincense,* and *myrrh.*

And having been *warned* in a *dream* not to return to *Herod,*
they departed for their *country* by *another* way.

king who attempts to keep anyone from honoring this child. One of the reasons for the change in tone is the change in authors. Up to this point we have been reading the nativity story primarily from the gospel of Luke; we now turn to the gospel of Matthew. But it is also time to recognize the demands placed on us by that sweet babe, for Epiphany is a challenging feast. There is great joy in the proclamation that God is made known to the entire world in Christ Jesus, and great challenge to us to be as open and accepting of those who are different from us as the child Jesus was of his visitors.

The story is familiar, yet it has a timeless quality. People of great wealth and education, able to see the signs of the times concentrated in a single star, come to honor a poor, unknown baby born to parents far from home. Naturally they begin by seeking him in a palace, since they recognize that he is to be the king of the Jews. When King Herod attempts to trick them, they accomplish their mission and return home, thwarting his jealous plot.

On this feast of Epiphany, we celebrate the mission of these foreign people who carried news of God's presence in Jesus back to their homelands. The significance of Jesus, unrecognized so often by his own people during his ministry, is clear to those who have never met him before.

Proclaim this gospel as the exciting story it is. Let the story challenge your listeners to be more accepting of those who are unfamiliar. We honor Jesus best today by resolving to do as the Magi did: bend our knees before the helpless; respect the young as well as the aged; offer our wealth to those with nothing.

BAPTISM OF THE LORD

Lectionary #21

READING I Isaiah 55:1–11

A reading from the book of the prophet Isaiah.

Thus says the LORD:
All you who are *thirsty*,
come to the *water!*
You who have no *money*,
come, receive *grain* and *eat*;
come, without *paying* and without *cost*,
drink *wine* and *milk!*
Why spend your *money* for what is not *bread*,
your *wages* for what fails to *satisfy?*
Heed me, and you shall eat *well*,
you shall *delight* in rich *fare*.
Come to me *heedfully*,
listen, that you may have *life*.
I will *renew* with you the everlasting *covenant*,
the *benefits* assured to *David*.

As I made him a *witness* to the *peoples*,
a *leader* and *commander* of *nations*,
so shall you summon a *nation* you knew *not*,
and *nations* that knew *you* not shall *run* to you,
because of the *LORD*, your *God*,
the *Holy One* of *Israel*, who has *glorified* you.

Seek the LORD while he may be *found*,
call him while he is *near*.

Speak gently and encouragingly.

The intensity builds as you repeatedly invite your listeners to partake of the sustenance offered.

Ask this as a sincere question; why would anyone be so foolish?

Sincerely encourage your listeners to turn to God. Speak with tender longing.

There are two choices for the first and second readings today. Speak with the liturgy coordinator or pastor to find out which readings will be used.

READING I **ISAIAH 55. A warm and welcoming invitation is offered in today's first reading, as well as an acknowledgment of the greatness of God. The promise of refreshing waters is especially appropriate for a feast celebrating baptism. It is God who speaks, drawing the listener to a banquet of great abundance. Those who thirst, those who hunger, those who have nothing, all are invited to indulge themselves. The banquet became a symbol in antiquity of the invitation of a god to humans, first offering food, then life, in exchange for faithful adherence. God here invites Israel to partake of good food and wine, then pledges love for the house of David. God's blessing of Israel through the monarchy is a constant theme of the book of Isaiah.**

Only those who have accepted the invitation from God will be able to recognize God's goodness and faithfulness. A contrast between the majesty of God and the simplicity of humans, especially the emptiness of the wicked, is provided. But the word of God enlivens, penetrating deeply in order to produce results, just as rain and snow penetrate the earth to bring forth fruit.

It is appropriate for one who proclaims this passage in the assembly to reflect on the concluding hymn to God's word. Know that God's declaration is true: This word will not return empty. Your task is to proclaim the word of God with power in order to bring forth new life in your listeners. Entice them

God invites this people into an intimate relationship, despite the chasm between heaven and earth.

Let the scoundrel *forsake* his way,
and the *wicked* man his thoughts;
let him *turn* to the LORD for *mercy*;
to our *God*, who is *generous* in *forgiving*.
For *my* thoughts are not *your* thoughts,
nor are *your* ways *my* ways, says the LORD.
As *high* as the *heavens* are above the *earth*
so high are *my ways* above *your ways*
and *my thoughts* above *your thoughts*.

Pause after the explanatory phrases you have just read before returning to the main theme of the sentence.

God's word is powerful and effective.

For just as from the *heavens*
the *rain* and *snow* come *down*
and do not *return* there
till they have *watered* the *earth*,
making it *fertile* and *fruitful*,
giving *seed* to the one who *sows*
and *bread* to the one who *eats*,
so shall my *word be*
that goes *forth* from my *mouth*;
my *word* shall not *return* to me *void*,
but shall do my *will*,
achieving the *end* for which I *sent* it.

Or:

READING I Isaiah 42:1–4, 6–7

A reading from the book of the prophet Isaiah.

Speak with firm conviction.

Thus says the LORD:
Here is my *servant* whom I *uphold*,
my *chosen* one with whom I am *pleased*,

with the promise of nourishment, so that all who hear you will want to learn more. You can do this by speaking with sincerity and conviction as you extend God's invitation to all.

ISAIAH 42. The servant of God in this passage is one who is pleasing to God and inspired by God's spirit, but also one who acts for justice without becoming the center of attention. The servant is gentle yet strong.

The servant songs of the book of Isaiah often depict Israel as God's faithful servant, chosen by God for a special mission. Here the mission is one with universal implications. The servant Israel will establish justice throughout the whole world and will instruct others, proclaiming liberty.

Christians understand this passage to refer not only to Israel but also to Jesus, the one who is a beacon of light for all the nations and who proclaims freedom for people from both real and metaphorical prisons. The opening lines sound much like the words spoken at Jesus' baptism, as recounted in the gospel reading.

Proclaim this passage as a way of remembering God's servants, whether the prophets of old, the Jewish people or Jesus. In addition, inspire your assembly to see itself as called to be this servant, to uphold righteousness for all the world to see, to follow Jesus' leadership in overturning systems of oppression, and to provide relief to those who suffer.

READING II **1 JOHN. The first letter of John deals with a schism in the Johannine community, and the author instructs the remaining members to be faithful and loving toward one another. The author**

upon whom I have put my *spirit*;
he shall bring forth *justice* to the *nations*,
not *crying* out, not *shouting*,
not making his voice *heard* in the *street*.
A *bruised reed* he shall not *break*,
and a *smoldering wick* he shall not *quench*,
until he *establishes justice* on the *earth*;
the *coastlands* will *wait* for his *teaching*.

Lower your voice a bit as you read of the servant's meekness, then speak forcefully again in the final lines of the paragraph.

I, the LORD, have *called* you for the victory of *justice*,
I have *grasped* you by the *hand*;
I *formed* you, and *set* you
as a *covenant* of the *people*,
a *light* for the *nations*,
to open the *eyes* of the *blind*,
to bring out *prisoners* from *confinement*,
and from the *dungeon*, those who live in *darkness*.

Speak this as a word of challenge to your community as well as a description of the servant.

READING II 1 John 5:1–9

A reading from the first letter of Saint John.

Beloved:
Everyone who *believes* that Jesus is the *Christ* is begotten by *God*,
and everyone who *loves* the *Father*
loves *also* the one *begotten* by him.
In *this* way we know that we love the *children* of God
when we love *God* and obey his *commandments*.

Pause briefly after "Christ."

For the *love* of God is *this*,
that we *keep* his *commandments*.

Pause after "God."

begins with a statement of truth: A person who truly loves another will love the child of the other. Since every Christian is born of God, anyone who loves God will love other Christians. Those born of God are known by their obedience to God's commandments. As in the gospel of John, the author affirms that the central command is to love.

Real love — and faith — can conquer any adversity. Love and faith are linked; a person cannot embrace one without the other. Faith enables one to accept God's testimony to the Son and to practice love.

In an affirmation of the full humanity of Jesus (against those who claimed that he simply appeared to be human), the author speaks of Jesus coming by "water and blood." The reference to water and blood has long been taken to refer to Jesus' baptism and the Last Supper, which is why this passage is proclaimed today.

Proclaim this difficult passage as clearly as possible, so that you can instill genuine belief in your listeners and inspire them to live lives modeled on that of Jesus, who demonstrated his love for us all in both his life and his death.

ACTS. According to the Acts of the Apostles, Cornelius was the first Gentile convert to Christianity. Before being summoned to the house of Cornelius, Peter had a vision in which he was instructed that what he had previously thought was unclean (both non-Jews and certain foods) has been declared clean by God. Peter understood it to mean that Gentiles could enter the community of God's chosen ones without first becoming Jewish; thus Peter became the first apostle to the Gentiles in Acts.

And his *commandments* are not *burdensome*,
for whoever is *begotten* by *God conquers* the *world*.
And the *victory* that conquers the *world* is our *faith*.

Raise your voice a bit as you continue.

Who indeed is the *victor* over the world
but the one who *believes* that Jesus is the *Son* of *God?*

This is the one who came through *water* and *blood*, Jesus *Christ*,
not by water *alone*, but by *water* and *blood*.
The *Spirit* is the one who *testifies*,
and the *Spirit* is *truth*.
So there are *three* that testify,
the *Spirit*, the *water*, and the *blood*,
and the *three* are of one *accord*.
If we accept human testimony,
the testimony of *God* is surely *greater*.
Now the testimony of *God* is *this*,
that he has *testified* on behalf of his *Son*.

Or:

READING II Acts 10:34–38

A reading from the Acts of the Apostles.

Peter speaks on behalf of accepting Gentiles into the community of Christians. The role of Gentile missionary actually went to Paul. Peter himself, although he may have accepted Gentiles, was never entirely comfortable with them.

Peter proceeded to speak to those gathered
in the house of *Cornelius*, *saying*:

In *truth*, I see that God shows *no partiality*.
Rather, in every nation whoever *fears* him and acts *uprightly*
is *acceptable* to him.

The speech in the present text is one that Peter delivers as soon as he arrives at the house of Cornelius. It summarizes both his new realization and Jesus' baptism and early ministry (which is why it is included today). Although the good news of Jesus was sent to Israel, God accepts any person who acts rightly. Cornelius was introduced earlier in Acts as a devout man who respected the Jewish Temple. Peter can claim, then, that he must surely have heard of Jesus and his deeds.

Your task today is to challenge your congregation to be as accepting of those who are different as Peter was. The inspiration for this is Jesus' own ministry to the outcasts of Israel. Read Peter's speech as though it is addressed directly to your congregation.

GOSPEL **The gospel of Mark, the earliest of the gospels, often gives a bare-bones account of events in Jesus' life. The present instance is no exception. John is introduced briefly, but his significance as forerunner of the "one with power" is made clear. The account of Jesus' baptism is brief and simple.**

Jesus' baptism by John posed a problem for early Christians. It seemed to imply that Jesus was a disciple of John, which is why all accounts of the event insist that John was the lesser of the two and prepared the way for Jesus. In addition, John preached a baptism for the forgiveness of sins, a statement removed from the gospel of Matthew

You *know* the word that he *sent* to the Israelites
as he proclaimed *peace* through Jesus *Christ*, who is Lord of *all*,
what has *happened* all over *Judea*,
beginning in *Galilee* after the *baptism*
that *John* preached,
how God *anointed* Jesus of Nazareth
with the *Holy Spirit* and *power*.

Emphasize this phrase; it is key. Throughout Acts, the Holy Spirit powerfully inspires the followers of Jesus.

He went about doing *good*
and *healing* all those *oppressed* by the *devil*,
for *God* was *with* him."

GOSPEL Mark 1:7–11

A reading from the holy gospel according to Mark.

John was addressing the crowds. Raise your voice similarly.

This is what John the Baptist *proclaimed:*
"One *mightier* than I is coming *after* me.
I am not *worthy* to stoop and *loosen* the *thongs* of his *sandals*.
I have baptized you with *water*;
he will baptize you with the *Holy Spirit*."

Emphasize this line; Jesus' baptism is not that of John, but is much more powerful.

It *happened* in those days that *Jesus* came from *Nazareth* of *Galilee*
and was *baptized* in the Jordan by *John*.
On coming up out of the *water* he saw the *heavens* being torn *open*
and the *Spirit*, like a *dove*, *descending* upon him.

Speak firmly and slowly, but resist adopting a booming voice for God's words.

And a *voice* came from the *heavens*,
"*You* are my beloved *Son*; with *you* I am well *pleased*."

because it seemed to imply sinfulness on the part of Jesus.

What happens when Jesus emerges from the water clarifies his special status. He is like the others baptized by John, sharing fully in John's conviction that repentance is necessary for salvation, but he is also unique. At his baptism Jesus was marked by the Spirit as the messianic servant of God. His followers will come to recognize him as the beloved Son as well.

God's presence in the event is made clear by the spectacular events that occur: The heavens open, a dove descends just as at the creation of the world, and a heavenly voice resounds. John's words that Jesus will baptize with the Holy Spirit are confirmed by the presence of the dove, the symbol of the Spirit, who rests upon Jesus.

The author makes it clear that Jesus is no ordinary preacher. He is the chosen one of God, with a special mission to accomplish. He is intimately united with God, and upon him God's favor rests.

Proclaim this short gospel passage with clarity and boldness. Encourage your listeners to reflect on Jesus' identity and its significance for his followers. Read John's words regarding the baptism Jesus will bring as a hint of things to come.

2ND SUNDAY IN ORDINARY TIME

Lectionary #65

READING I 1 Samuel 3:3b–10, 19

A reading from the first book of Samuel.

The ark of God was the holiest object of the Hebrews. Samuel's proximity to the ark places him in the proper place for receiving a divine revelation.

Eli = EE-lī

Samuel was sleeping in the *temple* of the LORD
where the *ark* of *God* was.
The LORD called to Samuel, who answered, "*Here* I am."
Samuel ran to *Eli* and said, "*Here* I am. You *called* me."
"*I* did not call you," Eli said. "Go *back* to *sleep.*"
So he went back to sleep.

Speak Eli's words with a note of impatience. Emphasize the "not."

Again the LORD called Samuel, who *rose* and went to *Eli.*
"*Here* I *am,*" he said. "You *called* me."
But Eli answered, "I did *not* call you, my son. Go *back* to *sleep.*"
At that time Samuel was not *familiar* with the LORD,
because the LORD had not *revealed* anything to him as *yet.*

Samuel must be getting impatient also.

Communicate a sense of discovery and gentle explanation in Eli's words.

The LORD called Samuel *again,* for the *third* time.
Getting up and going to *Eli,* he said, "*Here* I *am.* You *called* me."
Then Eli understood that the *LORD* was calling the youth.
So he said to Samuel, "*Go* to *sleep,* and if you are *called,* reply,
'*Speak,* LORD, for your *servant* is *listening.*'"
When Samuel went to *sleep* in his *place,*
the *LORD* came and *revealed* his presence,
calling out as before, "*Samuel, Samuel!*"
Samuel answered, "*Speak,* for your *servant* is *listening.*"

This is the most important line of the entire passage. Read it with clarity and conviction. Then pause before continuing.

Samuel grew *up,* and the *LORD* was *with* him,
not permitting *any* word of his to be *without effect.*

READING I Samuel was the model prophet and leader of the Hebrew people before they were organized under a monarchy. In fact, it was Samuel who anointed the first king of Israel, Saul, and his successor, David.

This passage is a classic story of the call of a prophet and provides a fitting introduction to the calling of Jesus' first disciples in today's gospel. Just before the beginning of today's selection, the text indicates that visions and the prophetic hearing of the word of God were rare, so it is not surprising that neither Samuel nor Eli initially understood what was happening. God calls three times before Eli understands who is speaking. Imagine Eli's exasperation at having his sleep repeatedly interrupted, and consider as well Samuel's frustration at not being understood. But after Samuel responds to the one who is calling him, he receives further revelations, which he guards with reverence. All of Israel eventually comes to recognize him as a prophet of God.

This tale makes for great storytelling. Allow your voice to express the emotions that seem appropriate: eagerness, tiredness, frustration, impatience, confusion and finally understanding. Encourage your listeners to respond to God with the same confident trust that Samuel displays: "Speak for your servant is listening."

READING II Paul's correspondence with the Corinthian community reveals a vibrant, if somewhat confused, group of enthusiastic new Christians. They were blessed with spectacular gifts but had apparently taken Paul at his word when he preached the freedom of the gospel of Christ,

READING II 1 Corinthians 6:13c–15a, 17–20

A reading from the first letter of Saint Paul to the Corinthians.

Brothers and sisters:
The *body* is not for *immorality,* but for the *Lord,*
and the *Lord* is for the *body;*
God *raised* the Lord and will also raise *us* by his power.

Stress the first two instances of "Lord." The point is that one's body is not one's own.

Do you *not know* that your bodies are *members* of *Christ?*
But whoever is *joined* to the Lord becomes *one Spirit* with him.
Avoid immorality.
Every *other* sin a person commits is *outside* the body,
but the *immoral* person sins *against* his *own* body.

Express this more as a statement than a question. Paul is actually arguing his point, but may also be shocked at the Corinthians' ignorance about this.

Do you *not know* that your body
is a *temple* of the *Holy Spirit* within you,
whom you have from *God,* and that you are *not* your *own?*
For you have been *purchased* at a *price.*
Therefore *glorify* God in your *body.*

This is a key thought. Speak with conviction and inspiration that the body is a temple of the Holy Spirit.

Paul has in mind Jesus' selfless act on the cross. Read this with a sense of awe.

misunderstanding and abusing their newfound freedom. Paul continually had to correct their misbehavior. He was shocked at their participation in pagan feasts, as well as at several examples of sexual misconduct.

It is this latter issue that comes to the fore in today's reading. Against those who argued that freedom in Christ meant doing whatever one wanted, Paul insists that the human body is holy and belongs to the Lord. There are three aspects to Paul's argument against sexual immorality.

First, Paul held an active hope in the resurrection of the body after death. The sanctity of the body, then, was of great import. According to Paul, the body will not simply be discarded at death, but will be transformed. As a result, it must be kept pure, just as the soul and spirit are.

Second, Paul says that Christians are united with Christ in body and spirit. By sinning with their bodies, Christians sin against the whole community, the body of Christ.

Paul concludes by asserting that the body is a temple, a place of honor and reverence for the Holy Spirit. This reality is the result of the great price paid by Christ. The body, then, must be used to give glory to God.

Paul's words remind us that our actions can adversely affect ourselves, our community and our relationship with God. Offer this reading as a challenge to all the members of your community to see their own bodies as holy, to be used in all ways, sexual or otherwise, to offer praise to God.

GOSPEL The call of Jesus' disciples in the gospel of John opens with John the Baptist not only pointing the way to Jesus, but introducing him. Two of the disciples of John leave him to follow

GOSPEL John 1:35–42

A reading from the holy gospel according to John.

John was *standing* with two of his *disciples*,
and as he watched Jesus walk *by*, he said,
"*Behold*, the *Lamb* of *God*."
The two *disciples heard* what he said and *followed* Jesus.

Pause to allow the question to sink in.

Jesus *turned* and saw them *following* him and said to them,
"What are you *looking* for?"
They said to him, "*Rabbi*"—which translated means *Teacher*—
"where are you *staying*?"
He said to them, "*Come*, and you will *see*."
So they went and *saw* where Jesus was *staying*,
and they stayed *with* him that day.
It was about *four* in the afternoon.

Andrew is clearly excited; express his enthusiasm.

Andrew, the brother of Simon *Peter*,
was *one* of the two who heard John and followed Jesus.
He *first* found his *own* brother *Simon* and told him,
"*We* have *found* the *Messiah*"—which is translated *Christ*.
Then he brought *him* to Jesus.
Jesus *looked* at him and said,
"You are *Simon* the son of *John*;
you will be called *Cephas*"—which is translated *Peter*.

Cephas = SEE-fuhs
The disciple we know as Peter was known by many names. His parents gave him a Hebrew name, Simon (or Simeon). Jesus here renames him Cephas, from the Aramaic word for "rock"; the name "Peter" comes from the Greek for "rock." Jesus apparently nicknamed him "Rocky."

Jesus. At first they are simply curious, but it later becomes clear that their "following" is permanent.

The title used of Jesus by John ("Lamb of God") recalls the one who is like a "lamb led to the slaughter" in Isaiah. It refers as well to the Passover lamb, whose blood preserved the lives of the Hebrew children in Egypt. In the gospel of John, Jesus is crucified at the same time as the lambs of the Passover celebration are slaughtered; he is the one who gives life and freedom to those who have been "washed in the blood of the Lamb" (Revelation 7:14).

Jesus asks John's disciples a question that must be asked of every person: "What are you looking for? "Whatever the response of the two might have been, they find the answer in Jesus. He invites them to "come," to "see," terms that signify discipleship and the special insight of faith.

After spending time with him, the two were so inspired that Andrew went looking for his brother to tell him the wondrous news: This one is the one for whom they have hoped and longed. He is the anointed one of God, the Christ. The evangelist does not give Peter a chance to question or even respond. Yet Jesus knows him. Jesus renames Peter, a sign that he has been chosen and given a new direction in life. Peter becomes a new person, a disciple of the Christ.

Convey to your listeners the excitement of the discovery made by the two new disciples of Jesus. Offer this reading to the members of your congregation as a call for each of them to choose once again whom they will follow, and to announce it to all the world.

3RD SUNDAY IN ORDINARY TIME

Lectionary #68

READING I Jonah 3:1–5, 10

A reading from the book of the prophet Jonah.

Nineveh = NIN-uh-vuh
There is no evidence for a city of the size implied in this reading. The entire story is exaggerated for greatest effect. Speak God's words as a strong command.

The *word* of the LORD came to *Jonah*, saying:
"*Set out* for the *great* city of *Nineveh*,
and *announce* to it the message that I will *tell* you."
So *Jonah* made ready and went to *Nineveh*,
according to the LORD's *bidding*.

Now *Nineveh* was an enormously *large* city;
it took *three* days to go *through* it.
Jonah *began* his journey through the city,
and had gone but a *single* day's *walk* announcing,

Jonah's words are yelled in the streets; attempt to convey this in your voice, then pause briefly.

"*Forty* days *more* and *Nineveh* shall be *destroyed*,"
when the people of Nineveh *believed* God;

Read in a tone of amazement at the repentance of the people.

they proclaimed a *fast*
and *all* of them, *great* and *small*, put on *sackcloth*.

When God *saw* by their actions how they *turned* from their evil *way*,
he *repented* of the evil that he had *threatened* to do to them;
he did *not* carry it out.

READING I Jonah, we are told earlier in the book, spent a great deal of time avoiding God's command to preach to the people of Nineveh. They were foreigners, and he thought himself better than they. As a result of his refusal to do God's will, he ended up in the belly of a large fish. But today's reading comes from later in the tale, after he has finally given in to God's persistent prodding.

Although the text presents Nineveh as a huge city, Jonah's warning changes the hearts of every inhabitant, from ruler to child, and all repent of their evil deeds. God also repents of the destruction planned for Nineveh.

Everything about the tale of Jonah is exaggeration, from the sizes of the fish and the city, to the attempts of Jonah to flee God's will, to the instant acknowledgment of Jonah's God by the sailors and all Nineveh's inhabitants. It is ironic that Jonah, who knows God, attempts to disobey, while the sailors and Ninevites instantly offer worship to Jonah's foreign God. People often surprise us.

Read this short story as the exciting tale of reversal that it is. Speak as a prophet, urging your listeners to turn from sinfulness and honor our God.

READING II Paul firmly believed in an imminent Parousia; that is, he thought that Jesus was going to be returning to earth in the immediate future. In light of this belief, we can understand his instructions to the Corinthians given in

READING II 1 Corinthians 7:29–31

A reading from the first letter of Saint Paul to the Corinthians.

There is an urgency in these words, but avoid reading them too quickly or falling into a sing-song voice. Try to vary the stress or speed in the last part of each phrase in order to keep the attention of your listeners.

I *tell* you, brothers and sisters, the time is running *out.*
From *now* on, let those having *wives* act as *not* having them,
those *weeping* as *not* weeping,
those *rejoicing* as *not* rejoicing,
those *buying* as *not owning,*
those using the *world* as *not* using it *fully.*

Pause before this line and proclaim it with solemnity.

For the world in its *present* form is passing *away.*

GOSPEL Mark 1:14–20

A reading from the holy gospel according to Mark.

After *John* had been *arrested,*
Jesus came to *Galilee* proclaiming the *gospel* of *God:*

We have heard this so many times that it is easy to lose its significance. Proclaim it as an urgent, life-changing command.

"This is the *time* of *fulfillment.*
The *kingdom* of *God* is at *hand.*
Repent, and *believe* in the *gospel.*"

As he passed by the Sea of Galilee,
he saw *Simon* and his brother *Andrew* casting their *nets* into the sea;
they were *fishermen.*
Jesus said to them,
"Come *after* me, and I will make you *fishers* of *men.*"

Convey a sense of wonder at how quickly these first disciples follow Jesus.

Then they *abandoned* their nets and *followed* him.

today's reading. Paul urges the Corinthians to put nothing before God and to be prepared always for the day when Christ will return. They are urged not to marry, not to mourn, not to care for day-to-day matters, but to focus on their faith and its priority in their lives. For the "world . . . is passing away," according to Paul.

It is clear that Christ did not return as Paul expected, or as many others have since predicted. However, although the urgency may have eased, the single-heartedness of Paul's message still holds. We are called to be ready always to meet the Lord. This may be difficult to remember when the baby is crying or dinner is burning, and it is natural to make plans and prepare for the future. But any person could be gone tomorrow, the present form of the world having passed away for that individual.

Inspire the members of your congregation, then, not to deny the lives they are living, but to recall always the fragility of life and the things that matter most. Encourage them to reflect on the possibility of death and to be prepared for it at all times—whether it comes tomorrow or years from now.

GOSPEL **Last week we heard from the gospel of John how Andrew was called to be a disciple of Jesus, and how he introduced his brother Simon (Peter) to Jesus. Today we encounter Mark's version of the story, in which two sets of brothers are called by Jesus; they instantly drop everything and follow him.**

Zebedee = ZEB-uh-dee
Their father certainly must have been startled. Stress again the immediacy, both of Jesus' call and of the brothers' response.

He walked along a little farther
and saw *James*, the son of *Zebedee*, and his brother *John*.
They *too* were in a boat *mending* their nets.
Then he *called* them.
So they *left* their father *Zebedee* in the *boat*
along with the hired men and *followed* him.

Jesus' early ministry is summed up in the proclamation that the kingdom of God has come near. It seems that Jesus continues the preaching begun by John. As Jesus' ministry progresses, we shall see that the kingdom of God has indeed come near. But this passage makes it clear that Jesus had hope in an imminent approach of God, perhaps the long-awaited Day of the Lord, and sought to prepare people for it by demanding repentance.

His words and manner must have been inspiring. The four who are named do not hesitate to leave their boats behind to become "fishers of people." We later learn that they do not entirely abandon their profession, although they do indeed seek to introduce others to the one who inspired them. But in today's story the action is sudden. This is not simply a hobby or a day's outing on the lake; these men leave behind the very source of their livelihood to follow an itinerant preacher.

It is through you that Jesus speaks to your community, saying, "Follow me." Seek to make his words as inspiring today as they were to his first followers. Call your assembly to value nothing greater than knowing the one who proclaims the good news of God.

4TH SUNDAY IN ORDINARY TIME

Lectionary #71

READING I Deuteronomy 18:15–20

A reading from the book of Deuteronomy.

Moses spoke to *all* the people, saying:
"A prophet like me will the *LORD, your God,* raise *up* for you
from among your *own kin;*
to *him* you shall listen.
This is *exactly* what you requested of the LORD, your God,
at *Horeb*
on the day of the *assembly,* when you said,
'Let us not *again* hear the voice of the *LORD, our God,*
nor see this great *fire* any more, lest we *die.'*

God confirms the people's request. Speak God's words firmly but without undue drama.

"And the LORD said to me, 'This was well *said.*
I will raise up for them a prophet like *you* from among their *kin,*
and will put my *words* into his *mouth;*
he shall tell them *all* that I *command* him.

This is a warning and bears greater emphasis than what has gone before.

"'Whoever will *not listen* to my words which he speaks
in my name,
I myself will make him *answer* for it.
But if a prophet presumes to *speak* in *my name*
an oracle that I have *not* commanded him to speak,
or speaks in the name of *other* gods, *he* shall *die.'"*

Speak these final words with solemnity, but without sounding morbid or flippant. Practice until you are satisfied that you can give the proper emphasis to them, especially to "die."

READING I Deuteronomy (Greek for "second law") gives instructions for Israel to live as God's holy people, according to the Law given to Moses. The present section comes from a series of instructions by Moses regarding the role of leaders in the community, including kings, Levites (those entrusted with ensuring proper worship) and, here, prophets.

Prophets are the medium through which God communicates with the people. Moses, who would die before leading Israel into the Promised Land, assures the people that God will provide other prophets to mediate divine revelation. He reminds them of their experience of God at Mount Horeb (Sinai), when direct encounter with God was too overpowering for them. The conclusion of the passage warns of the difficulties that can arise when prophets are not true to their vocation.

Proclaim this passage as a call to your assembly to be faithful to the communication of God in its midst. Reflect on prophetic voices within your community and encourage your listeners to honor such voices, even when the message is uncomfortable. Remind them as well to be wary of the "prophet" who preaches a message that is not from God. There must be a balance between listening and questioning.

READING II This passage from Paul's first letter to the Corinthians continues where last week's reading left off. Paul is convinced that Jesus will be returning to earth again in the very near future (he expects to be alive to witness it) and gives instructions for how to live with that in mind.

Paul instructs each person to live the life God has called that person to live; he

READING II 1 Corinthians 7:32–35

A reading from the first letter of Saint Paul to the Corinthians.

Speak sincerely.

Paul's words are actually quite radical. They defied a Roman law requiring men and women to marry; they were taxed heavily if they did not.

Brothers and sisters:
I should like you to be *free* of *anxieties.*
An *unmarried* man is anxious about the things of the *Lord,*
how he may *please* the Lord.
But a *married* man is anxious about the things of the *world,*
how he may please his *wife,* and he is *divided.*

The two titles perhaps refer to one who is engaged but unmarried, as well as to one who is not betrothed.

An unmarried *woman* or a *virgin* is anxious about the things
of the *Lord,*
so that she may be *holy* in both *body* and *spirit.*
A *married* woman, on the other hand,
is anxious about the things of the *world,*
how she may please her *husband.*

I am telling you this for your *own benefit,*
not to impose a *restraint* upon you,
but for the sake of *propriety*
and *adherence* to the Lord without *distraction.*

recognizes that God calls different individuals to different ways of life. Paul is trying to help the Corinthians live uprightly. The essence of his instruction is that a Christian should be free from anxieties in order to be devoted entirely to God.

The core of Paul's instruction is that people should not marry, lest the concerns of married life interfere with total devotion to the Lord. Even so, Paul does not prohibit marriage; he does not want to "restrain" anyone, but is attempting to help these new Christians live holy lives. Notice the almost perfect parallelism of Paul's words to men and to women; all Christians have an equal calling and an equal responsibility to be faithful to God's intentions for them.

Almost 2000 years have passed since Paul penned these words. Christ did not return on clouds of glory as Paul expected, and women and men have continued to marry and devote their lives to God at the same time. Still, Paul's words can speak to us today.

Encourage your listeners to consider how to live lives free of anxiety, trusting solely in God. Help them to see that their primary concern must always be to serve God in whatever they do. Make clear that God calls men and women alike, married or unmarried, to the same holy lives and sincere devotion.

GOSPEL **Jesus' early ministry centered in and around the city of Capernaum, on the shores of the Sea of Galilee. He and his followers regularly visited the synagogue there, the meeting place of Galilean Jews. As today's story suggests, it was also the scene of some of Jesus' spectacular deeds.**

GOSPEL Mark 1:21–28

A reading from the holy gospel according to Mark.

Capernaum = kuh-PER-nay-*m

Then they came to *Capernaum*,
and on the sabbath Jesus entered the *synagogue* and *taught*.

Stress the amazement of the people.

The people were *astonished* at his teaching,
for he taught them as one having *authority* and *not* as the *scribes*.
In their *synagogue* was a man with an *unclean spirit*;
he cried out, "What have you to do with us, Jesus of *Nazareth*?
Have you come to *destroy* us?

The unclean spirit's words are, ironically, strong and true; especially stress "I know."

I know who you are—the *Holy One* of *God!*"

Jesus rebuked him and said,
"*Quiet!* Come *out* of him!"
The unclean spirit *convulsed* him and with a *loud cry* came *out* of him.

Again, the people are overwhelmed.

All were *amazed* and asked one another,
"What is *this*?
A *new teaching* with *authority*.
He commands even the unclean *spirits* and they *obey* him."
His fame spread *everywhere* throughout the *whole* region of *Galilee*.

Jesus begins by teaching. His command of the Hebrew Scriptures and his ability to present himself in public must have been overwhelming, for all accounts agree that his listeners were amazed. He spoke with divine authority, fully and faithfully revealing God's communication; he can truly be said to be a prophet like Moses. In addition to teaching, Jesus performs many wonders, casting out unclean spirits (as in today's passage), healing, controlling nature, even raising his friend Lazarus from the dead.

The witnesses to the exorcism are amazed, but it is the unclean spirit itself that dares to identify Jesus as the "Holy One of God." This illustrates what scholars call the "messianic secret" in Mark—the fact that Jesus keeps his identity as God's chosen one a secret; only the demons know who he really is. Even when he does reveal who he is to his close followers, he finds that he must correct their mistaken belief that the Messiah's life would be marked by glory and devoid of suffering. Mark's gospel was written in this way to indicate that Christians must expect to suffer just as Jesus did.

Your task today is to convey the wonder of Jesus' deeds and teachings to your assembly, separated by time and culture from the events recorded here. Let the electricity that energizes today's story be heard in your voice. Finally, encourage your listeners to reflect on the fact that this powerful preacher ultimately submitted himself to become powerless on the cross. We who follow him are called to teach and preach with power as well, and also to be willing to suffer as he did.

5TH SUNDAY IN ORDINARY TIME

Lectionary #74

READING I Job 7:1–4, 6–7

A reading from the book of Job.

The entire reading has a mournful quality to it, but try not to sound self-pitying. Job's words are the genuine cries of one in anguish.

Job *spoke*, saying:
Is not man's *life* on earth a *drudgery*?
Are not his *days* those of *hirelings*?
He is a *slave* who longs for the *shade*,
a *hireling* who waits for his *wages*.
So *I* have been assigned *months* of *misery*,
and troubled *nights* have been *allotted* to me.

Allow the words to speak for themselves. Extend the phrase "drags on"; speak "restlessness" in a quick, tired tone.

If in bed I say, "*When* shall I *arise*?"
then the night *drags on*;
I am filled with *restlessness* until the *dawn*.

Similarly, "swifter" should be spoken quickly; pause briefly after "end," then finish the sentence in a tone of despair.

My days are *swifter* than a weaver's *shuttle*;
they come to an *end* without *hope*.
Remember that my *life* is like the *wind*;
I shall not see *happiness* again.

READING I The book of Job challenges the traditional Hebrew understanding that blessings were rewards for good behavior and misfortunes were punishments for sin. Job was a righteous man who suffered tremendous calamities in his life. The dramatic book that bears his name explores the question of God's justice in light of human suffering: How could a good God allow pain and hardship?

In today's passage, Job contemplates the painful existence that is human life. His days seem to fly by, but they do not bring contentment. Since Job was written prior to an active belief in an afterlife, he cannot even look forward to vindication after death. He despairs of his fate.

When we consider the lot of the majority of the people in the world, we see that life often consists of back-breaking toil, subhuman living conditions, repressive governments and meager living. Even in our own affluent culture, we know what it is to struggle for real meaning and happiness in life. Job's questions are timeless; his despair stabs at the heart.

Reflect on the deepest pains you have felt in your own life, then prepare to empathize with Job in his mournful lament. Speak slowly and with yearning. The reading ends without hope; some days, some lives are like that. Let Job's words stand as they are: stark and foreboding.

READING II Paul was proud of the fact that he supported himself even as he preached the gospel. But he says that he cannot really boast about it. Indeed, he is compelled to preach, making himself a

READING II 1 Corinthians 9:16–19, 22–23

A reading from the first letter of Saint Paul to the Corinthians.

Brothers and sisters:
If I preach the *gospel,* this is no *reason* for me to *boast,*
for an *obligation* has been imposed on me,
and *woe* to me if I do *not* preach it!
If I do so *willingly,* I have a *recompense,*
but if *unwillingly,* then I have been entrusted with a *stewardship.*
What then is my *recompense?*
That, when I *preach,*
I offer the gospel *free* of *charge*
so as *not* to make full use of my *right* in the *gospel.*

Speak the following lines with proud conviction.

Although I am *free* in regard to all,
I have made myself a *slave* to all
so as to win over as *many* as *possible.*
To the *weak* I became *weak,* to win *over* the weak.
I have become *all* things to *all,* to save at least *some.*
All this I do for the sake of the *gospel,*
so that I *too* may have a *share* in it.

Paul does not mean to indicate vacillation here, but rather empathy with the situations of those he meets.

"slave" to the recipients of his message. Since a key part of Paul's preaching was the freedom available in Christ, it is especially striking that he would choose a term of captivity and servitude to describe himself.

Everything Paul does is for the gospel. In an apparent reference to an earlier controversy regarding pagan worship, he identifies with the "weak," who do not have the same knowledge some Corinthians claimed to have. In order not to offend anyone, Paul does not eat food offered to idols, even though he knows the gods the idols represent do not really exist. He becomes "all things to all" for the sake of the gospel.

Speak with the zeal of a missionary as you read Paul's words in the assembly. Allow Paul's enthusiasm to inspire your listeners to be bold about their beliefs and to do everything to serve the gospel.

GOSPEL Following the exorcism of last week's gospel, Jesus performs a healing miracle in the gospel account given today. Jesus' popularity is growing, as evidenced by the many who come to him for healing or exorcism.

The healing of Simon's mother-in-law suggests that what Simon (Peter) gave up to follow Jesus was far more than his fishing boat; he also had a home and family. Crowds of people bring their sick and possessed friends to Simon's home; they gather at the door to the house, surely spilling out into the street. Jesus is popular—for now.

In last week's account of the exorcism, the unclean spirit proclaimed Jesus as the

GOSPEL Mark 1:29–39

A reading from the holy gospel according to Mark.

On leaving the *synagogue*
Jesus entered the house of *Simon* and *Andrew*
with *James* and *John.*

Fever was understood as a disease of its own, not as a symptom of other illnesses.

Simon's *mother-in-law* lay sick with a *fever.*
They *immediately* told him about her.
He *approached,* grasped her *hand,* and helped her *up.*
Then the fever *left* her and she *waited* on them.

Pause before beginning this new scene.

When it was *evening,* after *sunset,*
they brought to him *all* who were ill or possessed by *demons.*
The *whole town* was gathered at the *door.*
He cured *many* who were sick with various *diseases,*
and he drove out many *demons,*
not *permitting* them to *speak* because they *knew* him.

Pause again before this change of scene.

Rising very early before *dawn,* he *left*
and went off to a *deserted* place, where he *prayed.*
Simon and those who were with him *pursued* him
and on *finding* him said, "Everyone is *looking* for you."

Notice that Jesus does not return with the disciples to Capernaum but suggests continuing his ministry in the surrounding region.

He told them, "Let us go *on* to the nearby villages
that I may *preach there* also.
For *this* purpose have I *come.*"
So he went into their *synagogues,*
preaching and *driving* out *demons* throughout the *whole*
of Galilee.

Holy One of God. In today's story, Jesus does not allow the demons to speak. Perhaps Jesus knew that the crowds would want to seize him and make him king, or perhaps he knew that there was yet much more to his ministry. This silence is in keeping with the "messianic secret" in this gospel: Jesus does not claim to be the Messiah, and in the end admits it only reluctantly. Instead, he begins to teach about his own passion and death. His path is not simply one of acclaim and glory.

Jesus separates himself for prayer. He apparently knows that he needs quiet, needs to strengthen himself before he can cure so many others. Meanwhile the crowds seek him, and he responds by going to their towns, preaching in the synagogues and exorcising the demons from their midst.

Encourage your congregation to reflect not only on Jesus' miracles or the crowds who are attracted to him, but also on the source of his strength. Challenge your hearers to establish regular prayer rituals in order to have the same ability to go forth as Jesus did, preaching and offering assistance to those in need.

6TH SUNDAY IN ORDINARY TIME

Lectionary #77

READING I Leviticus 13:1–2, 44–46

A reading from the book of Leviticus.

The LORD said to *Moses* and *Aaron*,
"If someone has on his *skin* a *scab* or *pustule* or *blotch*
which appears to be the *sore* of *leprosy*,
he shall be *brought* to *Aaron*, the *priest*,
or to one of the *priests* among his *descendants*.
If the man is *leprous* and *unclean*,
the *priest* shall declare him *unclean*
by reason of the *sore* on his *head*.

In part because the disease could be eradicated without effort, it is clear that this ancient affliction was not leprosy. It must have been some type of fungus, since it could affect fabric and houses as well as humans.

"The one who bears the *sore* of *leprosy*
shall keep his garments *rent* and his head *bare*,
and shall *muffle* his *beard*;
he shall cry *out*, '*Unclean, unclean!*'
As *long* as the sore is *on* him he shall declare himself *unclean*,
since he is in *fact unclean*.
He shall dwell *apart*, making his abode *outside* the *camp*."

Changing one's appearance to signify illness is both practical and symbolic.

READING II 1 Corinthians 10:31—11:1

A reading from the first letter of Saint Paul to the Corinthians.

Brothers and sisters,
whether you *eat* or *drink*, or *whatever* you do,
do everything for the glory of God.

This is central to Paul's creed; all is for God's glory.

READING I The Hebrews considered a person afflicted with a skin disease not only contagious and a threat to the physical welfare of others but also a threat to the religious welfare of the community as a whole. An affliction was considered a visible punishment from God, and the person affected made the entire community impure. As a result, great care was taken to separate the individual from the community and to ensure that the disease was completely gone before the person was allowed to return.

Although the precise nature of the disease is unclear, this reading paves the way for the healing performed by Jesus in the gospel. Stress the description of the person's appearance and the fact that one with such a disease had to live apart from others. This will be contrasted with Jesus' openness and willingness to touch the man who presents himself to Jesus to be cured.

READING II The lively Corinthian community presented Paul with many challenges in his ministry. Adopting his declaration of freedom in Christ Jesus, the Corinthians engaged in practices that shocked Paul and defended their behavior using Paul's own words. Paul responds with further instruction, as he does here with the issue of food offered in sacrifice to idols.

Paul seems to be responding to a letter from the Corinthian community in which they asserted that "all things are lawful." He agrees with them, but points out that what is lawful is not necessarily helpful.

Apparently some Corinthians were freely eating of food that had been presented

Avoid giving *offense*, whether to the *Jews* or *Greeks* or
the church of *God*,
just as *I* try to please *everyone* in every *way*,
not seeking my *own* benefit but that of the *many*,
that they may be *saved*.

Be *imitators* of me, as *I* am of *Christ*.

Paul offers his own life as an example, not to build up his own ego, but to demonstrate how Christian behavior should look.

GOSPEL Mark 1:40–45

A reading from the holy gospel according to Mark.

Make the man's sincerity and trust in Jesus evident in your voice.

A *leper* came to Jesus and kneeling *down begged* him and said,
"If you *wish*, *you* can make me *clean*."
Moved with *pity*, he *stretched* out his hand,
touched him, and *said* to him,
"I *do* will it. Be made *clean*."
The leprosy *left* him *immediately*, and he was made *clean*.

Jesus offers healing by establishing human, even physical, contact with one who is shunned by others.

Then, warning him *sternly*, he *dismissed* him at *once*.
He *said* to him, "*See* that you tell *no* one *anything*,
but *go*, *show* yourself to the *priest*
and offer for your *cleansing* what Moses *prescribed*;
that will be *proof* for them."

The gospel passage includes an example of the "messianic secret" in Mark. However, as so often happens, the man simply cannot keep silent.

The man went *away* and began to *publicize* the whole *matter*.
He *spread* the report *abroad*
so that it was *impossible* for Jesus to enter a town *openly*.
He remained *outside* in deserted *places*,
and people kept *coming* to him from *everywhere*.

to idols in pagan temples; some even seem to have participated in the pagan ritual meals. Paul argues that, although it is permissible to eat food whose origin is unknown, one must refrain if eating the food will give scandal to other members of the community.

Speak boldly Paul's stirring exhortation to do all for God's glory, offending no one.

GOSPEL As we learned from the first reading, a person with a skin disease was to remain apart from the community. The man in the gospel approaches Jesus because he has learned of Jesus' healing power. He demonstrates his faith in Jesus both in his conviction that Jesus could heal him, and in his trust that Jesus would not shun him or flee.

In fact, Jesus' response to the man is one of compassion. Risking the possibility that he too would catch the disease, Jesus actually touches the man, extending an invitation to him to rejoin his human and religious family. The man is not only made well; he is made whole, a vibrant member of the community of Israel.

Share this happy story with warmth and a spirit of welcome. Challenge your listeners to extend a hand to anyone who is ostracized for physical, religious or economic reasons. Inspire your listeners to adopt Jesus' attitude of acceptance and love for all people, especially those who have been shunned by others.

7TH SUNDAY IN ORDINARY TIME

Lectionary #80

READING I Isaiah 43:18–19, 21–22, 24b–25

A reading from the book of the prophet Isaiah.

Thus says the LORD:
Remember *not* the events of the *past*,
the things of long *ago* consider *not*;
see, I am doing something *new!*
Now it springs *forth*, do you not *perceive* it?
In the *desert* I make a *way*,
in the *wasteland*, *rivers*.

There is joy and anticipation in these words; speak with excitement.

The people I *formed* for *myself*,
that they might *announce* my *praise*.

Yet you did not *call* upon me, O *Jacob*,
for you grew *weary* of me, O *Israel*.
You *burdened* me with your *sins*,
and *wearied* me with your *crimes*.

Express regret and sadness at the people's actions.

It is *I*, *I*, who wipe *out*,
for my *own* sake, your *offenses*;
your *sins* I remember no *more*.

This people was formed to give praise to God; God can override their transgression in order to allow them once again to offer the honor that is their vocation. Speak with conviction and forcefulness.

READING I Israel's identity has long been shaped by the Exodus from Egypt and the experience of God's guidance through the wilderness. This section of Second Isaiah, written as the exile in Babylon was coming to an end, declares that the people are to proclaim a new Exodus, through a different desert, that would lead them home to Jerusalem. God is providing refreshment and a smooth path for the people as they begin a new life after their captivity.

Yet they have not remembered God; they have not fully recognized that the exile was a punishment for sin. God declares that all sinfulness will be wiped out in this new creation. Since the purpose of God's people is to offer God praise, it is for God's own sake that they are declared free of sin and able to honor God again, demonstrating to the world their glorious new status.

This is a wonderful promise of newness offered by God. Read it with enthusiasm and excitement in your voice. Only when God describes the sinfulness of the people should your tone change, but end with a strong declaration of the loving forgiveness of God.

READING II Second Corinthians is a composite letter, reflecting some of the tensions between Paul and the enthusiastic, but sometimes misguided, Christians in Corinth. After writing First Corinthians, Paul visited Corinth but had an unpleasant encounter there. He left feeling that the community did not support him and wrote a letter that he refers to as "painful."

Although the letter was painful to write, it was successful in rallying the Corinthians and procuring their assistance. He writes now in joy, having been assured that the Corinthians had not abandoned the faith or

READING II 2 Corinthians 1:18–22

A reading from the second letter of Saint Paul to the Corinthians.

Silvanus = sil-VAY-nuhs

Let the "yes" ring out and fill the room.

All God's promises have been fulfilled in Christ Jesus.

Brothers and sisters:
As *God* is *faithful*,
our word to you is *not* "yes" *and* "no."
For the Son of *God*, Jesus *Christ*,
who was *proclaimed* to you by *us*, *Silvanus* and
Timothy and *me*,
was not "*yes*" and "*no*," but "*yes*" has been in him.

For however *many* are the promises of *God*, their *Yes* is in *him*;
therefore, the *Amen* from us also goes *through* him to *God*
for *glory*.
But the one who gives us *security* with you in *Christ*
and who *anointed* us is *God*;
he has also put his *seal* upon us
and given the *Spirit* in our hearts as a first *installment*.

GOSPEL Mark 2:1–12

A reading from the holy gospel according to Mark.

Capernaum = kuh-PER-nay-*m

When *Jesus* returned to *Capernaum* after some days,
it became *known* that he was at *home*.
Many gathered *together* so that there was no longer *room*
for them,
not even around the *door*,
and he *preached* the *word* to them.

their relationship with him, although he must still respond to some criticism.

Because Paul apparently changed his mind about earlier anticipated visits to the Corinthian community, there were some in the congregation who accused him of vacillating. Paul responds here by insisting that his word, like God's, is true. God's message in Christ Jesus is entirely positive, always a resounding "Yes!"

In a reference to early Christian liturgical practice, Paul refers to the community's "Amen," which gives glory to God through Christ. God's "yes" is answered by the Corinthians' "yes." God's promises in Christ are known to be true because the Corinthians have already been anointed and given the Spirit. But that is only the first part of God's fulfillment of promises; there is yet more to come.

Proclaim this passage as an affirmation of God's commitment to your congregation. Assure your listeners that God can be trusted, that good things await them. And remind them that they have already experienced the truth of God's promises by their experience of the Spirit, conferred in baptism and made known in their participation in the liturgy.

GOSPEL Although the story told in today's gospel selection is from early in Jesus' ministry, Jesus' reputation is already well established. In a vivid portrait of enthusiastic crowds, the evangelist states that there was not room for everyone. In order to approach Jesus, some people carrying a paralyzed man even have to climb onto the roof.

The four friends of the man clearly believe that Jesus can cure their friend; they

They came *bringing* to him a *paralytic* carried by *four* men.
Unable to get *near* Jesus because of the *crowd*,
they *opened* up the *roof* above him.
After they had broken *through*,
they let *down* the *mat* on which the *paralytic* was *lying*.

Indicate your amazement. This is not typical behavior but borders on desperation.

When Jesus saw their *faith*, he said to the paralytic,
"*Child*, your *sins* are *forgiven.*"
Now some of the *scribes* were sitting there *asking* themselves,
"*Why* does this man *speak* that way? He is *blaspheming*.
Who but God *alone* can forgive *sins*?"

Speak kindly but with authority.

Jesus *immediately* knew in his mind
what they were *thinking* to themselves,
so he said, "*Why* are you thinking such *things* in your *hearts*?
Which is *easier*, to say to the paralytic,
'Your *sins* are *forgiven*,'
or to say, '*Rise*, pick up your *mat* and *walk*?'

The text implies that Jesus did not hear the comment but sensed distrust and opposition.

"But that *you* may know
that the Son of *Man* has *authority* to *forgive* sins on *earth*"
—he said to the paralytic,
"I *say* to you, *rise*, pick up your *mat*, and go *home*."

He *rose*, picked up his mat at *once*,
and went *away* in the sight of *everyone*.
They were all *astounded*
and glorified *God*, saying, "We have *never* seen *anything*
like *this*."

Let their surprised joy ring out in your voice.

are prepared to stop at nothing in order to gain an audience with him. It is this determination and perseverance that elicits a positive response from Jesus. Indeed, Jesus does cure the man, to the amazement of the crowd, which then gives glory to God.

But the story of the paralyzed man as it stands is no simple healing story. Embedded within it is an account of a controversy with religious leaders regarding forgiveness. Perhaps the issue of forgiveness was an urgent one for the author's community. At any rate, this section of the story grabs the reader's attention even more than the healing. And here Jesus is accused of blasphemy for the first time, for which the religious leaders will later seek his death.

Juxtaposing these two stories illustrates to the reader that Jesus offers not only physical healing but also the deeper healing of forgiveness. Since the scribes in the story believe that only God can forgive sins, and then only through the established rituals of atonement, Jesus' claim appears to be blasphemous. Yet Jesus' self-identification as Son of Man and the paralyzed man's ability to walk again demonstrate Jesus' authority.

Share this story with your assembly with the same sense of awe that must have filled those who witnessed Jesus' words and deeds. Perhaps the account can stimulate interesting reflection on and discussion of the issue of forgiveness in our own day and culture.

8TH SUNDAY IN ORDINARY TIME

Lectionary #83

READING I Hosea 2:16b, 17b, 21–22

A reading from the book of the prophet Hosea.

Speak lovingly and tenderly, then hopefully, as God expresses the desire that the people will respond.

Thus says the *LORD:*
I will *lead* her into the *desert*
and *speak* to her *heart.*
She shall *respond* there as in the *days* of her *youth,*
when she came *up* from the land of *Egypt.*

The relationship between God and Israel is one characterized by justice and love. It is by responding to God in this way that fidelity is demonstrated.

I will *espouse* you to me *forever:*
I will *espouse* you in *right* and in *justice,*
in *love* and in *mercy;*
I will *espouse* you in *fidelity,*
and *you* shall *know* the *LORD.*

READING II 2 Corinthians 3:1b–6

A reading from the second letter of Saint Paul to the Corinthians.

Brothers and sisters:

Paul is a bit incredulous here.

Do *we* need, as *some* do,
letters of *recommendation to* you or *from* you?

Speak with fondness and pride.

You are our letter, *written* on our *hearts,*
known and *read* by *all,*
shown to be a letter of *Christ* ministered by *us,*

READING I **Hosea, like some other prophets, acted out the message God gave him to deliver to the people. Hosea married a prostitute; their children were given symbolic names, such as "Not pitied" and "Not my people." Hosea's fidelity to his faithless wife illustrates God's love and faithfulness to wayward Israel.**

Today's passage is a tender appeal from God to the people of Israel to return in faithfulness. The relationship between God and Israel is intimate, that of a marriage, and God seeks to revive the spark that had characterized it in the beginning. God's words allude to the Exodus experience; God intends to draw Israel out into the desert once again in order to rekindle the love and commitment that had once inspired Israel.

Offer this beautiful selection as a heartfelt plea from God to your congregation. Speak to the hearts of the people, so that they may recognize God's tremendous love and resolve always to respond in faithfulness and trust.

READING II **Written to a community that had embraced and then rejected Paul, Second Corinthians contains in large part Paul's expression of gratitude that the Corinthians have once again accepted him. At the same time, there is some defense of Paul's person and ministry. In contrast to those who might claim to be apostles and who offer "proof" of their status, Paul suggests that the Corinthians themselves are his proof. He displays his pride in the community by continuing the metaphor;**

written not in *ink* but by the *Spirit* of the living *God*,
not on tablets of *stone* but on tablets that are *hearts* of *flesh*.

Raise your voice in confidence, then speak in humility.

Such *confidence* we have through *Christ* toward *God*.
Not that of *ourselves* we are qualified
to take credit for *anything* as coming from *us*;

Let your voice grow stronger from here until the end.

rather, our *qualification* comes from *God*,
who has *indeed* qualified us as *ministers* of a *new* covenant,
not of *letter* but of *spirit*;
for the letter brings *death*, but the *Spirit* gives *life*.

GOSPEL Mark 2:18–22

A reading from the holy gospel according to Mark.

The disciples of *John* and of the *Pharisees* were accustomed to *fast*.
People came to him and objected,

Although fasting was required only on the Day of Atonement, the Pharisees adopted many more fast days, and others may have been popularly celebrated.

"*Why* do the disciples of *John* and the disciples of the *Pharisees fast*,
but *your* disciples do *not* fast?"

It would be rude to act in a manner of repentance and sorrow while purporting to help one celebrate a joyous occasion.

Jesus answered them,
"Can the *wedding* guests *fast* while the bridegroom is *with* them?
As *long* as they have the bridegroom *with* them they *cannot* fast.
But the days will *come* when the bridegroom is taken *away* from them,
and *then* they will fast on *that* day.

they indeed are his letter of support, written by the Spirit on the human heart.

Paul's defense of himself is really a defense of God, he says. It is not by his own strength that Paul has accomplished his work, but by God's. Paul is a minister of a new covenant that is not literal but spiritual, like the community itself. Keeping with Paul's characteristic emphasis on the Spirit rather than the Law, Paul suggests that the covenant of the Law brings destruction, but the new covenant in the Spirit brings life.

There is fondness in Paul's words to the Corinthian Christians that you would do well to convey to your community. Speak with the same warmth and pride that Paul uses in his letter. Finally, declare your humility as a minister of God's word, just as Paul insists that it is God who provides him with his abilities. Close with emphasis on the role of the life-giving Spirit.

GOSPEL **Picking up the image of marriage from the first reading, the gospel selection compares Jesus with a bridegroom celebrating with his friends. The story begins with a question: Why don't Jesus' disciples fast, as do others? There may be a hint of the tension that initially existed between the followers of John and those of Jesus. There is certainly a distinction in their behavior.**

Jesus' response perhaps hints at his messianic role as eschatological bridegroom and certainly suggests his impending death. Some have suggested that the

These parables represent ancient common sense. By using a new patch in an old cloth or putting new wine in old wineskins, one ran the risk of losing everything.

"No one sews a piece of *unshrunken* cloth on an *old cloak.*
If he does, its fullness *pulls away,*
the *new* from the *old,* and the tear gets *worse.*
Likewise, no one pours *new* wine into *old wineskins.*
Otherwise, the wine will *burst* the skins,
and both the *wine* and the *skins* are *ruined.*
Rather, *new* wine is poured into *fresh* wineskins."

disciples of John are fasting after their teacher's death; Jesus indicates that his fate will be similar. But as long as he is present, his friends must rejoice.

The parables about the cloth and the wineskins were originally independent. They comment on the folly of combining something fresh and new with something worn out and obsolete; the cloth will rip, the wineskin will burst. Taken together with the earlier story, the entire section suggests that Jesus is bringing something new in his declaration that the kingdom of God is a present reality; new behavior is also required. The new and the old cannot comfortably coexist.

Proclaim this passage as a teaching about the new life available in Christ. Inspire your listeners to rejoice that Christ remains present and to recognize that a new life requires different actions. Allow this reading to be an impetus for renewal in your community.

9TH SUNDAY IN ORDINARY TIME

Lectionary #86

READING I Deuteronomy 5:12–15

Deuteronomy = doo-ter-AH-nuh-mee

A reading from the book of Deuteronomy.

The seventh day of the week, the day of rest in Jewish practice, is the day we call Saturday. From the beginning, Christians revered Sunday as the day on which Jesus rose from the dead, but it was not until the fourth century that Christians in the Roman Empire could refrain from work on that day.

Thus says the Lord:
"Take *care* to keep *holy* the *sabbath* day
as the *LORD, your God, commanded* you.
Six days you may *labor* and do *all* your *work;*
but the *seventh* day is the *sabbath* of the *LORD*, your *God.*
No work may be done then, whether by *you,*
or your *son* or *daughter,*
or your male or female *slave,*
or your *ox* or *ass* or *any* of your beasts,
or the *alien* who lives *with* you.
Your male and female *slave* should rest as *you* do.

This is important; give it emphasis. Close with a stirring presentation of God's might.

"For *remember* that you *too* were once a slave in *Egypt,*
and the *LORD*, your *God, brought* you from there
with his *strong hand* and *outstretched arm.*
That is why the *LORD*, your *God,* has *commanded* you
to observe the *sabbath* day."

READING I **The Sabbath figures prominently in today's readings. First we hear of the importance of keeping holy one day of week from Deuteronomy's list of the Ten Commandments. Although the creation story attests to the importance of rest, here the Sabbath is understood against the background of the Exodus from Egypt. After toiling through the desert, the Israelites finally come to rest in the land promised to them. Keeping the Sabbath becomes a declaration of freedom from slavery, to rest without a master's consent. The Sabbath is not a major festival but a regular occurrence; it indicates that even ordinary life is holy before God.**

There is great concern in this passage that slaves also be allowed Sabbath rest. All levels of society are to be given the opportunity to give back to God in gratitude for what has been given them. There is no room for the harsh, continual demands of slave labor; everyone is to rest.

READING II **Paul needed to argue for his own legitimacy as an apostle, in light of the Corinthian community's earlier questioning of his authority and truthfulness. His status as a vehicle of God's grace is evident in the fact that the same God who spoke at creation now shines in the hearts of the Corinthians.**

The minister of the gospel is a vulnerable person. In a series of contrasts, Paul points out the tribulations he has faced; but the power of God sustains him. The treasure of knowing God and the salvation offered in Christ Jesus is stored in breakable vessels.

READING II 2 Corinthians 4:6–11

A reading from the second letter of Saint Paul to the Corinthians.

Brothers and sisters:
God who said, "Let *light* shine out of *darkness*,"
has *shone* in our hearts to *bring* to *light*
the knowledge of the *glory* of *God* on the face of Jesus *Christ*.

Consciously slow down through the many prepositional phrases so that you are able to do justice to each one.

But we hold this *treasure* in *earthen vessels*,
that the surpassing *power* may be of *God* and *not* from *us*.
We are *afflicted* in every way, but not *constrained*;
perplexed, but not driven to *despair*;
persecuted, but not *abandoned*;
struck *down*, but not *destroyed*;
always carrying about in the *body* the dying of *Jesus*,
so that the *life* of Jesus may also be *manifested* in our *body*.

Convey the inimitable power of God by raising your voice in amazement.

Throughout these, express the first clause quietly, but phrase the second with great conviction.

For we who *live* are constantly being given up to *death*
for the sake of *Jesus*,
so that the *life* of Jesus may be *manifested* in our mortal *flesh*.

This is intended to be encouraging, not frightening. Speak it as such.

GOSPEL Mark 2:23—3:6

A reading from the holy gospel according to Mark.

As Jesus was passing through a field of *grain* on the *sabbath*,
his *disciples* began to make a *path* while *picking* the heads
of *grain*.
At *this* the Pharisees *said* to him,
"*Look*, *why* are they doing what is *unlawful* on the *sabbath*?"

In this way, God's great power can be more clearly seen. Just as God's power and love are evident in the crucifixion of Jesus, so also the afflictions Paul and the Corinthians have experienced allow God's power to show forth.

Paul seems to have recently undergone a life-threatening experience that informs his outlook here. Paul lists several adversities he has faced, but at no time does he despair. Indeed, through all of it he seeks to reflect the death of Jesus, precisely so that Jesus' life might be evident in him. This is the paradox of the cross Paul preaches; an instrument of torture reveals the glory of God.

Your task today is to convey some of the excitement and enthusiasm of the earliest followers of the gospel to your community. Offer your listeners encouragement as they face their own trials and setbacks.

GOSPEL **Jesus comes into growing conflict with the religious authorities, and the issue now is the observance of Sabbath regulations. First, Jesus' disciples pluck grain on the Sabbath, raising the ire of the Pharisees, who were concerned with ensuring observation of the Law. In the second instance, Jesus heals on the Sabbath. By the end of today's gospel reading, the animosity between Jesus and the Pharisees is palpable.**

Since it was unlawful to bring in the harvest on the Sabbath, the Pharisees question the disciples' practice of pulling off heads of grain in the fields. Jesus' responds that his disciples were hungry. He appeals to

Abiathar = uh-BĪ-uh-thahr

He said to them, "Have you *never* read what *David* did
when he was in *need* and he and his companions were *hungry?*
How he went into the *house* of *God* when *Abiathar* was
high *priest*
and ate the *bread* of *offering*
that only the *priests* could lawfully eat,
and *shared* it with his *companions?*"

Then he said to them,
"The *sabbath* was made for *man, not* man for the *sabbath.*
That is why the *Son* of *Man* is lord *even* of the *sabbath.*"

Again he entered the synagogue.
There was a *man* there who had a *withered hand.*
They watched him *closely*
to see if he would *cure* him on the *sabbath*
so that they might *accuse* him.
He *said* to the man with the withered *hand,*
"Come *up* here *before* us."
Then he said to them,
"Is it *lawful* to do *good* on the sabbath rather than to do *evil,*
to *save* life rather than to *destroy* it?"
But they remained *silent.*

Looking around at them with *anger*
and *grieved* at their *hardness* of *heart,*
he *said* to the man, "Stretch *out* your *hand.*"
He stretched it *out* and his hand was *restored.*

Herodians = her-OH-dee-uhnz

The Pharisees went out
and immediately took *counsel* with the Herodians *against* him
to put him to *death.*

[Shorter: Mark 2:23–28]

the story of David, who broke another precept of the Law in order to feed his hungry companions. Jesus suggests that the Pharisees are more concerned about keeping the letter of the Law than with real human needs.

The same issue is raised in the cure of the man with a withered hand. Jesus is aware that his Sabbath behavior is under scrutiny, and he tries to engage the Pharisees in conversation about the impending event. Despite the strict laws regarding cessation of work on the Sabbath, exceptions can be made in order to save a life. Jesus extends the exception to cover "doing good," or healing.

As the scene ends, Jesus is angry with the Pharisees for strictly upholding the Law. The Pharisees, for their part, begin actively making plans for his death. Early in the gospel, the stage is set for rising conflict, culminating in Jesus' passion and death.

Today's gospel sometimes gives people pause because Jesus seems to be advocating a policy of breaking the law. Indeed, the mature believer must be able to discern between lazy, self-serving disregard for law and the acts of compassion that Jesus advocates, despite their prohibition.

ASH WEDNESDAY

Lectionary #219

READING I Joel 2:12–18

A reading from the book of the prophet Joel.

Draw attention to the present need for repentance; stress "now." Then speak slowly and sincerely.

Even *now*, says the Lord,
return to me with your *whole heart*,
with *fasting*, and *weeping*, and *mourning*;
Rend your *hearts*, not your *garments*,
and *return* to the *Lord*, your *God*.

Let the majestic nature of God's love shine through these words.

For *gracious* and *merciful* is he,
slow to anger, *rich* in kindness,
and *relenting* in punishment.

Speak with hope and awe.

Perhaps he will *again* relent
and leave behind him a *blessing*,
Offerings and *libations*
for the *Lord*, *your God*.

These lines are those of a herald, crying out to the people. The short phrases can be spoken forcefully and with a bit more speed than usual. Be careful not to sacrifice clarity or to become sing-song.

Blow the *trumpet* in *Zion!*
proclaim a *fast*,
call an *assembly*;
Gather the *people*,
notify the *congregation*;
Assemble the *elders*,
gather the *children*
and the *infants* at the breast;
Let the *bridegroom* quit his room,
and the *bride* her *chamber*.

READING I We begin our annual season of repentance, prayer and renewal with a stark reminder of our need to turn our hearts and minds to God. The first reading, from the prophet Joel, calls us to a heartfelt conversion, a return to the presence of a God who is compassionate and loving. But this God is also powerful, able to bring judgment to an erring people, using any means available to draw us back into a loving embrace.

Joel wrote during a time of crisis in Israel. The political situation was peaceful, but Israel faced a severe locust plague and drought. Joel understands these conditions to be indicative of the Day of the Lord, the judgment of God. He believes that the people of Israel and the cultic leaders have become complacent, relying too much on rituals without the accompanying sincerity of heart that God desires. As a result, the locusts were sent as a sign of God's judgment.

But just when utter destruction seems inevitable and the end appears to be imminent, God extends the invitation that we read today. It is still possible to return to God, to weep before the Lord, to fast and pray. Joel offers the hope that the Day of the Lord will be not only a day of judgment, but one of promise and vindication as well.

We gather today to acknowledge our own complacency before God, our own tendency to wander away from our home in the bosom of God, our own need to return to God with all our hearts. We too adopt the practices that Joel recommends: We fast and weep and repent, standing before God mindful of our sinfulness and trusting in God's mercy and love.

Between the porch and the altar
let the *priests*, the *ministers* of the Lord, *weep*,
And say, "*Spare*, O Lord, your *people*,
and make not your *heritage* a *reproach*,
with the nations *ruling over* them!
Why should they say among the peoples,
'*Where* is their *God*?'"

Proclaim this with sadness but also with dignity.

Then the Lord was *stirred* to *concern* for his land
and took *pity* on his people.

Pause, then let your voice ring with conviction as you proclaim God's compassionate response.

READING II 2 Corinthians 5:20—6:2

A reading from the second letter of Paul to the Corinthians.

We are *ambassadors* for *Christ*,
God as it were appealing *through* us.
We *implore* you, in Christ's name:
be *reconciled* to God!
For *our* sakes God made him who did *not* know sin to *be sin*,
so that in *him* we might become the very *holiness* of God.

Proclaim with wonder this willingness of Christ to take on responsibility for human sin.

As your fellow *workers*
we *beg* you not to receive the grace of God in *vain*.
For he says,
"In an *acceptable time* I have *heard* you;
on a *day* of *salvation* I have *helped* you."
Now is the *acceptable time!*
Now is the *day* of *salvation!*

You proclaim hope in God's promises, as well as the demand to put into practice the appeal for reconciliation. Speak with force and urgency.

Your task today is to proclaim, clearly and decisively, God's call to personal and communal conversion, and the urgency of leaving all else behind in order to respond. You have an awesome responsibility today; let the solemnity of the occasion resonate in your words.

READING II **The apostle Paul implores the Corinthians to turn to God and to recognize that salvation has been won in Christ. It is a fitting address to us as well, alerting us to our urgent need for reconciliation with God as we begin our journey through Lent.**

Paul's relationship with the Corinthian church was a stormy one. The community was prone to factionalism; sometimes Paul needed to be severe in his rebukes, resulting in strained relations with the Corinthians. Paul writes this letter after sending a delegate to the community to convey his message. He expresses in this letter his gratitude for their positive response.

Paul's appeal in this passage is urgent. Yet he does not clarify here what precipitates his message. This makes it especially available to us, living in a different time and place. The thrust of the appeal — "Be reconciled to God!"— applies to us just as to the Corinthians. But Paul also clarifies that we are not engaged in this process on our own. In fact, the opportunity for holiness, for being united with God, is offered because of the salvific action of Christ. He has taken on our sinfulness, that tendency to stray from

GOSPEL Matthew 6:1–6, 16–18

A reading from the holy gospel according to Matthew.

Introduce the gospel by reading these lines with solemn sincerity.

Jesus said to his disciples:
"Be on *guard* against performing religious *acts*
for people to *see.*
Otherwise expect *no recompense* from your heavenly Father.

synagogues = SIN-uh-gogz
hypocrites = HIP-uh-krits

Emphasize the contrast between what the hypocrites do and what is admonished here. Raise your voice at the beginning of each practice — almsgiving, praying, fasting — and stress "You can be sure," and so forth.

When you give *alms,* for example,
do *not* blow a *horn* before you in *synagogues* and *streets*
like *hypocrites* looking for *applause.*
You can be sure of *this* much, they are *already* repaid.
In giving *alms*
you are not to let your *left* hand
know what your *right* hand is doing.
Keep your deeds of mercy *secret,*
and your *Father* who *sees* in secret will *repay* you.

"When you are *praying,*
do *not* behave like the *hypocrites*
who love to *stand* and pray in *synagogues*
or on *street corners* in order to be *noticed.*
I give you my *word,* they are *already* repaid.
Whenever *you* pray, go to your *room,*
close your *door,* and pray to your Father in *private.*
Then your *Father,*
who sees what *no* man *sees,* will *repay* you.

"When you *fast,*
you are not to look *glum* as the *hypocrites* do.
They *change* the appearance of their faces
so that others may *see* they are fasting.
I *assure* you, they are *already* repaid.

God, so that we might be brought back into an intimate relationship with God. Quoting from the book of Isaiah regarding the servant of God, Paul indicates that divine aid is available to all those who serve God.

Paul says that he and his companions in ministry are ambassadors for Christ, as well as "fellow workers" with the members of the community. This is also an apt description of the role of the minister of the word, one who is part of the community but also entrusted with a noble task. You share with Paul the responsibility and the dignity inherent in proclaiming God's message. You too announce that the time for reconciliation, for acceptance of the salvation offered in Christ, for turning to God, is now.

GOSPEL The gospel of Matthew was written for a community of Jews who believed in the saving action accomplished in Jesus' death and resurrection. This community of Jewish Christians found itself at odds with the larger Jewish community. The entire gospel reflects a tension with the synagogue and its leaders, while preserving traditional Jewish practices and beliefs. Today's gospel passage adopts the hyperbole found in much of the gospel regarding the proper ways to act, in contrast to the deeds of the "hypocrites."

Prayer, fasting and almsgiving — the pillars of Lenten observance — were time-honored practices of the Jewish people. The author upholds them, suggesting that they are central to the Christian life as well. But

In reading this reversal of ordinary behavior, allow some amazement to enter your voice.

Slowly and warmly proclaim this promise.

When *you* fast,
see to it that you *groom* your hair and *wash* your face.
In *that* way no one can *see* you are fasting
but your *Father* who is *hidden*;
and your *Father* who *sees* what is hidden will *repay* you."

what is most striking is the author's insistence that all is to be done in secret.

These words challenge us as we solemnly begin a season in which we adopt practices of austerity and denial by marking our foreheads with ashes. We are called today to reflect on why we engage in these customs. Are we truly repenting, turning ourselves back to God with sincerity of heart? Or do we take pride in proclaiming to others what we are doing? Today's gospel insists that our duty is not so much to be examples for others, but rather to repent without drawing attention to ourselves: to care for the needs of others without recompense, to pray without being noticed, to fast and yet to keep up our spirits.

The emphasis on private devotion comes at a time when we gather as community to begin our journey of 40 days. We know that we need one another. We come together to acknowledge our failings; we resolve, in the presence of others, to turn back to the path of righteousness. We also go forth from today's gathering to put into practice the exhortations of this gospel. Your task in proclaiming the gospel is to place God's invitation and demands before the community. Then step back and allow God to work in people's lives.

1ST SUNDAY OF LENT

Lectionary #23

READING I Genesis 9:8–15

A reading from the book of Genesis.

Establish the setting with a tone of solemnity in your voice. As you proceed to describe the covenant, speak God's words warmly.

God said to *Noah* and to his sons *with* him:
"*See,* I am now establishing my *covenant* with *you*
and your descendants *after* you
and with *every* living *creature* that was with you:
all the *birds,* and the various *tame* and *wild animals*
that were *with* you and came out of the *ark.*
I will establish my *covenant* with you,
that *never again* shall all bodily creatures be *destroyed*
by the waters of a *flood;*
there shall *not* be *another flood* to *devastate* the earth."

Strongly proclaim this promise.

God added:
"*This* is the *sign* that I am giving for *all* ages to *come,*
of the *covenant* between *me* and *you*
and *every* living creature *with* you:
I set my *bow* in the *clouds* to serve as a *sign*
of the *covenant* between *me* and the *earth.*
When I bring *clouds* over the earth,
and the *bow* appears in the *clouds,*
I will *recall* the *covenant* I have made
between *me* and *you* and *all living beings,*
so that the *waters* shall *never again* become a *flood*
to *destroy* all mortal beings."

Stress the scope of the covenant.

READING I Ancient covenants usually involved an exchange of promises between two parties, ratified by the sacrifice of an animal. The covenant in today's reading is unilateral; it is God's promise always to care for the earth and its inhabitants.

Ancient Israel must have looked to the heavens after rains and understood the rainbow in the sky to be a link between God and the earth. It is an appropriate symbol for covenant, for the promise of unconditional love, acceptance and care. The beauty of the rainbow appearing after a rain also suggests the association of covenant with water. Christian baptism is, indeed, our supreme covenant with God.

We journey through Lent with parched lips. But we have hope, which you proclaim today, that the waters of life await us. Offer this encouraging message to the members of your assembly, reminding them that on Easter we will renew our baptismal promises and welcome new members into our community.

READING II The second reading today recalls God's promises to Noah outlined in the first reading. The story of Noah, who passed through the flood and lived while those around him perished, is explicitly presented as a prefigurement of baptism. The present passage comes from a letter that was written to strengthen Christians in the face of cultural pressures to compromise their faith.

The difficulty with this passage is understanding the preaching that Christ proclaimed to the "spirits in prison." It has been variously suggested that these spirits were

READING II 1 Peter 3:18–22

A reading from the first letter of Saint Peter.

The first line describes the great work Christ has done in suffering so that humans might return to God. Read it slowly and with forcefulness.

Beloved:
Christ *suffered* for sins *once*,
the *righteous* for the sake of the *unrighteous*,
that he might *lead* you to *God*.
Put to *death* in the flesh,
he was brought to *life* in the *Spirit*.

Read these difficult verses clearly but without drawing special attention to them.

In it he also went to *preach* to the *spirits* in *prison*,
who had *once* been *disobedient*
while *God* patiently *waited* in the days of *Noah*
during the building of the *ark*,
in which a *few* persons, *eight* in all,
were *saved* through water.

Baptism is the key idea here. We await the Easter renewal of baptism, our covenant with God.

Emphasize the importance of the resurrection and the authority given to Christ.

This prefigured *baptism*, which saves *you* now.
It is *not* a removal of *dirt* from the body
but an *appeal* to God for a *clear conscience*,
through the *resurrection* of Jesus *Christ*,
who has gone into *heaven*
and is at the *right hand* of God,
with *angels*, *authorities* and *powers subject* to him.

either those who died in the flood at the time of Noah or evil spirits whose sinful activity led to the flood. The "preaching" has been understood as an early reference to Christ's descent into hell to rescue the righteous dead, or, if to evil spirits, an announcement of Christ's triumph over them.

Whatever is intended by these verses, it is clear that the author believes that a decisive victory over evil has been won. The righteous one has died "once for all" in order to bring people to God. Just as the flood waters saved Noah from the evil world in which he lived, Christians too are saved from the surrounding evils in society through baptism.

During Lent we examine our involvement with our society and its pressures, often finding the need to reject some of its values. We discipline ourselves in order to become stronger, more committed people. Your task today is to proclaim the hope we retain throughout this season, a hope in Christ's resurrection, and in the promises of baptism. We thirst now, but trust that we will find refreshment when our Lenten journey ends at Easter.

GOSPEL **Today's first and second readings suggest the hope that Christians have by virtue of baptism. In the gospel, however, we learn that struggle is also necessary.**

Jesus is driven by the Spirit into the wilderness, where he remains for 40 days

GOSPEL Mark 1:12–15

A reading from the holy gospel according to Mark.

Read this short account of Jesus' time in the desert with care. Communicate the power of the Spirit.

The Spirit *drove* Jesus out into the *desert*,
and he *remained* in the desert for *forty* days,
tempted by Satan.

Pause before this line so that the contrast in Jesus' experiences will be more evident. Pause again at the end of the sentence.

He was among *wild beasts*,
and the *angels ministered* to him.

After *John* had been *arrested*,
Jesus came to *Galilee* proclaiming the *gospel* of God:

This is the promise for which Israel is waiting. But the promise carries also a demand. Speak Jesus' own call to repentance slowly and clearly.

"This is the *time* of *fulfillment*.
The *kingdom* of *God* is at *hand*.
Repent, and *believe* in the *gospel*."

(a symbolic reference to a long time). It is only after being tempted that he begins to preach, demanding repentance of those who listen to his words.

Our Lenten journey in the wilderness is also difficult. We enter it as baptized Christians, and we must be honest in acknowledging that following Christ is not always easy. We find that we must be continually called to repentance. This life is demanding; it is hard work.

Jesus began his ministry only after encountering Satan. In our desert experience, we too come face-to-face with temptation, with our own greed, arrogance, fear. This season is a time when we reflect on these struggles, recognizing them as tests that can strengthen us, so that we too can proclaim the good news.

This short gospel selection demands a careful, measured reading. Proclaim both the difficulties faced by Jesus and the strength he gained through his struggles. Let your listeners know that following Jesus means going where he goes, even into the barren desert.

2ND SUNDAY OF LENT

Lectionary #26

READING I Genesis 22:1–2, 9a, 10–13, 15–18

A reading from the book of Genesis.

Pause after this summary statement.

God put *Abraham* to the *test.*
He called to him, *"Abraham!"*
"*Here* I am!" he replied.

Abraham does not know what is coming.

Then God said:
"*Take* your son *Isaac*, your *only* one, whom you *love*,
and go to the *land* of *Moriah.*
There you shall *offer* him *up* as a *holocaust*
on a height that I will point *out* to you."

Emphasize with tenderness the words describing Isaac.
Moriah = moh-RĪ-uh

Allow the realization of the command to sink in for your listeners.
As you continue, do not be afraid to allow a certain dread to enter your voice.

When they *came* to the place of which God had *told* him,
Abraham built an *altar* there and arranged the *wood* on it.
Then he *reached out* and took the *knife* to *slaughter* his *son.*

Read slowly, with tension in your voice.
Pause.

But the LORD's *messenger* called to him from *heaven*,
"Abraham, Abraham!"
"*Here* I am!" he answered.
"Do *not* lay your hand on the boy," said the messenger.
"Do *not* do the *least* thing to him.
I *know now* how *devoted* you are to God,
since you did not *withhold* from me your *own beloved son."*

The emotion of the passage spirals downward from this point.

As Abraham looked about,
he spied a *ram* caught by its *horns* in the *thicket.*
So he went and *took* the ram
and *offered* it up as a *holocaust* in *place* of his son.

READING I The story of Abraham's willingness to sacrifice his son Isaac is high drama indeed. It is difficult to read or hear this account without a sense of horror at the thought of anyone attempting to kill a child. Allow tension to enter your voice in order to convey most effectively this suspense-filled story.

Abraham obeys God's command in silence. We are left to imagine what he was thinking. The sense of loss must have been unbearable. Lest we miss how special this child was, God's words clarify it: "Take your son, your only one, whom you love . . ." Perhaps Abraham could not speak because his heart was broken.

The drama intensifies when Abraham and Isaac reach the place of sacrifice; Abraham even binds Isaac to the wood on the altar. What must the boy have been feeling? What was Abraham experiencing as he grasped the knife?

But the angel interrupts and tells him not to harm the child, congratulating him for being willing to sacrifice his son. We breathe a sigh of relief. God's promise of numerous offspring to Abraham and Sarah seems to bring the drama to a satisfying end.

And yet the nagging question remains: Why would God demand the sacrifice of a child? It is a good question. In fact, the story is intended to illustrate just the opposite.

Human sacrifice was commonly practiced in the land of Canaan. Foreign kings offered their firstborn sons (their immediate heirs) in order to enlist help from their gods in battle. Even some kings of Israel are said to have sacrificed their children — but they are condemned as wicked and unfaithful to Israel's God.

Because of Abraham's faithfulness, God again declares this promise to Abraham.

God's blessings go beyond the chosen people to all the earth.

Again the LORD's messenger called to Abraham
from heaven and said:
"I *swear* by *myself*, declares the LORD,
that *because* you acted as you *did*
in *not withholding* from me your *beloved son*,
I will *bless* you *abundantly*
and make your *descendants* as *countless*
as the *stars* of the *sky* and the *sands* of the *seashore*;
your *descendants* shall take *possession*
of the gates of their *enemies*,
and in your *descendants all* the nations of the *earth*
shall find *blessing*—
all *this* because you *obeyed* my *command*."

READING II Romans 8:31b–34

A reading from the letter of Saint Paul to the Romans.

The answer to the first question ("No one!") should be made obvious to your hearers, even though it is left unsaid. Read all of these questions as if their answers are already known. Raise your voice at or near the end of each question.

Speak this line with a sense of conviction.

Brothers and sisters:
If *God* is *for* us, who can be *against* us?
He who did not spare his *own Son*
but *handed* him *over* for us *all*,
how will he not *also* give us everything *else* along with him?

Who will bring a charge against God's *chosen* ones?
It is *God* who *acquits* us, *who* will *condemn*?

Christ Jesus it is who *died*—or, rather, was *raised*—
who *also* is at the *right hand* of God,
who indeed *intercedes* for us.

The story of Abraham, then, challenges the idea that child sacrifice is acceptable to the divine. It is not selfishness or squeamishness that keeps the Hebrew people from engaging in such practices but rather the command of God. Abraham's willingness to give up his claim to God's promise is the ultimate demonstration of his faith and trust in God.

This passage is difficult and painful to read. It also provides plenty of suspense to keep the attention of your listeners. Practice the reading carefully, letting God's demand carry its full weight, building the tension and anxiety as Abraham grows closer to committing the act. Let your voice be filled with relief when the angel intervenes. Finally, speak God's promises with a firm voice.

READING II Paul, in his letter to the Romans, insists that God is fully supportive of the "elect" or "chosen ones," those justified in Christ. For any who might not readily recognize it, the proof lies in the fact that God was willing to suffer what Abraham did not: The life of God's Son was offered for our sake.

The image evoked by the next verses is that of the final judgment. The questions are ironic; there is no one to bring accusations against the chosen ones, surely not God, the judge who declares our innocence. There is also no one to condemn, since the only one who has such authority is precisely the one interceding for us. The only ones who could speak against us are those who are for us.

Read the questions genuinely, but give the responses ("God?", "Christ Jesus?") with a sense of "You've got to be kidding!"

GOSPEL Mark 9:2–10

A reading from the holy gospel according to Mark.

Jesus took *Peter*, *James* and *John*
and led them up a high *mountain apart* by themselves.

Pause before continuing. Then proceed in amazement.

And he was *transfigured* before them,
and his *clothes* became *dazzling* white,
such as no fuller on *earth* could *bleach* them.

Then *Elijah* appeared to them along with *Moses*,
and they were *conversing* with Jesus.

Read Peter's words a little more quickly and breathlessly, illustrating Peter's excitement.

Then *Peter* said to Jesus in reply,
"*Rabbi*, it is *good* that we are *here!*
Let us make *three* tents:
one for *you*, one for *Moses*, and one for *Elijah*."

This explains the absurdity of his proposal.

He hardly knew *what* to say, they were so *terrified*.

Then a *cloud* came, casting a *shadow* over them;
from the cloud came a *voice*,

Speak God's words with dignity and authority (but resist the temptation to deepen your voice). Pause briefly before this line; pause again after it.

"*This* is my *beloved Son*. *Listen* to him."
Suddenly, looking around, they no *longer* saw *anyone*
but *Jesus alone* with them.

As they were coming *down* from the mountain,
he *charged* them *not* to relate what they had seen to *anyone*,
except when the *Son* of *Man* had *risen* from the *dead*.

Slow down for the last line.

So they kept the matter to *themselves*,
questioning what *rising* from the *dead* meant.

GOSPEL The story of the transfiguration, read here in the dead of a Lenten winter, alludes to the Easter joy that awaits us. Just as the flowers and trees are beginning to show signs of life, so also our gospel hints that glory will once again prevail. But it is not without cost.

Jesus takes three of his most trusted followers with him as he climbs the mountain. Transformed, Jesus radiates splendor, just as Moses radiated in his body the awe of his encounter with God. Jesus is accompanied by Moses and Elijah, the Law and the prophets embodied. Both figures were understood in Hebrew tradition as having been taken up into heaven. The clouds and voice indicate God's presence, while the words echo those spoken about Jesus at his baptism.

The disciples, to whom Jesus had just made his first prediction of his passion, do not understand. Peter, who had tried to talk Jesus out of the idea of suffering, again wants to emphasize his glory. He wants to remain on the mountaintop, but Jesus is already on his way down, again speaking about death.

The gospel of Mark insists repeatedly that the glory of the resurrection, the glory of the Christian life, cannot be found through anything but suffering. Exaltation comes to Jesus only after taking the path of the cross. The same path lies ahead of us as well.

Today's gospel selection is a powerful one, to be conveyed with a sense of awe. Read the account of the transfiguration with excitement in your voice. Offer Peter's words as an interruption to the majesty of the scene, even as they attempt to preserve it. The closing lines have a sense of foreboding, and a sense of promise.

3RD SUNDAY OF LENT

Lectionary #29

READING I Exodus 20:1–17

A reading from the book of Exodus.

In those days, God delivered *all* these *commandments:*
"*I*, the *LORD*, am *your God*,
who brought you out of the *land* of *Egypt*, that *place*
of *slavery*.
You shall *not* have other *gods besides* me.
You shall *not* carve *idols* for yourselves
in the shape of anything in the *sky* above
or on the *earth* below or in the *waters beneath* the earth;
you shall *not* bow down *before* them or *worship* them.

Give equal emphasis to "I," "Lord" and "God."

For *I*, the *LORD*, *your God*, am a *jealous* God,
inflicting *punishment* for their fathers' *wickedness*
on the *children* of those who *hate* me,
down to the third and fourth *generation*;
but bestowing *mercy* down to the *thousandth* generation
on the children of those who *love* me
and keep my *commandments*.

Love will last indefinitely for the descendants of those who are faithful.

"You shall *not* take the name of the *LORD*, *your God*, in *vain*.
For the LORD will *not* leave *unpunished*
the one who takes his *name* in *vain*.

"*Remember* to keep *holy* the *sabbath* day.
Six days you may *labor* and do all your *work*,
but the *seventh* day is the *sabbath* of the LORD, your God.

"Sabbath" means cessation from work, and rest. Humans are to follow God's example. The word for "seven" in Hebrew is similar to "Sabbath."

READING I The commands of God given to Moses at Sinai are best known as the Ten Commandments, although their number, division and contents vary. They are the core moral teaching in both the Jewish and Christian traditions. In the book of Exodus, the Ten Commandments are of the same nature as the Covenant Code, a series of legal precepts dealing with particular offenses or specific commands.

The commandments begin with a reminder of the Israelites' deliverance from bondage in Egypt. Israel's response is to be single-hearted devotion. At this point in Israel's history, there is no insistence that there is only one god; it is assumed that there are many. But no other is to have the allegiance of this people.

The prohibition against idols, reverence for the name of God, and the practice of observing the Sabbath have been understood differently in the Jewish, Christian and Muslim traditions. Jews and Muslims shun decoration of houses of worship with images or statues, while Christians avoid images of foreign gods. Later Jewish tradition forbids any use of the divine name; Christians take the commandment to mean that they should avoid speaking God's name irreverently. Finally, many Christians have transferred their day of rest from the last day of the week to the first, Sunday, in honor of Jesus' resurrection.

Subsequent commandments are brief and direct, involving issues of honesty and reverence for life.

The reading of the commandments can be both a challenge and a joy. Think of them not as orders but as opportunities to offer love to God and to others, and offer this sentiment to your listeners. Resist speaking God's words in a deep, booming voice, but

No work may be done then either by *you*, or your
son or *daughter*,
or your male or female *slave*, or your *beast*,
or by the *alien* who lives with you.
In *six* days the LORD made the *heavens* and the *earth*,
the *sea* and all that is *in* them;
but on the *seventh* day he *rested*.
That is why the LORD has *blessed* the *sabbath* day and
made it *holy*.

This commandment has a reward attached.

"*Honor* your *father* and your *mother*,
that you may have a *long life* in the land
which the *LORD*, your *God*, is *giving* you.

Speak slowly and with emphasis on each word for these short commands.

You shall *not kill*.
You shall *not* commit *adultery*.
You shall *not steal*.
You shall *not* bear *false witness* against your *neighbor*.

"House" includes all that follows. Although humans and animals appear to be placed on the same level in the commandment, there were actually different degrees of importance assigned to wives, slaves and different types of animals. Yet all are considered items of the household and possessions of the (male) landowner.

You shall *not covet* your neighbor's *house*.
You shall *not covet* your neighbor's *wife*,
nor his male or female *slave*, nor his *ox* or *ass*,
nor *anything* else that *belongs* to him."

[Shorter: Exodus 20:1–3, 7–8, 12–17]

speak slowly and with authority. Say "You shall not" with great emphasis on each word throughout the reading, but in a tone of instruction rather than anger. The final commandments are brief and pose a special challenge. Pause generously before and after each command, emphasizing each word of the shortest commands.

READING II **Paul, apostle to the Gentiles, discusses at the outset of his first letter to the church in Corinth the views of non-Christians toward the gospel he preaches. At the center of his preaching is the cross.**

Paul claims that the Jews seek signs of power, a classification that certainly could not be applied to a man dying helplessly on the cross. Since Israel's God had often demonstrated power and might through visible signs, it is understandable that Jews would expect the same from God's anointed one. The reality of the cross is then a "stumbling block"; it is scandalous (the Greek word for "stumbling block" is *skandalon*) for Jews.

The Greeks were known for their love of philosophy and desire for knowledge. The claim that the execution of an uneducated man as a common criminal mediated divine revelation —indeed that the execution itself was central to the salvific message—must have seemed foolish. The cross was in fact an object of ridicule by pagans for centuries.

It is the cross, however, that Paul preaches. Paradoxically, Jesus' power is shown precisely by his refusal to claim power. By rejecting the common understanding of knowledge, God's wisdom can

READING II 1 Corinthians 1:22 – 25

A reading from the first letter of Saint Paul to the Corinthians.

Brothers and sisters:
Jews demand *signs* and *Greeks* look for *wisdom*,
but *we* proclaim *Christ crucified*,
a *stumbling* block to Jews and *foolishness* to Gentiles,
but to those who are *called*, Jews and Greeks *alike*,
Christ the *power* of God and the *wisdom* of God.
For the *foolishness* of *God* is *wiser* than human *wisdom*,
and the *weakness* of *God* is *stronger* than human *strength*.

It was Jewish practice to divide the world into "Jews and Greeks" (that is, non-Jews).

The key words here are "power" and "wisdom." Speak this line and the next with authority.

GOSPEL John 2:13 – 25

A reading from the holy gospel according to John.

Since the *Passover* of the Jews was *near*,
Jesus went up to *Jerusalem*.
He found in the *temple* area those who sold *oxen*,
sheep and *doves*,
as well as the *money* changers seated there.
He made a *whip* out of *cords*
and *drove* them all out of the temple area,
with the sheep and oxen,
and *spilled* the coins of the *money* changers
and *overturned* their tables,
and to those who sold *doves* he said,
"Take these *out* of here,
and *stop* making my Father's *house* a *marketplace*."

There is no question that Jesus is upset here; communicate this with great forcefulness in your voice.

This is the climax of the passage; convey Jesus' anger.

be made known. Human judgments are inadequate for understanding God.

Proclaim this passage with the same pride Paul felt in writing it. Encourage your listeners not to be ashamed of their faith but to seize every opportunity to proclaim it. The closing line is especially powerful; speak it with conviction.

GOSPEL The story of Jesus cleansing the Temple, although it appears early in the gospel of John, is the event that precipitates Jesus' arrest in the synoptic gospels. Jesus challenges not only the Jewish aristocracy, but seems to attack the central institution of Jewish life and thought: the Temple.

Jesus had entered Jerusalem at the time of the Jewish Passover. Jerusalem must have been bustling with preparations for the feast, and the Temple area would have been the center of activity. Not only were the sacrificial offerings brought to the Temple for slaughter, but those who did not have their own offering could purchase one near the Temple. The presence of animals in the Temple area is hardly surprising; they were necessary in order to fulfill the requirements of the Law.

Living under Roman occupation, the people ordinarily conducted business with Roman or Greek coins. However, these coins could not be used to pay the Temple tax because of the images on them. Money changers provided a service in supplying acceptable coins.

The reason the author gives for Jesus' action — driving out the animals for sacrifice, overturning tables — is zeal for the house of God. Jesus saw all the activity as turning the Temple area into a marketplace.

His disciples *recalled* the words of Scripture,
"*Zeal* for your *house* will *consume* me."

At *this* the Jews answered and said to him,
"What *sign* can you show us for *doing* this?"
Jesus answered and said to them,
"*Destroy* this temple and in *three days* I will *raise* it up."
The Jews said,
"This *temple* has been under construction for *forty-six* years,
and you will *raise* it up in *three days*?"
But he was speaking about the temple of his *body*.

Therefore, when he was *raised* from the *dead*,
his disciples *remembered* that he had said this,
and they came to *believe* the Scripture
and the *word* Jesus had *spoken*.

While he was in *Jerusalem* for the feast of *Passover*,
many began to *believe* in his name
when they saw the *signs* he was doing.
But Jesus would not *trust* himself to them because he *knew* them *all*,
and did not need *anyone* to testify about *human nature*.
He *himself* understood it *well*.

Precisely why the business of the Temple offended Jesus is not clear; it has been variously proposed that there was cheating against the poor, that Jesus was rejecting commercial activity in a sacred area, or that he opposed a carnival-like atmosphere. None of the suggestions is entirely satisfactory. What is clear is that Jesus feels justified in his actions and raises the ire of the Jewish leaders against him.

When the leaders (called "the Jews" throughout the gospel of John) ask for a sign, Jesus speaks harsh words against the Temple and designates his own body as a "temple," words that the evangelist interprets as a prediction of Jesus' passion. If Jesus' behavior and preaching were not enough to cause the Jewish leaders to dislike him, his popularity with the masses must have tipped the balance. But Jesus himself knows that public adulation is a fickle thing.

There is much drama in this account; Jesus' words and actions demonstrate his anger. There is tension as well between the Jewish leaders and Jesus, and even between Jesus and the "many." Read this account with all the skill you have in order to convey Jesus' volatile emotions and the leaders' challenge to his authority. The excitement peaks with his spoken words and gradually lessens until the end. Inspire your listeners to share in Jesus' zealous reverence for all things holy.

3RD SUNDAY OF LENT, YEAR A

Lectionary #28

READING I Exodus 17:3–7

A reading from the book of Exodus.

In those days, in their *thirst* for *water*,
the people *grumbled* against *Moses*,
saying, "*Why* did you ever make us leave *Egypt?*
Was it just to have us *die* here of *thirst*
with our *children* and our *livestock?*"
So Moses cried *out* to the LORD,
"What shall I *do* with this people?
A little *more* and they will *stone* me!"

The people are upset, almost ready to revolt. Let their exasperation be heard in your words.

Moses is desperate.

The LORD *answered* Moses,
"Go over there in *front* of the *people*,
along with some of the *elders* of Israel,
holding in your *hand*, as you *go*,
the *staff* with which you struck the *river*.
I will be standing there in *front* of you on the *rock* in *Horeb*.
Strike the rock, and the water will *flow* from it
for the people to *drink*."
This Moses *did*, in the presence of the elders of *Israel*.

Speak God's words calmly and firmly.

The place was called *Massah* and *Meribah*,
because the Israelites *quarreled* there
and *tested* the LORD, saying,
"Is the LORD in our *midst* or *not?*"

Massah = MAS-ah
Meribah = MAYR-ih-bah
Massah means "testing" and Meribah means "quarreling."

READING I Life-giving water figures prominently in today's readings, as we prepare to welcome new members of the community through the waters of baptism on Easter.

Despite God's continual intervention on behalf of the Israelites wandering in the desert, the Pentateuch records their constant grumbling against the Lord whenever they meet with adversity. At times they even plan to return to Egypt; freedom, with its attendant struggles, can be even more threatening than bondage. This might seem to be the case for us too, as we journey through the Lenten wilderness; we would prefer to turn back rather than continue wandering with parched lips, longing for home. So today we are given refreshment to strengthen us on the way.

Although they have just been fed with quail and manna, the Israelites find the absence of water in the desert too much to bear. Although Moses rightly fears that he, as God's mouthpiece, is in danger of losing his life to the mob, the Israelites' revolt is really against God. As so often before, God instructs Moses to take symbolic action, and the result is a physical benefit for the Israelites. Here their thirst is met with water in abundance, but their rebellious actions are recorded forever in the names given to the places where they questioned God.

There is plenty of drama in this passage to make for an interesting presentation. Let the people's words sound defiant, and express Moses' fear, but make God's control throughout the situation evident. Challenge your listeners also to reflect on their own times of rebellion. Do we really believe that God will provide for us everything that we need? Through the waters of baptism we

READING II Romans 5:1–2, 5–8

A reading from the letter of Saint Paul to the Romans.

Begin strongly, but with a genuine peacefulness in your voice.

Brothers and sisters:
Since we have been *justified* by *faith*,
we have *peace* with God through our Lord Jesus *Christ*,
through whom we have gained *access* by faith
to this *grace* in which we *stand*,
and we *boast* in hope of the *glory* of *God*.

The word translated "boast" here is related to words elsewhere translated "rejoice" or "exult." Paul has been contrasting the presumptuous boasting of one who is overconfident with the certainty of one who genuinely trusts in God.

And *hope* does not *disappoint*,
because the *love* of God has been poured *out* into our *hearts*
through the *Holy Spirit* who has been *given* to us.
For *Christ*, while we were still *helpless*,
died at the appointed *time* for the ungodly.

Stress words such as "difficulty," "just" and "perhaps" in order to emphasize how unusual it would be for someone to die for another — even for one who is good.

Indeed, only with *difficulty* does one die for a *just* person,
though *perhaps* for a *good person* one might even
find *courage* to die.

Pause briefly after "that." The reality expressed here is truly amazing; let your voice be filled with awe.

But *God* proves his *love* for us
in that while we were still *sinners* Christ *died* for us.

have become part of a community that commits itself to God, even as we know that God is completely committed to our welfare. Offer this reading to your congregation as a challenge to trust that God is indeed on our side.

READING II **This rich passage from Paul's letter to the Romans is filled with assurances about the great love of God. It spells out Paul's belief in the initiative taken by God for our sake, seen in the actions of Christ.**

Paul begins this section by affirming one of his most cherished principles: We are made right before God, brought back into relationship with God ("justified"), not through anything we ourselves have done, but through God's own gracious love. Because of this we can be at peace. Even in times of trial ("stand" in Paul always means firmness in the face of adversity), we can turn to God in faith, knowing that God's glory will be revealed.

Our hope is not a false one; we can be confident because we know that God's love for us has been demonstrated in Jesus' death. And that love has been poured out in abundance, filling our hearts to overflowing. It is through the Holy Spirit, given in baptism, that the overwhelming love of God for us is confirmed.

Jesus' actions demonstrate God's overflowing grace as well. Paul points out how rare it is for one person to die for another. We can think of instances when this happens, but usually it is a brave soul who saves a loved one or friend. It is much harder to imagine someone dying for the sake of an enemy. Yet that is what Jesus has done,

GOSPEL John 4:5–42

Sychar = SĪK-ahr

Jesus' statement sounds rude and demanding. The woman does not understand it to be so. Phrase it in such a way that it sounds like a request rather than a demand.

In the gospel of John, the term "Jew" is usually applied to the religious leaders of the Jews. It is used of Jesus only here in this gospel.

The woman is being practical and reasonable. In Greek the terms seem to refer to actual water.

Speak here with a bit of indignation and surprise at the notion.

A reading from the holy gospel according to John.

Jesus came to a town of *Samaria* called *Sychar*,
near the plot of land that *Jacob* had given to his son *Joseph*.
Jacob's well was there.
Jesus, tired from his *journey*, sat *down* there at the *well*.
It was about *noon*.

A *woman* of *Samaria* came to draw *water*.
Jesus said to her,
"*Give* me a *drink*."
His disciples had gone into the town to buy *food*.

The Samaritan woman said to him,
"How can *you*, a *Jew*, ask *me*, a *Samaritan woman*,
for a *drink*?"
—For *Jews* use nothing in common with *Samaritans*.—
Jesus answered and said to her,
"If you knew the *gift* of God
and *who* is saying to you, '*Give* me a *drink*,'
you would have asked *him*
and he would have given you *living* water."

The woman said to him,
"Sir, you do not even have a *bucket* and the cistern is *deep*;
where then can you get this *living water*?
Are you *greater* than our father *Jacob*,
who *gave* us this cistern and *drank* from it himself
with his *children* and his *flocks*?"

dying for us while we were caught in sin, having made ourselves enemies of God.

This is a solemn proclamation, yet the message is cause for great joy. Though we have done nothing to deserve it, God has given us the greatest gift of love. Inspire the members of your assembly to reflect on God's deep commitment and the tremendous love God offers us through Jesus. Encourage your listeners to stand firm in their faith in this season of Lent and always, knowing that God is always with us. In this there is truly a message of peace.

GOSPEL The encounter between Jesus and the Samaritan woman at the well centers on the question of living water and the related significance of Jesus' identity. As always in the gospel of John, Jesus has full knowledge of his mission and identity, but his companions (here primarily the woman, but also the disciples) have ordinary human knowledge, inadequate for fully comprehending what Jesus is saying. Here also, ordinary water—so important for sustaining life and for refreshment—gives way to living water, the kind of water necessary for eternal life. As we prepare to approach the waters of baptism on Easter, whether to renew our baptismal commitment or to receive the life-giving waters, we are reminded of the source of our sustenance. It is through Jesus that we receive the water of life, essential for our thirsty souls.

Although Jesus could have avoided traveling through Samaria on his way to Galilee from Jerusalem, he finds himself in the heart of Samaritan territory. Samaritans and Jews, despite common roots, had long felt great animosity toward one another. Jews were convinced that "salvation is from

Jesus' words are solemn and carry deep meaning. Let them build so that the words sound like the bubbling water they describe.

Jesus answered and said to her,
"*Everyone* who drinks *this* water will be thirsty again;
but *whoever* drinks the water *I* shall give will *never* thirst;
the water *I* shall give will become in him
a *spring* of water *welling up* to *eternal life.*"

Convey the woman's eagerness, although she still does not understand.

The woman said to him,
"Sir, *give* me this water, so that I may not be *thirsty*
or have to keep *coming* here to draw *water.*"

Jesus said to her,
"*Go* call your *husband* and come *back.*"
The woman answered and said to him,
"I do not *have* a husband."
Jesus answered her,
"You are *right* in saying, 'I do not have a *husband.*'
For you have had *five* husbands,
and the one you have *now* is *not* your husband.
What you have *said* is *true.*"

The woman said to him,
"*Sir,* I can *see* that you are a *prophet.*
Our *ancestors* worshiped on *this* mountain;
but *you* people say that the place to worship is in *Jerusalem.*"
Jesus said to her,
"*Believe* me, woman, the *hour* is *coming*
when you will worship the *Father*
neither on *this* mountain *nor* in Jerusalem.

"*You* people worship what you do not *understand;*
we worship what we understand,
because *salvation* is from the *Jews.*

the Jews," and Samaritans held fast to the Pentateuch and viewed later traditions — such as worship in Jerusalem — as accretions to the true faith. For a Jewish teacher to speak at length (or at all!) with a Samaritan was unheard of.

For a Jewish teacher to speak in public with a woman — even a Jewish woman — was also unknown. The disciples' surprise when they returned and saw Jesus conversing with the Samaritan woman is to be expected. Jesus was defying the tradition that kept strict social barriers in place between those of different nationalities, religious traditions and sexes. Jesus reached out to the woman and offered her what she did not even realize she needed.

The story begins simply; in one of the few instances in the Fourth Gospel in which he displays human weakness, Jesus is tired and thirsty after a morning of travel. When he requests a drink of the woman, she immediately hides behind the barriers she has always known. Jesus' response does not address her issues, but rather turns the conversation to the question of water.

The term for "living" water can also mean "flowing," referring to water that is not stagnant but fresh and pure. The woman misunderstands and is skeptical of Jesus' claims. Although she recognizes him as a teacher, she is convinced that he could not possibly be greater than Jacob, whose well they are using. The reader anticipates what is coming: Jesus is, of course, far greater. However, Jesus again does not reply directly but allows her to draw her own conclusions.

Jesus reveals that he has water for eternal life; the woman is intrigued. But she becomes convinced that he is no ordinary person when he has insight into her life and her character. Jesus brings her to fuller

But the hour is *coming*, and is now *here*,
when *true* worshipers will worship the Father
in *Spirit* and *truth*;
and indeed the Father *seeks such* people to worship him.
God is *Spirit*, and those who *worship* him
must worship in *Spirit* and *truth*."

The woman said to him,
"I *know* that the *Messiah* is coming, the one called the *Christ*;
when he *comes*, he will tell us *everything*."
Jesus said to her,
"*I* am *he*, the one *speaking* with you."

At that moment his disciples *returned*,
and were *amazed* that he was talking with a *woman*,
but still no one said, "*What* are you looking for?"
or "*Why* are you *talking* with her?"
The woman left her *water* jar
and *went* into the town and *said* to the people,

Express the woman's excitement.

"*Come see* a man who told me *everything* I have *done*.
Could he possibly *be* the *Christ*?"
They went *out* of the town and *came* to him.
Meanwhile, the disciples *urged* him, "*Rabbi, eat*."
But he said to them,
"I have *food* to eat of which *you* do not *know*."
So the disciples said to one another,
"Could someone have *brought* him something to *eat*?"

The disciples, like the woman, do not initially understand; this provides Jesus with an opportunity to teach them.

Jesus said to them,
"My food is to do the *will* of the one who *sent* me
and to *finish* his *work*.
Do you not say, 'In *four* months the *harvest* will be here'?
I tell you, *look up* and *see* the fields *ripe* for the *harvest*.

understanding of his identity by establishing a relationship with her.

It is especially appropriate to contemplate the "living water" offered by Jesus on this day when catechumens undergo their first scrutiny in preparation for Easter baptism. Recall that, as with the Samaritan woman, the life-giving water is something that is offered only through personal contact; one comes to know Jesus by encountering those who trust in him.

Just when it seems that their religious differences are irrelevant, Jesus affirms that "salvation is from the Jews." Here the gospel of John reveals itself as a document from a Jewish-Christian community. But, Jesus claims, the time soon approaches when true worship of God will be "in spirit and truth," rather than the rituals familiar to the Samaritans or the Jews. The evangelist is clearly alluding to Christian worship of the God who is revealed in Jesus; Jesus is truth, as the Johannine prologue asserts, and baptizes with the Holy Spirit. Although the old ways may have been valid in the past, the author leaves no doubt that a new way of living and worshiping is available through and in Jesus.

The woman's belief in a Messiah seems odd coming from a Samaritan. In fact, it is probably the Jewish expectation for a Davidic Messiah that is expressed, allowing Jesus to reveal himself as the fulfillment of that expectation.

The conversation is interrupted by the return of the disciples. Jesus continues his enigmatic claims by asserting that he has food of which they are unaware. He then launches into a discussion of ministry under the metaphor of harvest. As is so often true in agriculture and in life, the minister knows that it takes time for a seed to take root. The

The reaper is *already* receiving payment
and gathering *crops* for *eternal life*,
so that the *sower* and *reaper* can rejoice *together*.
For *here* the saying is *verified* that '*One sows* and *another reaps*.'
I sent you to *reap* what you have not *worked* for;
others have done the *work*,
and *you* are sharing the *fruits* of their *work*."

Many of the *Samaritans* of that town began to *believe* in him
because of the *word* of the *woman* who *testified*,
"He told me *everything* I have *done*."
When the Samaritans *came* to him,
they *invited* him to *stay* with them;
and he stayed there *two days*.
Many *more* began to believe in him because of *his word*,
and they *said* to the woman,
"We no *longer* believe because of *your* word;
for we have heard for *ourselves*,
and we *know* that this *is* truly the *savior* of the *world*."

[Shorter: John 4:5–15, 19b–26, 39a, 40–42]

Close with an emphasis on the personal nature of faith, and on the title given Jesus.

one who begins the work of evangelizing and nurturing faith is not always the one who sees that work come to fruition. We must recognize that no one individual or group can claim credit for success, precisely because we claim to be a community. One may plant the seed of faith, another may water it, and still another enjoy the fragrant blossoms of mature belief.

The Samaritan woman is sometimes remembered as the first evangelist. She ran to the town to tell others of her encounter with Jesus. Her neighbors came to believe, however, based on their own experience. Although others can introduce one to faith, each person must have his or her own encounter with Jesus.

This is an interesting and exciting story of faith. Allow the woman's sincerity and eagerness to be heard. Although Jesus' responses can be exasperating and elusive, use them as the teaching tools they are, drawing your listeners to a deeper level of understanding. Challenge your community of faith to reflect on its ministry and the necessity of coordinating efforts in order to witness the greatest gains. Finally, remember that it is often in quiet darkness that the seeds of faith are first sown. Trust that God is working even when all evidence seems to indicate otherwise.

APRIL 2, 2000

4TH SUNDAY OF LENT

Lectionary #32

READING I   2 Chronicles 36:14–16, 19–23

A reading from the second book of Chronicles.

In those days, *all* the princes of *Judah*, the *priests*, and the *people*
added *infidelity* to *infidelity*,
practicing all the *abominations* of the *nations*
and *polluting* the LORD's temple
which he had *consecrated* in *Jerusalem.*

The prophets were messengers of God's compassion. Speak here with sincerity.

Early and *often* did the LORD, the *God* of their *fathers*,
send his *messengers* to them,
for he had *compassion* on his people and his *dwelling* place.

Let your voice become harsh here.

But they *mocked* the messengers of God,
despised his warnings, and *scoffed* at his prophets,
until the *anger* of the LORD against his *people* was so *inflamed*
that there was *no remedy.*

Their enemies *burnt* the house of God,
tore down the walls of Jerusalem,
set *all* its palaces *afire*,
and *destroyed* all its precious *objects.*

Chaldeans = kal-DEE-uhnz

Those who *escaped* the sword were carried *captive* to *Babylon*,
where they became *servants* of the *king* of the *Chaldeans* and
his *sons*
until the kingdom of the *Persians* came to *power.*

READING I Today's account is essentially an accurate summary of the events surrounding the exile in Babylon, with a few significant errors. It was clearly written by an admirer of the prophet Jeremiah, for Jeremiah's predictions and perspective are used to interpret the exile.

God is depicted by the writer of Second Chronicles as one who repeatedly tried to call a wayward nation to faithfulness, but who finally saw no solution but to bring punishment upon it. A foreign people, the Chaldeans (or Babylonians), was allowed to wreak havoc on the chosen people, even destroying the holy city and its Temple. All this was in concert with the divine plan, however, as was the rise of Persia and the end of the exile. God's purpose, described as a lengthy observation of the Sabbath in order to make up for Sabbaths previously ignored, was accomplished as Jeremiah had foretold.

King Cyrus of Persia conquered the Babylonian empire and allowed the exiles to return. Cyrus was hailed as a savior, even called "messiah" in the book of Isaiah, and a great ruler. He was understood by the Jews as an instrument of God. The conclusion of today's reading, also the conclusion of the work, is told in the words of Cyrus, who blesses all of God's people as they return to their homeland.

The exile in Babylon is a fitting image of our Lenten journey. We are a wayward people, longing for home. This selection reminds us that everything is in God's control and that we shall be brought safely home in the end.

Because of the nature of this selection, it can be read as a straightforward historical

All *this* was to fulfill the word of the LORD spoken by *Jeremiah:*
"Until the land has *retrieved* its lost *sabbaths,*
during *all* the time it lies *waste* it shall have *rest*
while *seventy years* are *fulfilled.*"

Cyrus = SĪ-ruhs
Speak these lines, and those of Cyrus, with vigor and hope.

In the *first* year of *Cyrus,* king of Persia,
in order to *fulfill* the word of the LORD spoken by *Jeremiah,*
the LORD *inspired* King Cyrus of Persia
to issue this *proclamation* throughout his *kingdom,*
both by word of *mouth* and in *writing:*
"*Thus* says *Cyrus,* king of Persia:
All the kingdoms of the *earth*
the *LORD,* the God of *heaven,* has *given* to me,
and he has also *charged* me to build him a *house*
in *Jerusalem,* which is in *Judah.*
Whoever, therefore, among you belongs to *any part* of his *people,*
let him *go up,* and may his *God* be *with* him!"

READING II Ephesians 2:4–10

A reading from the letter of Saint Paul to the Ephesians.

Speak warmly of God's mercy and love.

Brothers and sisters:
God, who is *rich* in *mercy,*
because of the *great love* he had for us,
even when we were *dead* in our *transgressions,*
brought us to *life* with *Christ*—by *grace* you have
been *saved*—
raised us up with him,

This is a triumphant image; proclaim it so that your congregation can feel blessed.

account, despite its errors. Dwell, however, on the divine intent of the exile's end, and the graciousness of God's chosen agent in freeing the people. Call your own assembly to a recognition of God's hand in all human affairs.

READING II Paul's missionary zeal and extended correspondence with his churches inspired others who admired him to write in his name, borrowing some of his themes and seeking to further instruct readers in the Christian faith. The author of Ephesians is one such admirer.

The present passage is a celebration of God's goodness. It contrasts the Christians' former life—or rather death in sin—to the new life offered in Christ. Central to the writer's thought is the thesis that new life in Christ and all it entails is a gift from God. It is by this gift, this graciousness of God, that we have been saved.

The writer imagines this life as one in which the Christian has already been raised and enthroned with Christ—an idea that is clearly not Paul's. In Paul, such glorification is always held out as a future hope. But the author of Ephesians reflects Paul's thought in claiming that we are saved by God's goodness, not by our own merit. For this reason, there is no sense in boasting about salvation. Although good deeds cannot bring salvation, they remain the purpose of our creation. Doing good is not the cause of salvation but the result of it.

Midway through our Lenten journey, we run the risk of tiring and wanting to give up. This reading reminds us of all that

and *seated* us with him in the *heavens* in *Christ Jesus*,
that in the *ages* to *come*
he might show the *immeasurable riches* of his grace
in his *kindness* to us in *Christ Jesus*.

This is the central point; we have done nothing to deserve salvation, but God generously offers it. Read these lines with conviction and awe.

For by *grace* you have been *saved* through *faith*,
and this is not from *you*; it is the *gift* of *God*;
it is not from *works*, so *no* one may *boast*.
For *we* are his *handiwork*, *created* in *Christ Jesus* for the
good works
that God has *prepared* in *advance*,
that we should *live* in them.

GOSPEL John 3:14–21

A reading from the holy gospel according to John.

Jesus said to *Nicodemus*:
"Just as *Moses* lifted up the serpent in the *desert*,
so must the *Son* of *Man* be *lifted up*,
so that everyone who *believes* in him may have *eternal life*.

A lengthy pause should precede and follow this statement. Try to read it as though for the first time, so that your listeners will hear it anew.

The gospel passage is filled with contrasts from here until the end. Make clear the relationship between the contrasted elements — condemned/saved, believe/not believe, light/darkness, evil/truth.

"For God so *loved* the world that he gave his *only Son*,
so that everyone who *believes* in him might not *perish*
but might have *eternal life*.
For God did not send his Son into the world
to *condemn* the world,
but that the world might be *saved* through him.
Whoever *believes* in him will *not* be *condemned*,
but whoever does *not* believe has *already* been condemned,
because he has *not believed* in the name of the *only Son* of *God*.

God has given us and encourages us to move forward.

Your task today is to remind your listeners of the tremendous love of God, who has deemed us worthy of sharing in salvation. Dwell especially on the descriptions of all that God has done for us in Christ.

GOSPEL **Nicodemus was a Pharisee and Jewish leader, and perhaps belonged to the ruling council, the Sanhedrin. He had come to Jesus by night, recognizing Jesus as one who had come from God. He was receptive to Jesus, yet Jesus rebuked him, as he had not yet come to accept the new life offered to all who believe in Jesus as the Son of God.**

Nicodemus quickly recedes into the background in today's passage, however, while Jesus — or more precisely, the evangelist — expounds on the meaning of Jesus' life and actions. Nicodemus had recognized that God's presence was behind the signs that Jesus performed, and Jesus now appeals to another whose signs brought life to the people. While the Israelites were wandering in the desert, many were bitten by snakes and died. God instructed Moses to fashion a snake and lift it up on a pole, so that all who looked on it could live. Jesus claims that he too must be lifted up in order to give life. In the gospel of John, Jesus is "lifted up" and glorified on the cross. His death brings life to the people.

Although others had been messengers of God, Jesus' relationship with God is unique; he is "descended" from God; he is the very Son of God. In a well-known statement that summarizes the gospel message,

"And *this* is the *verdict*,
that the *light* came into the *world*,
but people preferred *darkness* to *light*,
because their works were *evil*.
For everyone who does *wicked* things *hates* the light
and does not come *toward* the light,
so that his *works* might *not* be *exposed*.
But whoever lives the *truth* comes to the *light*,
so that his *works* may be clearly *seen* as done in *God*."

the evangelist proclaims that "God so loved the world that he gave his only Son," offering life to those who believe. Indeed, God did not send Jesus to bring condemnation, but salvation. Such salvation is contingent upon faith.

In an unusual statement, the one who does not believe is said to have been judged already. Rejection of the gospel apparently brings judgment upon the nonbeliever, as the image of light and darkness clarifies. The nonbeliever, refusing the light, walks in darkness.

Central to the Johannine proclamation is the command to love; belief is demonstrated in action. Here the image of light is tied to moral demands; evil deeds are done in darkness, while the truth lives in the light. The Johannine community knew there were some who rejected their claims about Jesus. The author suggests that such unbelievers avoid the light that Jesus is because they do not want their evil deeds exposed.

Proclaim this rich passage slowly and carefully, allowing each claim to build on the one before it. At its core is a statement of God's tremendous love and the life offered in Jesus. Challenge your community to live always in the light, doing deeds that will serve to enlighten the world.

4TH SUNDAY OF LENT, YEAR A

Lectionary #31

READING I 1 Samuel 16:1b, 6–7, 10–13a

A reading from the first book of Samuel.

The LORD said to *Samuel:*
"*Fill* your horn with *oil*, and be on your *way.*
I am sending you to *Jesse* of *Bethlehem*,
for I have *chosen* my *king* from among his *sons.*"

As Jesse and his sons came to the *sacrifice*,
Samuel looked at *Eliab* and thought,
"Surely the LORD's *anointed* is *here* before him."
But the LORD said to Samuel:
"Do *not* judge from his *appearance* or from his lofty *stature*,
because I have *rejected* him.
Not as *man* sees does *God* see,
because man sees the *appearance*
but the *LORD* looks into the *heart.*"

In the *same* way Jesse presented *seven* sons before Samuel,
but Samuel said to Jesse,
"The LORD has not chosen *any one* of these."
Then Samuel asked Jesse,
"Are these *all* the sons you have?"
Jesse replied,
"There is still the *youngest*, who is tending the *sheep.*"
Samuel said to Jesse,
"*Send* for him;
we will *not begin* the sacrificial *banquet* until he *arrives* here."

Speak with confidence; Samuel is sure that this is God's chosen one.

Express Samuel's disappointment and confusion, then the exasperation in his next question.

Speak Jesse's words with an uncertain tone; he too must not have expected his youngest to be chosen over the others.

Samuel is firm.

READING I Saul, the first king of Israel, was chosen by the people against the advice of the prophet Samuel. But Samuel agreed to anoint him and supported him during his tenure as king, even while reprimanding him when he disobeyed God. But it was Saul's unwillingness to obey God in everything, and his inability to provide true leadership for the people, that led to his eventual downfall. In today's story, Samuel is sent to choose a successor for Saul, although the choice is kept secret and Saul remains in office until his death.

God sent Samuel to the insignificant town of Bethlehem to anoint the future king of Israel. Told that one of the sons of Jesse would be chosen by God to lead Israel, Samuel assumes that the first and tallest is the one. When God rejects that one, Samuel examines six others, but none is God's choice for king. Only when the youngest is brought in from the fields is Samuel convinced that he has found the one to anoint.

This reading introduces the reader to the greatest king of Israel, David. God promises everlasting favor to David and his descendants, and under David the kingdom prospers. But the blessings that await David are only hinted at here. In this passage, it is the importance of sight that dominates the discussion.

Just as the gospel reading will contrast the physical ability to see with genuine insight, so also this reading contrasts outward appearance with the qualities desired by God, qualities only God is able to see. For God does not see as humans do, but is able to look into the very heart of a person. The

Jesse sent and had the young man *brought* to them.
He was *ruddy*, a youth *handsome* to behold
and making a *splendid appearance.*

Speak with fondness; David was much loved.

The LORD said,
"*There* — *anoint* him, for *this* is the *one!*"

Speak slowly and emphasize this line.

Then Samuel, with the *horn* of oil in *hand*,
anointed David in the presence of his *brothers*;
and from *that* day *on*, the *spirit* of the LORD
rushed upon *David.*

David was anointed with God's spirit as well as with oil. Speak with excitement in your voice and emphasize David's name.

READING II Ephesians 5:8–14

A reading from the letter of Saint Paul to the Ephesians.

Brothers and sisters:
You were *once darkness*,
but *now* you are *light* in the *Lord.*
Live as *children* of light,
for light produces *every* kind of *goodness*
and *righteousness* and *truth.*

Speak encouragingly.

Try to *learn* what is *pleasing* to the Lord.
Take *no part* in the *fruitless* works of *darkness*;
rather *expose* them, for it is *shameful* even to *mention*
the things done by them in *secret*;
but everything *exposed* by the light becomes *visible*,
for everything that becomes *visible* is *light.*
Therefore, it says:
"*Awake*, O *sleeper*,
and *arise* from the *dead*,
and *Christ* will give you *light.*"

qualities within David's heart were those that made him a great leader.

Read this captivating story from the point of view of Samuel. Express Samuel's certainty when he sees Eliab, his confusion when none of the seven is chosen, and his conviction when he sees David. Stress also the words of God.

READING II Having discussed the fate of the disobedient, the author of Ephesians turns to discuss a positive way of life. Adopting the contrast of light and darkness found in Jewish writings and other Middle Eastern materials, the author encourages Christians to live in the light, to walk uprightly.

A contrast is made as well between the present life of the Christians at Ephesus and their former lives as pagans. In the past, the recipients of the letter did not see the proper way to behave. Now, living in the light of Christ, they can act rightly. Formerly, they had embraced the darkness of the world around them, so that they could be said to be darkness; as Christians, the author says, they are bearers of the light. Their former deeds are to be exposed — perhaps there is a reference to some type of public or private confession of sinfulness — so that they might be made light.

The final quotation from an unknown source is a vigorous call to live in the light of Christ. Mixing metaphors (as is done elsewhere in this passage), the author combines the idea that the former life was death as well as darkness. The quotation may come from a hymn or Christian prayer, or some other unknown document; it would have

GOSPEL John 9:1–41

A reading from the holy gospel according to John.

As Jesus *passed by* he saw a man *blind* from *birth.*
His disciples asked him,
"*Rabbi,* who sinned, *this man* or his *parents,*
that he was born *blind?*"

Jesus answered,
"*Neither* he *nor* his parents *sinned;*
it is so that the *works* of God might be *made visible*
through him.
We have to do the *works* of the one who *sent* me while it is *day.*
Night is coming when *no* one can *work.*
While I am in the *world,* I am the *light* of the *world.*"
When he had said this, he *spat* on the *ground*
and made *clay* with the *saliva,*
and *smeared* the *clay* on his eyes, and said to him,
"*Go wash* in the Pool of *Siloam*"—which means *Sent.*
So he went and *washed,* and came *back* able to *see.*

His *neighbors* and those who had seen him earlier
as a *beggar* said,
"Isn't *this* the one who used to *sit* and *beg?*"
Some said, "It *is,*"
but *others* said, "*No,* he just looks like him."
He said, "*I am.*"
So they said to him, "*How* were your eyes *opened?*"
He replied,
"The *man* called *Jesus* made clay and *anointed* my *eyes*
and told me, 'Go to *Siloam* and *wash.*'
So I *went* there and *washed* and was able to *see.*"

This was not a typical healing but an actual giving of light to one who had never seen it. Express the amazement of the man's neighbors. Their question implies not only that the man now had sight, but also that his former behavior of begging had been changed as well.

been especially appropriate for use in the celebration of baptism.

This reading applies to all of us as we strive to live lives that are pleasing to God. When we allow the brightness of Christ's love to shine in our hearts, we are able to see more clearly how to act justly and properly. Challenge your listeners to be fully alert in their Christian vocation, hiding nothing in darkness, but walking boldly in the light of day for all to see.

Offer this reading also for those who are preparing for initiation at Easter. We sometimes refer to initiation as "illumination," and we pray that those seeking baptism will always find a well-lit path on which to travel. Proclaim this message as encouragement, the hope that they will receive enlightenment. Charge them also to meet the challenge to practice deeds that can be exposed to the light rather than hidden away in shame.

GOSPEL **The giving of sight to the man born blind affirms one of the favorite truths of this gospel: Jesus is the light and brings the ability to see with the eyes of faith to all who trust in him. It is this gift of insight that we desire for those who approach initiation at Easter. We pray that their eyes, and the eyes of all the faithful, will be opened more fully to appreciate the brightness of God's love and the glory of God revealed in Jesus.**

Although the healing itself is told only briefly, great interest is shown in the question of Jesus' disciples. Traditional belief

And they said to him, "Where *is* he?"
He said, "I *don't know.*"

They *brought* the one who was once blind to the *Pharisees.*
Now Jesus had made clay and opened his *eyes* on a *sabbath.*
So then the *Pharisees* also asked him *how* he was able to *see.*
He said to them,
"He put *clay* on my *eyes,* and I *washed,* and *now* I can *see.*"
So *some* of the Pharisees said,
"This man is *not* from God,
because he does *not* keep the *sabbath.*"
But *others* said,
"How can a *sinful man* do such *signs?*"
And there was a *division* among them.

So they said to the *blind* man again,
"What do *you* have to say about him,
since he *opened your* eyes?"
He said, "He is a *prophet.*"

The blind man has an insight that is lost on the others; Jesus is a prophet because he performs signs.

Now the Jews did *not* believe
that he had been *blind* and gained his *sight*
until they summoned the *parents* of the one
who had *gained* his *sight.*
They asked them,
"Is *this* your *son,* who you say was *born blind?*
How does he *now see?*"
His parents answered and said,
"We *know* that this is our *son* and that he was *born blind.*
We do *not* know *how* he sees *now,*
nor do we know *who opened* his *eyes.*
Ask *him,* he is of *age;*
he can *speak* for himself."

Suspecting a fabrication, they try to investigate all possibilities.

held that a person was punished in this life for sins and rewarded with blessings for right behavior. In the absence of belief in an afterlife, affirmation of a just God required such belief. But, even before the development of hope in an afterlife, Jewish thought had been questioning the accuracy of this simple system of reward and punishment.

Jesus does not question the justice of the assertion that the man was being punished, whether for his own sin or that of his parents, nor does he appeal to the idea of an afterlife. Instead, the occasion provides an opportunity for Jesus to demonstrate God's power. The affliction of the man allows the familiar Johannine themes of light and darkness to be played out literally for the blind man. Surprisingly, those with both eyesight and knowledge, the Pharisees, are the ones who are "blind" to the light.

Not only is the man given sight for the first time, but his behavior is so changed that his neighbors do not even recognize him. He affirms that he is indeed the one who used to sit and beg, and recounts what has happened to him. He tells his story a second time, this time to the Pharisees. Although the Pharisees had no legal authority to declare a person cured, they were apparently consulted because of their religious knowledge.

The fact that the miracle occurred on the Sabbath immediately arouses suspicion in some of the Pharisees. After ascertaining what has happened, they accuse the man of being Jesus' disciple. Although some are open to the possibility that Jesus performs

His parents said this because they were *afraid*
of the *Jews,* for the Jews had already *agreed*
that if anyone *acknowledged* him as the *Christ,*
he would be *expelled* from the *synagogue.*
For this reason his parents said,
"*He* is of age; question *him.*"

So a *second* time they called the man who had been *blind*
and said to him, "Give *God* the *praise!*
We *know* that this man is a *sinner.*"
He replied,
"If he is a *sinner,* I do *not* know.
One thing I *do* know is that I was *blind* and *now* I *see.*"
So they said to him,
"What did he *do* to you?
How did he open your *eyes?*"
He answered them,
"I told you *already* and you did not *listen.*
Why do you want to hear it *again?*
Do *you* want to become his disciples, *too?*"
They *ridiculed* him and said,
"*You* are that man's *disciple;*
we are disciples of *Moses!*
We *know* that God spoke to *Moses,*
but we do *not know* where *this* one is from."

The man answered and said to them,
"*This* is what is so *amazing,*
that you do *not know* where he is *from,*
yet he opened my *eyes.*
We *know* that God does not listen to *sinners,*
but if one is *devout* and *does* his *will,* he *listens* to him.

The second questioning of the man is in a quasi-judicial hearing. The man speaks only of his own experience.

The man becomes sarcastic when they again ask questions he has already answered.

This is an accurate depiction of the Pharisees and a reason for them to be proud.

The man speaks with great strength and conviction here. Speak his words forcefully.

signs as one sent from God (perhaps reflecting an openness to Jesus on the part of some Jewish leaders in the author's own day), the majority turn against the man. He unwaveringly states his belief that Jesus is a prophet, one endowed with a divine ability to perform miraculous signs.

During the second questioning of the man, the atmosphere turns hostile. The Jewish leaders are harsh in their accusations and the man responds with sarcasm and contempt. He can tell only what he knows — that he was blind but can now see — and the Pharisees cling to their belief that they alone are best able to interpret the Law of Moses. Finally the man speaks a truth that they refuse to believe: God, who does not listen to sinners, has acted decisively through Jesus. Far from being a sinner, Jesus must be a man of God. The one who was blind has real insight into Jesus' heavenly origin, while those who supposedly have the light of God's favor are in fact blind.

Rather than assist those less fortunate, the religious leaders would prefer to follow blindly the dictates of the Law. Experts in the Law, they refuse to help others understand what God asks of them, choosing instead to leave others in the dark. Although they think of themselves as enlightened leaders, they are seen in the end to be stumbling in darkness, and those they accuse of being filled with sin hold the lantern to guide them, if they would only open their eyes to see its brilliance.

This is an especially appropriate reading for us as we struggle through the dark days of Lent. We know that the light is available for us, if we but acknowledge it. With

It is *unheard* of that anyone *ever opened* the *eyes*
of a person *born blind.*
If this man were not from *God,*
he would *not* be able to do *anything."*
They answered and said to him,
"You were born *totally* in *sin,*
and are *you* trying to teach *us?"*
Then they *threw* him out.

The man's strength of character is threatening, and they rely on the old line that he must have been sinful to have been born blind.

When Jesus *heard* that they had *thrown* him out,
he *found* him and said, "Do you *believe* in the Son of Man?"
He answered and said,
"Who *is* he, sir, that I may *believe* in him?"
Jesus said to him,
"You have *seen* him,
the one *speaking* with you is he."
He said,
"I *do* believe, *Lord,"* and he *worshiped* him.

The man is open to faith, although he does not yet understand the significance of what has happened to him.

Speak reverently and sincerely.

Then Jesus said,
"I came into this *world* for *judgment,*
so that those who do *not see* might *see,*
and those who do *see* might become *blind."*
Some of the *Pharisees* who were with him heard this
and said to him, "Surely *we* are not also *blind,* are we?"
Jesus said to them,
"If you were *blind,* you would have no *sin;*
but now you are saying, 'We *see,*' so your sin *remains."*

This summarizes the entire passage: Those who do not see can be healed, but those who insist that they have not only working eyes but insight into God's will are in the end proven to be blind.

[Shorter: John 9:1, 6–9, 13–17, 34–38]

the catechumens who are gradually being illuminated in their prayer and study, we pray that we will all grow in our ability to see Christ. Read this passage as a challenge to your community to proclaim Christ as the source of light for the world. Offer it also as encouragement to trust in the one who offers insight and enlightenment, even if those in power refuse to accept it. Finally, read this as a preparation for the baptismal promises of Easter, whether spoken for the first time by the newly initiated or renewed by the congregation.

APRIL 9, 2000

5TH SUNDAY OF LENT

Lectionary #35

READING I Jeremiah 31:31–34

A reading from the book of the prophet Jeremiah.

This is a solemn promise; speak with certainty.

The *days* are *coming*, says the LORD,
when I will make a *new* covenant with the *house* of *Israel*
and the *house* of *Judah*.
It will *not* be like the covenant I made with their *fathers*
the day I took them by the *hand*
to *lead* them *forth* from the land of *Egypt*;
for they *broke* my covenant,
and I had to show myself their *master*, says the LORD.

There is anger and disappointment in God's words here.

Pause before this line, then speak with renewed hope.

But *this* is the covenant that I will *make*
with the house of *Israel after* those *days*, says the LORD.
I will *place* my *law within* them and *write* it upon their *hearts*;
I will be their *God*, and *they* shall be my *people*.

Allow your voice to become gentler here.

No longer will they have need to *teach* their friends and relatives
how to *know* the LORD.

Speak with amazement in your voice. End with gentle firmness.

All, from *least* to *greatest*, shall *know* me, says the LORD,
for I will *forgive* their evildoing and *remember* their *sin*
no *more*.

READING I Jeremiah is often remembered as a prophet of gloom and doom. Indeed, he predicted the exile in Babylon and chastised the kings of Judah for their unfaithfulness. But he also spoke tender words of consolation and hope, including those in today's reading.

God speaks through Jeremiah, recalling the covenant made with Moses and the people at Sinai and lamenting its failure. Despite the intimate relationship God established with Israel, the people repeatedly forsook the commands of the covenant. So God promises a new covenant, one not written on stone tablets but on the very hearts of God's people. It can never be forgotten, but all will know it and put it into action.

This is indeed good news for us as well as for Jeremiah's listeners. We often seem to forget all that God has promised us and seek satisfaction and comfort in money, possessions and human honor. We need to know that God will pierce our hearts with the divine word, inscribing it permanently in our consciousness and will. Proclaim with joy this great promise from God.

READING II Hebrews establishes that Jesus is the high priest *par excellence*, one who offers sacrifice not in a temple on earth but in a heavenly sanctuary, who offers not an animal but himself, accomplishing complete forgiveness of sin. Within the context of that claim, today's passage establishes the full humanity of this high priest; by being human, just as we are, he is best able to intercede on our behalf before God.

This brief selection opens with a portrait of Jesus in anguish, reminiscent of his agony in the garden of Gethsemane, but also

READING II Hebrews 5:7–9

A reading from the letter to the Hebrews.

Jesus offers the perfect example of trust and sincerity in prayer.

The idea of obedience is central to this passage; stress it here and below.

In the days when *Christ Jesus* was in the *flesh*,
he offered *prayers* and *supplications* with loud *cries* and *tears*
to the one who was able to *save* him from *death*,
and he was *heard* because of his *reverence.*
Son though he *was*, he learned *obedience* from what he suffered;
and when he was made *perfect*,
he became the *source* of eternal *salvation* for *all* who
obey him.

GOSPEL John 12:20–33

A reading from the holy gospel according to John.

Your tone here can be relatively light.
Bethsaida = beth-SAY-ih-duh

Some *Greeks* who had come to *worship* at the *Passover* Feast
came to *Philip*, who was from *Bethsaida* in Galilee,
and asked him, "*Sir*, we would like to see *Jesus.*"

Philip went and told *Andrew*;
then Andrew and Philip went and told *Jesus.*

There is no indication that any question was asked. The setting prepared in the previous lines is dropped in favor of a discourse by Jesus. Let your voice resonate as you speak Jesus' words.

Jesus answered them,
"The *hour* has *come* for the Son of Man to be *glorified.*
Amen, amen, I say to you,
unless a *grain* of *wheat falls* to the ground and *dies*,
it remains just a *grain* of *wheat*;
but if it *dies*, it produces much *fruit.*

echoed in today's gospel passage, in which Jesus speaks of being troubled prior to his passion. The passion was necessary to make Christ perfect, so that he could learn obedience through suffering. Although we know that suffering can be a learning experience, Jesus did not need to learn obedience because he was disobedient; rather, his suffering brought salvation to all who are obedient to him. Today's selection establishes that Jesus is one with us, but able to save us because of his perfect obedience.

Proclaim this rich and difficult passage with care. It sets forth a doctrinal claim, but also offers Jesus as a model for believers. Suggest that your listeners turn to heartfelt prayer in the same way that Jesus did, following him in obedience, even in the midst of suffering.

GOSPEL The dark hour approaches, and Jesus reflects on his impending death. He speaks of it as a glorification, but one that he is tempted to avoid. Yet it is his purpose; it is the means by which he draws all to himself.

The opening verses of the passage appear to be introductory but are in fact significant. The "Greeks" who come for the Passover may be God-fearing Gentiles, those attracted to and interested in Judaism, or possibly Greek-speaking Jews. In either case, their inclusion indicates that Jesus' mission has universal import and will be proclaimed to all the world.

Jesus' reflection on his "glorification" indicates the paradoxical nature of the event. Just as a grain of wheat must die in order to grow, so also must one be willing to die in order to have life. Although the claim may

Whoever *loves* his life *loses* it,
and whoever *hates* his life in *this world*
will *preserve* it for *eternal* life.

"Whoever *serves* me must *follow* me,
and where *I* am, there *also* will my *servant* be.
The Father will *honor* whoever *serves* me.

Pause before this line, then continue with gravity. Convey the anguish that must have filled Jesus, knowing he was to die, yet fearing it and hoping to avoid it.

"I am *troubled* now. Yet *what* should I *say*,
'Father, *save* me from this *hour*'?
But it was for *this* purpose that I *came* to this *hour*.
Father, *glorify* your *name*."

Then a *voice* came from *heaven*,

Speak these words with power.

"I *have* glorified it and will *glorify* it *again*."

Convey some of the bewilderment of the crowd.

The crowd there *heard* it and said it was *thunder*;
but others said, "An *angel* has spoken to him."
Jesus answered and said,

Jesus' words again are weighty. But righteousness will claim victory over evil.

"This *voice* did not come for *my* sake but for *yours*.
Now is the time of *judgment* on this world;
now the *ruler* of this world will be driven *out*.
And when I am *lifted up* from the *earth*,
I will draw *everyone* to *myself*."
He said this indicating the kind of *death* he would *die*.

sound contradictory, its truth can be readily seen. Letting go of something in order to gain it is part of our reality as well, whether a dream, a friendship or the promise of life itself. We cannot try to hang on to something too tightly, lest we kill it by strangulation.

The same is true, says Jesus, of honor and service. To serve Jesus will result in divine honor. But to be Jesus' disciple means going where he goes, even on the road to death.

Although Jesus has spoken of "glorification," he contemplates avoiding his fate in a scene reminiscent of the garden of Gethsemane. But he cannot; it is his purpose, and it will glorify God.

The voice from heaven, although intended for the members of the crowd, confuses them. Jesus speaks of his death, as the evangelist indicates; the cross is both an instrument of judgment and an offer of salvation for all. Jesus will be "lifted up" literally and figuratively; his death on the cross is precisely the means by which he is glorified.

Although this passage appears to begin like any other narrative, it quickly becomes a speech by Jesus. Speak Jesus' words with great solemnity, giving weight especially to those describing his agony. The oscillation between death and glory — they are one and the same in this gospel — makes it difficult to do justice to the message simply by changing one's tone of voice. Try instead to proclaim the entire passage as a word of solemn importance given to Jesus' hearers and to yours.

5TH SUNDAY OF LENT, YEAR A

Lectionary #34

READING I Ezekiel 37:12–14

A reading from the book of the prophet Ezekiel.

Thus says the Lord GOD:
O my *people,* I will *open* your *graves*
and have you *rise* from them,
and bring you *back* to the land of *Israel.*
Then you shall *know* that I am the LORD,
when I *open* your *graves* and have you *rise* from them,
O my *people!*

I will put my spirit *in* you that you may *live,*
and I will *settle* you upon your *land;*
thus you shall *know* that I am the LORD.
I have *promised,* and I will *do* it, says the LORD.

This is a message of comfort and love; speak with encouragement in your voice.

The exiles longed for their homeland.

This promise is especially inspiring; lift your voice and speak slowly and with conviction from here until the end.

READING II Romans 8:8–11

A reading from the letter of Saint Paul to the Romans.

Brothers and sisters:
Those who are in the *flesh* cannot please *God.*
But *you* are not in the *flesh;*
on the contrary, *you* are in the *spirit,*
if only the *Spirit* of God *dwells* in you.

Pause slightly after the first line in order to provide a contrast with those (believers) who are not in the flesh.

READING I The prophet Ezekiel writes during the bleak years of Judah's exile in Babylon. Ezekiel's message is largely one of hope: God is with this people, wherever they are, and will one day restore them to their own land.

Coming right after Ezekiel's vision of dry bones, today's passage speaks of the new life that God will give to the people. Both the vision and this selection picture a people coming to life again after having been dead, a people filled with God's spirit. The message is one of hope: God will restore the nation and symbolically bring it back to life. The sad period of exile will end.

Although it was several hundred years before the belief in an actual resurrection of the dead developed, this passage certainly sounds as though it promises such. In fact, the graves are symbolic of the nation's current state, and the promise is that the people will once again live in their own land. But it has also inspired many who hope for an afterlife, and this is the reason it is used in our liturgy today. The picture of graves opening and living people emerging fittingly introduces the gospel story of the raising of Lazarus from the tomb.

Offer this reading to your listeners on several levels. For those who are struggling, it is a message of hope that God will take care of them. Read it compassionately as a firm promise. For many of us, the passage can affirm our belief that this life is not final; we have hope in something greater. Finally, encourage the catechumens to reflect on the new life they are receiving in their Easter profession of faith. Allow God's promise of

Whoever does *not* have the Spirit of *Christ*
does not *belong* to him.

But if Christ is *in* you,
although the *body* is *dead* because of *sin*,
the *spirit* is alive because of *righteousness*.

Pause briefly after "dead."

Proclaim this with hope and confidence.

If the *Spirit* of the one who *raised Jesus* from the *dead*
dwells in you,
the one who raised *Christ* from the *dead*
will give life to *your* mortal bodies *also*,
through his *Spirit* dwelling *in* you.

GOSPEL John 11:1–45

A reading from the holy gospel according to John.

Now a man was *ill*, *Lazarus* from *Bethany*,
the village of *Mary* and her sister *Martha*.

Mary is said to have anointed Jesus with costly oil, although the event has not yet been told in this gospel.

Mary was the one who had *anointed* the Lord with *perfumed oil*
and dried his *feet* with her *hair*;
it was *her* brother *Lazarus* who was ill.

Emphasize the love Jesus had for Lazarus here and wherever it occurs.

So the *sisters* sent *word* to Jesus saying,
"*Master*, the one you *love* is *ill*."
When Jesus *heard* this he said,

What Jesus says of Lazarus here is much the same as his attitude toward his own death as presented in this gospel.

"This *illness* is not to end in *death*,
but is for the *glory* of God,
that the *Son* of *God* may be *glorified* through *it*."

life in the Spirit to be addressed especially to them.

READING II **Paul writes to the Christian community in Rome, whose members he had never met, in a theoretical rather than a personal tone. Here he contrasts the new life available in Christ with life in the "flesh."**

When Paul speaks here of living in the flesh, he is talking about a mindset and a lifestyle. He contrasts living according to the dictates of the world with living as one who belongs to God. His addressees, he knows, are those who are committed to God, who are in the Spirit. The presence of the Spirit confirms whether one is Christian.

But Paul recognizes also that resurrected life remains in the future. We live in an age that is still under the rule of sin and death, but the Christian is also infused with the Spirit of life. We live in two worlds in a sense, the world of death and the world of life in Christ. Obviously Paul's audience is not actually dead, but was still dwelling in a world under the sway of death. Yet the Romans could have hope, not only while in this life, but also after death, when they would be raised as Christ was. The hope is for an actual afterlife, although the life of the Spirit begins before death for the Christian.

This passage offers the same hope in the indwelling of God's Spirit as the first reading, together with the same genuine belief in life after death evidenced in the gospel. Offer it to your community as an encouragement to recognize the life of the

Now Jesus *loved* Martha and her sister and *Lazarus.*
So when he *heard* that he was *ill,*
he *remained* for *two* days in the place where he *was.*
Then after this he said to his disciples,
"Let us go *back* to *Judea."*
The disciples said to him,

The disciples must have been afraid for themselves and for Jesus; express their dismay effectively.

"*Rabbi,* the *Jews* were just trying to *stone* you,
and you want to go *back* there?"
Jesus answered,
"Are there not twelve *hours* in a *day?*
If one walks during the *day,* he does not *stumble,*
because he sees the *light* of this *world.*

This evangelist often plays on the contrast between light and darkness. This obscure statement is apparently Jesus' claim that he will not be swayed by the powers of darkness.

But if one walks at *night,* he *stumbles,*
because the *light* is not in him."

He said this, and then told them,
"Our friend *Lazarus* is *asleep,*
but I am *going* to *awaken* him."
So the disciples said to him,

Although the euphemistic phrase "to fall asleep" for death is common, the disciples, as usual, misunderstand.

"Master, if he is *asleep,* he will be *saved."*
But Jesus was talking about his *death,*
while they thought that he meant ordinary *sleep.*
So then Jesus said to them *clearly,*
"*Lazarus* has *died.*
And I am glad for *you* that I was *not* there,
that *you* may *believe.*
Let us *go* to him."
So *Thomas,* called Didymus, said to his fellow disciples,
"Let us *also* go to *die* with him."

When Jesus *arrived,* he found that Lazarus

Pause briefly after "tomb."

had *already* been in the *tomb* for *four days.*
Now Bethany was *near Jerusalem,* only about two *miles* away.

Spirit within. It is an especially poignant promise to those who will be initiated into the community on Easter. But the new life offered is not contrasted only with the life prior to conversion or initiation, although it begins at initiation. We can all be more fully open to the Spirit of God in our hearts. Encourage your listeners to live more completely in Christ, with lives determined not by the values of the world around them, but by God's Spirit.

GOSPEL **The story of the raising of Lazarus is inspiring and touching, and, most of all, it reveals Jesus' power over death. It is a precursor to Jesus' own death and resurrection, and inspires the characters within the story, as well as the reader of it, to accept the message that the opportunity for life is offered in Jesus. We also use this passage as an indication of the life that will be available to the newly initiated this Easter, as well as a promise of life after death.**

The story, which appears only in the gospel of John, begins with an introduction of the sick man, Lazarus, later identified as especially beloved of Jesus, and his two sisters, Martha and Mary. Throughout, the author repeatedly insists on Jesus' profound love for Lazarus, Martha and Mary.

When Jesus learns of the illness of Lazarus, he responds with an enigmatic statement about giving glory to God. Oddly, he takes his time responding to the urgent message. The protests of the disciples when Jesus announces his decision to return to Judea make the reader aware of the perils

And many of the *Jews* had *come* to *Martha* and *Mary*
to *comfort* them about their *brother.*
When *Martha* heard that Jesus was *coming,*
she went to *meet* him;
but *Mary* sat at *home.*
Martha said to Jesus,
"*Lord,* if you had *been* here,
my brother would *not* have *died.*
But even now I know that *whatever* you *ask* of God,
God will *give* you."
Jesus said to her,
"Your *brother* will *rise.*"

Martha said to him,
"I *know* he will *rise,*
in the *resurrection* on the last *day.*"
Jesus told her,
"*I* am the *resurrection* and the *life;*
whoever believes in *me,* even if he *dies,* will *live,*
and everyone who *lives* and believes in me will n*ever die.*
Do you *believe* this?"
She said to him, "*Yes,* Lord.
I have come to *believe* that *you* are the *Christ,* the *Son* of *God,*
the *one* who is *coming* into the *world.*"

This is the central teaching of today's gospel; read slowly and forcefully in order to give it due emphasis.

Speak Martha's declaration of faith with quiet but firm assurance.

When she had said this,
she *went* and called her sister *Mary* secretly, saying,
"The *teacher* is here and is *asking* for you."
As soon as she *heard* this,
she *rose* quickly and *went* to him.
For Jesus had not yet come *into* the village,
but was still where Martha had *met* him.

inherent in the decision. The danger is underscored by Thomas' blustery remark, which indicates his willingness to die with Jesus.

As always in this gospel, Jesus speaks on a level deeper than that of his companions, and even his closest disciples misunderstand what he is saying. Jesus must finally spell out the situation, claiming that the entire event will be for their sake. Throughout this story, Jesus acts in order to instruct others, to inspire faith in the characters of the story and in the reader.

Both Martha and Mary seem to reproach Jesus for his delay, saying that Lazarus would not have died had he been present. But the statements may in fact be claims of faith; Martha's encounter with Jesus is especially telling. She immediately affirms that God will grant whatever Jesus asks, and the two discuss the resurrection of the dead, which leads to Martha's confession of faith in Jesus.

Whenever Jesus speaks, he offers fuller insight into his identity. Here he declares that he is the resurrection and the life. This is not simply a promise of a future resurrection of the dead, which Martha already accepts, but is a declaration of a present reality for the believer. Resurrected life begins now in faith, says the evangelist. Martha's response indicates a partial understanding; she recognizes that, in Jesus, the future hope has become present. Jesus is the Messiah for whom Israel has been waiting.

In a rare instance of human emotion in this gospel, Jesus is moved to tears when he sees the profound sadness of Mary. The reader, just like the Jewish visitors who were mourning with the family, is struck by the depth of Jesus' love for the dead man.

So when the *Jews* who were *with* her in the house *comforting* her
saw Mary get up *quickly* and go *out*,
they *followed* her,
presuming that she was going to the *tomb* to *weep* there.

When *Mary* came to where *Jesus* was and *saw* him,
she *fell* at his *feet* and said to him,
"*Lord*, if you had *been* here,
my brother would *not* have *died*."
When Jesus saw her *weeping* and the Jews who had come
with her *weeping*,
he became *perturbed* and *deeply troubled*, and said,
"*Where* have you *laid* him?"
They said to him, "*Sir*, come and *see*."
And Jesus *wept*.
So the Jews said, "See *how* he *loved* him."
But some of them said,
"Could not the one who *opened* the eyes of the *blind* man
have done *something* so that *this* man would *not* have *died*?"

Be sure to convey the great sorrow Jesus felt.

Pause after "wept." Jesus' love for Lazarus, and for Martha and Mary, ran deep. Let it sink in here for your listeners.

This is probably a wistful expression rather than criticism.

So Jesus, *perturbed again*, *came* to the *tomb*.
It was a *cave*, and a *stone* lay across it.
Jesus said, "Take away the *stone*."
Martha, the dead man's *sister*, said to him,
"*Lord*, by now there will be a *stench*;
he has been dead for *four days*."
Jesus said to her,
"Did I not *tell* you that if you *believe*
you will see the *glory* of *God*?"

So they *took* away the stone.
And Jesus *raised* his *eyes* and said,
"Father, I *thank* you for *hearing* me.

The mourners are not hostile to Jesus, evident in their expression of belief in his healing of the blind man.

The reality of Lazarus' death is affirmed once again through the words of Martha as Jesus approaches the tomb. As is typical in the Fourth Gospel, Jesus' prayer is not for himself but for his listeners. He thanks God in advance for hearing him and responding in the raising of Lazarus.

When the dead man emerges from the tomb against all human expectations, the event elicits a response of faith from those present. The giving of life, an activity reserved for God, leads directly to the plot against Jesus in the verses that follow today's reading. The revelation of Jesus' person and mission, indeed the affirmation of his declaration to Martha that he is the resurrection and the life, is too threatening to the religious leaders in this gospel. The raising of Lazarus was accomplished for the glory of God. Jesus' death will also serve as the supreme moment of his revelation, when he is raised up in glory for all to see.

The superhuman knowledge of Jesus in this story — indeed, throughout this gospel — often makes it difficult to employ the best story-telling techniques to Jesus' words and deeds. But in this passage you are offered the words of others as well, and an indication that Jesus was deeply moved after his friend's death. Capitalize on these comments and proclaim the story with all its drama and emotion. Read Jesus' declarations regarding his person as statements intended to elicit faith, as they are intended.

I know that you *always* hear me;
but because of the *crowd* here I have *said* this,
that they may *believe* that you *sent* me."

And when he had *said* this,
he cried out in a loud voice,
"*Lazarus*, come *out!*"

Speak this command firmly and with authority.

The *dead* man came *out,*
tied *hand* and *foot* with burial *bands,*
and his *face* was wrapped in a *cloth.*
So Jesus said to them,
"*Untie* him and let him *go.*"

The story is meant to inspire us with more profound faith as well.

Now *many* of the Jews who had come to *Mary*
and *seen* what he had done began to *believe* in him.

[Shorter: John 11:3–7, 17, 20–27, 33b–45]

PALM SUNDAY OF THE LORD'S PASSION

Lectionary #37

PROCESSION GOSPEL Mark 11:1–10

A reading from the holy gospel according to Mark.

Bethphage = BETH-fayj
Bethany = BETH-uh-nee

When *Jesus* and his *disciples* drew near to *Jerusalem*,
to *Bethphage* and *Bethany* at the Mount of *Olives*,
he sent *two* of his *disciples* and said to them,
"*Go* into the village *opposite* you,
and immediately on *entering* it,
you will find a *colt* tethered on which *no* one has ever *sat*.
Untie it and bring it *here*.
If anyone should *say* to you,
'*Why* are you *doing* this?' reply,
'The *Master* has *need* of it
and will send it *back* here at *once*.'"

Jesus knows what will happen; it is not clear if the evangelist means to imply that Jesus could predict the future or if he had already made arrangements.

So they went off
and found a *colt* tethered at a *gate* outside on the *street*,
and they *untied* it.
Some of the *bystanders* said to them,
"What are you *doing*, untying the *colt*?"
They answered them *just* as Jesus had *told* them to,
and they *permitted* them to do it.

So they brought the *colt* to *Jesus*
and put their *cloaks* over it.
And he *sat* on it.

Note that there are two choices for the procession gospel today.

PROCESSION GOSPEL MARK. The gospel of Mark consistently presents Jesus' actions as hidden or misunderstood by the crowds and even the disciples. Jesus does not claim titles for himself and urges those who do recognize his significance (often the demons) to remain silent about him. In this story, the crowd might still be oblivious to Jesus' significance.

The joyful procession that enters Jerusalem with Jesus accompanies a festival. Although the gospel of John and Christian tradition place this event one week before the Passover, the gospel of Mark makes no such claim. In fact, many elements of the story better fit the feast of Tabernacles, held in the fall.

For the feast itself, processions would have entered Jerusalem joyously, with pilgrims waving palm branches and reciting psalms of rejoicing, including Psalm 118, quoted here. This passage, then, is consonant with the rest of the gospel: Jesus acts humbly, riding a colt, while those around him celebrate but do not recognize the real reason for their rejoicing. Only the believer knows that the actions are those of the Messiah: Jesus arrives from the Mount of Olives, traditionally associated with the Messiah; he fulfills the words of Zechariah 9:9 ("Behold, your king comes to you; triumphant and victorious is he, humble and riding on a donkey, on a colt, the foal of a donkey"); he is greeted by shouts of "Hosannah" and the blessings for one who "comes in the name of the Lord."

Let your voice gradually build as you describe the processional scene.

Many people spread their *cloaks* on the *road*,
and *others* spread leafy *branches*
that they had *cut* from the *fields*.

Sing out in joy from here until the end. "Hosanna" means "please deliver" or "save"; it came to be understood as a cry of praise to God.

Those *preceding* him as well as those *following* kept crying out:
"Hosanna!
Blessed is he who *comes* in the *name* of the *Lord!*
Blessed is the *kingdom* of our father *David* that is to *come!*
Hosanna in the *highest!"*

Or:

PROCESSION GOSPEL John 12:12–16

A reading from the holy gospel according to John.

The reading begins with an excited crowd. Let your voice express eager anticipation, quickly giving way to shouts of joy.

When the great *crowd* that had come to the *feast* heard
that *Jesus* was coming to *Jerusalem*,
they took *palm* branches and went out to *meet* him,
and cried out:

"Hosanna" means "please deliver" or "save"; it came to be understood as a cry of praise to God.

"Hosanna!
Blessed is he who *comes* in the *name* of the *Lord*,
the *king* of *Israel."*

The scripture quoted is a combination of Zechariah 9:9 and Zephaniah 3:16.

Jesus found an *ass* and *sat* upon it, as is written:
"Fear no *more*, O daughter *Zion*;
see, your *king* comes, seated upon an *ass's colt."*

Speak this as explanation; even the disciples, not to mention the crowds, do not comprehend the significance of these events.

His disciples did not *understand* this at first,
but when Jesus had been *glorified*
they *remembered* that these things were *written* about him
and that they had *done* this for him.

The section concerning the colt, which occupies so much of today's selection, both demonstrates Jesus' foreknowledge and provides a prophetic link. But it is the procession that is most dramatic. We too will join in a joyous procession shortly after reading this gospel. In our retelling, this event almost immediately precedes the passion account. It is ironic that Jesus is greeted now with joy and song, but will later be abandoned by the same crowd during his hour of need.

Read the story of the colt as a straightforward narrative of events. Hold nothing back, however, when you recount the procession itself. Let your "Hosannah!" ring out, offering honor and praise to the Davidic king, our Messiah and Lord.

JOHN. There is no ambiguity in the account provided in the gospel of John. Jesus enters Jerusalem for the last time, on his journey to his passion and death. The events are said to have taken place only days before the Passover festival. The crowd's cries are clearly directed at Jesus, who is acclaimed "King of Israel." Although the story about the selection of the donkey is considerably shorter in John, the contrast is evident between the usual triumphant procession, in which the king rides in a chariot, and the humble entry of Jesus on a colt. The prophetic foretelling of the event is made explicit in the quote from Zechariah.

Lift your voice in praise as you tell of the reaction of the crowds to Jesus. Read the words of the prophet concerning the colt with encouragement and amazement. Close with a reflective tone, considering with the disciples the significance of these events.

Lectionary #38

READING I Isaiah 50:4–7

A reading from the book of the prophet Isaiah.

Practice "well-trained tongue" until you can say it without swallowing any letters.

The *Lord* GOD has given me
a *well*-trained *tongue*,
that I might know how to *speak* to the *weary*
a word that will *rouse* them.

Read this with certainty and an eagerness to speak God's word.

Morning after *morning*
he *opens* my ear that I may *hear*;
and I have *not rebelled*,
have *not* turned *back*.

Pause, then proceed in a tone of drama, emphasizing the torments experienced by the servant.

I gave my *back* to those who *beat* me,
my *cheeks* to those who *plucked* my *beard*;
my *face* I did not *shield*
from *buffets* and *spitting*.

Pause, then continue with a peaceful, trusting tone.

The Lord GOD is my *help*,
therefore I am *not disgraced*;
I have set my *face* like *flint*,
knowing that I shall *not* be put to *shame*.

READING II Philippians 2:6–11

A reading from the letter of Saint Paul to the Philippians.

Christ Jesus, though he was in the *form* of *God*,
did not regard *equality* with God
something to be *grasped*.

Stress the contrast of these lines with what has gone before.

Rather, he *emptied* himself,
taking the form of a *slave*,

READING I The servant songs from the book of Isaiah have long been understood to refer to Jesus' humility and willingness to endure pain and humiliation. This passage is especially poignant, followed in our liturgy a short time later by the reading of the passion narrative.

The servant sees himself as one who learns and then shares his knowledge with others. His task is to teach despite opposition. He knows that the people are exhausted, that they continue to be in pain, but his own pain cannot silence him. He listens attentively to God, then instructs those who fear God.

The gospel accounts of Jesus' passion echo the description of the servant's sufferings. Jesus, like the servant, is struck, abused and insulted. Yet he does not give up, but knows that he will ultimately be vindicated.

Your task is similar to that of the servant: You are entrusted with God's word and asked to present it to your assembly, teaching and encouraging, continuing at all costs. Offer this reading to your congregation with an eye to the sufferings of Jesus. Speak of the suffering in a dark tone of pain, and close with an air of conviction and courage.

READING II Paul offers encouragement to the Philippians to be humble and obedient, just as Christ was. As a demonstration of Christ's humility, Paul quotes this hymn, celebrating the willingness of Christ to give up his rightful exalted state and be humiliated.

The hymn in Philippians is one of the earliest Christian passages to refer to the preexistence of Christ Jesus. Rather than laying claim to the exaltation of heaven, he was humbled by becoming human and by being willing to die on the cross, only then to be glorified with God.

coming in *human likeness*;
and found *human* in *appearance*,
he humbled himself,
becoming *obedient* to the point of *death*,
even *death* on a *cross*.

Crucifixion is an extremely humiliating form of execution. Pause after this line, then change your tone to a lighter, joy-filled one.

Slow down and emphasize every phrase, allowing your voice to grow in intensity and wonder until you practically shout "Jesus Christ is Lord!" The final line is a bit more subdued, but still emphasized; be careful not to rush.

Because of this, God greatly *exalted* him
and *bestowed* on him the *name*
which is above *every* name,
that at the *name* of *Jesus*
every *knee* should *bend*,
of those in *heaven* and on *earth* and *under* the earth,
and every *tongue confess* that
Jesus Christ is *Lord*,
to the *glory* of God the *Father*.

PASSION Mark 14:1—15:47

The reading of the passion begins without the customary introduction

The feast of Unleavened Bread, although originally a separate feast, is another name for the week-long celebration of Passover. Both titles recall the Exodus of the Hebrews from Egypt.

The Passion of our Lord Jesus Christ according to Mark.

(1) The *Passover* and the Feast of *Unleavened Bread*
were to take place in *two* days' *time*.
So the *chief priests* and the *scribes* were seeking a way
to *arrest* him by *treachery* and put him to *death*.
They said, "Not during the *festival*,
for fear that there may be a *riot* among the *people*."

Pause before beginning this narrative; the scene has shifted.

(2) When he was in *Bethany* reclining at *table*
in the house of *Simon* the *leper*,
a *woman* came with an alabaster *jar* of perfumed *oil*,
costly genuine *spikenard*.
She *broke* the alabaster jar and *poured* it on his *head*.

What is most exciting in this hymn is the name accorded Jesus. At mention of his name, all honor will be given him, and everyone will proclaim that "Jesus Christ is Lord." The Greek word for "Lord" is the word that is used to translate the divine name revealed in the Hebrew Scriptures. Jesus can be addressed with the same title given to the creator of the world, the God who saved the Israelites from their oppressors in Egypt, who was revealed at Sinai, who spoke through the prophets and restored the people after the exile in Babylon. The same God who acted on behalf of the Jewish people has now acted decisively for all the world.

Begin your reading, as does Paul, with an exhortation to proper behavior. Then recount solemnly the "emptying" of Jesus, giving special weight to the reference to his death. Speak triumphantly of his exaltation, allowing your voice to reach a crescendo with the proclamation that Jesus is Lord.

PASSION The mood quickly darkens as we turn to the passion narrative from the gospel of Mark. After a joyous procession with palms, after the servant's expression of trust in God despite opposition, and after the proclamation of praise that closes the second reading, we now turn to the darkest hour of Jesus' life. We know that the gospel has been building to this point, that Paul proclaimed the cross with pride, that Jesus' passion and death are at the center of our proclamation of him as Savior, that he has conquered death. Yet we approach with trepidation.

The account of the passion in the gospel of Mark is the shortest and least embellished of all the gospels; it is the earliest written account that we have of these events. For

There were *some* who were *indignant.*
"*Why* has there been this *waste* of perfumed *oil?*
It could have been *sold* for more than *three hundred* days' *wages*
and the *money* given to the *poor.*"
They were *infuriated* with her.

This is almost a year's wages for a laborer. Let your voice express the indignation of the speakers. Jesus kindly defends the woman.

Jesus said, "Let her *alone.*
Why do you make *trouble* for her?
She has done a *good* thing for me.
The *poor* you will *always* have *with* you,
and whenever you *wish* you can do *good* to them,
but you will *not* always have *me.*
She has *done* what she *could.*
She has *anticipated* anointing my *body* for *burial.*
Amen, I say to you,
wherever the gospel is proclaimed to the *whole world,*
what *she* has done will be *told* in *memory* of her."

Even an act of extravagance designed to honor Jesus bespeaks the passion.

It is ironic that the woman, whose deed will be told wherever the gospel is proclaimed, is never named.

Iscariot = is-KAYR-ee-uht

The tone here is dark; the mood somber.

(3) Then Judas *Iscariot,* one of the *Twelve,*
went off to the chief *priests* to hand him *over* to them.
When they *heard* him they were *pleased*
and promised to pay him *money.*
Then he looked for an *opportunity* to hand him *over.*

Pause before beginning a new scene. The date is the 14th of Nisan on the Jewish calendar. In the evening (that is, at the start of the 15th of Nisan, since days begin at sundown in Jewish reckoning), families would celebrate the Passover meal. To say that the feast of Unleavened Bread began on the 14th of Nisan is unusual but not unknown among the evangelist's contemporaries.

(4) On the *first* day of the Feast of Unleavened *Bread,*
when they sacrificed the Passover *lamb,*
his disciples said to him,
"*Where* do you want us to go
and *prepare* for you to eat the *Passover?*"
He sent *two* of his disciples and said to them,
"Go into the *city* and a man will *meet* you,
carrying a jar of *water.*
Follow him.

the author, the passion is the central event of Jesus' ministry, the one which fully reveals him as the Messiah. The "messianic secret" no longer hides Jesus' true identity. The spectacular nature of the healings and exorcisms gives way to the stark reality that the anointed one, the hope of Israel, is reviled, beaten and crucified. The author's community is challenged, as we are, to walk with Jesus on his final journey. The author reminds us that true discipleship lies in suffering.

The story of Jesus' arrest and crucifixion is presented as a fulfillment of scripture. The evangelist places the claim that scripture must be fulfilled on Jesus' own lips, and presents the crucifixion itself in the words and images of Psalm 22. Jesus, like the suffering servant from Isaiah, is persecuted unjustly, suffers in silence, and will be vindicated by God in the end.

It is only in the passion account that Jesus' true identity is revealed. He seems to acknowledge for the first time that he is the Messiah. He would not accept the title when it bespoke glory and honor, but at his trial, helpless and derided, he makes the claim. After his death, the Roman centurion acknowledges as well that Jesus is the "Son of God." These titles must be understood in the light of the passion: The one who comes on the "clouds of heaven" is the one hanging on the cross.

We sometimes forget how offensive the idea of a suffering and dying Messiah was to Judaism. The cross was an instrument of torture, a symbol of degradation and humiliation. But it was also a sign of being cursed by God. And for the Jew awaiting a Messiah who would overthrow the occupying forces, or a Messiah who would demonstrate God's victory and righteousness, or a Messiah who would bring about peace and justice,

Wherever he *enters*, say to the *master* of the house,
'The *Teacher* says, "*Where* is my *guest* room
where I may eat the *Passover* with my *disciples*?"'
Then he will show you a *large* upper *room furnished* and *ready*.
Make the *preparations* for us *there*."
The disciples then went *off*, entered the *city*,
and found it *just* as he had *told* them;
and they prepared the *Passover*.

The Passover meal was eaten later than most meals, and guests reclined at table. Jesus' words should be spoken with solemnity.

(5) When it was *evening*, he *came* with the *Twelve*.
And as they *reclined* at table and were *eating*, Jesus said,
"Amen, I *say* to you, *one* of you will *betray* me,
one who is *eating* with me."
They began to be *distressed* and to *say* to him, one by one,
"*Surely* it is not *I*?"

He said to them,
"*One* of the *Twelve*, the one who *dips* with me into
the *dish*.

Jesus' words suggest what will happen to him in a very short time. Recall them quietly but firmly.

For the Son of Man *indeed* goes, as it is *written* of him,
but *woe* to that man by whom the Son of *Man* is *betrayed*.
It would be better for *that* man if he had *never* been *born*."

(6) While they were *eating*,
he took *bread*, said the *blessing*,
broke it, and *gave* it to them, and said,
"*Take* it; this is my *body*."
Then he took a *cup*, gave *thanks*, and *gave* it to them,
and they all *drank* from it.
He said to them,
"This is my *blood* of the *covenant*,
which will be *shed* for *many*.

the cross represents failure. Rather than acting decisively, God seems to be silent. Rather than celebrating victory, the true Messiah suffers helplessly. The idea of a suffering Messiah appears to be a contradiction in terms.

Although the gospel of Mark ends without a resurrection appearance by Jesus (later endings were appended to the gospel), the passion narrative — indeed the entire gospel — still proclaims the victory of the resurrection. Jesus speaks of the gospel being proclaimed throughout the world, of not drinking wine again until the reign of God, and says he will go ahead of his disciples to Galilee when raised up. We know, as does the evangelist, that the ugly events recounted here are not the last word; there is yet more to come.

The method of reading the passion varies from parish to parish. Your parish may choose to have a group of readers proclaim the passion, or have one well-prepared reader proclaim the entire reading. A group may choose to divide the reading by sections, or each individual might take a role. Sometimes the assembly is involved in the proclamation, although this unfortunately requires the entire assembly to read along rather than listen attentively. Perhaps a congregational antiphon will follow each section, indicating shifts in the narrative. However your community proclaims the passion, proper preparation is essential.

Readers should be chosen for their ability to make the reading come alive for their listeners. This involves reading the entire passion alone or in a group, discussing it and praying about it, allowing the tension and drama to sink into your bones. Remember that in sharing this important reading with the rest of the assembly, you

Amen, I say to you,
I shall *not* drink *again* the fruit of the *vine*
until the day when I drink it *new* in the *kingdom* of *God."*

Pause before indicating the change of location.

Then, after singing a *hymn,*
they went out to the *Mount* of *Olives.*
(7) Then Jesus *said* to them,

Convey Jesus' sadness.

"All of you will have your faith *shaken,* for it is written:
'I will *strike* the *shepherd,*
and the *sheep* will be *dispersed.'*
But after I have been raised *up,*
I shall go *before* you to *Galilee."*
Peter said to him,
"Even though *all* should have their faith *shaken,*
mine will *not* be."
Then Jesus *said* to him,
"Amen, I *say* to you,
this very *night* before the *cock* crows *twice*
you will *deny* me *three times."*

Speak Peter's words with assurance and a bit of bluster.

(8) But he *vehemently* replied,
"Even though I should have to *die* with you,
I will *not deny* you."
And they *all* spoke *similarly.*

Gethsemane = geth-SEM-uh-nee

Then they *came* to a place named *Gethsemane,*
and he said to his disciples,
"Sit *here* while I *pray."*
He took with him *Peter, James* and *John,*
and began to be *troubled* and *distressed.*

Speak with heartfelt distress and pain.

Then he said to them, "My *soul* is *sorrowful* even to *death.*
Remain *here* and keep *watch."*

are helping your entire community to participate in the events described, to make them ritually present today.

All of the readers should have strong voices and clear diction. Jesus' speech is central; whoever reads his words should have an especially strong voice. Determine in advance who will read what and practice together. Make sure each reader is comfortable with the terms and understands the details of the story. Finally, practice in the place of worship. Know when you will move and where you will stand; be comfortable with the text and with the microphone. If there is to be music, practice with the musicians so that you will all be familiar with the flow of proclamation and song.

(1) Jesus' passion, death and resurrection occurred at the time of the Jewish celebration of Passover, the commemoration of the Israelites' flight from Egypt. Passover is a celebration of new life, a proclamation of hope. It recalls God's action in preserving the lives of the Israelite children and of bringing the people out of slavery and leading them to the land of promise. Similarly, we recall the events of Jesus' passion, death and resurrection as a liberation from lives held captive by sin.

At the outset of the passion narrative, a plot is hatched. The religious leaders seek a means to arrest and kill Jesus. Throughout his ministry, Jesus had come into conflict with them. Such conflict reaches a climax here, as we approach his death.

(2) The anointing of Jesus' head with the oil is presented as a preparation for his burial. The unnamed woman pours oil on Jesus' head, anointing him in the same manner as kings were anointed. Jesus is the true Anointed One (this is the meaning of the

	He *advanced* a little and fell to the *ground* and prayed
Abba = AH-bah	that if it were *possible* the hour might pass *by* him;
Jesus is pleading. Let your voice be filled with anguish.	he said, "*Abba, Father, all* things are possible to *you.*
	Take this cup *away* from me,
Pause, then quietly speak these words with resignation. Pause again before continuing.	but not what *I* will but what *you* will."
	When he *returned* he found them *asleep.*
	He said to Peter, "*Simon,* are you *asleep?*
Jesus is disappointed, but also offers words of encouragement for the coming trial.	Could you not keep *watch* for *one* hour?
	Watch and *pray* that you may not undergo the *test.*
	The *spirit* is *willing* but the *flesh* is *weak.*"
Let this line stand on its own, pausing briefly before and after it.	Withdrawing *again,* he *prayed,* saying the same *thing.*
	Then he *returned* once more and found them *asleep,*
	for they could *not* keep their eyes *open*
	and did not know *what* to *answer* him.
	He returned a *third* time and said to them,
Now Jesus is disgusted. The mood darkens and the tension rises as he sees what is coming.	"Are you *still* sleeping and taking your *rest?*
	It is *enough.* The *hour* has *come.*
	Behold, the Son of *Man* is to be handed *over* to *sinners.*
	Get *up,* let us *go.*
	See, my *betrayer* is at *hand.*"
The pace of the narrative picks up here, and the arrest, trial and crucifixion follow in rapid sequence.	(9) *Then,* while he was still *speaking,*
	Judas, one of the *Twelve,* arrived,
	accompanied by a *crowd* with *swords* and *clubs*
	who had come from the *chief priests,*
	the *scribes,* and the *elders.*
	His betrayer had arranged a *signal* with them, saying,
Speak Judas' words with a tone of conspiracy.	"The man I shall *kiss* is the *one;*
	arrest him and lead him away *securely.*"
	He came and *immediately* went over to him and said,
His "Rabbi" should sound genuine.	"*Rabbi.*" And he *kissed* him.
Pause briefly before continuing.	At *this* they laid *hands* on him and *arrested* him.

terms "Messiah" and "Christ"), chosen and honored by God.

The value of the ointment and its apparent waste causes a stir. Jesus' response ("the poor you will always have with you") is not a disregard for the poor; rather, it expresses the reality that there will always be poor for them to assist, but his time with them is limited.

(3) Judas had been described as Jesus' betrayer from the first time he was mentioned in the gospel. Here he acts in collusion with the religious leaders, agreeing to betray his friend in exchange for money. The assistance of Judas made it possible for the religious leaders to arrest Jesus by night, without causing a stir among the people.

(4) Jesus' foreknowledge (or previous arrangement) and instructions to his disciples recall the similar story of the colt heard earlier, in the procession gospel. In the synoptic gospels, Jesus' last meal with his disciples is a Passover celebration; in the gospel of John, Jesus dies on the day the Passover meal would have been prepared.

(5) At the meal, Jesus reveals to his disciples that one of their intimate company will be his betrayer. Judas is not mentioned, but we know his identity. The disciples, however, are preoccupied with protesting their innocence.

(6) The account of the eucharistic words of Jesus here differs somewhat from that which is more familiar to us. In the liturgy, we use a different tradition, preserved in the gospel of Luke and in the first letter of Paul to the Corinthians, the earliest recorded account of this event. The description of Jesus' actions fits with an abbreviated description of a Passover celebration, in which a blessing would be spoken over

One of the *bystanders* drew his *sword*,
struck the high priest's *servant*, and cut off his *ear*.

Jesus is indignant but does not resist; in the end, he is resigned to his fate.

Jesus said to them in reply,
"Have you come out as against a *robber*,
with *swords* and *clubs*, to *seize* me?
Day after *day* I was *with* you teaching in the temple *area*,
yet you did not *arrest* me;
but that the Scriptures may be *fulfilled*."

Pause briefly after "fled.".

And they all *left* him and *fled*.
Now a young man *followed* him
wearing *nothing* but a linen *cloth* about his body.
They *seized* him,
but he left the cloth *behind* and ran off *naked*.

A lengthy pause follows here.

(10) They led Jesus *away* to the high *priest*,
and *all* the *chief priests* and the *elders* and the *scribes*
came *together*.

The mention of Peter here serves to introduce his denial, recounted later.

Peter *followed* him at a *distance* into the high priest's *courtyard*
and was seated with the *guards*, *warming* himself at the *fire*.

Sanhedrin = san-HEE-druhn

The chief *priests* and the entire *Sanhedrin*
kept trying to obtain *testimony against* Jesus
in order to put him to *death*, but they found *none*.
Many gave *false* witness against him,
but their *testimony* did not *agree*.

Mosaic Law required the testimony of at least two witnesses to convict someone. It is not clear why the evangelist represents the testimony of the witnesses as false, when it sounds very much like claims made by Jesus.

Some took the stand and testified *falsely* against him,
alleging, "We heard him say,
'I will *destroy* this *temple* made with *hands*
and within *three* days I will build *another*
not made with *hands*.'"
Even *so* their testimony did not *agree*.
The *high priest rose* before the *assembly* and *questioned* Jesus,
saying, "Have you no *answer*?

unleavened bread and several cups of wine would be blessed and shared.

Jesus does not simply offer blessings or recall Israel's experience in Egypt, however, but reinterprets the event. He links the bread and wine to his imminent passion and death. His death is understood as a ratification of Israel's covenant with God. The bread is broken and the wine poured, just as his body will be broken and his blood poured out on the cross. The evangelist includes Jesus' prediction regarding drinking wine in the reign of God; one early understanding of eucharist was that it symbolized an eschatological gathering of all peoples for a heavenly banquet.

(7) After moving outside the city walls, Jesus sadly announces that his friends will desert him and responds to Peter's hearty protest with a prediction that Peter's own betrayal of Jesus will be repeated three times. In the gospel of Mark, Peter is the disciple often at the center of action. Yet he is not treated with the reverence that later came to be applied to the disciples and to him in particular. He is often a bumbling fool, rash and headstrong. Here he appears too self-assured and protests too much. Yet the sincerity of his words is evident; he is lovable despite his shortsightedness.

(8) With Jesus' agony in the garden, the narrative rises in intensity. His anguish is palpable as he prays to be spared the death he has come to expect. His disappointment in his disciples is also clear. Despite the fact that Jesus is joined by his closest friends, he is utterly alone.

Three times Jesus goes to pray; three times he finds the disciples asleep. The number signifies completeness; he prayed with all his might, and the disciples failed him utterly. The "cup" in Jesus' prayer is a

The high priest attempts to provoke an incriminating statement from Jesus.

These terms are probably understood to be synonymous.

What are these men *testifying* against you?"
But he was *silent* and answered *nothing.*
Again the high priest asked him and said to him,
"Are you the *Christ*, the *son* of the *Blessed* One?"
Then Jesus answered, "*I am*;
and 'you will see the Son of *Man*
seated at the *right hand* of the *Power*
and *coming* with the *clouds* of *heaven.*'"

At *that* the high priest *tore* his *garments* and said,
"What further *need* have we of *witnesses?*
You have *heard* the *blasphemy.*
What do you *think?*"
They all *condemned* him as deserving to *die.*
Some began to *spit* on him.
They *blindfolded* him and *struck* him and said to him,
"*Prophesy!*"
And the *guards* greeted him with *blows.*

The maid realizes that associates of Jesus could be held as accomplices; her statement is an accusation. Peter feigns innocence.

(11) While *Peter* was below in the *courtyard*,
one of the high priest's *maids* came along.
Seeing Peter *warming* himself,
she looked *intently* at him and said,
"You *too* were with the Nazarene, *Jesus.*"
But he *denied* it saying,
"I neither *know* nor *understand* what you are *talking* about."
So he went *out* into the outer *court.*
Then the cock *crowed.*

Speak the maid's words with force; she is alerting the crowd.

This scene reaches its climax here and in Peter's response; speak quickly (but clearly) in forceful tones.

The maid *saw* him and began *again* to say to the bystanders,
"*This* man is *one* of them."
Once *again* he *denied* it.
A little *later* the bystanders said to Peter once *more*,
"*Surely* you are one of *them*; for you *too* are a *Galilean.*"

metaphor for divine judgment and punishment. It signifies the redemptive nature of his suffering. Jesus' passion is presented as carrying implications beyond his own life. He bears the sins of the world on his shoulders.

Let us not too easily dismiss the pain and heartbreak Jesus must have felt by focusing too quickly on his resurrection. Fully human, Jesus recoils in fear and sorrow at the thought of what awaits him. He can turn for support to no one but God, whom he recognizes as having the power to intervene. Jesus' resignation to God's will is not reached easily, and his return to prayer suggests that he must have struggled repeatedly to accept his fate. But in the end, there is no escape.

(9) Events move quickly now. The sleeping disciples awaken to see a crowd sent by the religious authorities. Judas indicates who Jesus is with an embrace; his act of treason is made even more bitter by his audacious use of a gesture of friendship and an address conveying respect. The violent confrontation turns bloody when someone cuts off the ear of the high priest's servant. There is no healing of the ear (as in Luke); only the stark details are recounted in all their savagery.

Jesus addresses the armed gang with anger. He was not an armed robber, he had never hidden from the authorities, yet they treat him as a common criminal. In the end, as when he was praying, he resigns himself to what awaits him, recognizing it as fulfillment of scripture. In fulfillment of his predictions, his friends flee, leaving him to face death alone.

(10) In Jesus' trial before the supreme Jewish council, the Sanhedrin, the evangelist supports the claim made earlier that the

He began to *curse* and to *swear*,
"I do not *know* this man about whom you are *talking*."
And *immediately* a cock crowed a *second* time.
Then Peter *remembered* the word that Jesus had *said* to him,
"*Before* the cock crows *twice* you will *deny* me *three times*."
He broke *down* and *wept*.

Pause. Continue in a hushed, sad voice.

Speak this final line slowly, solemnly, then observe a lengthy pause.

(12) As soon as *morning* came,
the *chief priests* with the *elders* and the *scribes*,
that is, the whole *Sanhedrin* held a *council*.
They *bound* Jesus, led him *away*, and handed him over to *Pilate*.
Pilate *questioned* him,
"Are *you* the king of the *Jews*?"
He said to him in reply, "*You* say so."
The chief priests *accused* him of many things.
Again Pilate questioned him,
"Have you no *answer*?
See how many *things* they *accuse* you of."
Jesus gave him *no* further *answer*, so that Pilate was *amazed*.

The author asserts that the Jewish leaders bear responsibility, although the decision to crucify and the execution itself are carried out by Roman authorities.

Now on the *occasion* of the *feast* he used to *release* to them
one prisoner whom they *requested*.
A man called *Barabbas* was then in prison
along with the *rebels* who had committed *murder* in a *rebellion*.
The *crowd* came *forward* and began to *ask* him
to *do* for them as he was *accustomed*.
Pilate answered,
"Do you want me to *release* to you the *king* of the *Jews*?"
For he *knew* that it was out of *envy*
that the chief *priests* had handed him *over*.

Barabbas = buh-RAB-uhs
The name, ironically, means "son of the father."

Pilate's question may be spoken out of frustration, or it may be mocking or even hopeful. The author makes Pilate appear to be indecisive and reluctant.

But the chief *priests stirred* up the *crowd*
to have him release *Barabbas* for them *instead*.

Jewish leaders were plotting to have Jesus put to death. They do so by soliciting testimony from witnesses, but the evangelist claims that the testimony was false and the accusers did not agree. As a result, the high priest questions Jesus directly. Jesus affirms his messianic status; having refused throughout his ministry to allow others to claim publicly that he was the Messiah, he now openly accepts the designation for the first time. The Messiah is one who is broken, humiliated; no one can misunderstand now.

Jesus then combines Psalm 110:2 ("Sit at my right hand") with the reference to the messianic figure in Daniel 7 to acknowledge that he will come as a heavenly judge, having received dominion and glory. It is ironic that, while completely powerless, Jesus makes claims of total power. Clearly his authority is not the kind we are accustomed to recognizing.

The high priest tears his clothes, later a sign of a formal judicial act, but perhaps here simply an indication of anger. He is convinced that Jesus has blasphemed against God. Those present abuse Jesus, fulfilling the words spoken by the suffering servant in the first reading. The council deems Jesus worthy of death and sends him to the governing authority (Rome, in the person of Pilate).

The evangelist presents Jesus as one wrongly charged and convicted, maltreated and subsequently executed as a criminal by the Romans. He is alone, stripped of dignity, yet claiming ultimate power.

(11) The tension of the preceding section gives way only slightly in the account of Peter's denial. Just as Jesus had foretold, Peter turned his back on his friend and three times denied knowing him. He begins by feigning ignorance, but finally resorts to cursing and swearing in order to save his

Pilate *again* said to them in reply,
"Then what do you want me to *do*
with the man you call the *king* of the *Jews?*"
They shouted again, "*Crucify* him."
Pilate said to them, "*Why?* What *evil* has he done?"
They only shouted the *louder*, "*Crucify* him."
So *Pilate*, wishing to *satisfy* the crowd,
released *Barabbas* to them and, after he had Jesus *scourged*,
handed him *over* to be *crucified*.

It is not difficult to imagine a mob becoming bloodthirsty and violent. Little prodding would be necessary.

Pause briefly.

(13) The soldiers led him *away* inside the *palace*,
that is, the *praetorium*, and assembled the whole *cohort*.
They *clothed* him in *purple* and,
weaving a *crown* of *thorns*, placed it *on* him.
They began to *salute* him with, "*Hail*, *King* of the *Jews!*"
and kept *striking* his head with a *reed* and *spitting* upon him.
They *knelt* before him in *homage*.
And when they had *mocked* him,
they *stripped* him of the purple *cloak*,
dressed him in his *own* clothes,
and led him *out* to *crucify* him.

praetorium = prih-TOHR-ee-uhm

This is similar to the salutation with which Caesar was greeted.

Begin to slow down after the tense moments you have just described; lower your voice.

Observe a lengthy pause.

(14) They pressed into service a *passer-by*, *Simon*,
a *Cyrenian*, who was coming in from the *country*,
the father of *Alexander* and *Rufus*,
to carry his *cross*.

Cyrenian = sī-REE-nee-uhn
Cyrene was a city in northern Africa. Alexander and Rufus were apparently known to (or members of) the Markan community.

They *brought* him to the place of *Golgotha*
—which is translated *Place* of the *Skull*.
They gave him *wine* drugged with *myrrh*,
but he did not *take* it.
Then they *crucified* him and *divided* his garments
by casting *lots* for them to see what *each* should *take*.

Golgotha = GOL-guh-thuh

own hide. At the cock's crow, he is filled with remorse.

(12) When Jesus is brought before Pilate, he again resumes his silent stance, responding only with an ambiguous "You say so" to Pilate's query. The gospel depicts Pilate as reluctant to crucify Jesus, although his cruelty and hatred for the Jewish people are well documented. Here, he appears as a pawn of the chief priests and the crowd.

The practice of releasing a prisoner during the feast is unknown outside the gospels, as is the insurrection, although the Jews were often rebellious under Roman rule. Perhaps the crowd was disappointed that Jesus did not take up arms against the Romans and preferred one whose defiance of the Romans had been demonstrated. But it is hard to imagine why the Roman governor would agree with them and release a dangerous rebel.

(13) Jesus, given the title "King of the Jews," is abused by the soldiers, who clothe him in a royal robe, place a crown on his head, and salute him. Instead of honoring him, the soldiers mock him, insult him and spit on him. No response from Jesus is heard; his silence continues.

By offering mock homage the soldiers attempt to turn upside down the claim of royalty accorded Jesus. What they do not realize is that the gospel inverts all claims to power and authority. The one who will come to judge the world is the one standing in silence, pelted with abuses. The one for whom Israel had waited, the ruler of justice, wears no crown but thorns. He who rejected honor now dons a royal garment, only to have it stripped off him. Jesus had never asked for glory; the soldiers misunderstand that he desires it. The bitter cup that he anticipated is his.

Crucifixion was a cruel but not unusual form of execution in Roman-occupied Palestine. It was used by the Romans to control rebellious Jews.

(15) It was *nine* o'clock in the *morning* when they *crucified* him.
The inscription of the charge *against* him read,
"The *King* of the *Jews*."
With him they crucified two *revolutionaries*,
one on his *right* and one on his *left*.
Those passing by *reviled* him,
shaking their heads and saying,
"*Aha! You* who would destroy the *temple*
and *rebuild* it in *three days*,
save yourself by coming *down* from the *cross*."
Likewise the chief *priests*, with the *scribes*,
mocked him among *themselves* and said,
"He saved *others*; he cannot save *himself*.
Let the *Christ*, the King of *Israel*,
come *down* now from the *cross*
that we may *see* and *believe*."
Those who were crucified *with* him *also* kept abusing him.

Even the criminals crucified with him verbally abuse Jesus; he is utterly alone.

(16) At *noon darkness* came over the *whole land*
until *three* in the *afternoon*.
And at *three* o'clock Jesus cried out in a *loud voice*,
"*Eloi, Eloi,* lema *sabachthani*?"
which is translated,
"My *God*, my *God*, *why* have you *forsaken* me?"
Some of the bystanders who heard it said,
"*Look*, he is calling *Elijah*."
One of them *ran*, soaked a sponge with *wine*, put it on a *reed*
and gave it to him to *drink* saying,
"*Wait*, let us see if *Elijah* comes to take him *down*."
Jesus gave a *loud cry* and breathed his *last*.

[Here all kneel and pause for a short time.]

Eloi, Eloi, lema sabachthani = el-oh-EE, el-oh-EE, luh-MAH sah-bahk-TAH-nee

Elijah = ee-LĪ-juh

Observe an especially lengthy pause. It is customary to bow or kneel for a moment at this point. Allow the hideous nature of the events just recounted to sink in.

(14) The evangelist describes Jesus' path to crucifixion with few details, placing the horror of the event in sharp relief. The accused was customarily assigned to carry his own cross, but Jesus is apparently so weakened by the scourging that he needs assistance.

The claim that Jesus' clothes were divided by the rolling of dice provides the first of several references to Psalm 22, through which the crucifixion is interpreted. What happens to Jesus is a fulfillment of scripture, especially the words spoken by the psalmist, who suffers the taunts of the people but relies on God for strength.

(15) The inscription above the cross detailing the crime is in accord with Roman custom. Again, it is ironic that Jesus was condemned as a king and understood as a political insurrectionist, when Christians claim him to the be true ruler of the world.

As he was dying, suffering a supremely cruel form of execution, Jesus becomes a spectacle for the crowds. The charges brought before the Sanhedrin that Jesus spoke about destroying the Temple and rebuilding it in three days are repeated by the crowd, which goads him to prove his might by coming down from the cross.

(16) The momentous nature of Jesus' crucifixion is evident in the supernatural phenomena that accompany it. At the sun's highest point, the sky is darkened, and when Jesus dies, the Temple curtain is torn. This event is not simply an execution; it is a fulfillment of divine intent, a sign of the presence of God. The darkness indicates that the final Day of the Lord, the judgment of God, has arrived.

It is painful and exhausting to hear, and still more difficult to read publicly, the

There were two curtains in the Temple, an inner one before the Holy of Holies, and an outer, more visible one. Jesus' death is portrayed as having lasting significance for Judaism and the Temple cult.

(17) The *veil* of the *sanctuary* was torn in two from *top* to *bottom.*
When the *centurion* who stood *facing* him
saw how he *breathed* his *last* he said,
"Truly this man was the *Son* of *God!"*

Three women are mentioned; pause after "Magdalene" and after "Joses."
Magdalene = MAG-duh-luhn
Joses = JOH-seez
Salome = suh-LOH-mee
These women, who were with Jesus as he died, were the first to learn that he was risen.

There were also *women* looking on from a *distance.*
Among them were Mary *Magdalene,*
Mary the mother of the younger *James* and of *Joses,*
and *Salome.*
These women had *followed* him when he was in *Galilee*
and *ministered* to him.
There were also many *other* women
who had come *up* with him to *Jerusalem.*

The crucifixion took place on a Friday. If the body were to be buried, it needed to be accomplished before the arrival of the Jewish Sabbath at sunset, or it would have to remain on the cross over the Sabbath.
Arimathea = ayr-ih-muh-THEE-uh

(18) When it was already *evening,*
since it was the day of *preparation,*
the day before the *sabbath, Joseph* of *Arimathea,*
a *distinguished* member of the *council,*
who was *himself* awaiting the kingdom of *God,*
came and *courageously* went to *Pilate*
and asked for the *body* of *Jesus.*

It often took several days for someone to die by crucifixion.

Pilate was *amazed* that he was already *dead.*
He summoned the *centurion*
and *asked* him if Jesus had already *died.*
And when he *learned* of it from the *centurion,*
he *gave* the body to *Joseph.*
Having bought a linen *cloth,* he took him *down,*
wrapped him in the linen cloth,
and *laid* him in a *tomb* that had been hewn out of the *rock.*
Then he rolled a *stone* against the entrance to the *tomb.*
Mary *Magdalene* and *Mary* the mother of *Joses*
watched where he was *laid.*

[Shorter: Mark 15:1–39]

account of Jesus' anguish and pain. Do not shrink from the pain but let it inform your rendering of this section. Although you and your community have heard these words many times, your reading must make the horror of the event present for every member of the congregation.

(17) The rending of the Temple veil probably indicates an abrogation of Jewish cultic practice. The evangelist knew of the destruction of the Temple in 70 CE by the Romans and saw it foretold in the events surrounding Jesus' death. It is also connected with the story about the centurion.

The centurion was the Roman official overseeing the crucifixion; he is emblematic of the Gentile occupiers of Judea. For both Jewish and Gentile worlds, the cosmic nature of Jesus' death becomes evident. The centurion confesses, and draws the reader to acknowledge as well, the claim of Jesus' identity made in the first verse of the gospel: Jesus is the "Son of God."

(18) The story of Joseph of Arimathea requesting the body of Jesus serves several purposes. Although it was not uncommon for victims of crucifixion to rot on the cross, Jesus is buried before sundown in accord with Jewish tradition. The story also indicates that there were Jewish religious leaders who were receptive to Jesus' message, despite the actions of some to have him executed. Against any who might deny the Christian claim that Jesus was risen by saying that he had not truly died, Pilate confirms that Jesus has indeed died. The stage is set for the visit of the women to the empty tomb on Easter morning, to hear the news of Jesus' resurrection.

HOLY THURSDAY: EVENING MASS OF THE LORD'S SUPPER

Lectionary #39

READING I Exodus 12:1–8, 11–14

A reading from the book of Exodus.

The *LORD* said to *Moses* and *Aaron* in the land of *Egypt,*
"*This* month shall stand at the *head* of your *calendar;*
you shall reckon it the *first* month of the *year.*
Tell the whole community of *Israel:*
On the *tenth* of this *month* every one of your *families*
must procure for *itself* a *lamb, one* apiece for each *household.*
If a family is too *small* for a whole *lamb,*
it shall join the nearest *household* in *procuring* one
and shall *share* in the lamb
in proportion to the *number* of persons who *partake* of it.

"The *lamb* must be a year-old *male* and without *blemish.*
You may take it from either the *sheep* or the *goats.*
You shall *keep* it until the *fourteenth* day of this *month,*
and *then,* with the *whole* assembly of Israel *present,*
it shall be *slaughtered* during the evening *twilight.*
They shall take some of its *blood*
and apply it to the two *doorposts* and the *lintel*
of every house in which they *partake* of the *lamb.*
That *same* night they shall *eat* its roasted *flesh*
with *unleavened* bread and *bitter* herbs.

"*This* is how you are to *eat* it:
with your loins *girt, sandals* on your *feet* and your *staff*
in *hand,*

Nisan, in the spring, is the first month of the Jewish calendar.

Passover has long been celebrated as a feast of hospitality.

The prescriptions concerning the sacrifice ensure that the animal is healthy and is consumed immediately after slaughter.

The foods recall the Exodus from Egypt. Unleavened bread was used because the people did not have time to allow the dough to rise; bitter herbs recall the bitterness of slavery.
Stress the urgency of the situation; this is a people escaping by night.

READING I **Because the synoptic gospels recall Jesus' last meal with his friends as a Passover meal, we too remember the origins of Passover on this night before we commemorate Jesus' death.**

The passage from the book of Exodus tells of the instructions God gave the Israelites in Egypt before visiting the final and most severe plague, the death of the firstborn child, on the Egyptians. Adopting ancient rituals and reinterpreting them in light of the Exodus, the account recalls the preparations for the Passover meal, as well as the fulfillment of God's promises in freeing the Israelites from their oppressors.

The blood of an animal on the door of a dwelling was long understood as a means of warding off evil and protecting a household. In this case, it serves to keep the Israelite houses safe from the devastating plague brought by God. Blood is a sign of life; here it becomes a symbol of death being thwarted and of the "new" life now available.

The Hebrew people were instructed to remember this event always and to celebrate it faithfully. Indeed, Jews today continue to tell this story of their deliverance from tyranny. The events of long ago become present in the retelling and ritual sharing of the Passover meal.

Christians too recall Jesus' words at his last meal and celebrate them in a similar fashion, participating again at every eucharist in the meal Jesus shared with his friends. And just as the blood of the Passover lamb promised life for those protected by it, so also we celebrate the life available to us who share in the eucharistic meal of the Lamb of God, who died for our sake.

you shall *eat* like those who are in *flight.*
It is the *Passover* of the LORD.

"For on this *same* night I will go through *Egypt,*
striking down every *firstborn* of the *land,* both *man* and *beast,*
and executing *judgment* on all the *gods* of Egypt—*I,* the LORD!

The blood, a sign of life, ensures that those in the houses marked by it will be allowed to live.

"But the *blood* will mark the houses where *you* are.
Seeing the *blood,* I will *pass over* you;
thus, when I *strike* the land of *Egypt,*
no destructive *blow* will come *upon* you.

Pause, then conclude in a strong voice; these words have proven true for the Jewish people of every generation.

"*This day* shall be a memorial *feast* for you,
which *all* your generations shall *celebrate*
with *pilgrimage* to the LORD, as a perpetual *institution.*"

READING II 1 Corinthians 11:23–26

A reading from the first letter of Saint Paul to the Corinthians.

Brothers and sisters:

Pause after "you," then continue slowly and clearly.

I *received* from the *Lord* what I also handed *on* to you,
that the Lord *Jesus,* on the *night* he was *handed over,*
took *bread,* and, after he had given *thanks,*
broke it and *said,* "This is my *body* that is for *you.*
Do this in *remembrance* of me."

Pause briefly.

In the *same* way also the *cup,* after *supper,* saying,
"This *cup* is the new *covenant* in my *blood.*
Do this, as often as you *drink* it, in *remembrance* of me."

Take a breath before continuing with the last line. Speak it as though it was written for your assembly.

For *as often* as you eat this *bread* and drink the *cup,*
you *proclaim* the *death* of the Lord until he *comes.*

Take care to give this passage the attention it deserves. Make the urgency and significance of the Passover story apparent. Speak with forcefulness God's promise not to destroy the Israelites. Close with firmness and confidence in a God who keeps that promise.

READING II **Paul, quoting here from traditional material, gives us the earliest account of the eucharistic words of Jesus. The passage looks back to the death of Jesus but also looks forward to his coming again. Just as the Hebrew people celebrating Passover make present events of long ago, so also we participate in the ancient ritual of eucharist that becomes new every time we celebrate it. We too tell a story of freedom, a story that recalls the shedding of the blood of the Lamb for the safety and well-being of others, a story of God's love for this people.**

Central to Paul's proclamation, here and elsewhere, is the death of Christ. An embarrassment, a source of confusion and ridicule, it is Jesus' death that is paradoxically the source of life for the world. It cannot be ignored or glossed over; it is to be proclaimed at every eucharist. As the Passover lamb was slaughtered and the bread broken, so too was Jesus' body broken on the cross. As the covenants of old were ratified in the blood of animals, the new covenant in Christ was ratified in his blood.

This is an extremely important selection and should be read with all solemnity. The beginning and ending lines are less familiar than the rest and should be emphasized. Speak Jesus' words quietly and

GOSPEL John 13:1–15

A reading from the holy gospel according to John.

Before the feast of *Passover*, Jesus *knew* that his *hour* had come
to *pass* from this world to the *Father.*
He *loved* his *own* in the *world* and he *loved* them to the *end.*

Iscariot = is-KAYR-ee-uht

The *devil* had already induced *Judas*, son of Simon the *Iscariot*,
to hand him *over.*
So, during *supper*,
fully *aware* that the Father had put *everything* into his power
and that he had *come* from God and was *returning* to *God*,
he rose from *supper* and took off his outer *garments.*
He took a *towel* and tied it *around* his waist.
Then he poured *water* into a *basin*
and began to *wash* the disciples' *feet*
and *dry* them with the *towel around* his waist.

For a Passover meal, the group would have been reclining on couches. The gospel of John does not claim to be describing a Passover meal, but the solemnity of the occasion may indicate that it was no ordinary meal.

He came to Simon *Peter*, who said to him,
"*Master*, are you going to *wash* my *feet?*"
Jesus answered and said to him,
"What I am *doing*, you do not understand *now*,
but you will *understand later.*"
Peter said to him, "You will *never* wash *my* feet."
Jesus answered him,
"Unless I *wash* you, you will have no *inheritance* with *me.*"
Simon Peter said to him,
"*Master*, then not only my *feet*, but my *hands*
and *head* as *well.*"

Read Peter's words with a sense of both surprise and objection to the proposed action.

Jesus explains the meaning later in the narrative.

Continue speaking Peter's words with enthusiasm.

forcefully, but without exaggeration. To you is given the task of reminding your congregation of the importance of what we do in every eucharist, when we gather to remember Jesus' death.

GOSPEL Washing the feet clean of the dust of the road when entering a home was common in Jesus' day. Usually one washed one's own feet, although another might wash the feet of a revered teacher. Jesus, acknowledging his role as teacher, reverses the custom and thus honors his disciples.

The account of Jesus washing his disciples' feet is found only in the gospel of John. It is placed in a setting in which Jesus' death is imminent, a death that gives Jesus the opportunity to show his love for "his own."

There are two interpretations of the footwashing within the passage. One emphasizes the importance of sharing in Jesus' life and especially in his death. Peter goes from refusing to permit Jesus to wash his feet to enthusiastic and excessive acceptance. The second section of the story stresses Jesus' revered status and his humility in serving the disciples in this manner. Jesus calls on the disciples to join in the action; he has set the example.

The footwashing then has two meanings: It is both a sign of sharing in Jesus' fate and one of humble service to another. The second is usually emphasized in modern celebrations of the rite, but the use of this selection on the day preceding our commemoration of Jesus' passion and death suggests that we are asked to share in Jesus'

The author here interprets Jesus' words (which on their own simply distinguish between a clean body and dirty feet) in terms of the presence of his betrayer within the community of disciples.

Stress the parallel between what Jesus does and what those who follow him are expected to do. Close with solemnity.

Jesus said to him,
"Whoever has *bathed* has no *need*
except to have his feet washed,
for he is *clean* all over;
so *you* are clean, but not *all.*"
For he *knew* who would *betray* him;
for this reason, he said, "Not *all* of you are *clean.*"

So when he had *washed* their *feet*
and put his *garments* back on and *reclined* at table *again,*
he said to them, "Do you *realize* what I have *done* for you?
You call me '*teacher*' and '*master,*' and *rightly* so, for indeed I *am.*
If *I*, therefore, the *master* and *teacher*, have washed *your* feet,
you ought to wash *one another's* feet.
I have given you a *model* to follow,
so that as *I* have done for you, *you* should also do.

death as well. Just as Paul insists on proudly proclaiming Jesus' death, so also does participation in the footwashing rite lead us directly into the darkness of Good Friday.

There is an ominous tone throughout the first part of the selection, but the words of Peter provide comic relief. Stress Peter's enthusiastic embrace of anything that brings him close to Jesus. Close with an exhortation to your own community to be willing to stoop before even the most lowly in whatever act of humble service is required.

In many parishes, the impression is sometimes given that these words are directed only to the ordained or those in liturgical ministries. They are not; they are for all Christians.

GOOD FRIDAY: CELEBRATION OF THE LORD'S PASSION

Lectionary #40

READING I Isaiah 52:13—53:12

A reading from the book of the prophet Isaiah.

God is speaking here.

See, my *servant* shall *prosper,*
he shall be raised *high* and greatly *exalted.*
Even as *many* were *amazed* at him—
so *marred* was his look beyond *human* semblance
and his *appearance* beyond that of the *sons* of *man*—
so shall he *startle* many *nations,*
because of him *kings* shall stand *speechless;*
for those who have not been *told* shall *see,*
those who have not *heard* shall *ponder* it.

The people speak now.

Who would believe what we have *heard?*
To *whom* has the arm of the LORD been *revealed?*
He grew *up* like a *sapling* before him,
like a *shoot* from the parched *earth;*
there was in him no stately *bearing* to make us *look* at him,
nor *appearance* that would *attract* us to him.

The tone becomes very serious. Because the servant was not attractive in appearance, people treated him poorly.

He was *spurned* and *avoided* by people,
a man of *suffering,* accustomed to *infirmity,*
one of *those* from whom people hide their *faces,*
spurned, and we held him in no *esteem.*

Speak now with some hope, but also regret for how the servant was regarded. Emphasize the strong verbs in this section.

Yet it was our *infirmities* that he *bore,*
our *sufferings* that he *endured,*
while we thought of him as *stricken,*
as one *smitten* by God and *afflicted.*

READING I One of the suffering servant songs of Second Isaiah, this passage depicts first God and then the people of Israel discussing one who served God so faithfully, despite ridicule and punishment, that others were able to benefit from it. The death does not appear to have been a literal one, but represents the pain and anguish of the Babylonian exile, when the rulers and elite of the Kingdom of Judah were deported to Babylon. The servant accepted the exile, obediently experiencing it as just punishment for Israel's former sins. Others tried to flee the exile or settled in Babylon, but the servant, representing all of Israel, knew that it was a punishment for wrongdoing. The servant's actions allow the nation to continue to exist and to eventually return to Palestine. In the end, the servant is vindicated.

This passage has long been understood to foreshadow the work of the servant of God *par excellence:* Jesus. It is especially appropriate to read today, when we also hear the account of Jesus' passion from the gospel of John. There Jesus suffers, but is exalted through his suffering, just as God promises for the servant in this reading. The words of the people describing the servant can easily be applied to Jesus. He was of lowly appearance, yet was esteemed by God. He was rejected, he wrongly suffered, he died. But he did so in order that others might benefit. He silently offered his life for the sin of others. His punishment brought healing; it fulfilled God's will. In the end, God rewarded him.

On this solemn occasion, offer this selection to your assembly as a meditation

But he was *pierced* for our *offenses,*
crushed for our *sins;*
upon him was the *chastisement* that makes us *whole,*
by his *stripes* we were *healed.*

We had *all* gone *astray* like *sheep,*
each *following* his own *way;*
but the LORD laid upon *him*
the guilt of us *all.*

One who accepts mistreatment without objecting can be inspiring; such a one certainly catches people's attention.

Though he was harshly *treated,* he *submitted*
and opened *not* his *mouth;*
like a *lamb* led to the *slaughter*
or a *sheep* before the *shearers,*
he was *silent* and opened *not* his *mouth.*

This perhaps refers to the exile and the plight of the servant, and all of Israel, separated from their homeland.

Oppressed and *condemned,* he was taken *away,*
and who would have thought any *more* of his *destiny?*
When he was cut *off* from the land of the *living,*
and *smitten* for the *sin* of his *people,*
a *grave* was assigned him among the *wicked*
and a *burial* place with *evildoers,*
though he had done no *wrong*
nor spoken any *falsehood.*
But the LORD was pleased
to *crush* him in *infirmity.*

If he gives his life as an *offering* for *sin,*
he shall see his *descendants* in a long *life,*
and the *will* of the LORD shall be *accomplished* through him.

Pause before beginning this line. It is God who is again speaking.

Because of his *affliction*
he shall see the *light*
in *fullness* of *days;*

on the consequences that await one who truly serves God. Speak clearly and forcefully, inspiring your listeners to think especially of Jesus, but also to reflect on their own roles as God's servants.

READING II **Jesus, as the great high priest, did what every high priest of the Temple did: He offered a sacrifice in expiation for the people's sin. Yet he is enthroned in heaven, not as one unable to understand our human frailties but as one who knows our weaknesses, who himself suffered and turned to God in prayer. It was through his suffering that he was perfected and because of it that he can offer salvation to all.**

It is appropriate to reflect on this passage today. Jesus' passion was not without purpose. Read this as a reminder to your assembly of the fact that Jesus understands pain and can identify with the struggles of your community. Read also the discussion of the part of this passage that is used on the Fifth Sunday of Lent, April 9.

PASSION **The gospel of John presents a distinctive portrait of Jesus, a portrait that reaches a climax in the passion narrative. In this gospel, Jesus does not hesitate to reveal himself, to speak of his mission and his relationship with God.**

The Fourth Gospel diverges from the others in recounting Jesus' ministry, but is more in line with them regarding the details of his passion and death. The accounts of the passion in the gospels show greater agreement than accounts of other events in Jesus'

through his *suffering*, my servant shall justify *many*,
and their *guilt* he shall *bear.*

Speak triumphantly; the servant is vindicated, even honored.

Therefore I will give him his *portion* among the *great*,
and he shall divide the *spoils* with the *mighty*,
because he *surrendered* himself to *death*
and was *counted* among the *wicked*;
and he shall take *away* the sins of *many*,
and win *pardon* for their *offenses.*

READING II Hebrews 4:14–16; 5:7–9

A reading from the letter to the Hebrews.

Brothers and sisters:
Since we have a *great high priest* who has passed
through the *heavens*,
Jesus, the Son of *God*,
let us hold *fast* to our *confession.*

Though heavenly high priest, Jesus was fully human and underwent trials and temptations.

For we do not have a *high priest*
who is *unable* to sympathize with our *weaknesses*,
but one who has similarly been *tested* in *every* way,
yet *without* sin.

Speak confidently, with a light, sure voice.

So let us *confidently* approach the throne of *grace*
to receive *mercy* and to find *grace* for timely *help.*

Jesus prayed to God with trust and sincerity, just as we can.

In the *days* when Christ was in the *flesh*,
he offered *prayers* and *supplications* with loud *cries* and *tears*
to the *one* who was able to *save* him from *death*,
and he was *heard* because of his *reverence.*

life. Jesus' suffering, death and resurrection formed the earliest core of the Jesus story. But the meaning of the events is told here in the distinctive style and with the particular interpretation and theological outlook of the fourth evangelist.

Throughout the gospel, Jesus hints at his own passion. He will be "lifted up"—in glory, on the cross. He lays down his life freely; he is not an abused victim but in control of events, the ruler of all. The cross provides the opportunity for Jesus to be revealed as king; it is his exaltation, his throne.

The suffering of Jesus is not denied but is his to embrace. The silent, pained Jesus of the synoptics is gone. The Jesus of the Fourth Gospel boldly approaches the soldiers, heals while being arrested, discusses his fate and his person with the religious and civil authorities. He is sure of himself, advancing to the cross as a victorious king marches to the triumphant shouts of throngs of admiring subjects.

The Fourth Gospel is marked by artful composition; the scenes of the arrest and trial are intertwined, and the crucifixion and death follow quickly. Peter's denial does not appear as a discrete unit but is embedded in the trial. The trial itself presents Pilate moving back and forth between the unruly crowd outside and the peaceful, composed figure of Jesus within the praetorium. The contrast is further heightened by the ugly demands of the religious leaders and the controlled discussion of Pilate and Jesus regarding kingship and truth.

The idea of obedience is central to this passage.

Son though he was, he learned *obedience* from what he *suffered*;
and when he was made *perfect*,
he became the *source* of eternal *salvation* for all who
obey him.

PASSION John 18:1—19:42

The Passion of our Lord Jesus Christ according to John.

Kidron = KID-ruhn

(1) Jesus went out with his *disciples* across the Kidron *valley*
to where there was a *garden*,
into which he and his disciples *entered*.
Judas his *betrayer* also *knew* the place,
because Jesus had *often* met there with his *disciples*.

The group was made up of Roman soldiers and guards from the Jerusalem Temple.

So Judas got a *band* of *soldiers* and *guards*
from the *chief priests* and the *Pharisees*
and went there with *lanterns*, *torches*, and *weapons*.

Jesus is calm and in control, as he is throughout the passion narrative.

Nazarene = naz-uh-REEN

Jesus, knowing *everything* that was going to *happen* to him,
went out and said to them, "*Whom* are you *looking* for?"
They answered him, "*Jesus* the *Nazarene*."
He said to them, "*I AM*."
Judas his *betrayer* was also *with* them.
When he said to them, "*I AM*,"
they *turned* away and *fell* to the *ground*.

From the outset of this story, Jesus' power is evident. Rather than being dragged off by these armed guards, he controls their behavior.

So he *again* asked them,
"*Whom* are you *looking* for?"
They said, "*Jesus* the *Nazarene*."
Jesus answered,
"I *told* you that *I AM*.

Jesus is identified early in the gospel of John as the Lamb of God, and the image is especially apparent in the passion account. Jesus does not celebrate Passover with his disciples as in the other three gospels, but dies on the day of preparation for the feast. As a result, Jesus is crucified at the same time as the Passover lambs are being sacrificed in the Temple. He is presented as the true Lamb whose blood offers life for those who believe. The evangelist even quotes from the regulations regarding the paschal lamb, noting that Jesus' legs were not broken, as were those of the criminals crucified with him.

The assertion that Jesus is the Passover lamb is combined with the image of the scapegoat from Leviticus. On the Day of Atonement, the scapegoat bore the sins of the Jewish people, cleansing them. The high priest's suggestion that Jesus die for the people is significant. As the one who presided over the Day of Atonement rituals, Caiaphas symbolically sent Jesus into the wilderness, bearing the sins of the people, just as he sent the scapegoat on Yom Kippur.

Although all the gospels suggest complicity between the Jewish religious authorities and the Roman governor in Jesus' execution, the Fourth Gospel insists that the Jewish leaders are actually responsible; Pilate is presented as a pawn in their hands. This can be misleading.

All four gospels attest to the conflict between Jesus and the Jewish religious leaders. Indeed, the Sadducee party, in power at the time, may have been frightened by Jesus' popularity. The Sadducees were

So if you are looking for *me*, let *these* men *go*."
This was to *fulfill* what he had *said*,
"I have not lost *any* of those you *gave* me."

Then Simon *Peter*, who had a *sword*, *drew* it,
struck the *high priest's* slave, and *cut off* his right *ear*.
The slave's *name* was *Malchus*.
Jesus said to Peter,
"Put your sword *into* its *scabbard*.
Shall I *not* drink the *cup* that the Father *gave* me?"

Malchus = MAL-kuhs

(2) So the *band* of *soldiers*, the *tribune*, and the Jewish *guards* *seized* Jesus,
bound him, and brought him to *Annas* first.
He was the father-in-law of *Caiaphas*,
who was *high priest* that year.
It was *Caiaphas* who had *counseled* the Jews
that it was *better* that *one* man should die
rather than the *people*.

The tribune was the chief officer of the cohort.

Annas = AN-uhs
Caiaphas = KĪ-uh-fuhs

Caiaphas said this after the raising of Lazarus; see John 11:49–50.
Pause briefly.

(3) Simon *Peter* and *another* disciple *followed* Jesus.
Now the *other* disciple was *known* to the high priest,
and he entered the *courtyard* of the high priest *with* Jesus.
But *Peter* stood at the *gate* outside.
So the *other* disciple, the *acquaintance* of the high priest,
went *out* and *spoke* to the *gatekeeper* and brought Peter *in*.
Then the *maid* who was the *gatekeeper said* to Peter,
"*You* are not one of this man's *disciples*, are you?"
He said, "*I* am not."
Now the *slaves* and the *guards* were standing around a charcoal *fire*
that they had made, because it was *cold*,
and were *warming* themselves.
Peter was *also* standing there keeping *warm*.

surely offended by his preaching about the resurrection of the dead, which they did not accept. But the fact remains that Jesus was crucified by the Romans for political reasons, as the placard on the cross indicates, rather than stoned as a blasphemer by the Jewish authorities. In addition, although Pilate is known from other sources as having been particularly cruel to and contemptuous of the Jews, each gospel portrays Pilate somewhat sympathetically. This is particularly true of John's gospel, although it is unlikely that Pilate acted solely at the request of the Jewish leaders. Jesus may indeed have been delivered to Pilate by the Jewish authorities, but the extra-biblical evidence strongly suggests an execution carried out by the Romans for political reasons.

The negative portrait of the Jews in the gospel of John must also be qualified by the situation in the community of the evangelist. The Johannine Christians were Jews who proclaimed their belief in Jesus. At some point, the Jewish religious leaders had expelled these Jewish Christians from the synagogue for their unorthodox beliefs. The polemic against "the Jews" in this gospel, and against the Jewish leaders in particular, must be read in light of this conflict.

Reading the passion effectively is a challenging task. Due to its length, it is helpful to encourage the congregation to be seated. Take your time in order to do justice to the message you present. Allow a bit of wonder to enter your voice at the power and authority demonstrated by Jesus. Remember that Jesus is always in control, and attempt

Pause before continuing, to indicate a change in scene.

(4) The high priest *questioned* Jesus
about his *disciples* and about his *doctrine.*
Jesus answered him,
"I have spoken *publicly* to the *world.*
I have *always* taught in a *synagogue*
or in the *temple* area where all the Jews *gather,*
and in *secret* I have *said* nothing. *Why* ask *me?*
Ask those who *heard* me what I *said* to them.
They know what I *said."*

The high priest does not bring charges to be refuted, illustrating once again the total ineffectiveness of the Jewish authorities in this passion account. Instead, Jesus challenges why he is being questioned at all.

When he had said this,
one of the temple *guards* standing there *struck* Jesus and said,
"Is *this* the way you answer the high *priest?"*
Jesus answered him,
"If I have spoken *wrongly, testify* to the wrong;
but if I have spoken *rightly,* why do you *strike* me?"
Then Annas *sent* him *bound* to *Caiaphas* the high priest.

Jesus does not flinch but responds in a calm, composed manner.

Pause briefly.

(5) Now Simon *Peter* was standing there keeping *warm.*
And they said to him,
"*You* are not one of his disciples, *are* you?"
He *denied* it and said,
"I am *not."*
One of the *slaves* of the high priest,
a *relative* of the one whose *ear* Peter had *cut* off, said,
"Didn't I *see* you in the *garden* with him?"
Again Peter denied it.
And *immediately* the *cock crowed.*

A connection is drawn between the encounter in the garden and this incident.

Observe a lengthier pause here.

(6) Then they brought Jesus from *Caiaphas* to the *praetorium.*
It was *morning.*
And they themselves did not *enter* the *praetorium,*
in order not to be *defiled* so that they could *eat* the *Passover.*

praetorium = prih-TOHR-ee-uhm

to convey that in your manner of speaking. Even on this dark day, when the vicious cries of the crowd attempt to drown out any seeds of compassion, this reading is triumphant at its core.

(1) The meal Jesus had shared with his disciples is not a Passover meal in the gospel of John. This allows the evangelist to present Jesus as the paschal lamb *par excellence.* There is also no agony in Gethsemane. The garden is simply a familiar meeting place for Jesus and the disciples. Jesus is in command in this scene; his self-assurance and power are visible.

Judas brings Roman soldiers and Temple police with him to arrest Jesus. Simply by speaking, Jesus causes them all to fall to the ground in awe or fear. His enemies are powerless in his presence. He does not avoid arrest, but neither does he resign himself to it. In this gospel, Jesus offers himself for arrest. His only concern is for his companions; their safety is preserved, not because they flee but in order to fulfill Jesus' own words.

The violent encounter between one of Jesus' followers and the slave of the high priest is given more detail in this gospel than elsewhere. The combatants are identified: Peter strikes the slave, whose name is Malchus. But Jesus rejects any attempts to deny him his opportunity for glory; he willingly drinks the cup of death.

(2) There is no trial of Jesus before the Sanhedrin in the Fourth Gospel. Jesus is instead taken to the home of the former high

So *Pilate* came out to them and said,
"What *charge* do you bring *against* this man?"
They answered and said to him,
"If he were not a *criminal*,
we would *not* have handed him *over* to you."
At *this*, Pilate said to them,
"*Take* him yourselves, and *judge* him according to your *law*."
The Jews answered him,
"We do *not* have the right to *execute* anyone, "
in order that the *word* of Jesus might be *fulfilled*
that he *said* indicating the kind of *death* he would die.

(7) So Pilate went *back* into the *praetorium*
and summoned *Jesus* and said to him,
"Are *you* the *King* of the *Jews?*"
Jesus answered,
"Do *you* say this on your *own*
or have others *told* you *about* me?"
Pilate answered,
"*I* am not a *Jew*, am I?
Your own *nation* and the chief *priests* handed you *over* to me.
What have you *done?*"
Jesus answered,
"My *kingdom* does not belong to *this* world.
If my kingdom *did* belong to *this* world,
my *attendants* would be *fighting*
to *keep* me from being handed *over* to the *Jews*.
But as it *is*, my kingdom is *not here*."
So Pilate said to him,
"Then you *are* a *king?*"
Jesus answered,
"*You* say I am a *king*.

In this gospel, Pilate is sincerely trying to get information. The title has not been suggested yet in the passion narrative, but is the charge for which Jesus is crucified.

It is not clear if Pilate is speaking contemptuously or simply indicating his distance from the accusation.

This question could be spoken either by raising the voice at the end (indicating a genuine query) or by lowering it at the end (suggesting that the questioner knows that the answer is affirmative).

priest, Annas. In addition to being the father-in-law of the current high priest, Annas also had five sons who served in the high priestly office. Therefore, he was still an influential figure in the management of the Temple.

Caiaphas' proposal that one person die on behalf of the people ironically makes him suggest that Jesus fulfill the role of the scapegoat on Yom Kippur, the Day of Atonement. On that feast, the high priest symbolically placed the sins of the people on the back of a goat that was sent into the wilderness to die. Caiaphas continues to perform his high priestly function, but does so not with a goat but with Jesus. Jesus dies bearing the sins of the people.

(3) Although Peter is unknown to the high priest, the fourth evangelist provides a means to get him into the high priest's courtyard. The unnamed disciple is probably the same as the "one whom Jesus loved," and apparently represents John, son of Zebedee, who was revered by the community that produced this gospel. The scene is set for the first of Peter's three denials of Jesus.

(4) In this gospel, no witnesses are brought against Jesus; there is no charge of blasphemy or questions regarding Jesus' messianic status. Annas asks about his disciples and his teaching. Jesus responds somewhat impudently but truthfully, suggesting that the high priest consult those who have heard him preach. Jesus does not challenge the secretive nature of the arrest, as in the other three gospel accounts, but challenges the questioning itself.

(5) Peter denies that he knows Jesus two more times. The cock then begins to crow, confirming Jesus' words. The denial

Pilate demonstrates that he is not one of those who knows the truth or he would listen to Jesus. Pause briefly.

For *this* I was *born* and for *this* I came into the *world*,
to *testify* to the *truth*.
Everyone who *belongs* to the truth *listens* to my *voice*."
Pilate said to him, "What is *truth?*"

(8) When he had said *this*,
he again went *out* to the Jews and said to them,
"I find *no guilt* in him.
But you have a custom that I *release* one prisoner
to you at *Passover*.

Pilate is probably mocking the crowd with this question.

Barabbas = buh-RAB-uhs

Do you want me to *release* to you the *King* of the *Jews?*"
They cried out again,
"Not *this* one but *Barabbas!*"
Now *Barabbas* was a *revolutionary*.

The abuse of the soldiers lacks the bite of what is recorded in the other gospels. Jesus' response to it is not detailed.

(9) *Then* Pilate *took* Jesus and had him *scourged*.
And the *soldiers* wove a *crown* out of *thorns*
and placed it on his *head*,
and *clothed* him in a *purple* cloak,
and they *came* to him and said,
"Hail, King of the *Jews!"*
And they *struck* him repeatedly.

(10) Once *more* Pilate went out and said to them,
"Look, I am bringing him *out* to you,
so that you may *know* that I find no *guilt* in him."
So Jesus came *out*,
wearing the crown of *thorns* and the purple *cloak*.
And he said to them, *"Behold*, the *man!"*

Again, Pilate is probably mocking. His statement seems to be, "Look at this guy! How could he be dangerous?"

When the chief *priests* and the *guards* saw him they *cried* out,
"Crucify him, *crucify* him!"
Pilate said to them,
"Take him *yourselves* and crucify him.

is not as forceful here as in the synoptics, but the threefold rejection is underscored after Jesus' resurrection, when Jesus asks Peter three times if he loves him. Thus Peter is given the opportunity to right his wrong.

(6) During the trial, Pilate moves between the inner court and the public space, between dialogue with Jesus and discussion with the Jewish officials eager to see the captive die. There are no charges brought against Jesus (implying that none were valid), only the weak claim that he must be a criminal or they would not have brought him to Pilate. The claim that they could not put anyone to death does not fit the evidence from other periods but might have been true during Roman occupation.

(7) Pilate asks Jesus if he is the king of the Jews. The evangelist understands the ministry of Jesus in entirely non-revolutionary terms: He is king, but not of an earthly realm. Anyone who recognizes the truth will recognize that Jesus bears witness to the truth. Pilate refuses to acknowledge the truth.

(8) Pilate appears as one who wants to save Jesus' life, offering to release Jesus. He mentions a custom known only to the gospels of releasing a prisoner at Passover. But the crowd demands the release of Barabbas instead. They choose a fighter over one who has just rejected violence.

(9) The abuse received by Jesus is told with less detail here than in the other gospels. Never is Jesus a spectacle for pity or revulsion. The royal fixtures — crown, royal robe and homage — are given to one whose kingdom lies elsewhere.

I find *no guilt* in him."
The Jews answered,
"We have a *law*, and *according* to that law he ought to *die*,
because he *made* himself the *Son* of God."

(11) Now when Pilate heard *this* statement,
he became even more *afraid*,
and went back into the *praetorium* and said to Jesus,
"*Where* are you *from?*"
Jesus did *not answer* him.

Pilate's question was apparently suggested by the statement that Jesus claimed to be God's Son.

So Pilate said to him,
"Do you not *speak* to me?
Do you not *know* that I have power to *release* you
and I have power to *crucify* you?"
Jesus answered him,
"You would have *no power* over me
if it had not been *given* to you from *above*.
For this reason the one who handed me *over* to you
has the *greater* sin."
(12) *Consequently*, Pilate *tried* to *release* him; but the Jews
cried out,
"If you *release* him, you are not a *Friend* of *Caesar*.
Everyone who makes himself a *king opposes* Caesar."

"Friend of Caesar" was a title held by Pilate; here the crowd suggests that it is in jeopardy. Pause slightly before reading it to clarify the formal nature of the title.

When Pilate *heard* these words he brought Jesus *out*
and seated him on the *judge's* bench
in the place called Stone *Pavement*, in Hebrew, *Gabbatha*.
It was *preparation* day for *Passover*, and it was about *noon*.
And he said to the *Jews*,
"*Behold*, your *king!*"
They cried out,
"Take him *away*, take him *away! Crucify* him!"

Gabbatha = GAB-uh-thuh

Now Pilate mocks the crowd.

(10) Pilate repeatedly tries to free Jesus, but becomes fearful at the crowd's vehemence and claim that Jesus made himself God's Son. Responsibility for Jesus' death is placed squarely on the shoulders of his Jewish accusers. In the gospels Jesus is executed for religious reasons rather than political ones.

(11) Pilate questions Jesus once again in an attempt to ascertain his origins, perhaps afraid that Jesus was a divine figure appearing as a human. Trying to assert his authority, Pilate is met with Jesus' calm discussion of power; there is no real power on earth, but all comes from God. It is evident that Jesus is the one endowed with divine authority, and from his lips comes a statement placing blame for his fate not on Pilate but on the Jewish authorities.

(12) This makes Pilate even more eager to free Jesus, but he is compelled to give in to the crowd, according to this evangelist. They no longer bring religious charges against Jesus but appeal to Pilate's political vulnerability; if he frees this "king" he is aligning himself with an opponent of Caesar. Although Pilate taunts the crowd, he eventually consents to their wishes. The Jewish authorities profess their allegiance to Caesar, the ruler of the forces occupying their land and the chief obstacle to Jewish political, social and religious freedom. The collusion of Jewish leaders with Rome is accurate; the Romans had originally been welcomed into the region to settle disputes.

(13) Jesus remains in control even on his path to crucifixion. He carries his own cross. Nothing is said about taunts directed

At the time of Jesus' death there was no local king. The statement attributed to the chief priest is theological (denying Jesus' kingship). Pause before continuing.

Pilate said to them,
"Shall I *crucify* your *king?*"
The chief priests answered,
"We have *no king* but *Caesar.*"

(13) Then he handed him *over* to them to be *crucified.*

Golgotha = GOL-guh-thuh

So they took Jesus, and, carrying the *cross himself,*
he went *out* to what is called the *Place* of the *Skull,*
in Hebrew, *Golgotha.*
There they *crucified* him, and *with* him two others,
one on either *side,* with Jesus in the *middle.*

Pilate also had an *inscription* written and put on the cross.
It *read,*
"*Jesus* the *Nazarene,* the *King* of the *Jews.*"
Now *many* of the Jews read this *inscription,*
because the *place* where Jesus was *crucified* was near the *city;*
and it was written in *Hebrew, Latin,* and *Greek.*

So the *chief priests* of the Jews said to *Pilate,*
"Do *not* write 'The *King* of the *Jews,*'
but that he *said,* 'I am the *King* of the *Jews*'."
Pilate answered,
"What I have *written,* I have *written.*"

For once, Pilate refuses to give in to the demands of the Jewish leaders.

(14) When the soldiers had *crucified* Jesus,
they took his *clothes* and *divided* them into four *shares,*
a *share* for each *soldier.*
They also took his *tunic,* but the tunic was *seamless,*
woven in *one piece* from the top *down.*
So they said to one another,
"Let's not *tear* it, but cast *lots* for it to see *whose* it will be,"

at him or abuse from the other criminals. Only the chief priests raise their voices, but this is in opposition to the title "King of the Jews" placed above the cross. Once again, Pilate dismisses them.

The crucifixion is recounted without great detail and lacks the emotional intensity of the account from the gospel of Mark heard last Sunday. Far from being a pathetic figure, Jesus is accorded honor. The religious leaders and, to a lesser extent, Pilate, are the characters to be pitied in this gospel.

(14) Only the gospel of John mentions a seamless garment in the story of the soldiers dividing Jesus' clothing. Roman soldiers were allowed to confiscate the possessions (including the clothes) of those they executed; here, the action is seen as a fulfillment of Psalm 22:18, alluded to in the other passion accounts.

(15) The words of Jesus to his mother and the unnamed disciple make a statement about the church. The Acts of the Apostles indicates that Mary was present with the disciples in the early days of the Christian community. Jesus' words can be understood literally—that the disciple is to take Jesus' place and care for Jesus' mother—and figuratively. The disciple thus becomes the individual believer, while Mary represents the Christian church as a whole. Both interpretations have been a part of Christian tradition.

Although the other disciples are absent, Jesus is not alone. The women do not watch from afar but are close enough to speak with Jesus. In this gospel the disciple whom Jesus loved does not abandon Jesus but faithfully stands with the women.

in *order* that the passage of Scripture might be *fulfilled*
that says:
"They *divided* my garments *among* them,
and for my *vesture* they cast *lots.*"
This is what the soldiers *did.*

(15) Standing by the cross of Jesus were his *mother*
and his mother's *sister*, *Mary* the wife of *Clopas*,
and Mary of *Magdala.*

Clopas = KLOH-puhs
Magdala = MAG-duh-luh
There are four women here (three named Mary!). Adjust your phrasing so there is no mistake that Mary the wife of Clopas is not identified with the sister of Jesus' mother.

When Jesus saw his *mother* and the *disciple* there whom he *loved*
he said to his mother, "*Woman, behold,* your *son.*"
Then he said to the *disciple,*
"Behold, your mother."
And from *that* hour the disciple *took* her into his *home.*

Pause again.

(16) After this, aware that *everything* was now *finished,*
in order that the Scripture might be *fulfilled,*
Jesus said, "I *thirst.*"
There was a *vessel* filled with common *wine.*
So they put a *sponge* soaked in wine on a sprig of *hyssop*
and put it up to his *mouth.*
When Jesus had *taken* the wine, he said,
"It is *finished.*"
And *bowing* his head, he handed over the *spirit.*

hyssop = HIS-uhp
The use of hyssop here is odd; the plant is too small to be employed in this way. Hyssop was used to apply the blood of the Passover lamb to the doorposts of the Hebrews before they fled from Egypt.

[Here all kneel and pause for a short time.]

(17) Now since it was *preparation* day,
in order that the bodies might not *remain*
on the *cross* on the *sabbath,*
for the sabbath day of *that* week was a *solemn* one,
the *Jews asked* Pilate that their *legs* be *broken*
and that *they* be taken *down.*

Jesus died on a Friday and the Sabbath began that evening. This Sabbath, according to the gospel of John, was also the feast of Passover.

(16) Even to his death, Jesus is in command of events. He determines that his time to die has come; he ensures that scripture is fulfilled. There is no cry of abandonment or pain. The author does not deny the reality of Jesus' death, but it remains a glorification rather than an ignominious fate.

Traditionally, a moment of reverent silence accompanied by bowing or kneeling follows at this point.

(17) In Jewish practice, a dead body was buried before sunset, although the Romans had no such sensibilities; crucified corpses could be left on crosses to rot. Breaking the legs of the crucified was a merciful act, designed to hasten death. The fact that Jesus' legs were not broken because he was already dead allows the evangelist to apply to him the image of the Passover lamb; it was to be unblemished, with no broken bones. Once again the Jewish authorities are responsible. Pilate acts at their request.

The blood and water that flowed from Jesus' side have long been understood to refer to Christian eucharist and baptism, rituals connected with the saving death of Jesus. The author insists that a reliable witness observed the occurrence so that the reader might recognize its truth. The witness is probably the beloved disciple.

(18) The other gospels also attest to Joseph of Arimathea's role in burying the body of Jesus. Here he becomes a full-fledged follower of Jesus. Joining him in honoring the body is Nicodemus, whose nocturnal visit to Jesus is told only in this gospel. He anoints the body here, an act of tribute the women in the other gospels intended to do on Sunday morning. The stage is set for Mary Magdalene to arrive and find the empty tomb.

Breaking the legs of the crucified hastened death; they could no longer support their bodies and so suffocated from their own weight.

So the soldiers came and *broke* the *legs* of the *first*
and then of the *other* one who was crucified *with* Jesus.
But when they came to *Jesus* and saw that he was *already* dead,
they did *not* break his legs,
but *one* soldier thrust his *lance* into his *side*,
and immediately *blood* and *water* flowed out.

An *eyewitness* has testified, and his *testimony* is *true*;
he *knows* that he is speaking the *truth*,
so that you also may come to *believe*.

For this *happened* so that the *Scripture* passage might be *fulfilled:*
"*Not* a *bone* of it will be *broken*."
And again *another* passage says:
"They will *look* upon him whom they have *pierced*."

Arimathea = ayr-ih-muh-THEE-uh

(18) *After* this, Joseph of *Arimathea*,
secretly a *disciple* of Jesus for fear of the *Jews*,
asked Pilate if he could *remove* the body of *Jesus*.
And Pilate *permitted* it.
So he *came* and took his *body*.

Nicodemus = nik-oh-DEE-muhs

aloes = AL-ohz

Nicodemus, the one who had *first* come to him at *night*,
also came bringing a mixture of *myrrh* and *aloes*
weighing about one hundred *pounds*.
They took the *body* of Jesus
and *bound* it with burial *cloths* along with the *spices*,
according to the Jewish *burial* custom.
Now in the *place* where he had been *crucified* there was a *garden*,
and in the *garden* a new *tomb*, in which *no* one
had yet been *buried*.
So they laid Jesus *there* because of the Jewish *preparation* day;
for the tomb was *close* by.

Only this gospel indicates that the tomb was near the place of crucifixion.

EASTER VIGIL

Lectionary #41

READING I Genesis 1:1—2:2

A reading from the book of Genesis.

In the *beginning*, when God created the *heavens* and the *earth*,
the *earth* was a formless *wasteland*, and *darkness*
covered the *abyss*,
while a mighty *wind swept* over the *waters*.

Make "swept" sound like what it means.

Then God said,
"Let there be *light*," and there was *light*.
God saw how *good* the light was.
God then separated the *light* from the *darkness*.
God called the *light* "*day*" and the *darkness* he called "*night*."
Thus *evening* came, and morning *followed*—the *first* day.

Speak God's words in a strong, commanding tone.
Stress the word "good."

Pause slightly between "light" and "day."
Lower your voice in a concluding, satisfied tone.

Then God said,
"Let there be a *dome* in the middle of the *waters*,
to separate *one* body of water from the *other*."
And so it *happened:*
God made the *dome*,
and it separated the water *above* the dome
from the water *below* it.
God called the *dome* "the *sky*."
Evening came, and morning *followed*—the *second* day.

Declare the success of God's command slowly and decisively.

Pause slightly after "dome."
Practice this line with a microphone until you are able to speak the difficult "second day" clearly, without swallowing any letters or sounding stilted.

Then God said,
"Let the *water* under the *sky* be gathered into a *single basin*,
so that the dry land may appear."

READING I **When you proclaim the creation story to your community, you set the mood for the readings and prayers that follow. You tell the story of primeval beauty and the plan of God in forming the earth. Read it with wonder and awe, inspiring your listeners to accept their role in protecting the earth, preserving it unblemished, reflecting its original goodness. Convey God's power over everything in being able to bring about such a wondrous creation, a universe twirling in a cosmic dance, carefully balanced, reflecting the greatness and goodness of its maker.**

The story of the creation is poetic. It is similar to creation myths from other traditions, but unique as well. It establishes a six-day "work week," with a day devoted to rest. For the human the day of rest is appropriately devoted to marveling at the beauties of creation and giving praise to God for them and for all God's deeds.

In the creation story recounted here, God reigns supreme from beginning to end. There is no cosmic struggle for control, as in other creation accounts. The world begins in chaos, but God's spoken word brings order and beauty. As Christians we proclaim that God most fully communicates through God's Son, the incarnate Word, through whom the world was made.

This story of creation announces the origins of the world from a dark void. God

Pause slightly after "land."

Speak sincerely and with satisfaction.

Take care not to swallow the "d" in "third."

And so it *happened:*
the *water* under the *sky* was gathered into its *basin,*
and the dry land *appeared.*
God called the *dry land* "the *earth,*"
and the basin of the *water* he called "the *sea.*"
God saw how *good* it was.
Then God said,
"Let the *earth* bring forth *vegetation:*
every kind of *plant* that bears *seed*
and *every* kind of *fruit* tree on earth
that bears *fruit* with its seed *in* it."
And so it *happened:*
the earth brought forth every kind of *plant* that bears *seed*
and every kind of *fruit* tree on earth
that bears *fruit* with its seed *in* it.
God saw how *good* it was.
Evening came, and morning *followed*—the *third* day.

Then God said:
"Let there be *lights* in the *dome* of the *sky,*
to separate *day* from *night.*
Let them mark the fixed *times,* the *days* and the *years,*
and serve as *luminaries* in the *dome* of the *sky,*
to shed *light* upon the *earth.*"
And so it *happened:*
God made the *two* great *lights,*
the *greater* one to govern the *day,*
and the *lesser* one to govern the *night;*
and he made the *stars.*
God *set* them in the *dome* of the *sky,*
to shed *light* upon the *earth,*
to govern the *day* and the *night,*
and to separate the *light* from the *darkness.*

forms the world, beginning in the broadest possible way, by making light and darkness. From here, God proceeds to refine the work, making it ever more specific and detailed until finally reaching the creation of humanity. Human beings are the crown of creation because God declares them made in the divine image. This is both a declaration and a promise. We must fulfill God's word and reflect the divine in our words and actions.

Begin your proclamation by imagining the sound of a rushing wind and try to convey that image as you read the introductory verses of this selection. Throughout the description of creation, speak as slowly and clearly as you can, careful always not to swallow any words or phrases. Never rush the repetition in the passage but draw attention to it. Emphasize the words describing the elements of creation: light, waters, earth, plants, fruit, birds, animals, and so on. Give special emphasis to the creation of humans. Close with a quiet, satisfied voice.

There is a natural rhythm to this passage. Allow it to guide your proclamation, but try not to sound sing-song or too formal. Speak in a strong voice, and lift it a bit as you speak the words of God. Declare with warmth in your voice how good each aspect of creation is. Each "and so it happened"

Once again, speak sincerely and with satisfaction.

God saw how *good* it was.
Evening came, and morning *followed*— the *fourth* day.

Draw out "teem" in order to convey how many there were, then lift your voice and sound a bit excited as you describe the birds.

Then God said,
"Let the *water teem* with an abundance of living *creatures*,
and on the earth let *birds* fly beneath the *dome* of the *sky*."
And so it *happened*:

Practice this sentence until the phrasing is clear.

God created the great *sea* monsters
and *all* kinds of *swimming* creatures with which
the water *teems*,
and *all* kinds of winged *birds*.

Say "blessed" in a confident tone and with the same satisfaction that you display when declaring the goodness of God's creation.

God saw how *good* it was, and God *blessed* them, saying,
"Be *fertile*, *multiply*, and *fill* the water of the *seas*;
and let the birds *multiply* on the *earth*."
Evening came, and morning *followed*— the *fifth* day.

Then God said,
"Let the *earth* bring forth *all* kinds of living *creatures:*
cattle, *creeping* things, and wild *animals* of all *kinds*."
And so it *happened:*
God made all kinds of wild *animals*, all kinds of *cattle*,
and all kinds of *creeping* things of the *earth*.

All of creation is made by God and is good, even those creatures we consider less than noble.

God saw how *good* it was.

Pause before beginning this important proclamation, then lift your voice anew as you describe humanity.

Then God said:
"Let us make *man* in our *image*, after our *likeness*.
Let them have *dominion* over the *fish* of the sea,
the *birds* of the air, and the *cattle*,
and over all the wild *animals*
and *all* the creatures that *crawl* on the *ground*."

Stress "God."

God created *man* in his *image*;
in the *image* of *God* he created *him*;

Men and women both are made in God's image.

male and *female* he *created* them.

should be spoken after a slight pause and in a voice that expresses confidence rather than surprise. Pause slightly before and after the announcement of the day of the week ("evening" and "morning," "the first day," and so on). Read slowly, but with a tone of finality and satisfaction. Be sure to enunciate each word. Then pause before beginning the account of the succeeding day.

Your community might have the practice of beginning this reading in partial darkness, or the reading may be accompanied by a choral refrain or visual presentation. Be sure you understand what your liturgy committee or director has planned, and practice until you are confident that you can proceed smoothly, giving your entire attention to proclaiming the word of God. You are given the task of announcing that the light has dawned, a message that will also be imparted through song and ritual. Pray about the passage. After you have reflected on the beauty of God's creation, you will be better able to convey your wonder and awe to your listeners.

God *blessed* them, saying:
"Be *fertile* and *multiply*;
fill the earth and *subdue* it.
Have *dominion* over the fish of the *sea*, the birds of the *air*,
and *all* the living *things* that move on the *earth*."

There is a purpose for everything, and all creation is in harmony.

God *also* said:
"*See*, I give you every *seed*-bearing *plant* all over the *earth*
and every *tree* that has seed-bearing *fruit* on it to be your *food*;
and to all the *animals* of the land, all the *birds* of the air,
and all the living *creatures* that crawl on the *ground*,
I give all the green *plants* for *food*."
And so it *happened*.

Slow down as you read this and stress the great goodness of creation.

God looked at *everything* he had *made*, and he found it
very good.
Evening came, and morning *followed*—the *sixth* day.

Conclude the passage by reading slowly and with finality.

Thus the *heavens* and the *earth* and *all* their *array*
were *completed*.
Since on the *seventh* day God was *finished*
with the work he had been *doing*,
he *rested* on the *seventh* day from *all* the *work*
he had *undertaken*.

[Shorter: Genesis 1:1, 26–31a]

READING II **During our celebration of the Triduum, we reflect on the new covenant established in Jesus. It is appropriate, then, to learn about the covenant God first established with the patriarch Abraham. Today's passage follows the fulfillment of God's promise to Abraham and Sarah that they would have a child even though they were beyond child-bearing years. Abraham's part of the covenant was to institute circumcision, while God promised to bless Abraham and his descendants. In today's passage, the breadth of God's promise is evident: Abraham and Sarah will have descendants as numerous as the stars of the sky and the sands of the seashore.**

Before that promise is reiterated, Abraham demonstrates his faith in God by being willing to follow God's commands, even when they seem to contradict God's promises. The chilling story of the binding of Isaac shows just how far Abraham is willing to go. There is no doubt that Abraham loves his son; God's words make that clear. Yet he responds in faith, and it is for that faith that he is rewarded with the promise of many descendants. Written before a belief in an afterlife developed, this is the closest the text can come to speaking of immortality.

READING II Genesis 22:1–18

A reading from the book of Genesis.

Speak Abraham's name as if someone is calling him, then pause before giving his response.

God put Abraham to the *test.*
He called to him, *"Abraham!"*
"Here I am," he replied.
Then God said:
"Take your *son Isaac,* your *only one,* whom you *love,*
and go to the land of *Moriah.*
There you shall *offer* him up as a *holocaust*
on a *height* that I will point *out* to you."

Speak slowly and stress "only" and "love" in order to emphasize what a great gift this child was to Abraham and Sarah.
Moriah = moh-RĪ-uh

Early the next *morning* Abraham *saddled* his donkey,
took with him his son *Isaac* and two of his *servants* as *well,*
and with the *wood* that he had cut for the *holocaust,*
set *out* for the place of which God had *told* him.

The tension begins to mount as Abraham and Isaac approach the mountain.

On the *third* day Abraham got *sight* of the place from *afar.*
Then he said to his servants:
"Both of you *stay* here with the *donkey,*
while the *boy* and I go on over *yonder.*
We will *worship* and then come *back* to you."
Thereupon Abraham took the *wood* for the *holocaust*
and *laid* it on his son Isaac's *shoulders,*
while he *himself* carried the *fire* and the *knife.*

Isaac carries the wood just as Jesus will carry his cross.

As the two *walked* on *together,* Isaac spoke
to his father Abraham:
"Father!" Isaac said.
"Yes, son," he replied.
Isaac continued, "Here are the *fire* and the *wood,*
but where is the *sheep* for the *holocaust?"*

Although Isaac's words can be spoken lightly, allow some sadness to fill Abraham's responses.

Although the idea of a father sacrificing his son to God is horrifying, the purpose of the story is actually to claim that the God of Abraham does not require such an action. The gods of neighboring peoples accepted human sacrifice, but this God does not. God wants a demonstration of faith, but rejects the violence practiced by the nations.

Read this dramatic account with a tone of tension and horror just below the surface. Although it begins matter-of-factly, the story quickly threatens our sensibilities and causes us anxiety. Be aware of the discomfort that may be present in your congregation, but do not attempt to soften the message. When reading the dialogue, speak Isaac's words innocently, but allow some sorrow as well as nervousness to enter your voice as you read Abraham's words. Let the suspense build until the angel intervenes. Allow your voice to reflect relief when Abraham finds the ram, but continue to speak God's promise in a strong yet comforting tone.

This is not to be spoken matter-of-factly. Let your voice display some tightness in order to indicate what is coming.

"Son," Abraham answered,
"God *himself* will provide the *sheep* for the *holocaust."*
Then the two continued going forward.

Read these four lines slowly and allow tension to fill your voice.

When they came to the *place* of which God had *told* him,
Abraham built an *altar* there and arranged the *wood* on it.
Next he *tied* up his son *Isaac*,
and put him on *top* of the wood on the *altar.*

Read this first sentence very slowly and deliberately, with a tone of subdued horror. Then pause at length. When you begin again, speak with urgency and pick up your pace.

Then he *reached* out and took the *knife* to *slaughter* his son.
But the LORD's *messenger called* to him from *heaven*,
"Abraham, Abraham!"
"Here I am," he answered.
"Do *not* lay your *hand* on the boy," said the messenger.
"Do not do the *least* thing to him.

Although these are solemn words, you may speak with relief.

I know *now* how *devoted* you are to God,
since you did not *withhold* from me your *own* beloved son."
As Abraham looked *about*,

The tension continues to subside.

he spied a *ram* caught by its *horns* in the *thicket.*
So he went and *took* the ram
and *offered* it up as a holocaust in *place* of his *son.*

Yahweh-yireh = YAH-way-YEER-ay

Abraham named the site *Yahweh-yireh;*
hence people *now* say, "On the *mountain* the LORD will *see."*

Again the LORD's messenger *called* to Abraham from *heaven*
and said:
"I swear by *myself*, declares the LORD,
that because you *acted* as you *did*
in not *withholding* from me your beloved *son*,

This is a solemn promise, spoken with great sincerity.

I will *bless* you *abundantly*
and make your descendants as *countless*
as the *stars* of the *sky* and the *sands* of the *seashore;*
your *descendants* shall take possession
of the *gates* of their *enemies*,

READING III **The book of Exodus is the story of the plight of the Israelites in Egypt and their escape from the army of the Pharaoh as it chased them into the desert. Today's passage begins shortly after the journey has begun, just as the Pharaoh's army is approaching the Israelite procession. As they would do so many times on this journey to their Promised Land, the Israelites turn against Moses and lose heart. They regret the decision to flee Egypt, preferring to live in slavery than to die in the wilderness. The current selection follows immediately after Moses tries to reassure the people.**

The Israelites know that Pharaoh's army is near, but God seems far away. But the divine presence is manifested when the two camps approach the sea. The presence of God in the angel and in the pillar of cloud separates the Egyptians from the Israelites and protects them, then strikes the Egyptians and frightens them. When Moses follows God's instructions, the waters of the sea open for the Israelites but close again over the army of Pharaoh.

and *in* your descendants *all* the nations of the *earth*
shall find *blessing*—
all *this* because you *obeyed* my *command*."

Speak the final line slowly and with emphasis.

[Shorter: Genesis 22:1–2, 9a, 10–13, 15–18]

READING III Exodus 14:15—15:1

A reading from the book of Exodus.

Moses receives the criticism for the Israelites who were complaining.

The *LORD* said to *Moses*, "*Why* are you crying *out* to me?
Tell the Israelites to go *forward*.
And *you*, lift up your *staff* and, with hand outstretched
over the *sea*,
split the sea in *two*,
that the Israelites may pass *through* it on dry *land*.
But I will make the Egyptians *so obstinate*
that they will go in *after* them.
Then I will receive *glory* through *Pharaoh* and *all* his army,
his *chariots* and *charioteers*.
The Egyptians shall *know* that *I* am the LORD,
when I receive *glory* through *Pharaoh*
and his *chariots* and *charioteers*."

It is for God's glory that these events have been recorded. That is also the reason we recall them today.

The *angel* of God, who had been *leading* Israel's camp,
now *moved* and went around *behind* them.
The column of cloud *also*, leaving the *front*,
took up its place *behind* them,
so that it came *between* the camp of the *Egyptians*
and that of *Israel*.

The angel and the pillar of cloud had signified God's presence, leading the Israelites on the journey. Now they separate the Israelites from the Egyptians, offering protection and assistance.

The spectacular account of God's intervention during the flight from Egypt ends with a song of praise to God. It is appropriate for us to join our voices with those of the Israelites today, for God's promise to care for the Israelites gives glory to God and brings favor to the Israelites. In addition to giving God glory, the Exodus event provides salvation for the Hebrew people and convinces them of the great power of God.

This key reading is understood by Christians as being especially important on this holy night, when we proclaim that Jesus has passed through death to life. In addition, the Israelites' crossing of the sea is understood as an image of baptism, when the Christian passes through the waters to new life. Paul's understanding of baptism in his letter to the Romans, which follows shortly, speaks of dying in baptism with the promise of new life. Paul uses the Exodus event to explain Christian baptism. For the Israelites and for Christians, going through the waters and leaving the former life behind acknowledges the salvation offered by God.

There is a great deal of excitement in the story about the Israelites' flight from Egypt. Begin by speaking God's words forcefully; emphasize the glory that rightfully belongs to God. Let your voice reflect some of the anxiety that must have accompanied the Israelites as they passed through the

But the *cloud* now became *dark*, and thus the night *passed*
without the rival camps coming any closer *together*
all night *long*.

Raise your voice and speak majestically of God's intervention.

Then Moses stretched out his *hand* over the *sea*,
and the LORD *swept* the sea
with a strong east *wind* throughout the *night*
and so turned it into *dry land*.
When the *water* was thus *divided*,
the Israelites *marched* into the midst of the sea on *dry land*,
with the *water* like a *wall* to their *right* and to their *left*.

Pick up the pace a bit, as the Egyptians follow in hot pursuit.

The *Egyptians* followed in *pursuit*;
all Pharaoh's *horses* and *chariots* and *charioteers*
went *after* them
right into the midst of the *sea*.

This line can be tricky; prepare your phrasing well.

In the *night* watch just before *dawn*
the *LORD cast* through the column of the *fiery* cloud
upon the Egyptian force a *glance* that threw it into a *panic*;
and he so *clogged* their *chariot* wheels
that they could hardly *drive*.

Two explanations are given for Pharaoh's defeat. Here the wheels of the chariots became clogged, but in the next paragraph, the Egyptians drown when the waters return.

With *that* the Egyptians sounded the *retreat* before *Israel*,
because the *LORD* was fighting for them *against* the Egyptians.

Then the *LORD* told *Moses*, "*Stretch* out your *hand* over the *sea*,
that the water may flow *back* upon the *Egyptians*,
upon their *chariots* and their *charioteers*."
So Moses *stretched* out his *hand* over the *sea*,
and at *dawn* the sea flowed *back* to its normal *depth*.

Increase your speed here.

The Egyptians were fleeing *head on* toward the *sea*,
when the LORD *hurled* them into its *midst*.

sea, and allow it to grow in intensity until the Egyptians are finally vanquished. Speak triumphantly of the safety of the Israelites, and proclaim joyfully the victory song of the people.

The key theme of this reading is God's constant presence and care for the people, despite their grumbling. Offer it to your assembly as a commentary on God's continual care and the necessity of passing through tribulations, even death, on the path to true life.

READING IV

Chapters 40–55 of Isaiah are often called Second Isaiah because they were written centuries after the prophet Isaiah was active. The prophet Isaiah had counseled the king of Judah when Jerusalem was threatened by the Assyrians. Second Isaiah comes from a time near the end of the Babylonian exile, when the people were eagerly awaiting the chance to return to their homeland. Jerusalem had been destroyed and its inhabitants led away, but they kept alive the hope that they would one day return. As the political events of the day indicated that the time was drawing near, a prophet wrote these reassuring words. God speaks of the exile as a time of punishment that is drawing to a close. God also eagerly awaits the return of the chosen people to Jerusalem, to the holy mountain of Zion.

As the water flowed *back,*
it *covered* the *chariots* and the *charioteers*
of Pharaoh's *whole* army
which had *followed* the Israelites into the *sea.*
Not a *single one* of them *escaped.*

This is spoken with finality. The danger has passed.

But the *Israelites* had marched on *dry land*
through the *midst* of the sea,
with the water like a *wall* to their *right* and to their *left.*
Thus the LORD *saved* Israel on that day
from the *power* of the *Egyptians.*
When Israel *saw* the Egyptians lying *dead* on the *seashore*
and beheld the great *power* that the LORD
had *shown* against the *Egyptians,*
they *feared* the LORD and *believed* in him
and in his servant *Moses.*

As will so often happen on this journey, Israel is in awe of God's tremendous deeds.

Then *Moses* and the *Israelites* sang this *song* to the *LORD:*
I will *sing* to the *LORD,* for he is *gloriously* triumphant;
horse and *chariot* he has cast into the *sea.*

Speak this with great joy, giving glory to God.

READING IV Isaiah 54:5–14

A reading from the book of the prophet Isaiah.

Convey the intimacy of the relationship between God and Israel.

The One who has become your *husband* is your *Maker;*
his name is the *LORD* of *hosts;*
your *redeemer* is the *Holy* One of *Israel,*
called *God* of *all* the *earth.*
The *LORD* calls you *back,*
like a *wife forsaken* and grieved in *spirit,*

There is hope here, but sadness in the following lines.

God speaks throughout today's reading, first as a husband filled with love for a wife he had abandoned. Brimming with compassion, he calls her back. God was angry, but the moment of anger was brief and has passed. The image of Israel as a bride of God is expressed most poignantly in another prophet, Hosea; there God is faithful always, despite Israel's waywardness. Here God seems to regret the momentary anger, although elsewhere the exile is seen as a necessary period of instruction and testing.

God's word is forceful in the next section of the passage, as the author recalls the story of the flood in the days of Noah. At that time God also spoke, declaring never again to destroy the earth. Now the prophet proclaims that nothing can interfere with God's tremendous love for this people. Even if the mountains move and the hills quake, God will remember the covenant with Israel.

Finally, God addresses the city of Jerusalem directly. The city is lying in waste after the defeat by the Babylonians, and God promises to renew its splendor, decorating it with precious stones. Israel thought of the city of Zion as the one place that could not be defeated by the enemies of God. Even with Jerusalem in ruins, that hope is renewed here, for God will care for the city.

The people will also be renewed, taught by God and established in righteousness. In everything, God will offer protection and love.

Speak quietly but joyfully as you read these reassuring promises. Address this beautiful statement of God's commitment

a wife married in *youth* and then cast *off*,
says your God.

Speak as though with regret.

For a *brief* moment I *abandoned* you,
but with great *tenderness* I will take you *back*.
In an outburst of *wrath*, for a *moment*
I hid my *face* from you;

Convey the tender love of God in a warm but firm voice.

but with enduring *love* I take *pity* on you,
says the LORD, your *redeemer*.

A new idea begins here; lift your voice as though starting afresh.

This is for me like the days of *Noah*,
when I *swore* that the *waters* of Noah
should *never* again *deluge* the earth;
so I have *sworn* not to be *angry* with you,
or to *rebuke* you.

Speak this as a solemn oath.

Though the *mountains* leave their *place*
and the *hills* be *shaken*,
my *love* shall never *leave* you
nor my *covenant* of *peace* be *shaken*,
says the LORD, who has *mercy* on you.

God speaks tenderly to Jerusalem.

Let your voice grow in intensity as you describe the majesty of Jerusalem.

O *afflicted* one, *storm*-battered and *unconsoled*,
I lay your *pavements* in *carnelians*,
and your *foundations* in *sapphires*;
I will make your *battlements* of *rubies*,
your *gates* of *carbuncles*,
and all your *walls* of precious *stones*.

Speak these final lines in a sure, commanding voice. They are a promise of peace and justice.

All your *children* shall be *taught* by the LORD,
and *great* shall be the *peace* of your *children*.
In *justice* shall you be *established*,
far from the fear of *oppression*,
where *destruction* cannot come *near* you.

directly to the members of your assembly. Offer it as an assurance that God always wants to live in intimacy and love with this people. Remind them that times when God may seem distant are temporary, but God's love is eternal.

READING V This section of Isaiah follows almost immediately after the verses in the fourth reading. It was also used on the feast of the Baptism of the Lord (see that commentary).

This reading is an invitation to eat and drink and be satisfied. It is offered to all, even to those who cannot afford to purchase the food necessary to prepare the feast. This food is available to anyone because it is not food for physical sustenance but nourishment for the spirit. Just as we often gather together to celebrate momentous occasions by sharing in a banquet, so also the banquet is spread here in order to invite people to consume the food of wisdom.

In fact, the invitation to come and eat sounds very much like the invitation of Wisdom in the book of Proverbs. There, Lady Wisdom entices her listeners, inviting them to share a meal with her and drawing them especially to embrace her and act always in accordance with her instruction.

In today's passage, God invites a people living in exile to feast. The author recognizes that the end of the exile is near and the people will soon be restored to their homeland. The covenant that God established with David is still valid despite the exile; it will be renewed as an everlasting covenant.

READING V Isaiah 55:1–11

A reading from the book of the prophet Isaiah.

Thus says the LORD:
All you who are *thirsty*,
come to the *water!*
You who have no *money*,
come, receive *grain* and *eat*;
come, without *paying* and without *cost*,
drink *wine* and *milk!*
Why spend your money for what is *not bread*,
your *wages* for what *fails* to *satisfy?*
Heed me, and you shall eat *well*,
you shall *delight* in rich *fare*.
Come to me *heedfully*,
listen, that you may have *life*.
I will *renew* with you the everlasting *covenant*,
the *benefits* assured to *David*.

Speak this invitation quietly but clearly. Stress "come" throughout the reading in a way that sounds like you are eager for the guests to arrive.

Sound eager and encouraging. It is free!

These are reassuring words; continue to sound inviting, but in a firmer tone.

Speak these words with great promise.

As I made him a *witness* to the *peoples*,
a *leader* and commander of *nations*,
so shall *you* summon a nation you knew *not*,
and nations that knew *you* not shall *run* to you,
because of the LORD, your *God*,
the *Holy* One of *Israel*, who has *glorified* you.

Seek the LORD while he may be *found*,
call him while he is *near*.
Let the scoundrel *forsake* his *way*,
and the wicked man his *thoughts*;
let him *turn* to the LORD for *mercy*;
to our *God*, who is generous in *forgiving*.

Pause before beginning this line, and lower your voice again, gently urging your listeners to seek God.

This is meant to be encouraging, not disdainful. Do not give undue emphasis to "scoundrel" or "wicked."

Israel will once again be a light to all the nations of the world.

One of the lessons of the exile was the necessity to repent for wrongdoing. God again invites the wicked to forsake their deeds, to turn to God and learn. All of Israel needs to hear this (as do we), and to recognize that God's ways are fundamentally different from the ways of humans. But those who listen to God's word will recognize this, for like the rain and the snow that cause the earth to produce vegetation, God's word is effective and brings forth new life.

We accept God's call today to come to the waters. We come not for physical refreshment, but to reaffirm our commitment to the one who provides life-giving water. For those in your community who are approaching the waters of baptism, as well as for those renewing their baptismal commitment, offer this selection as an invitation to approach with confidence and trust, knowing that God will teach them and work through them. God has also spread a feast in the eucharist that we will soon share. Invite your community to partake of the sustenance that satisfies more than physical hunger. Read with a welcoming tone and a reassuring voice as you become the vessel through whom God's word is sown.

Pause before this line, then speak with majesty.

For *my* thoughts are not *your* thoughts,
nor are *your* ways *my* ways, says the LORD.
As *high* as the *heavens* are above the *earth,*
so high are *my* ways above *your ways*
and my *thoughts* above *your thoughts.*

This final section is a promise. It is one long complex sentence and will have to be carefully prepared. Read it slowly, knowing when you will pause for breath.

For just as *from* the *heavens*
the *rain* and *snow* come *down*
and do not *return* there
till they have *watered* the *earth,*
making it *fertile* and *fruitful,*
giving *seed* to the one who *sows*
and *bread* to the one who *eats,*

With "so shall," you begin the fulfillment of the promise. Pause before this line and speak it and what follows slowly and forcefully.

so shall my *word* be
that goes forth from my *mouth;*
my word shall not *return* to me *void,*
but shall do my *will,*
achieving the *end* for which I *sent* it.

READING VI Baruch 3:9–15, 32—4:4

Baruch = buh-ROOK

A reading from the book of the prophet Baruch.

Speak as though a herald, calling from the rooftops.

Hear, O *Israel,* the commandments of *life:*
listen, and know *prudence!*
How *is* it, Israel,

Do not end this long question by raising your voice at the end. It is rhetorical; God knows how and why the people went into exile.

that you are in the *land* of your *foes,*
grown *old* in a foreign *land,*
defiled with the *dead,*
accounted with those destined for the *netherworld?*

READING VI **The book of Baruch, like Second Isaiah, was written in connection with Israel's exile in Babylon and expresses a hope for return to the promised land. The present section is a poem in honor of wisdom, a pastiche of quotes from the Hebrew scriptures designed to draw the reader to recognize that wisdom is found in living according to the commandments of God.**

The author begins by declaring that Israel's exile is a punishment for forsaking God and disobeying God's commands. Exile is such a humiliation that it can be compared with dwelling among the dead. Such is the destiny of those who abandon wisdom.

Wherever there is wisdom, there is strength and understanding, but also a long and happy life. Wisdom is a grammatically feminine term and is elsewhere personified as a woman. Yet wisdom is not easy to find. Fortunately for Israel, God has found her and given her as a gift to this chosen people.

Wisdom literature speaks of Lady Wisdom as the joint creator of the universe with God. Although that specific teaching is not present in this passage, it does recall the creation account in Genesis. The one who created the universe knows Wisdom and bestowed her upon Israel. Through this people she has dwelt on earth.

Here is the answer to the question. Speak it forcefully.

You have *forsaken* the fountain of *wisdom!*
Had you walked in the way of *God,*
you would have *dwelt* in enduring *peace.*

Lower your voice a bit and speak encouragingly.

Learn where *prudence* is,
where *strength,* where *understanding;*
that you may know *also*
where are length of *days,* and *life,*
where *light* of the eyes, and *peace.*

Wisdom is hard to find.

Who has found the place of *wisdom,*
who has *entered* into her *treasuries?*

The One who *knows* all *things* knows *her;*
he has *probed* her by his *knowledge*—
the One who established the *earth* for all *time,*

What follows is a brief recapitulation of the Genesis creation account. As in Genesis, God is the one in control of everything.

and filled it with four-footed *beasts;*
he who *dismisses* the *light,* and it *departs,*
calls it, and it *obeys* him trembling;
before whom the *stars* at their posts
shine and *rejoice;*

The stars speak eagerly and joyfully.

when he *calls* them, they answer, "*Here* we *are!*"
shining with *joy* for their *Maker.*

Pause before beginning this section, then read with great conviction.

Such is our *God;*
no *other* is to be *compared* to him:
he has traced out the *whole* way of *understanding,*
and has *given* her to *Jacob,* his servant,
to *Israel,* his beloved *son.*

Since then she has *appeared* on *earth,*
and *moved* among *people.*

Israel believes that wisdom resides in the Law.

She is the *book* of the *precepts* of *God,*
the *law* that endures *forever;*

In a move that is somewhat surprising (developed to an even greater extent in the book of Sirach), Lady Wisdom is now identified with the Torah, the Law given to Moses. The gift of wisdom is the same as the gift of the Law. To keep the commandments of the Law is to hold on to wisdom and to have life.

Israel can rejoice in having received the Law. Through it Israel knows how to please God.

Christians have long understood the reference to Lady Wisdom living on earth among humans to refer to the incarnate Son of God, Jesus. He is truly Wisdom, from whom we learn about God and ourselves. We embrace the gift God has given us in Jesus and pledge our commitment to hold fast to him, so that we might live.

This is both an invitation and a bold challenge to the members of your community. Speak in encouraging tones as you coax them ever closer to the source of all life and knowledge.

all who *cling* to her will *live*,
but those will *die* who *forsake* her.

Slow your pace and speak tenderly, joyfully and encouragingly from here to the end.

Turn, O Jacob, and *receive* her:
walk by her light toward *splendor*.
Give not your *glory* to *another*,
your *privileges* to an *alien* race.
Blessed are *we*, O *Israel*;
for what *pleases* God is *known* to us!

READING VII Ezekiel 36:16–17a, 18–28

A reading from the book of the prophet Ezekiel.

"Son of man" simply refers to someone who is human. It is God's favorite form of address to Ezekiel.

Lower your voice and let anger enter into it as you express God's wrath.

Let "scattered" sound like what it means.

The *word* of the LORD *came* to me, saying:
Son of *man*, when the house of *Israel* lived in their *land*,
they *defiled* it by their *conduct* and *deeds*.
Therefore I poured out my *fury* upon them
because of the *blood* that they *poured* out on the *ground*,
and because they *defiled* it with *idols*.
I *scattered* them among the *nations*,
dispersing them over foreign *lands*;
according to their *conduct* and *deeds* I *judged* them.

Give emphasis to the statement about profaning God's name. As if their lawless deeds were not enough, the exile itself served to sully God's name.

But when they *came* among the *nations wherever* they came,
they served to *profane* my holy *name*,
because it was said of them: "*These* are the people of the LORD,
yet they had to *leave* their land."

READING VII **Ezekiel was a prophet during the Babylonian exile. He rebukes Israel for its unfaithfulness to God, which resulted in the destruction of Jerusalem and the deportation of its leaders to a foreign land. Yet his is also a strong voice of hope that the exile would soon end and Israel would be restored.**

The present passage is written entirely in God's words. God details the sins for which the punishment of the exile occurred. A new claim is added: The people in exile have profaned God's name simply by the fact that they are living in exile. God gave them a land, but the exile made it appear that God was unable to care for the chosen people as promised. As a result, God pledges to return them to their homeland regardless of their worthiness. Israel's God acts to protect the divine name, to display holiness for all the nations to see.

The passage closes with a beautiful promise that God would not only restore the people to the land but would there make them worthy, cleansing them and removing idols from their midst. God vows to place within the people a new heart, a heart of

Pause before this line and then speak calmly and reassuringly.

So I have *relented* because of my holy *name*
which the house of Israel *profaned*
among the *nations* where they came.

Speak forcefully, increasing your volume.

Therefore *say* to the house of *Israel: Thus* says the *Lord GOD:*
Not for *your* sakes do I act, house of *Israel,*
but for the *sake* of my holy *name,*
which you *profaned* among the *nations* to which you came.

This is a solemn promise.

I will *prove* the *holiness* of my great *name,*
profaned among the *nations,*
in whose *midst* you have *profaned* it.
Thus the *nations* shall *know* that *I* am the LORD,
says the Lord GOD,
when in their *sight* I prove my *holiness* through *you.*

The emphasis returns to what God will do for Israel. Speak with comfort.

For I will take you *away* from among the *nations,*
gather you from all the foreign *lands,*
and bring you *back* to your *own* land.

The sprinkling of water symbolizes purity. It reminds Christians of baptism.

I will *sprinkle* clean *water* upon you
to *cleanse* you from all your *impurities,*
and from all your *idols* I will *cleanse* you.

Speak tenderly and encouragingly.

I will give you a *new heart* and place a *new spirit within* you,
taking from your *bodies* your *stony* hearts
and giving you *natural* hearts.
I will put my spirit *within* you and make you *live* by my *statutes,*
careful to *observe* my *decrees.*

Close with a tone of solemn satisfaction.

You shall *live* in the land I gave your *fathers;*
you shall be my *people,* and *I* will be your *God.*

flesh to replace their stone-cold heart. God will also put God's own spirit in them, instructing them in the correct ways to live.

See this selection both as a historical lesson and as a challenge to your listeners to recognize God's greatness and to pledge to live as God's people. Raise your voice to read the final fifteen or so lines—the promise of God to reestablish the people. Inspire your community to open its heart to God, to rejoice in its homecoming and to be willing to live according to the statutes of God.

EPISTLE

In keeping with his emphasis on the cross of Christ, Paul's classic treatment of baptism also emphasizes the death of Christ and the believer's share in that death. In baptism, the old self is left behind, indeed crucified, in order to embrace the promise of a new life. And the resurrection life is, for Paul, always a future hope, something to be sought.

On this night, we begin our celebration in the darkness of death. But we are expectant and hopeful, knowing that our Lord is risen. Tonight we welcome into our community new members who have long been preparing for this day. We recall as well our own baptism and renew our baptismal promises. It is fitting that we be reminded of

EPISTLE Romans 6:3–11

A reading from the letter of Saint Paul to the Romans.

This is a rhetorical question and can be read either with or without raising your voice at the end.

Brothers and sisters:
Are you *unaware* that we who were *baptized* into Christ *Jesus*
were *baptized* into his *death?*
We were indeed *buried* with him through *baptism* into *death,*
so *that,* just as *Christ* was raised from the *dead*
by the *glory* of the *Father,*
we *too* might live in *newness* of *life.*

This is the hope that Paul has; lighten your voice and read with an expectant expression.

For if we have grown into *union* with him
through a *death* like his,
we shall also be *united* with him in the *resurrection.*
We know that our *old* self was *crucified* with him,
so that our sinful *body* might be done *away* with,
that we might no *longer* be in slavery to *sin.*
For a *dead* person has been *absolved* from sin.
If, then, we have *died* with *Christ,*
we believe that we shall also *live* with him.

Paul begins with what is past and moves on to the hope of sharing life with Christ. Stress the contrasts.

Speak with firm conviction.

We know that *Christ,* raised from the *dead,* dies no *more;*
death no longer has *power* over him.
As to his *death,* he died to *sin once* and for *all;*
as to his *life,* he lives for *God.*
Consequently, you *too* must think of *yourselves*
as being *dead* to *sin*
and *living* for *God* in Christ *Jesus.*

Make clear all of the contrasts: between Christ's death and his life in God, between the believer's "death" and new life.

Paul's understanding of baptism and reflect on its significance in our lives.

It is your task tonight to remind the members of your community of their baptismal pledge to leave sin behind. Urge them also to look forward, as does Paul, to the promise of being united with Christ in his resurrection. Proclaiming that Christ is risen allows us also to acknowledge that we shall rise with him.

This passage is not easy to proclaim and will require careful preparation. Stress the central concepts and terms: death, life, resurrection, freedom from sin. Close by offering Paul's exhortation to the Romans to be alive in Christ Jesus as a direct appeal to your own community.

GOSPEL The account of the resurrection in the gospel of Mark is distinct from those in the other gospels. There are no appearances of Jesus to his friends, no words of instruction or comfort, no real sense of finality. The story—and the gospel—ends with the women leaving the tomb frightened. Against some in the community of Mark's gospel, the author claims that the followers of Jesus must embrace suffering as well as glory. Jesus is risen indeed. We can rejoice and enthusiastically proclaim that death has been conquered by the author of life, that evil is

GOSPEL Mark 16:1–7

A reading from the holy gospel according to Mark.

These are the same women who watched the crucifixion from afar.
Salome = suh-LOH-mee

When the sabbath was *over*,
Mary *Magdalene*, *Mary*, the mother of *James*, and *Salome*
bought *spices* so that they might go and *anoint* him.

The reason Christians observe Sunday and not the Sabbath as our holy day is this gospel claim. It was on a Sunday that Jesus was revealed as having risen from the dead.

Very *early* when the sun had *risen*,
on the first day of the *week*, they came to the *tomb*.
They were *saying* to one another,
"*Who* will roll back the *stone* for us
from the entrance to the *tomb*?"
When they looked *up*,
they saw that the *stone* had been rolled *back*;
it was very *large*.

Note this with surprise. Let amazement fill your voice as you continue.

On *entering* the tomb they saw a young *man*
sitting on the right *side*, *clothed* in a white *robe*,
and they were utterly *amazed*.
He said to them, "Do *not* be *amazed!*

Pause, then proclaim the next line with a combination of joy, awe and certitude.

You *seek* Jesus of *Nazareth*, the *crucified*.
He has been *raised*; he is not *here*.
Behold the place where they *laid* him.

Although there are no resurrection appearances in this gospel, the author was clearly familiar with the tradition that Jesus had appeared to his followers after his death.

"But *go* and tell his *disciples* and *Peter*,
'He is going *before* you to *Galilee*;
there you will see him, as he *told* you.'"

overcome by good, that our God is victorious. But the forces of darkness still remain potent; our lives are not without struggle. It is left to us to finish the story.

Today's gospel reading begins serenely, but tension quickly builds. Surprising events have taken place. The mysterious young man who announces to the women that Jesus has been raised assures them that they have nothing to fear. For those of us who know how the story ends, who are recipients of a faith founded on this event, it is sometimes hard to appreciate what the women experienced. They had come to anoint a corpse; now their friend's body is missing. They were in mourning; he is said to be alive. They had wondered how they alone could move the stone from the tomb; not only is the stone moved when they arrive, but they find that they are not alone. A stranger announces Jesus' resurrection and predicts that he will appear to his followers. These are unusual events indeed.

Read this drama, the central proclamation of the entire church year, with full recognition of its importance in the ritual of the Easter Vigil and in the life of your community. You proclaim a text that witnesses to the triumph of the cross, the victory of Christ over death, the defeat of hatred and evil by the profound love of God. We go forth from this night not in fear, as did the women, but in amazement, fully aware of the task before us and of the strength God gives us to meet it.

EASTER SUNDAY

Lectionary #42

READING I Acts 10:34a, 37–43

A reading from the Acts of the Apostles.

Peter proceeded to *speak* and said:
"*You know* what has happened all over *Judea,*
beginning in *Galilee* after the baptism
that *John preached,*
how God *anointed* Jesus of *Nazareth*
with the *Holy Spirit* and *power.*
He *went about* doing *good*
and *healing* all those oppressed by the *devil,*
for God was *with* him.

Peter's speech begins here. Lift your voice and speak slowly, especially at the beginning, in order to make this sound like a speech.

"*We* are *witnesses* of all that he *did*
both in the country of the *Jews* and in *Jerusalem.*
They put him to *death* by hanging him on a *tree.*
This man God *raised* on the third *day* and granted
that he be *visible,*
not to *all* the people, but to *us,*
the *witnesses* chosen by God in *advance,*
who *ate* and *drank* with him after he *rose* from the *dead.*

Pause.

The proclamation of the core of the Christian faith begins here and continues in the following lines; emphasize it, especially stressing "raised."

"He *commissioned* us to *preach* to the people
and *testify* that *he* is the one *appointed* by *God*
as *judge* of the *living* and the *dead.*
To *him* all the *prophets* bear *witness,*
that *everyone* who *believes* in him
will receive *forgiveness* of sins through his *name.*"

Everyone who believes — both Jew and Gentile — is a recipient of the salvation wrought by Jesus.

READING I The speech of Peter to the household of Cornelius, the first Gentiles to be included among the followers of Christ, contains in a nutshell the truths of the Christian faith. Peter speaks about the ministry of Jesus on earth, as well as the core of Christian faith — Jesus' death and resurrection and his appearances to the disciples — and closes with a statement of belief in Christ as the heavenly judge in whom sins are forgiven. It is appropriate to proclaim this message on this central feast of our liturgical year.

Peter's speech follows his realization that the salvation offered in Christ is available to all people, Jews and Gentiles alike. He also claims to be a witness to Jesus' ministry, as well as to Jesus' death, and claims to have experienced the risen Jesus. The author makes it clear that Peter's testimony is reliable.

The command to preach about Jesus paves the way for the readings at our liturgies during the Easter season. In the coming weeks, we will hear about the early growth of the new community of believers and will be challenged to share the message of the risen Christ with those we meet.

Read this speech as a direct proclamation to your assembly. It provides you with a chance to remind your listeners of the core of their faith, a faith based on the testimony of prophets, apostles and "everyone who believes in him."

READING II Colossians 3:1–4

A reading from the letter of Saint Paul to the Colossians.

Brothers and sisters:

Challenge your listeners to set their sights on heavenly goals.

If then you were *raised* with Christ, seek what is *above*,
where Christ is *seated* at the *right hand* of *God*.
Think of what is *above*, *not* of what is on *earth*.

The great things of earth should be insignificant to one whose true home is with God.

For you have *died*, and your life is *hidden* with Christ in *God*.
When *Christ* your life *appears*,
then you *too* will appear with him in *glory*.

Or:

READING II 1 Corinthians 5:6b–8

A reading from the first letter of Saint Paul to the Corinthians.

Brothers and sisters:

The ideas progress quickly here. Pause before continuing.

Do you not *know* that a *little* yeast leavens *all* the *dough*?
Clear *out* the *old* yeast,
so that you may become a *fresh* batch of dough,
inasmuch as you are *unleavened*.

Pause again.

For our paschal *lamb*, *Christ*, has been *sacrificed*.

Speak with enthusiasm.

Therefore, let us *celebrate* the feast,
not with the *old* yeast, the yeast of *malice* and *wickedness*,
but with the *unleavened* bread of *sincerity* and *truth*.

There is a choice of second readings today. Speak with the liturgy coordinator or pastor to find out which reading will be used.

READING II **COLOSSIANS. For Paul, resurrection is always in the future. But here, in an apparent reference to the experience of baptism, the author (an admirer of Paul, who wrote in his name) claims that the Christian has already been raised with Christ. "You have died"—probably in the waters of baptism, but surely to a past sinful life—and must therefore live as one who is already sharing in the heavenly life of Christ enthroned with God. The splendor of resurrected life is not yet revealed to all but will be when Christ appears in glory.**

Offer this exhortation to your community as it was first offered to the Colossians: Encourage your listeners to strive for high goals in their behavior, remembering always that they have a share in the life available in Christ.

1 CORINTHIANS. Paul exhorts the Corinthians to live new, pure lives by referring to the feast of Passover and using the metaphor of leavened and unleavened bread. Even Gentiles would understand the domestic metaphor, although they probably did not understand leaven to be impure as the Jews did.

Paul assumes that his readers understand the way in which yeast or leaven is used: A small amount of leavened dough is saved and used to start a new loaf, providing the agent that will make the new dough rise. If left too long, the dough will ferment too much and begin to smell, thus leading to the negative connotations associated with

GOSPEL John 20:1–9

A reading from the holy gospel according to John.

Magdala = MAG-duh-luh

The passage began quietly, but the pace picks up with this line. Increase your speed slightly and allow your voice to indicate amazement.

Mary is a bit distraught; reflect this in your voice.

Emphasize this line; read slowly and forcefully.

On the *first* day of the *week*,
Mary of *Magdala* came to the *tomb early* in the morning,
while it was still *dark*,
and saw the *stone removed* from the tomb.
So she *ran* and went to Simon *Peter*
and to the *other* disciple whom Jesus *loved*, and *told* them,
"They have taken the *Lord* from the *tomb*,
and we don't know *where* they *put* him."

So *Peter* and the *other* disciple went out and came to the *tomb*.
They both *ran*, but the *other* disciple ran *faster* than Peter
and arrived at the tomb *first*;
he bent *down* and *saw* the burial cloths there, but did
not go in.

When Simon *Peter* arrived *after* him,
he went *into* the tomb and saw the burial *cloths* there,
and the *cloth* that had covered his *head*,
not with the burial *cloths* but rolled up in a *separate* place.
Then the *other* disciple also went *in*,
the one who had arrived at the tomb *first*,
and he *saw* and *believed*.
For they did not yet *understand* the Scripture
that he had to *rise* from the *dead*.

leaven. If the old dough is discarded and new dough prepared, it produces unleavened bread, a flat bread whose dough does not rise. Every Passover, Jews discard all yeast products from their homes and prepare unleavened bread, just as the Israelites did before fleeing Egypt.

Paul suggests that the moral life of the Christian is like the dough used to make bread. Wicked thoughts and actions can mushroom, negatively affecting a person or an entire community. Paul encourages the Corinthians to be like unleavened bread, free of any undesirable qualities. The mention of unleavened bread reminds him of the feast of Passover, when Jesus was crucified and became the "paschal lamb," the one who brought freedom through his death.

Encourage your community to purify itself this Easter season, to recognize the new life available to it, and to live as those free of any corruption or impurity. We too are celebrating the feast on which our paschal lamb gave us life; let us live lives worthy of our calling.

The gospel from the Easter Vigil may be read at any Mass on Easter Sunday, at any time of the day. The gospel for the Third Sunday of Easter, Year A, may be used at an afternoon or evening Mass (see Lectionary #46).

GOSPEL The gospel of John recounts several appearances of the risen Jesus to his followers. They, together with the witness of the empty tomb, provide touching, powerful testimony to our Easter proclamation: Jesus is risen. Alleluia!

Lectionary #46

AFTERNOON GOSPEL Luke 24:13–35

A reading from the holy gospel according to Luke.

That *very* day, the *first* day of the *week,*
two of Jesus' *disciples* were going
to a *village* seven miles from *Jerusalem* called *Emmaus,*
and they were *conversing* about *all* the things
that had *occurred.*
And it happened that while they were *conversing* and *debating,*
Jesus himself *drew near* and walked *with* them,
but their eyes were *prevented* from *recognizing* him.

Emmaus = eh-MAY-uhs

All the resurrection appearances of Jesus indicate that he had been transformed; he was no longer easily recognizable.

He asked them,
"What are you *discussing* as you walk *along?*"
They *stopped,* looking *downcast.*
One of them, named *Cleopas,* said to him in reply,
"Are you the *only* visitor to Jerusalem
who does not *know* of the things
that have *taken place* there in these *days?*"

Jesus' question seems innocent, but the response is one of frustration and sorrow.

Cleopas = KLEE-oh-puhs

And he replied to them, "What *sort* of things?"
They said to him,
"The *things* that happened to *Jesus* the *Nazarene,*
who was a *prophet mighty* in *deed* and *word*
before *God* and all the *people,*
how our *chief priests* and *rulers* both *handed* him *over*
to a sentence of *death* and *crucified* him.
But we were *hoping* that *he* would be the one to *redeem* Israel;
and besides all this,
it is now the *third* day since this *took place.*

They recognized him as a prophet, and had hoped that he was the Messiah.

Mary Magdalene, remembered in many sources as an especially close friend of Jesus and the first to encounter the risen Christ in the gospel of John, approaches the tomb but runs away when she sees that the stone has been removed. Understandably, she believes that the body has been stolen. Peter and the beloved disciple (probably John), the most prominent of the Twelve in this gospel, follow. Although the author indicates that the beloved disciple "saw and believed," the statement that the disciples did not yet understand that Jesus was to rise from the dead, as well as the witness of the other gospels, suggests that the women—in this gospel, Mary Magdalene—were the first to encounter both the empty tomb and the risen Lord.

The story of Peter and the beloved disciple racing to the tomb is exciting. This gospel passage moves quickly, with much to catch the congregation's attention. Read it as though for the first time, and make the story come alive with your telling. This reading provides not only a testimony of faith to the resurrection of Jesus, but most of all shows the tender love shared by Jesus and his followers.

AFTERNOON GOSPEL The beautiful story of the encounter between Jesus and two of his disciples on the road to Emmaus is touching, inspiring and revealing. It recounts the disciples' sadness and confusion in the beginning, their joy at recognizing Jesus, and their

Women were clearly members of the group of Jesus' disciples and were the first to recognize that Jesus had risen.

Some *women* from our group, however, have *astounded* us:
they were at the *tomb* early in the morning
and did *not* find his *body*;
they *came back* and *reported*
that they had indeed seen a *vision* of *angels*
who announced that he was *alive.*

"Then *some* of those with us *went* to the tomb
and found things *just* as the women had described,
but *him* they did not *see."*

Speak Jesus' words with tired sadness and a bit of frustration.

Although we know the answer, speak this as a real question.

And he said to them, "Oh, how *foolish* you are!
How slow of heart to believe *all* that the prophets *spoke!*
Was it not necessary that the *Christ* should *suffer* these things
and *enter* into his *glory?"*

Then beginning with *Moses* and all the *prophets*,
he *interpreted* to them what *referred* to him
in *all* the Scriptures.
As they *approached* the village to which they were *going*,
he gave the impression that he was going on *farther.*
But they *urged* him, "*Stay* with us,
for it is nearly *evening* and the day is almost *over."*
So he went in to *stay* with them.

Speak with amazement. It is through sharing food that the disciples come to know who their companion is.

And it happened that, while he was *with* them at *table*,
he took *bread*, said the *blessing*,
broke it, and *gave* it to them.
With *that* their eyes were *opened* and they *recognized* him,
but he *vanished* from their sight.

Then they said to each other,
"Were not our hearts *burning within* us
while he spoke to us on the *way* and *opened* the *Scriptures*
to us?"

need to understand what the prophets had said about Jesus, as well their recognition of his presence in their lives. It is written for Christians of any age or era, and provides inspiration for embracing an Easter faith.

On the first Easter, two disciples discuss all they have experienced. The evangelist suggests that the events of the crucifixion and death of Jesus were known to the residents of Jerusalem and to the pilgrims who had traveled there for the Passover festival. They proceed to tell Jesus about himself: his deeds in life, their belief in him as a prophet, and his death, which crushed their hopes that he was the Messiah. Even though they knew the story of the empty tomb and of angels saying that Jesus was alive, they did not understand its meaning. They were clearing pondering these matters as they walked along the road.

When Jesus appears to them as a stranger and expounds on the scriptures, they experience their hearts "burning within" them. The disciples' need to have Jesus' mission explained to them suggests how important it is to comprehend the faith in order to believe truly. Education is imperative in order to have informed believers who really understand what they claim. But knowing that the prophets had predicted all that had to happen to the Messiah is not enough for these disciples. It is only through a personal encounter with Jesus that their faith is able to come to life.

There is great excitement in this announcement. Apparently the male disciples, previously unwilling to believe the women, now accept what Peter says.

End on a quiet note.

So they set out *at once* and returned to *Jerusalem*
where they found *gathered* together
the *eleven* and those with them who were *saying*,
"The *Lord* has *truly* been *raised* and has *appeared* to *Simon!*"

Then the *two* recounted
what had *taken place* on the *way*
and how he was made *known* to them in the *breaking* of *bread*.

Although Jesus appears to be continuing through the village, the disciples reach out to him in hospitality, inviting him to join them for a meal. It is this meal encounter that finally opens their eyes. Sharing in something as ordinary as a meal provides a powerful opportunity for enlightenment to occur. It is for this reason that we gather to share the eucharist: to read the scriptures, to teach and understand, and finally to recognize Jesus in the breaking of the bread.

Your task today is made particularly enjoyable by the interesting, exciting story you are privileged to share with your community. Read it with plenty of expression, conveying the diciples' surprise that the stranger did not know about the events that had recently occurred. Express the disciples' disappointment and Jesus' exasperation at their lack of understanding, and finally the joy of the encounter and of the other disciples. Offer the story to your community as a loving challenge to recognize Jesus in its midst, especially in the eucharist and the assembly gathered to share it.

APRIL 30, 2000

2ND SUNDAY OF EASTER

Lectionary #44

READING I Acts 4:32–35

A reading from the Acts of the Apostles.

The opening line sets the stage for what follows. Proclaim it forcefully and with wonder and awe at the unity of this early community.

The community of *believers* was of *one heart* and *mind,*
and *no one* claimed that any of his *possessions* was his *own,*
but they had *everything* in *common.*

Let the power of the Spirit be heard in your words.

With great *power* the apostles bore *witness*
to the *resurrection* of the Lord *Jesus,*
and great *favor* was accorded them *all.*

Emphasize the lack of want due to the practice of sharing possessions.

There was no *needy* person *among* them,
for those who owned *property* or *houses* would *sell* them,
bring the *proceeds* of the *sale,*
and put them at the *feet* of the *apostles,*
and they were distributed to *each* according to *need.*

READING II 1 John 5:1–6

A reading from the first letter of Saint John.

Read these lines very slowly and with dignity, so that the weight of their message can sink in. Pause solemnly after each line.

Beloved:
Everyone who believes that *Jesus* is the *Christ* is *begotten*
by *God,*
and everyone who loves the *Father*
loves also the one *begotten* by him.

READING I Throughout these 50 days of Easter, we read of the experiences of the earliest Christian community, as told in the Acts of the Apostles. Today's passage gives a picture of the communal life shared by those first followers of the risen Lord, indicating the power of the Spirit in their lives. They spoke boldly of their faith in the resurrection; there is here no hint of danger in such a proclamation, as there is in other texts. Through both their accord ("one heart and mind") and their practice of sharing all goods, the community demonstrates its unity and love.

Today's reading is to be proclaimed not only with Easter joy at the success of the gospel but also as a challenge to our consumerist society. Proclaim to your listeners that we too can be moved by the Spirit to share our resources, believing that all people are deserving of care. Read this story not as a simple recollection of what might have been, but as a vision of what is possible if we strive to create a world in which no one has any need.

READING II Just as the first reading spoke of the unity of the early Christians, so also this reading discusses the love that infuses the life of each "child of God" — love for God and for other members of the community. The first letter of John was directed against those causing division within the Christian community. The letter emphasizes the power of love. Today's passage argues for the primacy of faith, which gives victory over the world, assumed to be evil. It is faith demonstrated in love that conquers the world.

In this section words are repeated and the meaning grows in an upward spiral. Stress the linking (repeated) words, such as "God," "children," "commandments," and so on.

In *this* way we *know* that we love the *children* of God
when we love *God* and obey his *commandments.*
For the *love* of God is *this,*
that we *keep* his *commandments.*
And his commandments are not *burdensome,*
for whoever is begotten by *God* conquers the *world.*

The crucial point is the phrase about faith. Pause both before and after it to emphasize its importance.

And the *victory* that conquers the *world* is our *faith.*
Who indeed is the *victor* over the *world*
but the one who *believes* that *Jesus* is the Son of *God?*

This is the one who came through *water* and *blood,* Jesus *Christ,*
not by water *alone,* but by water and *blood.*

Speak this final line slowly and clearly, to allow its significance to be heard by all.

The *Spirit* is the one that *testifies,*
and the *Spirit* is *truth.*

GOSPEL John 20:19–31

A reading from the holy gospel according to John.

The early lines set the stage. They are to be read clearly but without special emphasis.

On the *evening* of that *first* day of the *week,*
when the doors were *locked,* where the *disciples* were,
for *fear* of the Jews,
Jesus came and stood in their *midst*
and said to them, "*Peace* be with *you.*"
When he had *said* this, he showed them his *hands* and his *side.*
The disciples *rejoiced* when they saw the *Lord.*

Speak Jesus' words with gentleness, love and solemnity.

Jesus said to them again, "*Peace* be with *you.*
As the *Father* has sent *me,* so *I* send *you.*"

The author makes clear the content of the faith. The two titles applied to Jesus, "the Christ" and "the Son of God," were titles from the Hebrew tradition. The "Christ" or "Messiah" refers to the anointed one of God, one who would set the world straight on its path toward God. Christians claim that Jesus is the Anointed One. "Son of God" was a title also applied to Israel's kings. In Christian belief, it meant that Jesus was so intimately united with God as to be divine.

But the problem the author addresses is not the interpretation of these titles. The notion that the Christ, the Son of God, was also the Jesus who had walked on the earth and who suffered and died was problematic for some members of the community. The author insists that indeed this is so: Jesus was not simply anointed or infused with the Spirit at his baptism, but also suffered a horrible death.

The last few lines of today's reading allude to Jesus' baptism, during which the Spirit descended on Jesus. The Spirit gives the power to testify to the truth, for the Spirit of God is truth.

This is a powerful passage, proclaiming the importance of faith, love and the working of the Holy Spirit. Proclaim it with boldness and assurance that the one who gives the power to conquer the world is speaking through you.

GOSPEL **Despite Mary Magdalene's encounter with the risen Jesus, today's gospel finds the disciples cowering in fear behind locked doors. This does not deter Jesus from entering and bestowing on them the peace of God and the gift of the Spirit.**

The peace that Jesus gives is not simply the absence of conflict or even an inner

And when he had *said* this, he *breathed* on them and said to them,
"*Receive* the Holy *Spirit.*
Whose *sins* you forgive are *forgiven* them,
and whose sins you *retain* are *retained.*"

Pause before beginning the story about Thomas.
Didymus = DID-ih-muhs
Express the enthusiasm of the disciples here, and the disbelief of Thomas upon hearing their words.

Thomas, called *Didymus,* one of the *Twelve,*
was not *with* them when Jesus *came.*
So the *other* disciples said to him, "We have *seen* the *Lord.*"
But he said to them,
"Unless I see the mark of the *nails* in his *hands*
and put my *finger* into the *nailmarks*
and put my *hand* into his *side,* I will not *believe.*"

Pause again.

Now a week *later* his disciples were *again* inside
and Thomas was *with* them.
Jesus came, although the doors were *locked,*
and stood in their midst and said, "*Peace* be with *you.*"

Again convey Jesus' love and sincerity, and his challenge to Thomas.

Then he said to *Thomas,* "Put your finger *here* and see my *hands,*
and bring *your* hand and put it into my *side,*
and do *not* be *unbelieving,* but *believe.*"

This is one of the high points of today's reading and of the entire gospel. Pause before and after Thomas' words and proclaim them with faith and awe.

Thomas answered and said to him, "My *Lord* and my *God!*"
Jesus said to him, "Have you come to *believe* because you have *seen* me?
Blessed are those who have *not* seen and have *believed.*"

These final lines are a summary of today's reading and of the gospel as a whole.

Now Jesus did many *other* signs in the presence of his *disciples*
that are not *written* in this *book.*
But *these* are written that *you* may come to *believe*
that *Jesus* is the *Christ,* the Son of *God,*
and that through this *belief* you may have *life* in his *name.*

tranquility. It is rather the peace encompassed by the Hebrew term *shalom:* perfect harmony, oneness with God and with neighbor, with the earth — indeed, complete harmony throughout the cosmos. This *shalom* represents salvation; it is what God has always wanted for people.

Jesus then breathes on the disciples, imparting the gift of the Holy Spirit. The Spirit of God conveys power; the disciples to whom it is given (clearly not simply the Twelve) have the power to forgive sins, the opportunity to heal broken relationships, to restore lost *shalom.*

This gift of the Holy Spirit gives the disciples the courage to go forth, sent by Jesus, to proclaim the faith instilled in them by the events of Easter. However, Thomas was absent when Jesus inspired ("breathed into") the others. He demands evidence in order to believe that Jesus is truly alive.

The disciples' doubt in Jesus' resurrection is more strongly emphasized in the other gospels than here. The story of Thomas witnesses to this tradition and the need to affirm the reality of Jesus' risen life. The gospels assert that the disciples did not simply see a vision of Jesus but in fact touched his risen body. The fourth evangelist uses the story of doubt to provide another message as well. Faith is possible for those who have not seen Jesus directly: "Blessed are those who have not seen and yet believe." Finally, the story provides an opportunity for the evangelist to make a claim about Jesus as the Christ; indeed, Thomas' confession is one of the strongest statements of Jesus' divinity in the New Testament.

Inspire your own listeners with this interesting story, so that they too can join in Thomas' profession of faith.

3RD SUNDAY OF EASTER

Lectionary #47

READING I Acts 3:13–15, 17–19

A reading from the Acts of the Apostles.

Raise your voice as you address the crowd. Stress especially the word "glorified."

Peter said to the *people:*
"The God of *Abraham,*
the God of *Isaac,* and the God of *Jacob,*
the God of our *fathers,* has *glorified* his servant *Jesus,*
whom you handed *over* and *denied* in Pilate's *presence*
when he had decided to *release* him.

Emphasize the contrasts between the holy one and the murderer chosen, between "life" and "death."

You *denied* the *Holy* and *Righteous* One
and asked that a *murderer* be released to you.
The author of *life* you put to *death,*
but God *raised* him from the *dead;* of *this* we are *witnesses.*

Speak with a tone of understanding.

"Now I *know,* brothers,
that you acted out of *ignorance,* just as your *leaders* did;
but *God* has thus brought to *fulfillment*
what he had announced *beforehand*
through the mouth of all the *prophets,*
that his *Christ* would *suffer.*

Forgiveness is always available to those who turn to God.

"*Repent,* therefore, and be *converted,*
that your *sins* may be wiped *away.*"

READING I The Acts of the Apostles tells the story of the early days of Christianity, when the first followers of Jesus preached in his name so that many came to believe in him. Throughout the work, the power of the Spirit is evident, inspiring speakers, freeing those unjustly imprisoned, bringing many to see the truth of the disciples' words.

Peter gives the speech in today's selection just after he and John cured a lame man in the Temple. The action caught the attention of a crowd of Jews worshiping in the Temple. Peter roots his message firmly in the Jewish tradition, but challenges the crowd by claiming that they were responsible for Jesus' crucifixion, choosing a murderer (Barabbas) over the giver of life. But God is stronger than any human action.

Peter does not simply accuse his listeners of wrongdoing but points to their ignorance: They do not understand their own prophetic tradition. But now they have the opportunity to turn to God and be forgiven.

Despite adversity, the new movement flourishes. Although Peter and John are arrested following this event, Peter's words are successful, bringing many to faith. His speech is directed not only to the audience in the Temple area, but to us as well.

As you present Peter's words, raise your voice as one giving a speech. Emphasize the contrasts between what the people chose and what they rejected, challenging your own community to know the implications of their choices. Finally, close with a strong call to repentance, with the invitation to begin anew.

READING II Against those who denied that one's actions affected one's relationship with God, the author of

READING II 1 John 2:1–5a

A reading from the first letter of Saint John.

Speak warmly and with encouragement.

My *children*, I am *writing* this to you
so that you may not commit *sin*.
But if anyone *does* sin, we have an *Advocate* with the *Father*,
Jesus *Christ* the *righteous* one.
He is *expiation* for our *sins*,
and not for our sins *only* but for those of the whole *world*.

Pause before continuing.

Emphasize the word "know."

The way we may be sure that we *know* him
is to *keep* his *commandments*.
Those who say, "I *know* him," but do *not* keep
his *commandments*
are *liars*, and the *truth* is not *in* them.
But whoever *keeps* his word,
the *love* of God is truly *perfected* in him.

Pause briefly after "commandments" before delivering the harsh pronouncement of dishonesty.

Stress the contrast between such people and the liars mentioned above.

GOSPEL Luke 24:35–48

A reading from the holy gospel according to Luke.

The *two* disciples recounted what had taken *place* on the *way*,
and how *Jesus* was made *known* to them
in the *breaking* of *bread*.

Pause to recall the story.

While they were still *speaking* about this,
he *stood* in their midst and *said* to them,
"*Peace* be with *you*."

Speak Jesus' words warmly and firmly.

this work insists that knowledge of God is evident through concrete action. In strong language, the author condemns anyone who does not keep God's commands yet claims to "know" God.

The author begins by asserting that the instruction presented here is in an attempt to keep the community from sinning but acknowledges that people do commit sin. Fortunately, Jesus' sacrifice on the cross wipes out all sin, offering the opportunity to be reconciled with God.

There is a timeless quality to these words. We too need to be assured that all is not lost when we act wrongly. At the same time, we need to be challenged to put our words and faith into action. Remind the members of your assembly of the importance of allowing God's love to be evident in their lives through their actions. But assure them as well that all failures are forgiven.

GOSPEL Today's selection picks up the end of the story we read on Easter Sunday afternoon. But in many ways it resembles the story from the gospel of John read last Sunday. Jesus seems to appear out of nowhere, the disciples are afraid, and Jesus convinces them of his identity by showing them his hands and feet. Finally, he interprets the scriptures for them so that they can understand that his suffering and death had been foretold by the prophets and was necessary for the salvation of humanity.

The evangelists knew several stories of appearances by the risen Jesus to his followers. The touching story of Jesus' appearance to two disciples on the road to Emmaus ends with them recognizing Jesus in the breaking of bread. Today's passage also connects the revelation of the risen Christ to a

Convey something of the surprise and fear of the disciples in your tone.

But they were *startled* and *terrified*
and thought that they were seeing a *ghost.*

Jesus is reassuring.

Then he said to them, "*Why* are you *troubled?*
And why do *questions* arise in your *hearts?*
Look at my *hands* and my *feet*, that it is *I myself.*
Touch me and *see*, because a *ghost* does not have *flesh* and *bones*
as you can see *I* have."

And as he *said* this,
he showed them his *hands* and his *feet.*

Again, express the amazement of the disciples, but also stress the word "joy."

While they were still *incredulous* for *joy* and were *amazed*,

Jesus speaks matter-of-factly, but his action is convincing.

he asked them, "Have you *anything* here to *eat?*"
They gave him a piece of baked *fish*;
he took it and *ate* it in *front* of them.

He said to them,
"*These* are my *words* that I *spoke* to you while I was still
with you,
that *everything* written about me in the law of *Moses*
and in the *prophets* and *psalms* must be *fulfilled.*"

Jesus remains a teacher to the end.

Then he *opened* their minds to understand the *Scriptures.*
And he said to them,
"*Thus* it is *written* that the *Christ* would *suffer*
and *rise* from the *dead* on the *third* day
and that *repentance*, for the forgiveness of sins,
would be *preached* in his *name*
to all the *nations*, beginning from *Jerusalem.*

Address this to your listeners.

You are *witnesses* of these *things.*"

meal: Jesus requests and receives something to eat. The risen Jesus is the same—having flesh and bones, requiring food, reminding his followers of his earlier teachings—and yet different. He is not easily recognizable and he can come and go at will, leading some of his followers to assume he is a ghost.

It is clear that resurrection does not simply mean resuscitation. Jesus was transformed, changed. Precisely how he was changed and yet remained the same person is difficult to convey, but all of the resurrection appearances involve some element of confusion or doubt on the part of his followers. However, by speaking with them, eating, holding out his hands for their inspection, Jesus convinces his friends that he is truly alive. He has been changed but has not been defeated.

Before Jesus leaves his followers for the last time in this gospel, he returns to his role of teacher, explaining the scriptures that predicted his own suffering and death. Then he commands his followers to preach that message to all people and to announce the possibility of forgiveness for sin. In today's first reading Peter did precisely as Jesus commanded.

Share this fascinating story with your congregation as another tale of the joy and awe felt by the first followers of Jesus when they realized that he was alive. It is not a "proof" of the resurrection, but a creative retelling of a powerful experience. Invite your listeners to enter into that experience, so that they might join with Jesus' earliest followers in proclaiming the good news of salvation to all the world.

4TH SUNDAY OF EASTER

Lectionary #50

READING I Acts 4:8–12

A reading from the Acts of the Apostles.

Peter is inspired by the Holy Spirit; speak his words with forcefulness.

Peter, filled with the Holy *Spirit*, said:
"*Leaders* of the people and *elders:*
If we are being *examined* today
about a *good deed* done to a *cripple,*
namely, by what *means* he was *saved,*
then all of *you* and all the people of *Israel* should know
that it was in the *name* of Jesus *Christ* the *Nazarene*
whom you *crucified,* whom God *raised* from the *dead;*
in *his* name this man stands *before* you *healed.*

Pause after "today" and again after "cripple."

Take a deep breath after "saved," and continue as though starting a new sentence.

Pause, then allow the next sentence to be set off by itself before continuing.

"*He* is 'the stone *rejected* by you, the *builders,*
which has become the *cornerstone.*'
There is no *salvation* through anyone *else,*
nor is there any *other* name under *heaven*
given to the human *race* by which we are to be *saved.*"

READING I The story proclaimed last Sunday is continued here (see that commentary). Peter's proclamation of Jesus' resurrection roused the anger of the Sadducees, who controlled the Temple and did not accept the idea of the resurrection of the dead. The Jewish leaders arrested Peter and John, then brought them to be examined. Peter's speech in their judicial assembly forms the core of today's reading.

The content of the speech proclaims the importance of the "name" through which the man was healed and by which all people are saved. It also recalls the central tenets of the Christian faith and the Easter events we have recently celebrated. Read with confidence these words of a man at his trial.

READING II The author's assurance that Christians are children of God is encouraging. God, the source of life and greater than anything we can imagine, loves us so much that we are privileged to be called God's children. We share an intimacy with God that we can never deserve and are promised all the good things that belong properly to God.

Although this is good news, the author acknowledges that it is not always recognized, precisely because Jesus' significance is not recognized. But, in the end, the truth will be revealed.

Baptism makes us children of God, but the relationship must be renewed and reclaimed every day. Not everyone wants to accept that the Christian is a child of God. The newly baptized may find that others cannot accept the changes in their lives. And any Christian may become unpopular when trying to live up to high ideals. Popular

READING II 1 John 3:1–2

A reading from the first letter of Saint John.

Beloved:

Speak this with the awe and amazement that it deserves.

See what *love* the Father has *bestowed* on us
that we may be called the *children* of God.
Yet so we *are.*
The *reason* the world does not *know* us
is that it did not know *him.*

Convey the warmth and love of the author to your community.

Beloved, we are *God's* children *now;*
what we *shall* be has not yet been *revealed.*

Close with a sense of hopefulness.

We *do* know that when it *is* revealed we shall be like *him,*
for we shall *see* him as he *is.*

GOSPEL John 10:11–18

A reading from the holy gospel according to John.

Jesus said:

Read these first lines especially slowly and clearly.

"*I* am the good *shepherd.*
A *good* shepherd lays down his *life* for the *sheep.*

Pick up the pace a bit as you describe the flight of the hired hand and the devastation wrought by the wolf.

A *hired* man, who is *not* a shepherd
and whose *sheep* are not his *own,*
sees a *wolf* coming and *leaves* the sheep and runs *away,*
and the wolf *catches* and *scatters* them.
This is because he works for *pay* and has no *concern*
for the *sheep.*

culture tends to turn away from anything that might challenge the status quo.

Convey to your listeners the tremendous love of God, who has adopted us as children. Encourage your community also to remain firm in its commitment to God despite rejection by others.

GOSPEL In ancient Israel, the metaphor of the shepherd was used to describe rulers caring for the people, or to describe the Messiah, or God's love for the people. Even in Jesus' day, when there were fewer shepherds, the image is adopted as an apt means of expressing love and guidance.

Jesus contrasts himself, the good shepherd who acts out of love for the sheep, with the hired hand, who does not have the same commitment. The hired hand probably represents the religious leaders, who act primarily for their own benefit rather than for the good of the people. Jesus, on the other hand, loves his followers so much that he is willing even to lose his life in order to save them. Knowing what happened to Jesus, we see how appropriate the image is.

The next section of the passage discusses the intimate knowledge shared by the shepherd and the sheep and the close relationship between Jesus and the Father. That relationship is unique because of Jesus' willingness to die for the flock. As always in this gospel, Jesus is in complete control. His life is not taken from him; he chooses to give it up.

Offer this passage to your hearers as a reminder of the tremendous love God has for them.

Pause before beginning this line and speak solemnly.

Read this very slowly, with great emphasis.

Taking up his life requires laying it down first.

"*I* am the *good shepherd,*
and I know *mine* and *mine* know *me,*
just as the *Father* knows *me* and *I* know the *Father;*
and I will lay *down* my *life* for the *sheep.*
I have *other* sheep that do *not* belong to this fold.
These also I must lead, and they will *hear* my *voice,*
and there will be *one* flock, *one* shepherd.

"*This* is why the Father *loves* me,
because I lay down my *life* in order to take it *up* again.
No one takes it *from* me, but I lay it *down* on my *own.*
I have *power* to lay it *down,* and *power* to take it up again.
This *command* I have received from my *Father.*"

MAY 21, 2000

5TH SUNDAY OF EASTER

Lectionary #53

READING I Acts 9:26–31

According to Paul himself, he went to Jerusalem three years after his encounter with Jesus on the road to Damascus, but met only with Peter and James.

Barnabas = BAHR-nuh-buhs

Damascus = duh-MAS-kuhs

The Hellenists were Greek-speaking Jews.

Caesarea = sez-uh-REE-uh
Tarsus = TAHR-suhs

Fear here is not cowering fright, but respectful awe.

A reading from the Acts of the Apostles.

When *Saul* arrived in *Jerusalem* he tried to *join* the *disciples*,
but they were all *afraid* of him,
not *believing* that he was a *disciple.*
Then *Barnabas* took charge of him and *brought* him
to the *apostles*,
and he *reported* to them how he had *seen* the *Lord*,
and that he had *spoken* to him,
and how in *Damascus* he had spoken out *boldly* in the name
of *Jesus.*

He moved about *freely* with them in *Jerusalem*,
and spoke out *boldly* in the name of the *Lord.*
He also *spoke* and *debated* with the *Hellenists*,
but they tried to *kill* him.
And when the brothers *learned* of this,
they *took* him down to *Caesarea*
and sent him on his way to *Tarsus.*

The church throughout *all Judea*, *Galilee*, and *Samaria* was
at *peace.*
It was being *built up* and walked in the *fear* of the *Lord*,
and with the *consolation* of the Holy *Spirit* it grew in *numbers.*

READING I Saul is better known as Paul, the name he adopted after becoming a follower of Jesus. He had previously persecuted the Christians but had an encounter with Jesus that changed his life. The Christians in Jerusalem, who had suffered at his hands, were understandably cautious about accepting him, fearing that he had an ulterior motive for joining their group.

In his own writings, Paul suggests that he is far more independent of the Jerusalem church than this account from Acts suggests. He acknowledges that he visited the community in Jerusalem, but insists that nothing was added to his message by the leaders there. Instead, he discusses a controversy regarding the question of Gentile inclusion among the followers of Jesus. The earliest communities were not as harmonious as the author of Acts would have us believe.

Today's reading begins with a story about acceptance of one who has changed. Paul needed to prove himself, to show his credentials as a follower of Jesus, before he was welcomed into the group of disciples. It is human nature to be suspicious of a sudden transformation in a person, especially a transformation as drastic as Paul's. But it can also be painful for the one who is being questioned and shunned. Offer this story as a challenge to your listeners to be open to genuine changes in a person's life and character.

Although this story does not involve dialogue, it is still a tale with plenty of action. Make the tensions come alive for your listeners by expressing them with your voice, from the fears of the Jerusalem disciples in the beginning to the arguments Paul had with Hellenists, and their plot against him. Close in a tone of peacefulness; in the end, the church prospered.

READING II 1 John 3:18–24

A reading from the first letter of Saint John.

Pause briefly after "love."

Children, let us *love* not in *word* or *speech*
but in *deed* and *truth.*
Now *this* is how we shall *know* that we *belong* to the *truth*
and *reassure* our hearts *before* him
in whatever our hearts *condemn,*
for *God* is greater than our *hearts* and knows *everything.*

Beloved, if our *hearts* do *not* condemn us,
we have *confidence* in God
and *receive* from him whatever we *ask*,
because we *keep* his commandments and do what *pleases* him.

Slow down so that you might deliver the commandment to love most effectively.

And his *commandment* is *this:*
we should *believe* in the name of his *Son*, Jesus *Christ*,
and *love* one *another* just as he *commanded* us.

Close in a quiet, reassuring tone.

Those who *keep* his commandments *remain* in him, and *he*
in *them*,
and the way we know that he *remains* in us
is from the *Spirit* he *gave* us.

READING II The gentle passage from First John that forms today's second reading is actually quite demanding. The topic is love, but it is not warm-fuzzy, feel-good affection, but the kind of love that is put into action, as the first sentence makes clear. Claiming to love is not the same as loving; one's heart is most clearly visible through concrete actions.

The author also encourages the reader who is faithful to God to be bold in asking for whatever is needed, assured that God will provide. The confidence that God does so stems from the believer's dedication to keeping God's commandments. Returning to the original topic, the author asserts that God's commandment is precisely to love and believe in Jesus. Although the author does not identify particular deeds with the commandments of God, that does not mean that righteous deeds are irrelevant. Love is concrete, demonstrating itself in a person's behavior. Living in love brings one into an intimate relationship with God, evident in the presence of the Spirit in the believer's life.

Offer this selection to your community as a gentle and encouraging reminder to live according to God's intentions. Read quietly but firmly, addressing your own listeners with the endearing terms "Children" and "Beloved."

GOSPEL The gospel selections for the next several Sundays are taken from the last discourse of Jesus to his disciples in the gospel of John. Jesus speaks at length about himself, his relationship with God, and his relationship with his followers. Most importantly, he discusses his commandment — to love — and the means by which it is demonstrated, the

GOSPEL John 15:1–8

A reading from the holy gospel according to John.

Jesus said to his disciples:
"*I* am the true *vine,* and my *Father* is the *vine* grower.
He takes away every *branch* in me that does not bear *fruit,*
and every one that *does* he *prunes* so that it bears *more* fruit.
You are *already* pruned because of the *word* that I *spoke* to you.

Although pruning sounds painful, it is necessary for a plant to survive.

"*Remain* in me, as *I* remain in *you.*
Just as a *branch* cannot bear fruit on its *own*
unless it remains on the *vine,*
so neither can *you* unless you remain in *me.*
I am the *vine, you* are the *branches.*
Whoever *remains* in me and *I* in him will bear much *fruit,*
because *without* me you can do *nothing.*

If we are not connected to our source of life, we will wither and die.

"Anyone who does *not* remain in me
will be thrown *out* like a branch and *wither;*
people will *gather* them and *throw* them into a *fire*
and they will be *burned.*

If we are faithful, we can be confident that God will care for all our needs.

"If *you* remain in *me* and my *words* remain in *you,*
ask for whatever you *want* and it will be *done* for you.
By *this* is my Father *glorified,*
that you *bear* much *fruit* and become my *disciples.*"

The process of becoming a disciple is similar to that of bearing fruit; it takes time. Speak encouragingly.

willingness of one person to "lay down one's life for one's friends." Today's reading uses agricultural imagery to describe what the second reading calls "remaining in"; Jesus says he is the vine from which the branches, his followers, receive life.

The image of God as a gardener is a familiar one from the Hebrew Scriptures; now Jesus claims to be the true vine, from which God prunes away unproductive branches. He asserts that his disciples are fruit-bearing branches and encourages them to continue to live in him. The relationship is intimate and essential; the branches must be united with the vine or else they will wither and die. In the same way, the follower of Jesus must remain united with him in order to continue to thrive. The passage closes with Jesus asserting that his followers give glory to God when they are fruitful.

Jesus does not specify in today's selection precisely what he means by bearing fruit. But we know intuitively—and because we know that Jesus' command to love will follow—that he is suggesting the actions of the moral life.

Reflect on this passage before reading it in front of the assembly. The more closely you are united with the true vine, the more effectively you will be able to encourage your listeners to cling to the source of love and life. Offer the passage as an encouragement to nurture daily a friendship with Christ, knowing that such a relationship is not only essential but gives glory to God.

6TH SUNDAY OF EASTER

Lectionary #56

READING I Acts 10:25–26, 34–35, 44–48

A reading from the Acts of the Apostles.

Cornelius = kohr-NEEL-yuhs

When Peter entered, *Cornelius met* him
and, falling at his *feet*, paid him *homage.*
Peter, however, raised him *up*, saying,
"Get *up*. I *myself* am also a human *being.*"

Speak Peter's words to Cornelius firmly but kindly.

Then Peter proceeded to *speak* and said,
"In *truth*, I see that *God* shows no *partiality.*
Rather, in every *nation* whoever *fears* him and acts *uprightly*
is *acceptable* to him."

While Peter was still *speaking* these things,
the *Holy Spirit* fell upon *all* who were *listening* to the word.
The *circumcised* believers who had *accompanied* Peter
were *astounded* that the gift of the Holy *Spirit*
should have been poured out on the *Gentiles also*,
for they could *hear* them speaking in *tongues* and
glorifying *God.*

Let their astonishment be heard. They have apparently not yet come to accept that Gentiles are heirs to God's promises just as the Jews are.

Then Peter responded,
"Can anyone *withhold* the water for *baptizing* these people,
who have received the Holy *Spirit* even as *we* have?"
He ordered them to be *baptized* in the name of Jesus *Christ.*

Peter clearly expects no one to deny that the new believers should be baptized.

Dioceses in the United States are able to decide by region to move the celebration of the Ascension of the Lord from this Thursday, June 1, to next Sunday, June 4. In that case, the second reading and the gospel from the Seventh Sunday of Easter may be read today. Check with your liturgy coordinator or pastor to find out which readings will be used today.

READING I The visit of Peter to the house of Cornelius was told in part on Easter Sunday (see that discussion). Today's selection emphasizes the reception of the Holy Spirit by those who were previously considered too impure to be included among the believers of Jesus.

Peter, who was staunchly opposed to associating with Gentiles or risking any action that might make him unclean, had a vision in which God revealed to him that his understanding of purity was in error. As a result, Peter realized that God did not reject those who were not Jewish, but welcomed them as followers of Jesus, together with the original Jewish disciples.

In today's selection, Peter acts on his vision and enters the house of a Gentile, claiming that God accepts anyone who displays the proper reverence. As he speaks, the Holy Spirit comes down upon the Gentile believers, amazing the Jews who were present, including Peter. Peter recognizes God's action and asks for baptism for the family of Cornelius.

Since most Christians today are Gentiles, the reading's precise concern is foreign to us. However, we know well the struggles we face to include all people. This

READING II 1 John 4:7–10

A reading from the first letter of Saint John.

Speak affectionately to your community.

Beloved, let us *love* one *another*,
because *love* is of *God*;
everyone who *loves* is *begotten* by God and *knows* God.
Whoever is *without* love does *not* know God, for *God* is *love.*

Speak "God is love" slowly and with great emphasis, carefully enunciating each.

In *this* way the love of God was *revealed* to us:
God sent his only *Son* into the *world*
so that we might have *life* through him.
In *this* is *love:*
not that *we* have loved *God*, but that *he* loved *us*
and sent his *Son* as *expiation* for our *sins.*

Read this last sentence firmly, but reassuringly.

text is an exciting one for Sunday proclamation, filled as it is with a supernatural event and a stirring speech. Read it with plenty of enthusiasm, expressing the reverence of Cornelius, the confidence of Peter and the astonishment of the Jewish Christians.

READING II **We continue to read through the first letter of John during the Easter season, with the letter's beautiful description of the Christian life grounded in love. Today's passage provides the foundation for everything else that is said about love in this treatise, for it insists that the origin of love is God. Indeed, love does not only come from God; God, in essence, is love.**

God bestows love on us, in ways more profound than we can imagine, simply because God chooses to do so. For the Christian to love another is to participate in the creative flow of God's love. Knowing God involves knowing this deep love, and true loving can be done only in relationship to God.

The most profound evidence of God's love is that God sent the Son into the world to give us life by removing all taint of sin. This is what love is. All we can do is respond in heartfelt gratitude, loving one another and loving God, as God first loved us.

Offer this important selection to your assembly as a sincere reminder that God is the source of all good things, including love. You are reminding your listeners of the evidence for God's love, which we are celebrating this Easter season: Christ's death and vindication. Speak with genuine affection for the members of your community, and encourage them to share the love that has been so freely poured out on them.

GOSPEL John 15:9–17

A reading from the holy gospel according to John.

There is a natural rhythm to these lines, created by the contrasts presented. Try not to become sing-song.

Jesus said to his disciples:
"As the *Father* loves *me*, so *I* also love *you.*
Remain in my *love.*
If you *keep* my *commandments*, you will *remain* in my love,
just as *I* have kept my *Father's* commandments
and *remain* in *his* love.

"I have *told* you this so that my *joy* may be in *you*
and *your* joy might be *complete.*
This is my *commandment: love* one another as *I* love *you.*
No one has greater love than *this*,
to *lay* down one's *life* for one's *friends.*

Speak this key sentence slowly. Because it is so familiar, it is easy to fall into a familiar cadence and rush through it. Practice it carefully, so that you can present it to your hearers in a fresh way.

"*You* are my friends if you do what I *command* you.
I no longer call you *slaves*,
because a *slave* does not know what his *master* is *doing.*
I have called you *friends*,
because I have told you *everything* I have heard
from my *Father.*

"It was not *you* who chose *me*, but *I* who chose *you*
and *appointed* you to go and bear *fruit* that will *remain*,
so that whatever you ask the *Father* in my *name* he may
give you.
This I *command* you: *love* one *another.*"

GOSPEL Following directly after last Sunday's gospel reading about the vine and the branches, today's passage continues the last discourse of Jesus to his disciples in the gospel of John. Jesus expounds on last week's theme of bearing fruit by describing what he means. As in the second reading, the meaning is at once both simple and profoundly demanding: Jesus gives the command to love.

But first Jesus makes it clear that the Father has first loved him and he loves his followers. As in the second reading, God's love comes first; we are asked to recognize it, accept it and share it. Indeed, Jesus says to live in his love, suggesting a close, intimate bond between the one who gives love and the recipient of that love.

Love is not simply a feeling but is of moral consequence, as is clear when Jesus links living in his love with keeping his commandments. But the commandment he gives circles back to its source: Living in Jesus' love involves loving others. The demand of love is evident in Jesus' claim that laying down one's life for one's friends is the greatest expression of love. This is what Jesus has done and what we proclaim with awe and gratitude. The declaration is both self-descriptive and a command for us to follow.

We are to love others, being willing to offer our lives as Jesus has done. And Jesus has chosen his followers; we did not choose him. Our responsibility is to respond, to offer what has been lovingly bestowed on us to others.

In order to do this, the follower of Jesus must be deeply engaged with him. Read Jesus' words in such a way that they convey the intimacy that God desires, as well as the joy that such love brings.

JUNE 1, 2000

ASCENSION OF THE LORD

Lectionary #58

READING I Acts 1:1–11

A reading from the Acts of the Apostles.

Theophilus = thee-OF-uh-luhs
The first book was the gospel of Luke, also written by this author. Theophilus is a Greek name that means "lover of God."

In the *first* book, *Theophilus,*
I dealt with *all* that Jesus *did* and *taught*
until the *day* he was taken *up,*
after giving *instructions* through the Holy *Spirit*
to the *apostles* whom he had *chosen.*
He presented himself *alive* to them
by many *proofs* after he had *suffered,*
appearing to them during *forty days*
and *speaking* about the *kingdom* of *God.*

While *meeting* with *them,*
he enjoined them *not* to depart from *Jerusalem,*
but to *wait* for "the *promise* of the *Father*
about which you have heard me *speak;*
for *John* baptized with *water,*
but in a *few* days *you* will be baptized with the *Holy Spirit."*

When they had gathered *together* they *asked* him,
"Lord, are you at *this* time going to restore
the *kingdom* to *Israel?"*
He answered them, "It is *not* for you to *know* the *times*
or *seasons*
that the *Father* has *established* by his own *authority.*

These are important words. Speak this sentence slowly and forcefully.

But you will receive *power* when the Holy *Spirit* comes *upon* you,
and *you* will be my *witnesses* in *Jerusalem,*

Dioceses in the United States are able to decide by region to move the celebration of the Ascension of the Lord from today to Sunday, June 4, in which case today's readings are used.

READING I **The opening section of the Acts of the Apostles tells of Jesus' presence with the disciples after the resurrection, and of his ascension into heaven. Because he is said to have appeared among them for 40 days, this feast has been fixed on the calendar 40 days after Easter. In biblical terminology, 40 days indicates a considerable length of time; it is not to be taken at face value. In fact, this dating contradicts the gospel of Luke, to which the Acts of the Apostles is a sequel. In the gospel, Jesus ascends to heaven on the evening of Easter Sunday.**

The events described in the opening chapters of the Acts of the Apostles (including the ascension and Pentecost) are not told as historical occurrences. Rather, the author is creatively making claims of faith about Jesus and his followers. The story of the ascension conveys that Jesus is glorified, that his rightful home is with God in heaven. Similarly, the story of Pentecost describes the disciples' experience of the Spirit of God in their lives.

What is important is that the 50 days from Easter to Pentecost are all included in the Easter season. This is the time when we ritually celebrate for an extended period the victory of Christ over death, his vindication

The Acts of the Apostles is written as a fulfillment of this prediction. The gospel is successful first in Jerusalem and its environment, and it eventually reaches Rome, understood by a first-century Palestinian to be the end of the earth.

throughout *Judea* and *Samaria*,
and to the *ends* of the *earth*."

When he had *said* this, as they were looking *on*,
he was lifted *up*, and a *cloud* took him from their *sight*.
While they were looking *intently* at the sky as he was *going*,
suddenly two men dressed in white *garments*
stood *beside* them.

The expectation that Jesus would soon return on the clouds of heaven was strong in the early years of Christianity.

They said, "Men of *Galilee*,
why are you standing there looking at the *sky*?
This *Jesus* who has been taken *up* from you into *heaven*
will *return* in the same way as you have seen him
going into *heaven*."

READING II Ephesians 4:1–13

A reading from the letter of Saint Paul to the Ephesians

Brothers and sisters,
I, a *prisoner* for the *Lord*,
urge you to live in a manner *worthy* of the *call*
you have *received*,

Read each emphasized word quietly but clearly.

with all *humility* and *gentleness*, with *patience*,
bearing with one another through *love*,
striving to preserve the *unity* of the *spirit*
through the *bond* of *peace*:

Slow down and stress each word that indicates unity.

one body and *one* Spirit,
as you were also called to the one *hope* of your *call*;
one Lord, *one faith*, *one baptism*;
one *God* and *Father* of *all*,
who is *over* all and *through* all and *in* all.

after being executed, his exaltation and his continued presence, through the working of the Holy Spirit, with his followers on earth. The Easter season is one extended feast, although we concentrate on different aspects of Christ's triumph at different times during the season.

Today's reading is an awe-inspiring account of Jesus' exaltation to his rightful place with God. As a good teacher, he instructs his followers right to the end, and closes by giving them a commission to go forth in his name. In a manner similar to the women's discovery of the empty tomb, two men (presumably angels) appear to the apostles and tell them where Jesus is. Because they have yet to receive the gift of the Holy Spirit, the disciples remain confused, even after all that they have seen and heard.

There are several "voices" to adopt in the reading of this selection. It opens on a historical note, summarizing the gospel; this can be read in a straightforward manner. Raise your voice to proclaim the words of Jesus to his followers. Their question to him is asked innocently enough, ignorant though it may sound to us. Finally, the ascension itself is exciting, and the proclamation of the angels should be given due emphasis. Throughout, your goal is to make real to your listeners the great majesty of Jesus, now enthroned in heaven.

But *grace* was given to *each* of us
according to the *measure* of Christ's *gift*.
Therefore, it says:
"He *ascended* on high and took *prisoners captive*;
he gave *gifts* to *men*."

What does "he *ascended*" mean except that he also *descended*
into the lower *regions* of the *earth*?
The one who *descended* is also the one who *ascended*
far above all the *heavens*,
that he might *fill* all *things*.

Give each ministry due attention and emphasis, stressing that all are for the building up of the community.

And he gave some as *apostles*, others as *prophets*,
others as *evangelists*, others as *pastors* and *teachers*,
to *equip* the holy ones for the work of *ministry*,
for *building up* the body of *Christ*,
until we *all* attain to the *unity* of *faith*
and *knowledge* of the *Son* of *God*, to *mature* to manhood,
to the extent of the *full* stature of *Christ*.

[Shorter: Ephesians 4:1–7, 11–13]

Or:

There is a choice of second readings today. Speak with the liturgy coordinator or pastor to find out which reading will be used.

READING II **EPHESIANS 4:1–13. This reading from the letter to the Ephesians was chosen for today because of its reference to Christ's ascension. It is also a beautiful discussion of the unity we share because of our common faith, and the integrity and importance of each Christian ministry.**

The author's concern in these verses is proper conduct for those in the Lord, but the instruction is grounded always in foundational Christian beliefs. All Christians are initiated into the same faith, for there is one Lord over all. There are many and varied gifts given to individuals, but one Spirit who inspires each believer. The various ministries have as their common goal to build up the community, the body of Christ, until all are drawn together in unity of faith.

Inserted into the instruction on Christian gifts is a discussion of how Christ ascended into heaven and how he came down to the "lower regions" of earth. This phrase has been interpreted in different ways: to refer to the Incarnation, to the reality of Christ's death, or to the tradition of Christ freeing the dead spirits trapped in hell. Most likely the reference is to the reality of Jesus' death, and to his triumph over death.

As you share these words with the members of your assembly, speak with love and encouragement. Inspire your listeners to strive for the unity of faith that is upheld here,

READING II Ephesians 1:17–23

A reading from the letter of Saint Paul to the Ephesians.

This is a prayer; read it as such.

Brothers and sisters:
May the *God* of our Lord Jesus *Christ*, the Father of *glory*,
give you a Spirit of *wisdom* and *revelation*
resulting in *knowledge* of him.
May the *eyes* of your *hearts* be *enlightened*,
that you may *know* what is the *hope* that belongs to his *call*,
what are the *riches* of *glory*
in his *inheritance* among the *holy* ones,
and what is the surpassing *greatness* of his *power*
for us who *believe*,
in accord with the *exercise* of his great *might*,
which he *worked* in *Christ*,
raising him from the *dead*
and *seating* him at his *right hand* in the *heavens*,
far above every *principality*, *authority*, *power*, and *dominion*,
and every *name* that is *named*
not only in *this* age but also in the one to *come*.

The author prays for the reader to know three things: the hope of God's call, the riches of glory and the greatness of God's power. Plan your phrasing in order to make these three points stand out.

Steadily raise your voice from here until the end.

Christ has conquered all the heavenly powers that were believed to hold sway over the universe.

And he put *all* things *beneath* his *feet*
and gave him as *head* over *all* things to the *church*,
which is his *body*,
the *fullness* of the one who *fills* all things in every *way*.

The Christian church shares in Christ's dominion over all things.

always recognizing what really matters, despite individual differences. Finally, draw attention to the many roles available to followers of Christ, encouraging your community to value the skills of every member.

EPHESIANS 1:17–23. The author of Ephesians prays for the community in much the same way that you can offer to God your hopes and prayers for your community before you read this selection. The enlightenment for which you pray is that of knowing God better and receiving all that God has to give, including God's awesome power. Mention of that power leads the author to utter a prayer of praise to the glorified Christ.

The power of God was manifest most fully in raising Christ from the dead and exalting him. He is honored to such a degree that he rules over every power; he is worthy of every honorary title imaginable.

Raise your voice to sing your praises with those of the author. Slow down in the second half of the reading, and speak forcefully and with expression.

GOSPEL Today's gospel selection was added on to the original abrupt ending of Mark in order to correspond with the endings of the other gospels. Jesus commissions his followers and claims that certain signs will confirm the true believer. The glorification of Jesus in heaven is briefly recorded. Most striking are the claims about spectacular deeds that believers can do; this is an exaggerated reference to the power of the Spirit that infuses Christians.

Emphasize to your hearers the commissioning by Jesus. Do not draw particular

GOSPEL Mark 16:15–20

A reading from the holy gospel according to Mark.

Jesus said to his *disciples:*
"*Go* into the whole *world*
and proclaim the *gospel* to every *creature.*

This is our mission as well as that of the eleven.

Whoever *believes* and is *baptized* will be *saved;*
whoever does *not* believe will be *condemned.*
These *signs* will accompany those who *believe:*
in my *name* they will drive out *demons,*
they will speak new *languages.*
They will pick up *serpents* with their *hands,*
and if they *drink* any deadly *thing,* it will not *harm* them.
They will lay *hands* on the *sick,* and they will *recover."*

Emphasize this; it is the reason we choose this reading for today.

So then the Lord *Jesus,* after he spoke to *them,*
was taken *up* into *heaven*
and took his *seat* at the *right hand* of *God.*
But they went *forth* and preached *everywhere,*
while the Lord *worked* with them
and *confirmed* the word through accompanying *signs.*

Speak with a joyful, satisfied air.

attention to the "signs," but read them matter-of-factly as evidence of the belief that God's power is greater than any opposing force or natural danger. Conclude with a satisfied tone; proclamation of the gospel has prospered under the Lord's guidance.

7TH SUNDAY OF EASTER

Lectionary #60

READING I Acts 1:15–17, 20a, 20c–26

A reading from the Acts of the Apostles.

Peter stood up in the *midst* of the *brothers*
—there was a group of about one *hundred* and twenty *persons*
in the one *place*.
He said, "My *brothers*,
the *Scripture* had to be *fulfilled*
which the Holy Spirit spoke *beforehand*
through the mouth of *David*, concerning *Judas*,
who was the *guide* for those who *arrested* Jesus.
He was numbered *among* us
and was allotted a *share* in this *ministry*.

For the author of Luke-Acts, it is especially important to tie everything in Jesus' life and the life of the early Christian community to earlier prophecy.

"For it is *written* in the Book of *Psalms:*
'May *another* take his *office*.'

"Therefore, it is *necessary* that *one* of the men
who *accompanied* us the *whole* time
the Lord Jesus *came* and *went among* us,
beginning from the baptism of *John*
until the *day* on which he was taken *up* from us,
become with us a *witness* to his *resurrection*."

So they proposed *two*, *Judas* called *Barsabbas*,
who was also known as *Justus*, and *Matthias*.

Barsabbas = bahr-SAB-uhs
Justus = JUS-tuhs
Matthias = muh-THĪ-uhs

Dioceses in the United States are able to decide by region to move the celebration of the Ascension of the Lord from Thursday, June 1, to today. In that case, the readings of the Ascension replace the readings of the Seventh Sunday of Easter.

READING I Because this Sunday falls between the two feasts celebrating the ascension of Jesus and the coming of the Spirit at Pentecost, we interrupt our progression through Acts to hear about a decision made in the time between those two events, the decision to choose another apostle to take Judas' place among the Twelve. Peter emerges as the leader of the small community, and he will remain the principal figure throughout the first part of Acts.

It is important to the narrator of this account to maintain the number twelve for the core of Jesus' followers. The author of Luke-Acts was probably a Gentile Christian, but one who had been deeply interested in the history and traditions of Judaism before coming to Christianity; he retains that interest and commitment. The author keeps the early Christian movement rooted in Judaism.

The person chosen to replace Judas needed to be someone who had known Jesus personally and had been part of the group from the start. By choosing such a person, the continuity between the historical Jesus and the growing community is retained. Matthias could join with the eleven in providing eyewitness testimony of all the events that had taken place. He becomes one of the twelve "pillars" upon which the church is built.

Offer this reading to your community as a straightforward narrative of one of the events in the early church.

Speak sincerely, inspiring your listeners to examine their own hearts.

Lots were cast by shaking stones of different colors in a container until one fell out. God, not fate, was understood to determine how the lots fell.

Then they prayed,
"*You*, Lord, who know the *hearts* of *all*,
show which *one* of these two you have *chosen*
to take the *place* in this apostolic *ministry*
from which *Judas* turned *away* to go to his *own* place."
Then they gave *lots* to them, and the *lot* fell upon *Matthias*,
and he was *counted* with the eleven *apostles*.

READING II 1 John 4:11–16

A reading from the first letter of Saint John.

The source of and inspiration for Christian love is the love of God. Stress how greatly God loves us.

Beloved, if God *so loved* us,
we *also* must love one *another*.

God is present when we love one another.

No one has ever *seen* God.
Yet, if we *love* one *another*, God *remains* in us,
and his *love* is brought to *perfection* in us.

Read this line as a comment on the certainty of our faith.

This is how we know that we *remain* in him and *he* in *us*,
that he has *given* us of his *Spirit*.
Moreover, we have *seen* and *testify*
that the *Father* sent his *Son* as *savior* of the *world*.

Confessing Jesus as the Son of God allows one to abide in God.

Whoever acknowledges that *Jesus* is the *Son* of *God*,
God *remains* in him and *he* in *God*.
We have come to *know* and to *believe* in the love God *has* for us.

End the reading with this gentle but firm summary statement.

God is *love*, and whoever *remains* in love
remains in *God* and *God* in *him*.

READING II This passage is the last in a series of selections from the first letter of John read this Easter season. The topic is love: God's love for humans, made known by the sending of Jesus into the world to bear human sin and to give us life; and our love for God and for one another. Continuing the theme from last Sunday, the author begins today by reminding us of the deep love of God and encourages the community to share that love with one another.

Since no one can actually see and observe God, it becomes necessary for the believer to make God's presence known through the concrete reality of human behavior. Because God is love, God is present when humans love one another. When we do so, God lives within us. The proof of this is the presence of the Holy Spirit in the Christian's life.

The final section of today's reading discusses faith in Jesus as the Son of God. Jesus is the proof of God's love, so that believing in Jesus is equated with knowing God's love. Those who believe in Jesus, just as those who live in love, abide in God. The image is of a divine heart so huge that it encompasses all people, and allows them to experience the love that originates from God.

Reflect on this passage before attempting to proclaim it to your assembly. Allow the depth of God's love to fill your heart. Then attempt to convey that reality to your listeners, instilling also the burning desire to respond faithfully in love to the greatest gift that has ever been given.

GOSPEL Near the end of Jesus' last meal with his disciples as recounted in the gospel of John, he utters a

GOSPEL John 17:11b–19

A reading from the holy gospel according to John.

Read this entire selection as the solemn prayer of one who is saying good-bye to his friends.

Lifting up his eyes to *heaven*, Jesus *prayed*, saying:
"Holy *Father*, *keep* them in your *name* that you have *given* me,
so that they may be *one* just as *we* are *one*.
When I was *with* them I *protected* them in your *name* that you *gave* me,
and I *guarded* them, and *none* of them was *lost*
except the son of *destruction*,
in order that the *Scripture* might be *fulfilled*.

Even Judas' betrayal was understood to be predicted by scripture.

"But *now* I am coming to *you*.
I *speak* this in the *world*
so that they may *share* my *joy completely*.
I gave them your *word*, and the world *hated* them,
because they do not *belong* to the *world*
any more than *I* belong to the *world*.
I do not *ask* that you take them *out* of the world
but that you *keep* them from the *evil* one.

Jesus' followers share many things with Jesus, including a sense of alienation from the world around them.

"They do not *belong* to the world
any more than *I* belong to the *world*.
Consecrate them in the *truth*. Your *word* is *truth*.
As you *sent* me into the *world*,
so I sent *them* into the *world*.
And I consecrate *myself* for *them*,
so that they *also* may be *consecrated* in *truth*."

Despite not belonging in the world, Jesus' disciples have a task, a mission to accomplish. For this they must remain in the world.

prayer for his own glorification (in this gospel, identical to his crucifixion) and for his disciples. Some earlier themes return. Jesus again depicts himself as a shepherd, and he speaks of his oneness with the Father and of the opposition his disciples will face. There is a tone of anguish in his words, as can be expected of one about to part from his friends and go to his death. But despite everything, Jesus is in control.

Jesus prays that God will continue to watch over his disciples after his death, as he himself had been keeping watch. In keeping with the strong contrasts of this gospel, Jesus distinguishes between his followers and "the world," a world in which they live but to which they do not belong, a world that hates and rejects them, a world in which they are destined to stay, filled though it is with evil. For this reason Jesus prays that God may protect them. They will be made holy in truth, just as Jesus himself is holy.

Many cultures of the ancient Near East thought good and evil forces battled — on fields both earthly and celestial — for control of the world. The key was to align oneself with the correct forces: with light against darkness, with truth against error. The gospel of John comes down firmly on the side of light, life and truth.

Since our worldview is generally more benign than this, it might be tempting to reject such images altogether and thus lose some of the force of Jesus' prayer today. But we also know that there are forces of violence, greed, manipulation and apathy that threaten our own well-being and that of those we love.

PENTECOST VIGIL

Lectionary #62

READING I Genesis 11:1–9

A reading from the book of Genesis.

The *whole* world spoke the same *language*, using the
same *words*.
While the people were *migrating* in the *east*,
they came upon a *valley* in the land of *Shinar* and *settled* there.
They *said* to one another,
"*Come*, let us mold *bricks* and harden them with *fire*."
They used *bricks* for *stone*, and *bitumen* for *mortar*.

Shinar = SHĪ-nahr

bitumen = bih-TYOO-m*n

Then they said, "*Come*, let us *build* ourselves a *city*
and a *tower* with its top in the *sky*,
and so make a *name* for ourselves;
otherwise we shall be *scattered* all over the *earth*."

The sin is threefold: building a tower to the sky; seeking a great reputation; and remaining in one place.

The LORD came down to *see* the *city* and the *tower*
that the people had *built*.
Then the LORD said: "If *now*, while they are *one* people,
all speaking the *same* language,
they have started to do *this*,
nothing will later stop them from doing
whatever they *presume* to *do*.
Let us then go *down* there and *confuse* their language,
so that one will not *understand* what another *says*."

God has to nip the presumptuous actions of the people in the bud, or they might make even more outrageous claims for themselves.

Thus the LORD *scattered* them from there *all* over the *earth*,
and they *stopped* building the *city*.

There is a choice of first readings today. Speak with the liturgy coordinator or pastor to find out which reading will be used.

READING I GENESIS. The story of the Tower of Babel is a story about human sin and alienation from God. The writer recalls a time at the origins of human history when human relations were not characterized by division, and when there was no enmity between the divine and the human realms. But the writer's own experience is of a world inhabited by many peoples who cannot communicate with one another and who are scattered widely over the earth. Today's reading explains what caused the change to occur.

The story of the Tower of Babel follows the tale of Noah, who was saved from the waters of the flood with his family because of his devotion to God. But they were not without sin, as Genesis makes clear. Noah's descendants build a city and a tower for the express purpose of "making a name" (that is, gaining fame) for themselves, and to remain together against the command of God. The result was disastrous and their hope for unity destroyed; God scattered them and they ceased to speak the same language.

At the root of the crime committed by the people was a desire to go beyond human limitations, to make themselves as great as God (the phrase "to make a name" is reserved for actions of a ruler or of God).

Babel = BAB-*l
There is a play on words here between the name of the city and the Hebrew word for "confuse." It is somewhat like the English play on the words "Babel" and "babble."

That is why it was called *Babel,*
because *there* the LORD confused the *speech* of all the *world.*
It was from *that* place that he *scattered* them all over the *earth.*

Or:

READING I Exodus 19:3–8a, 16–20b

A reading from the book of Exodus.

Speak these words solemnly, but do not try to represent God by using a deep, booming voice.

Lighten your voice as you read this beautiful image of how God rescued the people.

Moses went up the *mountain* to *God.*
Then the LORD *called* to him and said,
"*Thus* shall you say to the house of *Jacob;*
tell the *Israelites:*
You have *seen* for *yourselves* how I treated the *Egyptians*
and how I bore you *up* on *eagle* wings
and *brought* you here to *myself.*

"Therefore, if you *hearken* to my voice and *keep* my covenant,
you shall be my *special* possession,
dearer to me than *all* other *people,*
though *all* the earth is *mine.*
You shall *be* to me a kingdom of *priests,* a *holy* nation.
That is what you must tell the *Israelites.*"

Pause.

Proclaim this slowly, so that your listeners can join in silently. Pause.

So *Moses* went and summoned the *elders* of the *people.*
When he set *before* them
all that the LORD had *ordered* him to *tell* them,
the people all answered *together,*
"*Everything* the LORD has said, we will *do.*"

We know also that Near Eastern cultures built towers to the heavens in order to enter the realm of the gods. God acts to punish the pride of the humans and to keep them in their proper realm. As a result, they resume moving into the land as God had commanded, but without the ability to communicate with each other. Division and lack of understanding result.

Pentecost provides a reversal of the Babel story. At Pentecost, the misunderstandings that occur because of language differences are nullified; the Spirit opens the hearers to understand Jesus' disciples speaking in their own languages. Unity is restored, but it is a unity under God's rule, not one that threatens to usurp divine authority.

Proclaim the reading with expression, communicating the arrogance of the people and the determination of God to correct their waywardness. Inspire your own community to seek unity and open communication, always acting under divine guidance.

EXODUS. God's presence is sometimes revealed in spectacular ways, as the appearance of the Holy Spirit on Pentecost will demonstrate. In that story, there is a sound like rushing wind, and tongues as of fire appear over the believers' heads. In today's reading God's direct presence is also signaled by fire and smoke, by a loud trumpet and by the mountain shaking. Although it is true that God is always present, we can sometimes forget this truth. The dramatic

God's presence is announced unmistakably. Speak with awe in your voice.

On the morning of the third *day*
there were peals of *thunder* and *lightning*,
and a heavy *cloud* over the *mountain*,
and a very loud *trumpet* blast,
so that all the *people* in the camp *trembled*.
But *Moses* led the people out of the camp to meet *God*,
and they *stationed* themselves at the foot of the *mountain*.

These images convey the awesome nature of God.

Mount *Sinai* was all wrapped in *smoke*,
for the *LORD* came down upon it in *fire*.
The smoke *rose* from it as though from a *furnace*,
and the whole *mountain* trembled *violently*.
The *trumpet* blast grew *louder* and *louder*,
while Moses was *speaking*,
and *God* answering him with *thunder*.

Close quietly, with a sense of finality.

When the LORD came *down* to the top of Mount *Sinai*,
he summoned *Moses* to the top of the *mountain*.

Or:

READING I Ezekiel 37:1–14

A reading from the book of the prophet Ezekiel.

The image is striking: God picks up Ezekiel and moves him into the valley.

The *hand* of the LORD came *upon* me,
and he led me out in the *spirit* of the *LORD*
and set me in the *center* of the *plain*,
which was now *filled* with *bones*.

Imagine a scene of utter destruction in the middle of the desert. Try to convey this image to your listeners.

He made me *walk* among the bones in every *direction*
so that I saw how *many* they were on the *surface* of the *plain*.

signs described in these readings make God's presence unmistakable, both to those who experienced them and to us.

The present passage details part of Israel's encounter with God at Sinai. Immediately following this passage is the giving of the Ten Commandments by God. It is especially appropriate to hear this s tory today, since the feast of Pentecost (or Shavuot, the Feast of Weeks) is celebrated by our Jewish friends in memory of the giving of the Law at Sinai. For both Christians and Jews, Pentecost is a time to recall the establishment of a covenant with God. But covenant also involves accepting responsibility. The Israelites were to obey God and keep the Law, while the first Christians were to go forth under the guidance of the Spirit and preach to all the good news of salvation in Christ.

Israel is reminded of all that God has already done for it before being asked to keep God's covenant. The people respond with a statement of profound commitment: "All that the Lord has said, we will do." This is our inspiration today, as we renew our pledge of faith.

The passage you are reading contains plenty of drama. Summon up your skills to convey the great love of God for the people in choosing them, the positive response on the part of Israel, and the magnificence of God evident in the signs. Challenge your listeners as well to proclaim with Israel a willingness to obey and serve God in whatever is asked of them.

EZEKIEL. Ezekiel's vision of dry bones was also used on the Fifth Sunday of Lent, Year A (see that commentary). Ezekiel wrote

How *dry* they were!
He *asked* me:
Son of *man*, can these *bones* come to life?
I answered, "Lord GOD, you *alone* know that."

Then he said to me:
Prophesy over these bones, and say to them:
Dry *bones*, *hear* the *word* of the *LORD!*
Thus says the Lord GOD to these *bones:*
See! I will bring *spirit* into you, that you may come to *life.*
I will put sinews *upon* you, make *flesh* grow *over* you,
cover you with *skin*, and put *spirit* in you
so that you may come to *life* and *know* that *I* am the *LORD.*

Lift your voice and speak more loudly these words. They are a call to newness of life.

sinews = SIN-yooz

The purpose of the bones coming to life is to acknowledge God. This is our purpose too, just as it was for Israel.

I, Ezekiel, *prophesied* as I had been *told*,
and even as I was *prophesying* I heard a *noise;*
it was a *rattling* as the bones came *together*, *bone* joining *bone.*
I saw the *sinews* and the *flesh* come *upon* them,
and the *skin* cover them, but there was no *spirit* in them.

Then the LORD *said* to me:
Prophesy to the *spirit*, *prophesy*, son of man,
and *say* to the spirit: *Thus* says the Lord *GOD:*
From the four winds *come*, O spirit,
and *breathe* into these *slain* that they may come to *life.*
I *prophesied* as he *told* me, and the spirit came *into* them;
they came *alive* and stood *upright*, a vast *army.*

prophesy = PROF-uh-sī

Then he said to me:
Son of *man*, these *bones* are the whole house of *Israel.*
They have been *saying*,
"Our *bones* are dried *up*,
our *hope* is *lost*, and we are cut *off.*"

Although the bones appear human, they have life only with the coming of God's spirit.

during the Babylonian exile, when the leaders of the kingdom of Judah were separated from their beloved land and forced to live in exile. It was a time of near despair, when many lost hope that they would ever return or that they would again live freely as a people.

The vision of dry bones is fundamentally a vision of hope. Ezekiel sees a valley filled with dry, lifeless bones. When Ezekiel speaks the word of the Lord, the bones come together and take on human form. But only when Ezekiel calls upon the breath or spirit to breathe into them do they truly come to life. It is God's Spirit that gives life.

The renewed life accorded the bones is a symbol of the life that will come to Israel. God promises in this vision that Israel will be reconstituted, that it will once again exist as a nation. God has not abandoned Israel, but will always take care of the chosen people.

The life of the church also begins when the Spirit breathes into the disciples on Pentecost. It is a powerful Spirit, one that can bring life where there is only death. Read this story as it was first offered to the people in exile, as a promise of new life under God's care. Inspire your readers to be renewed and filled with life and energy, as they reflect on the power of the Spirit in their lives.

JOEL. The prophet Joel believed that the people of Israel had become complacent and as a result deserved to experience the

Therefore, *prophesy* and *say* to them: *Thus* says the Lord GOD:
O my *people,* I will *open* your *graves*
and have you *rise* from them,
and bring you *back* to the land of *Israel.*

This is a message of great hope to Israel, which considered itself dead in a foreign land.

Then you shall know that *I* am the LORD,
when I *open* your *graves* and have you *rise* from them,
O my *people!*
I will put my *spirit* in you that you may *live,*
and I will *settle* you upon your *land;*
thus you shall know that *I* am the LORD.
I have *promised,* and I will *do* it, says the LORD.

Speak this solemn vow with firmness. Convey to your community that God's word can be trusted.

Or:

READING I Joel 3:1–5

A reading from the book of the prophet Joel.

Thus says the Lord:
I will *pour out* my *spirit* upon *all* flesh.
Your *sons* and *daughters* shall *prophesy,*
your *old* men shall dream *dreams,*
your *young* men shall see *visions;*
even upon the *servants* and the *handmaids,*
in those days, I will *pour out* my *spirit.*
And I will work *wonders* in the *heavens* and on the *earth,*
blood, fire, and columns of *smoke;*
the *sun* will be turned to *darkness,*
and the *moon* to *blood,*

The Spirit is for everyone.
prophesy = PROF-uh-sī

Emphasize "wonders," then darken your tone to describe the awesome things that will occur on that day. These are signs of the greatness of God.

judgment of God on the "great and terrible" Day of the Lord. But God chose not to act in wrath but to draw Israel close, and to give this promise: God's spirit will be given to all people, regardless of nationality, age, sex or social status. Then, when the Day of the Lord arrives, those who respond to God's spirit and are faithful will be saved. It is a promise of hope and a fitting introduction to the feast of Pentecost, when the Holy Spirit is poured out on believers.

Offer this reading as a great promise of God's love and the inspiration of the Spirit. It is to be spoken forcefully, as a pledge made by God. Even the section about the sun turning to darkness and the moon to blood is a statement of God's sovereignty over all, including nature. Inspire your listeners to respond to the Spirit in their lives and to strive to be part of the faithful remnant.

READING II For Paul, all of creation awaits fulfillment in God. Despite any sufferings he currently experiences, he is convinced that there is a glorious future to be revealed. In the present, the "first fruits" of the Spirit (like a first installment) have been given, but this is simply a promise of what lies ahead. "Adoption" is both a present reality and something not yet

at the *coming* of the *day* of the LORD,
the *great* and terrible *day.*

Those who are faithful have nothing to fear.

Then *everyone* shall be *rescued*
who *calls* on the *name* of the LORD;
for on Mount *Zion* there shall be a *remnant,*
as the LORD has *said,*
and in *Jerusalem survivors*
whom the LORD shall *call.*

READING II Romans 8:22–27

A reading from the letter of Saint Paul to the Romans.

Read this as though you are in pain.

The "firstfruits" were the portions of a grain sacrifice that were harvested first and offered in the Temple as a promise of what was to come.

Brothers and sisters:
We know that all *creation* is *groaning* in *labor* pains
even until *now;*
and not only *that,* but we *ourselves,*
who have the *firstfruits* of the *Spirit,*
we also groan *within* ourselves
as we wait for *adoption,* the *redemption* of our *bodies.*

For in *hope* we were *saved.*
Now hope that *sees* is not *hope.*
For who *hopes* for what one *sees?*
But if we hope for what we do *not* see, we wait with *endurance.*

While we are waiting in hope, the Spirit inspires us and prays through us.

In the *same* way, the *Spirit too* comes to the aid of our *weakness;*
for we do not *know* how to *pray* as we *ought,*
but the Spirit *himself* intercedes with inexpressible *groanings.*

completed. Paul often claims that Christians have been adopted into the family of God that is Israel, but in this passage, he says we still await adoption. This isn't all there is!

But the belief that there is more to come is part of the hope that saves us. We await it with patience; in the meantime, the Spirit moves through us, helping us to pray and interceding for us before God. In the end, everything will work for the good, and we will share in the glory of God.

The reading is straightforward, but filled with reassurances. It is a reflection on what is and what is to be. Paul intends it as a way to instill hope in his readers. Offer it to the members of your community in the same manner, drawing them into a vision for the future in which all creation is united and at peace.

GOSPEL **The festival in question in today's gospel is the Feast of Tabernacles or Booths, an important pilgrimage feast in the first century. It was associated with the triumph of God on the Day of the Lord, but retained some of its agricultural origins as an occasion of prayer for rain. The importance of water was emphasized during the feast; each day, water was carried in procession from a spring to the**

And the one who searches *hearts*
knows what is the intention of the *Spirit*,
because he *intercedes* for the *holy* ones
according to God's *will*.

GOSPEL John 7:37–39

A reading from the holy gospel according to John.

On the *last* and *greatest* day of the *feast*,
Jesus stood up and *exclaimed*,
"Let anyone who *thirsts* come to me and *drink*.
As Scripture says:
'*Rivers* of living *water* will flow from *within* him
who *believes* in me.'"

He said this in reference to the *Spirit*
that those who came to *believe* in him were to *receive*.
There was, of course, no *Spirit* yet,
because Jesus had *not* yet been *glorified*.

Jesus is proclaiming this for all to hear. Lift your voice and speak invitingly.

Flowing water is often used to indicate the presence of the Spirit.

The evangelist intends to say that Jesus had not yet breathed the Spirit on the disciples; that was a gift that had to wait until after his resurrection.

Temple. At the Temple, it was poured out and flowed onto the ground.

The emphasis on water apparently inspired Jesus to announce a truth about himself. He describes himself as a fountain from which the believer could drink in order to receive refreshment. The image of drinking from a fountain is used often in connection with Lady Wisdom, who satisfies the thirst for knowledge and right behavior. The Jewish scriptures hold Wisdom in high esteem; she co-creates the world with God, and dwells in the heavenly heights. Jesus is the font of wisdom, or even Lady Wisdom herself in the flesh.

It should be noted that there has long been discussion about the source of the flowing waters; the Greek is unclear. Either the believer is the source of the water, as in some translations, or Jesus is, implied here. Either way, the waters represent wisdom, a wisdom given by Jesus to those who seek it.

The water is a symbol of the teaching of Jesus, but it is also specifically identified by the redactor of the gospel as representing the Spirit, who will be given by Jesus after his death and resurrection. We proclaim on the feast of Pentecost that the Spirit indeed fills our lives and inspires our actions.

Emphasize the words of Jesus in this short passage. Invite your listeners to approach him in confidence and to learn from him, filled with the fervent hope and faith inspired by God's gift of the Spirit.

PENTECOST

Lectionary #63

READING I Acts 2:1–11

A reading from the Acts of the Apostles.

Pentecost (which means "fifty" and falls 50 days after Easter) is Jewish in origin and celebrates the giving of the Law at Sinai.

This is a spectacular event; make it sound almost as though you are reading the most exciting part of a mystery novel.

When the *time* for *Pentecost* was *fulfilled*,
they were *all* in one place *together*.
And *suddenly* there *came* from the *sky*
a *noise* like a strong driving *wind*,
and it *filled* the entire *house* in which they *were*.
Then there *appeared* to them *tongues* as of *fire*,
which *parted* and came to rest on each *one* of them.
And they were *all* filled with the Holy *Spirit*
and began to *speak* in different *tongues*,
as the *Spirit* enabled them to *proclaim*.

Two claims are made regarding what the miracle of Pentecost involved. Here the believers speak in different languages; later, they are said to speak in their own language, but their hearers are able to understand them.

Express their confusion in your voice.

Galileans = gal-ih-LEE-uhnz

Now there were devout *Jews* from every nation under *heaven*
staying in *Jerusalem*.
At this *sound*, they gathered in a large *crowd*,
but they were *confused*
because each one heard them *speaking* in his own *language*.
They were *astounded*, and in *amazement* they asked,
"Are not all these people who are speaking *Galileans*?
Then *how* does each of us *hear* them in his native *language*?

READING I The presence of God at Pentecost is manifested in several ways. There is a roaring sound, tongues as of fire and a distinct change in the disciples' ability to communicate. The description in Acts recalls the ancient predictions that God would pour out the Spirit upon all people and that God would renew the people and give them hope. The dramatic symbols of God's presence (the tongues as of fire and the sound like wind) remind one of similar events when the Law was given at Sinai. Most significant, the divisions created by differences in communication, said to have begun after the building of the Tower of Babel, are reversed. All people are able to hear about the wondrous deeds God has done in Jesus.

In the Pentecost account, people from many nations can understand the disciples' preaching. The differences between Jews and Gentiles are wiped out. This is important for us today to recall as well; we Christians do not have ownership of God's Spirit. We need to remember that God is much bigger than we are; God is able to include all peoples in a loving embrace.

Share the excitement of this story with your listeners so that they might also experience God's Spirit in their lives. Read the first part of the reading a bit breathlessly, in order to convey the sweeping movement of the Spirit and the astonishment of the disciples. Slow down a bit in the second part, but continue to allow your voice to be filled with amazement. Stress in the final line the power of God. You are a vehicle through whom God's

Parthians = PAHR-thee-uhnz
Medes = meedz
Elamites = EE-luh-mīts
Mesopotamia = mes-uh-poh-TAY-mee-uh
Judea = jo͞o-DEE-uh
Cappadocia = kap-uh-DOH-shuh
Pontus = PON-tuhs
Phrygia = FRIJ-ee-uh
Pamphylia = pam-FIL-ee-uh
Libya = LIB-ee-uh
Cyrene = sī-REE-nee
Cretans = KREE-tuhnz
Slow down and emphasize the final line.

We are *Parthians*, *Medes*, and *Elamites*,
inhabitants of *Mesopotamia*, *Judea* and *Cappadocia*,
Pontus and *Asia*, *Phrygia* and *Pamphylia*,
Egypt and the districts of *Libya* near *Cyrene*,
as well as travelers from *Rome*,
both *Jews* and *converts* to Judaism, *Cretans* and *Arabs*,
yet we hear them *speaking* in our own *tongues*
of the *mighty* acts of *God*."

READING II Galatians 5:16–25

A reading from the letter of Saint Paul to the Galatians.

Brothers and sisters, *live* by the *Spirit*
and you will certainly not *gratify* the desire of the *flesh*.
For the *flesh* has desires *against* the *Spirit*,
and the *Spirit* against the *flesh*;
these are *opposed* to each other,
so that you may *not* do what you *want*.

"What you want" here means acting without discipline or patience. It does not mean that anything that a person wants is wrong.

Lower your voice and read these words with some disdain. Proclaim them clearly, but a little quickly.

But if you are *guided* by the *Spirit*, you are not *under* the *law*.
Now the works of the *flesh* are *obvious*:
immorality, *impurity*, *lust*, *idolatry*,
sorcery, *hatreds*, *rivalry*, *jealousy*,
outbursts of *fury*, acts of *selfishness*,
dissensions, *factions*, occasions of *envy*,
drinking bouts, *orgies*, and the *like*.

I *warn* you, as I warned you *before*,
that those who *do* such things will not *inherit*
the kingdom of *God*.

Spirit moves in your community on this day. Inspire your listeners to open their hearts to God and to work to break down barriers to communication in their own lives.

There is a choice of second readings today. Speak with your liturgy coordinator or pastor to find out which reading will be used.

READING II **GALATIANS. Paul contrasts a life of the flesh with a life guided by the Spirit, providing clear examples of the vices and virtues that characterize them. Paul is not speaking here of "flesh" in the literal sense; he does not disparage the body but indicates a way of living that gives priority to material things. It involves moral as well as physical laziness and greed. It is an undisciplined life, the opposite of the life lived in the Spirit.**

Paul joins his contemporaries, especially teachers of ethics, in providing lists of virtues and vices. For Paul, however, everything must be ordered by recognition of the new life offered in Christ. The old way of living is gone; in place of it is one into which the Spirit breathes life.

The most difficult aspect of proclaiming this passage is reading the lists of words clearly without boring your listeners. Pause slightly after each word or phrase in order to keep the terms separate. Read with a different quality, enlivening your voice for each list. Give special attention to the list of virtues inspired by the Spirit. Practice until you feel confident that you can proclaim Paul's words effectively and can help your listeners embrace lives guided by the Spirit of God.

Brighten your voice and read slowly, emphasizing each positive gift.

In *contrast*, the fruit of the *Spirit* is *love, joy, peace,*
patience, kindness, generosity,
faithfulness, gentleness, self-control.
Against *such* there is no *law.*
Now those who belong to Christ *Jesus* have *crucified* their flesh
with its *passions* and *desires.*
If we *live* in the *Spirit*, let us also *follow* the *Spirit.*

Or:

READING II 1 Corinthians 12:3b–7, 12–13

A reading from the first letter of Saint Paul to the Corinthians.

Read these lines slowly and solemnly in order to avoid sounding sing-song. Concentrating on the meaning—that there is unity in the faith, despite great diversity—will help.

Brothers and sisters:
No one can say, "*Jesus* is *Lord*," except by the Holy *Spirit.*
There are different kinds of spiritual *gifts* but the same *Spirit*;
there are different forms of *service* but the same *Lord*;
there are different *workings* but the same *God*
who produces *all* of them in *everyone.*
To each *individual* the *manifestation* of the *Spirit*
is given for some *benefit.*

This is an extremely important statement of equality in Christ.

As a body is *one* though it has many *parts,*
and *all* the parts of the body, though *many*, are *one* body,
so also *Christ.*
For in one *Spirit* we were all baptized into one *body*,
whether *Jews* or *Greeks*, *slaves* or *free* persons,
and we were *all* given to drink of one *Spirit.*

1 CORINTHIANS. The Corinthian community was an exuberant one, with lively worship services and energetic members. Paul needed to expend much effort to guide this energetic but sometimes confused congregation on the right path. The present passage was written in response to a Corinthian question regarding testing the actions of members of the community to see whether they were indeed inspired by God.

Because the Corinthians placed undue emphasis on the more spectacular gifts of the Spirit, such as speaking in tongues and prophesying, Paul insists that the Spirit works in many ways and all gifts of the Spirit should be appreciated. But despite such variety of gifts, the Spirit is not divisive. There is one Spirit who unites all people.

It is the Spirit who gives a person the ability to proclaim Jesus as Lord, a sure confession of faith and sign of the presence of the Spirit. Such a confession, which gives Jesus a title of honor applied to God, distinguishes the Christian from a nonbeliever. Beyond that common confession, the Spirit inspires each person according to what the good of the community requires.

The one Spirit of God unites people from various religious persuasions or from different social and economic circumstances into one body. The differences that had been so important before are no longer significant. This is an important message for us to take to heart, living in a society that sometimes makes it hard to cross the barriers that are established along racial, economic or educational lines.

GOSPEL John 15:26–27; 16:12–15

The Spirit comes from the Father and is sent by Jesus. There is unity among them in action and in glory.

A reading from the holy gospel according to John

Jesus said to his disciples:
"When the *Advocate* comes whom I will *send* you
from the *Father,*
the *Spirit* of *truth* that *proceeds* from the *Father,*
he will *testify* to me.
And you *also* testify,
because you have been *with* me from the *beginning.*

"I have much *more* to tell you, but you cannot *bear* it *now.*
But when he *comes,* the *Spirit* of *truth,*
he will *guide* you to all *truth.*
He will not *speak* on his *own,*
but he will speak what he *hears,*
and will *declare* to you the things that are *coming.*
He will *glorify* me,
because he will *take* from what is *mine* and *declare* it to you.

"*Everything* that the Father has is *mine;*
for *this* reason I told you that he will *take* from what is *mine*
and *declare* it to you."

Or:

Address this reading to your assembly so that each person might recognize the ways in which the Spirit is active in each member of your community. Inspire your listeners to look inside themselves to see the ministries they have to offer, whether visible and acknowledged or quiet but necessary. Challenge them to work always for unity with all other Christians, from many walks of life, believing sincerely that there is one Spirit who inspires us all.

Note that there is a choice of gospel readings today.

GOSPEL **JOHN 15.** Today's selection is part of Jesus' teaching to his disciples at the Last Supper. He indicates here that, although he will be departing from them, he will not leave them entirely. He will send the Spirit to guide them and to inspire them to bear witness to him.

Apparently recognizing that many of the claims Christians made about Jesus after his death and resurrection were not made about him before his death, the author insists that this is part of the divine plan. Jesus' followers simply could not have understood everything in advance. They needed to live through the horror of the passion and the wondrous experience of Jesus' resurrection before they would be ready to learn more. At that point, however, the Spirit would teach them, guide them and strengthen them, thus glorifying Jesus. Throughout his speech Jesus clarifies the unity that exists between himself, the Spirit and the Father.

GOSPEL John 20:19–23

A reading from the holy gospel according to John.

Although Jesus is recognizable, he has been transformed. He is able to entered a locked room.

On the *evening* of that *first* day of the week,
when the *doors* were *locked*, where the disciples were,
for *fear* of the *Jews*,
Jesus came and *stood* in their *midst*
and *said* to them, "*Peace* be with *you.*"
When he had *said* this, he showed them his *hands* and his *side.*
The disciples *rejoiced* when they saw the *Lord.*

Jesus said to them *again*, "*Peace* be with *you.*
As the *Father* has *sent* me, so I send *you.*"

In the Hebrew Scriptures, the Spirit of God is represented as the breath of God.

And when he had *said* this, he *breathed* on them
and said to them,
"*Receive* the Holy *Spirit.*
Whose *sins* you *forgive* are *forgiven* them,
and whose sins you *retain* are *retained.*"

Forgiveness is a hallmark of the new people of God.

Read this passage as a straightforward teaching of Jesus to his friends, but address it as well to the members of your assembly.

JOHN 20. The experience of the Spirit's presence in the lives of the evangelists was difficult to describe in concrete terms, leading to the two very different accounts we read in the Acts of the Apostles and here in the gospel of John. Here, the Spirit is given on Easter Sunday, with Jesus still present. The spectacular occurrence of wind and fire has changed; now it is the unprecedented ability of Jesus to enter a locked room that brings amazement and awe. What matters is not how the event is described but the reality that the Spirit has indeed been given to believers, drawing Christians of every way of life into one church.

And what Jesus brings, what the Spirit inspires, is peace. It is the deep, heartfelt peace of knowing that one is in right relationship with God, despite what might be happening in one's life or in the world. It is a peace that gives the strength to change the world. Jesus sends us, his followers, just as he was sent, and says that the hallmark of the life in the Spirit is to forgive. Enmity and strife are realities, but in the Spirit we can heal wounds and bring forgiveness and unity to a broken world.

Speak Jesus' words gently but firmly. Pray that the members of your community might receive the Spirit just as Jesus' first disciples did, then address your hearers directly.

HOLY TRINITY

Lectionary #165

READING I Deuteronomy 4:32–34, 39–40

A reading from the book of Deuteronomy.

Moses said to the *people:*
"*Ask* now of the days of old, before your time,
ever since *God* created *man* upon the earth;
ask from one end of the sky to the other:
Did anything *so great* ever happen before?
Was it ever *heard* of?

"Did a *people* ever hear the *voice* of *God*
speaking from the midst of *fire*, as you did, and *live*?
Or did *any god* venture to go and take a *nation* for himself
from the *midst* of another *nation*,
by testings, by *signs* and *wonders*, by war,
with *strong hand* and *outstretched arm*, and by great terrors,
all of which the *LORD*, *your God*,
did for you in *Egypt* before your very eyes?

"*This* is why you must now *know*,
and *fix* in your *heart*, that the *LORD is God*
in the *heavens* above and on *earth* below,
and that there is *no other.*
You must keep his *statutes* and *commandments* that I enjoin on
you today,
that *you* and your *children* after you may *prosper*,
and that you may have *long life* on the land
which the *LORD*, your *God*, is giving you *forever.*"

Pause before voicing the questions.

Pause again before recounting the spectacular things God has done.

Slowly and dramatically emphasize each word of "Lord your God."

Let your voice become lighter, yet resonating with authority as you convey both God's expectations and God's promises.

READING I The book of Deuteronomy is a summary of the ancient Law of Israel as told by the great intermediary between God and the people, Moses. Throughout the book, as in today's reading, Moses speaks to the people, reminding them of the precious gift given them in the commandments of God.

Moses reminds the people how the Law was given to them as they stood at the foot of Mount Sinai and saw it enveloped in fire and smoke. He reminds them as well of God's many saving deeds on their behalf during their flight from Egypt and journey through the wilderness. Their response is to be an acknowledgment of the supreme nature of this God and a commitment to abide by God's statutes. Your task when proclaiming this reading is to remind the members of your congregation of the work of God in their lives.

The questions posed by Moses are rhetorical; surely no other god could ever be said to have done such wondrous things. Not only is God greater than all other gods, but there is in fact "no other." The unique contribution of the Hebrew people in the religious history of the world is their monotheism. We inherit and proclaim monotheism as well today—even as we affirm that this one God is a union of three persons, Father, Son and Spirit.

READING II Just as Israel was chosen by God in the covenant at Sinai, Christians are brought into relationship with God through baptism. All those who are "led by the Spirit" are entitled to share in the relationship Jesus has with the one he called "Abba," Father. We are adopted children of God, deemed worthy of

READING II Romans 8:14–17

A reading from the letter of Saint Paul to the Romans.

Brothers and *sisters:*
For those who are led by the *Spirit* of *God* are *sons* of *God.*
For you did *not* receive a spirit of *slavery* to fall back into fear,
but you received a Spirit of *adoption,*
through whom we cry, *"Abba, Father!"*
The *Spirit himself* bears witness with *our spirit*
that we are *children* of *God,*
and if children, then *heirs,*
heirs of God and *joint heirs* with Christ,
if only we *suffer with him*
so that we may also be *glorified with him.*

Being made children of God by virtue of baptism entitles us to call on God in the same way that Jesus did.

Being "joint heirs" with Christ entitles us to blessings and glory but also requires willingness to suffer as he did. Be careful not to swallow "with Christ" or "with him" at the end of these lines.

GOSPEL Matthew 28:16–20

A reading from the holy gospel according to Matthew.

The eleven disciples went to *Galilee,*
to the *mountain* to which Jesus had *ordered* them.
When they all saw him, they *worshiped,* but *they doubted.*

Then Jesus approached and said to them,
"All power in *heaven* and on *earth* has been *given* to me.
Go, therefore, and *make disciples* of *all nations,*
baptizing them in the *name* of the *Father,*
and of the *Son,* and of the *Holy Spirit,*
teaching them to *observe all* that I have commanded you.

"And *behold,* I am *with* you *always,* until the *end* of the *age."*

Pause before "but they doubted."

Proclaim Jesus' words with vigor and solemnity.

Give each of the three commands — to make disciples, to baptize and to teach — equal emphasis.

inheriting all the blessings and glory that belong rightfully to the Son.

But being made "heirs with Christ" involves more than simply looking forward to sharing in Christ's blessings. It also means we must share in his suffering. Being part of a family involves difficult times as well as joyful ones. Inspire your hearers to accept the privileges, as well as the difficulties, of being part of God's family.

GOSPEL **God enters into communion with the people of Israel and with the community of the church, passionately loving, teaching and admonishing, tenderly holding them in a loving embrace. But God's love is not only directed outward. God enters into communion with us precisely because God is community: God is relationship; God is love.**

Today's gospel, chosen because of its baptismal formula invoking Father, Son and Spirit, is a commissioning — of Jesus' immediate followers and of us as well — to draw others into this family relationship with God. In reading today's gospel passage, you proclaim the common responsibility of all Christians to make disciples, to baptize and to teach what Jesus has commanded. It is up to you to inspire your assembly to share the good news of God's compassion, to bring others into the warm embrace of God's family, to let the world know that God is love.

It is not easy. There are responsibilities, even suffering, involved. As you proclaim this text, take comfort in Jesus' promise that he remains always with us. We are not alone, but are guided also by a Spirit who proclaims that we are, with Jesus, able to call upon God as "Abba."

BODY AND BLOOD OF CHRIST

Lectionary #168

READING I Exodus 24:3–8

A reading from the book of Exodus.

When *Moses* came to the *people*
and related all the *words* and *ordinances* of the LORD,
they all answered with *one voice*,
"We will do everything that the *LORD* has *told* us."

Speak with conviction, recalling the conviction of Israel.

Moses then wrote down all the *words* of the *LORD* and,
rising early the next day,
he *erected* at the foot of the mountain an *altar*
and *twelve pillars* for the *twelve tribes* of Israel.
Then, having sent certain *young men* of the Israelites
to offer *holocausts* and sacrifice *young bulls*
as *peace offerings* to the LORD,
Moses took *half* of the blood and put it in large *bowls*;
the *other half* he *splashed* on the *altar*.

Speak slowly, emphasizing the people's response.

Taking the *book* of the *covenant*, he read it aloud to the people,
who answered, "*All* that the LORD has *said*, we will
heed and *do*."

Then he took the *blood* and *sprinkled* it on the *people*, saying,
"This is the *blood* of the *covenant*
that the *LORD* has made with *you*
in accordance with all these *words* of his."

READING I **The account of the covenant between God and Israel reaches its high point in the actual commands given to Israel. These commands are of two types: general rules for right behavior (the Ten Commandments; in today's reading called "words"), and regulations for handling specific cases (the "ordinances"). Moses here reminds the people of these commandments, twice eliciting a positive response of obedience.**

The sacrifice of animals was understood as part of Israel's response to God. Sacrifice ratified treaties between two parties. The sprinkling of the lifeblood of an animal was also the means by which Israel could atone for its sinfulness in the presence of God. Here it confirms the covenant between God and Israel. Blood, the symbol of life, is also a sign of holiness. The altar is sanctified by being splashed with blood; the people too are declared to be God's holy people by the sprinkling of blood, drawn into a unique relationship with God through this covenant. The blood confirms the covenant and declares this people to be God's own, to be sacred.

Your goal as reader today is to call forth from the people of God in your community the same heartfelt response described here. In addition, you introduce the concepts upon which the following readings are based. Christians understand the ultimate covenant-establishing sacrifice to be that made by Jesus, who offered his own life. Remind your assembly of the foreshadowing of Christ's sacrifice in the sacrifices of Israel.

READING II Hebrews 9:11–15

A reading from the letter to the Hebrews.

Brothers and *sisters:*
When Christ came as *high priest*
of the *good things* that have come to be,
passing through the *greater* and more *perfect tabernacle*
not made by hands, that is, *not* belonging to this *creation,*
he entered *once* for *all* into the *sanctuary,*
not with the blood of *goats* and *calves*
but with *his own blood,* thus obtaining *eternal redemption.*

Emphasize the uniqueness of Christ's role as high priest.

For if the blood of *goats* and *bulls*
and the sprinkling of a *heifer's ashes*
can *sanctify* those who are *defiled*
so that their flesh is *cleansed,*
how *much more* will the *blood* of *Christ,*
who through the *eternal Spirit offered himself* unblemished
to God,
cleanse our *consciences* from dead works
to worship the *living God.*

This is a difficult line to read. Lower your voice slightly throughout the clause following "Christ," and speak a bit more quickly (but pause briefly after "Spirit"). This parenthetical clause should not interrupt the flow of the entire sentence.

For this reason he is *mediator* of a *new covenant:*
since a *death* has taken place for deliverance
from *transgressions* under the *first covenant,*
those who are *called* may receive the *promised*
eternal inheritance.

Proclaim this triumphantly.

READING II The letter to the Hebrews imagines a heavenly temple, of which the earthly Temple in Jerusalem was a reflection. The heavenly temple is perfect in every way. Its high priest is Jesus, whose own blood establishes a new covenant between God and the chosen people.

The Temple in Jerusalem, destroyed by the Romans in the year 70 CE and never since rebuilt, was the center of Israel's worship and its understanding of itself as the chosen people. The ark of the covenant, the repository of the commandments of God, was kept within the Temple's innermost chamber. Although sacrifices could be offered at the Temple by other priests, only the high priest could enter this Holy of Holies, and then only once a year, on the Day of Atonement. Sprinkling blood in the Holy of Holies recalled and confirmed the covenant made between God and Israel.

The author of Hebrews indicates that the earthly Temple is superseded by a heavenly temple in which Christ serves as the high priest. Only he could enter into the holy sanctuary, the very reality of God's presence. Instead of offering the blood of animals to sanctify the people, he offered his own blood, shed on the cross. He became the perfect offering, pure and undefiled. He was both the high priest who made the offering and the one offered. And through offering himself, Christ established a new covenant, sealed in his own blood. Finally, unlike the high priest in Jerusalem, Christ did not need to enter into the holy sanctuary annually, but

GOSPEL Mark 14:12–16, 22–26

A reading from the holy gospel according to Mark.

On the *first* day of the Feast of *Unleavened Bread,*
when they *sacrificed* the *Passover lamb,*
Jesus' disciples said to him,
"*Where* do you want us to go
and prepare for you to *eat* the *Passover?*"

Read this odd story as a simple introduction to the central event: the sharing of the bread and cup.

He sent two of his disciples and said to them,
"Go *into* the *city* and a man will meet you,
carrying a *jar* of *water.*
Follow him.
Wherever he enters, say to the *master* of the house,
'The *Teacher* says, "*Where* is my *guest* room
where I may eat the *Passover* with my *disciples?*"'
Then he will show you a *large* upper *room* furnished and ready.
Make the *preparations* for us *there.*"

The disciples then went off, entered the city,
and found it *just* as he had told them;
and they *prepared* the *Passover.*

Slow down in this section. Speak quietly but firmly. Because these words are so familiar, it is easy to lose their significance. Read them as though for the first time, but avoid dramatization.

While they were eating,
he *took bread,* said the *blessing,*
broke it, *gave* it to them, and said,
"*Take* it; *this* is *my body.*"

Then he took a *cup,* gave *thanks,* and *gave* it to them,
and they all drank from it.

offered himself once only, thus effecting an eternal covenant in his blood.

Today's passage is as difficult to read as it is rich in imagery. When you feel confident that you understand the parallels being drawn here between what Christ does and the ritual of ancient Israel, proclaim it to your assembly with due reverence. Read slowly, so that your hearers can comprehend each aspect of the comparison being made.

GOSPEL **The core of our gospel reading today, and the reason it was chosen for this feast, is the account of Jesus' words about his body and blood, spoken as he shared his last meal with his disciples. The breaking of the bread and the sharing of a cup signify the body of Jesus, soon to be broken and wounded, and his blood, to be poured out on the cross. This blood recalls the blood sprinkled in the first reading, when the covenant between God and Israel was ratified by the blood of an animal. This blood is also alluded to in the second reading, the blood of Jesus that established a new and eternal covenant.**

Every time we share in the eucharist, we recall these words of Jesus. It is by sharing in the eucharist that we are formed as God's people. In it we proclaim, as did the people Israel, "All that God has said, we will do." It is also by sharing in this meal that we enter into communion with one another, that we become the "body of Christ." Just as

Sharing in the eucharist not only recalls Jesus' words and sacrificial death, but looks ahead to the future reign of God.

He said to them,
"*This* is my *blood* of the *covenant*,
which will be shed for many.
Amen, I say to you,
I shall *not* drink again the *fruit* of the *vine*
until the day when I drink it *new* in the *kingdom* of *God.*"

Then, after singing a *hymn*,
they went out to the *Mount* of *Olives.*

Jesus was willing to be broken and battered, so too must we be open to suffering. But we are not alone. We cannot be his body in isolation, but only as we draw together to celebrate our common identity.

Your task today is to proclaim the importance of this event in Jesus' life, as well as its significance for your own community. Challenge your hearers to become Christ's body.

When we come together to celebrate the eucharist, we look back at the event recounted here today. But this is not the only way that the eucharist has been understood by Christians. It has also been seen as that which has the power to bring God's people together in a great eschatological celebration. The words of Jesus in today's gospel invoke this understanding. Just as Jesus looks forward to a heavenly banquet at which God reigns, so also we can proclaim our hope for sharing in such a banquet.

13TH SUNDAY IN ORDINARY TIME

Lectionary #98

READING I Wisdom 1:13–15; 2:23–24

A reading from the book of Wisdom.

Speak with conviction about God's purpose in creation: life, not death.

God did *not* make *death,*
nor does he *rejoice* in the *destruction* of the *living.*

This is an independent thought; begin again as though it is a new sentence.

For he *fashioned* all things that they might *have being;*
and the *creatures* of the world are *wholesome,*
and there is *not* a *destructive* drug among them
nor any *domain* of the *netherworld* on *earth,*

Pause before and after this key line, and speak it slowly and firmly.

for *justice* is *undying.*

For *God formed* man to be *imperishable;*
the *image* of his *own nature* he made him.

Pause briefly before "death" and again before "experience."

But by the *envy* of the *devil, death* entered the world,
and they who belong to *his company experience* it.

READING II 2 Corinthians 8:7, 9, 13–15

A reading from the second letter of Saint Paul to the Corinthians.

Brothers and sisters:

Pause after each item in the list.

As you *excel* in *every* respect, in *faith, discourse,*
knowledge, all *earnestness,* and in the *love* we have for you,

Speak encouragingly.

may you excel in *this* gracious act *also.*

READING I Today you have the pleasant task of communicating God's desire for human health and eternal happiness. The beautiful passage from the Wisdom of Solomon in today's first reading leaves no doubt that the most certain of all human experiences—death—does not come from God. Instead, God creates a world in which everything, if used in accord with its original design, is good and wholesome.

We know, of course, that human beings do experience "corruption" (that is, death) and that the natural world is not always safe. But the author makes clear that this reality is the result of evil having entered the world. God has created us in the divine image and desires that we share in eternal life. Death, though a reality, is not part of God's original plan. Even when death would seem to be a blessing, it is not so much the end of living that is desired, but the cessation of suffering. God, the author of life, does not bring about death. God gives life.

Speak this message to the assembly with conviction, trust and hope, as well as sensitivity to those who are grieving the death of a loved one.

READING II During the period of Paul's mission in Greece and Asia Minor (modern day Turkey), there was a famine in the region of Judea. Paul took up a collection to assist the Jews most afflicted by the famine in Jerusalem.

In today's reading, Paul details some of the abundance enjoyed by the Corinthian community. Because they excel in so many

Proclaim this sentence with a full voice. Pause briefly after "Christ," and again after "rich" and "poor."

For you know the *gracious act* of our *Lord Jesus Christ*,
that though he was *rich*, for *your* sake he became *poor*,
so that by his *poverty you* might become *rich*.

Not that *others* should have *relief* while *you* are *burdened*,
but that as a matter of *equality*
your *abundance* at the present time should supply their *needs*,
so that *their abundance* may also supply *your needs*,
that there may be *equality*.

As it is written:
"Whoever had *much* did not have *more*,
and whoever had *little* did not have *less*."

GOSPEL Mark 5:21–43

A reading from the holy gospel according to Mark.

When *Jesus* had *crossed* again in the *boat*
to the *other side*,
a *large crowd* gathered around him, and he stayed *close*
to the *sea*.

Jairus = JĪ-ruhs

One of the *synagogue officials*, named *Jairus*, came forward.
Seeing him he *fell* at his *feet* and *pleaded earnestly* with him,
saying,

Without overdramatization, convey the desperation — and faith — of this father.

"My *daughter* is at the *point* of *death*.
Please, come *lay* your *hands* on her
that she may get *well* and *live*."
He *went* off *with* him,
and a large crowd *followed* him and *pressed* upon him.

Pause before proceeding with the following independent story.

things, Paul encourages them to excel also in their generosity toward the inhabitants of Jerusalem. He presents Christ as the example of complete generosity.

In a passage recalling the beautiful hymn of Philippians 2:6–11, Paul points to Christ as one who had wealth — namely, heavenly glory — who sacrificed his honored place and took on humanity ("became poor") for the sake of others. Paul's claim foreshadows the later Christian claim that "God became human so that humans might become divine." Compared with the glory of heaven, human life seems impoverished. But God became human in Jesus, willing to experience all that we experience, including suffering and death, precisely so that we might also know what it is to share in heavenly life.

There is a timeless quality about the words you proclaim today. There is always much for which we can be grateful, just as there are always people in need around us. Proclaim these words of Paul to your own community as though they were written expressly for it. Speak warmly of the assembly's gifts and encourage it to reflect on the example of Christ, so that it might be eager to share its abundance. Although Christ has acted in a unique manner, allow his example to stand before the assembly as an inspiration. Finally, stress the fact that even those blessed with plenty may at some time find themselves in need, whether financial, spiritual, emotional or physical.

GOSPEL **Today's gospel consists of two separate stories, one sandwiched within the other. Together they**

There was a *woman* afflicted with *hemorrhages* for *twelve* years.
She had *suffered greatly* at the hands of many doctors
and had spent *all* that she had.
Yet she was *not helped* but only *grew worse.*
She had *heard* about *Jesus* and came up *behind* him in the *crowd*
and *touched* his *cloak.*

Speak with sincerity and confidence in order to show the trust of the woman.

She said, "If I but *touch* his *clothes*, I shall be *cured."*
Immediately her flow of blood *dried up.*
She *felt* in her body that she was *healed* of her *affliction.*

Jesus, aware at once that *power* had gone out from him,
turned around in the *crowd* and asked,
"Who has *touched* my *clothes?"*

Jesus does not seem to be indignant, but rather curious and aware that power has gone out from him.

But his *disciples* said to Jesus,
"You see how the *crowd* is *pressing* upon you,
and yet you ask, *'Who touched me?'"*

Raise your voice in a question at the end of this line to convey some of the incredulity of the disciples.

And he looked *around* to see who had done it.

The *woman*, realizing what had *happened* to her,
approached in *fear* and *trembling.*
She *fell* down *before* Jesus and *told* him the *whole truth.*

Speak warmly.

He said to her, *"Daughter*, your *faith* has *saved* you.
Go in *peace* and be *cured* of your *affliction."*

Speak strongly but encouragingly.

While he was still *speaking*,
people from the *synagogue* official's *house* arrived and said,
"Your *daughter* has *died*; why *trouble* the *teacher* any longer?"
Disregarding the message that was reported,
Jesus said to the *synagogue official*,
"Do not be *afraid*; just have *faith."*

He did *not* allow *anyone* to *accompany* him inside
except *Peter*, *James*, and *John*, the brother of James.

demonstrate Jesus' extraordinary power and the importance of faith for those who turn to him. Jesus unwittingly heals a woman with a flow of blood and restores to life a young girl said to be dead. The account ends with the author's characteristic emphasis on the "messianic secret": Jesus' spectacular deeds are kept hidden. The author is careful to emphasize not the glory and majesty of Jesus but the suffering — shared by those who follow him — that Jesus experienced.

The account of the hemorrhaging woman begins with details of the woman's plight: The bleeding had continued for twelve years, the woman had suffered much and had spent all her funds. Yet her confidence in Jesus' abilities is clear: She does not even approach him directly but seeks only to touch his clothing. The author presents Jesus as one who knew when his power was tapped. His response is to praise the woman's faith and to declare that she is saved, that is, filled with health and wholeness. The message to the reader of the gospel is clear: The one who trusts completely in the healing power of Jesus is the one who is granted salvation.

The story of Jairus and his daughter is also a story of faith, in this case the faith of a Jewish official. Even a powerful member of

When they arrived at the *house* of the *synagogue official*,
he caught sight of a *commotion*,
people *weeping* and *wailing loudly*.
So he *went in* and said to them,
"Why this *commotion* and *weeping*?
The *child* is *not dead* but *asleep*."

Pause before and after this line.

And they *ridiculed* him.

Then he put them all *out*.
He took along the child's *father* and *mother*
and those who were *with* him
and entered the room where the *child* was.

Talitha koum = TAH-lee-thah KOOM

He took the child by the *hand* and said to her, "*Talitha koum*,"
which means, "*Little girl*, I *say* to you, *arise!*"
The girl, a child of twelve, arose *immediately* and
walked around.

Pause before continuing. The closing line of the story is rather anti-climactic and needs no special emphasis.

At that they were *utterly astounded*.

He gave *strict orders* that *no one* should *know* this
and said that she should be given something to eat.

[Shorter: Mark 5:21–24, 35b–43]

the religious establishment is willing to humble himself before Jesus and appeal for help. In this account, Jesus' power is shown to be even greater than before: His power extends even over the forces of death, so that he is able to restore the young girl to life. As in the Wisdom of Solomon, God brings not death but life.

In both stories, Jesus was not afraid to have contact with impurity. If, as seems likely, the woman's bleeding was vaginal, she was ritually unclean under the Jewish Law and had been so for 12 years. Anyone who came in direct contact with her was made unclean as well. If the girl was really dead, Jesus' act of taking her by the hand also made him unclean. These stories demonstrate that Jesus' strength was greater than the unclean forces of the world.

As you proclaim this passage, draw attention to the complexity of these stories. Emphasize both the power of Jesus and the faith of those who trusted in him. But note also the tenderness Jesus conveys in his words and actions to those who need his help, especially to those who are considered unclean and are shunned by society. Finally, note the gospel author's unwillingness to emphasize only the spectacular, even while detailing Jesus' divine powers.

14TH SUNDAY IN ORDINARY TIME

Lectionary #101

READING I Ezekiel 2:2–5

A reading from the book of the prophet Ezekiel.

In an earlier verse (not printed here), Ezekiel was told to stand, but he was unable to do so until God's spirit moved him.

Literally, "son of humanity," Here it simply means "human one."

The words of God are harsh; speak them firmly.

As the LORD *spoke* to me, the *spirit* entered into me
and *set* me on my *feet*,
and I *heard* the *one* who was *speaking* say to me:
Son of *man*, I am *sending* you to the *Israelites*,
rebels who have *rebelled against* me;
they and their *ancestors* have *revolted* against me to this very day.
Hard of face and *obstinate* of heart
are *they* to whom I am *sending* you.

Speak these words as a prophet would: slowly, firmly and with conviction.

But *you* shall *say* to them: *Thus says* the *Lord GOD!*
And whether they *heed* or *resist*—for they are a *rebellious* house—
they shall *know* that a *prophet* has been *among* them.

READING I Ezekiel, prophet and visionary, prophesied in Babylon during the Babylonian exile. Here we read one of the accounts of his call from God. Ezekiel understood himself to be directly, even physically, guided by God's spirit as he took God's message to a hard-hearted people. As proof of the authenticity of his message, Ezekiel is unable to speak or even move until enabled to do so by God's spirit. When he does speak, it is a message filled with power.

In proclaiming this short passage, stress the power of God's spirit as the true agent in a prophet's life. Proclaim strongly the beginning of God's message ("Thus says the Lord God") which confirms Ezekiel's role as God's prophet. Allow these words to inspire the prophets among you (and the prophet in each of us) to follow God's spirit and to speak the word of God boldly despite opposition.

READING II In this letter, Paul must attempt to balance a defense of himself with a spirit of humility. He defends himself so that his community will not be led astray by those who may appear more interesting or authoritative. After recounting his various tribulations, as well as his mystical experiences, he writes the passage in today's reading. In it Paul shares an intimate detail of his life and his conviction that the power of Christ is manifested through Paul's own weakness.

This is a difficult but inspiring message. Most of us do not care to dwell on our weaknesses or resign ourselves to them, but rather seek to "overcome" them. Reflect on a way in which God's love and strength have been present in your life, despite—or perhaps through—your own weakness. Keep that in

READING II 2 Corinthians 12:7–10

A reading from the second letter of Saint Paul to the Corinthians.

Brothers and sisters:
That *I, Paul,* might not become *too elated,*
because of the *abundance* of the *revelations,*
a *thorn* in the *flesh* was given to me, an *angel* of *Satan,*
to *beat* me, to *keep* me from being *too* elated.

Three times I *begged* the Lord about this, that it might *leave* me,
but he *said* to me, *"My grace* is *sufficient* for you,
for *power* is made *perfect* in *weakness."*
I will *rather* boast most *gladly* of my *weaknesses,*
in order that the *power* of *Christ* may *dwell with* me.

Therefore, I am *content* with *weaknesses, insults,*
hardships, persecutions and *constraints,*
for the *sake* of *Christ;*
for when I am *weak, then* I am *strong.*

Proclaim these words with a strong, clear voice; they are the key to the passage.

Pause briefly before and after each item, but do not dwell on them.

Pause after "weak"; read this final line with certainty, but also as if confiding in someone. Try lowering your voice and speaking quietly but firmly.

mind as you proclaim today's reading, and allow the power of Christ to speak through you. It takes strength to admit one's weakness; speak with conviction, yet humility.

GOSPEL **As is so often the case, it is difficult for Jesus to speak to those who have known him best and longest. Earlier in this gospel his family thought he was crazy, and in the end his community—Israel—rejects him.**

The gospel begins on a positive note. Jesus was presumably invited to teach, and his listeners were struck by his wisdom. But then jealousy crept in as they reflected on his humble beginnings among them. Who did he think he was?

It is interesting that Jesus' powers can be diminished by the lack of faith of the people, at least in this gospel. It is Jesus' turn to be astonished and perplexed.

The experience of Jesus is not uncommon. It can, however, encourage each of us to listen more closely to the people in our midst, to the most humble and the most familiar, and to seek the wisdom they share.

As you proclaim today's gospel, allow your voice to reflect the relative calm in the beginning and to grow as the conflict ensues, ending with a tone of regret at the people's unbelief. The words of Jesus describe his situation and are the central challenge to us. Is Jesus' message a retort to his challengers? Or is he simply quoting a popular saying to explain their rejection of him? How you understand his attitude will determine how you read his words.

GOSPEL Mark 6:1–6

A reading from the holy gospel according to Mark.

Jesus departed from there and *came* to his *native* place,
accompanied by his *disciples.*
When the *sabbath* came he began to *teach* in the *synagogue,*
and *many* who *heard* him were *astonished.*

Allow the people's wonder and astonishment to be heard in your voice, but without being overly dramatic.

They said, "*Where* did this man *get all* this?
What kind of *wisdom* has been *given* him?
What *mighty deeds* are *wrought* by his *hands!*

There is a change in tone here from amazement to suspicion.
Joses = JOH-seez

Is he not the *carpenter*, the *son* of *Mary*,
and the *brother* of *James* and *Joses* and *Judas* and *Simon?*
And are not his *sisters here* with us?"
And they took *offense* at him.

Speak Jesus' words slowly and firmly, with whatever emotion you deem appropriate.

Jesus said to them,
"A *prophet* is not without *honor except* in his *native place*
and among his *own* kin and in his *own* house."

So he was *not* able to perform any *mighty deed* there,
apart from *curing* a few *sick* people by *laying* his hands
on them.
He was *amazed* at their *lack* of *faith.*

15TH SUNDAY IN ORDINARY TIME

Lectionary #104

READING I Amos 7:12–15

A reading from the book of the prophet Amos.

Amaziah = am-uh-ZĪ-uh

Amaziah speaks impatiently and forcefully. In this context, his word for Amos ("visionary") is almost a term of contempt.

Amaziah, priest of *Bethel*, said to *Amos*,
"*Off* with you, *visionary*, *flee* to the land of *Judah!*
There earn your bread by *prophesying*,
but *never again* prophesy in *Bethel*;
for it is the *king's sanctuary* and a *royal temple*."

Read the response of Amos with dignity and sincerity.

Amos answered Amaziah, "*I* was *no prophet*,
nor have I belonged to a *company* of *prophets*;
I was a *shepherd* and a dresser of *sycamores*.

Pause before quoting the words of the Lord; then read this for what it is — a command from God.
prophesy = PROF-uh-sī

The LORD took me from *following* the *flock*, and said to me,
Go, prophesy to my people *Israel*."

READING II Ephesians 1:3–14

A reading from the letter of Saint Paul to the Ephesians.

This is a prayer of joyous praise to God; lift your voice and proclaim it with gladness.

Blessed be the *God* and *Father* of our *Lord Jesus Christ*,
who has *blessed* us in *Christ*
with *every* spiritual *blessing* in the *heavens*,
as he *chose* us in him, before the *foundation* of the *world*,
to be *holy* and *without blemish* before him.

READING I Amos was a shepherd from the southern kingdom of Judah who prophesied in Israel, the northern kingdom of the Hebrew people, in the eighth century BCE. His sharp criticisms of social injustice continue to stir readers' hearts.

Amos criticizes the economic situation in Israel, perhaps causing social unrest as a result. His words are directed at the wealthy and powerful, as well as against the religious cult, which he believed was a farce in light of the injustice he witnessed. Amos claims that wealthy merchants observed religious feasts insincerely, looking forward to returning to their businesses and cheating their customers.

The priest Amaziah saw himself as God's representative and his function in the sanctuary at Bethel as the proper response to God's calling. He saw the words of the prophet as a threat to good order and the proper worship of God. In Amaziah's mind, the king was God's agent on earth; anything that threatened unity in the kingdom was an affront to the king and therefore to God as well.

The response Amos gives to Amaziah is a description of the mission of the prophet. Amos insists that he is not a "professional" prophet but one called directly by God to declare God's will. As such, his responsibility is first to God and not to the king. When God calls someone to speak, it is essential to respond.

In *love* he *destined* us for *adoption* to himself
through *Jesus Christ*,
in *accord* with the *favor* of his *will*,
for the *praise* of the *glory* of his *grace*
that he *granted* us in the *beloved*.

Again, raise your voice in praise of God.

In him we have *redemption* by his *blood*,
the *forgiveness* of *transgressions*,
in accord with the *riches* of his *grace* that he *lavished upon* us.
In *all wisdom* and *insight*, he has made *known* to us
the *mystery* of his *will* in *accord* with his *favor*
that he set *forth* in him as a plan for the *fullness* of *times*,
to sum up all things in Christ, in *heaven* and on *earth*.

Speak these words with awe at God's graciousness.

Emphasize the authority given to Christ.

In him we were also *chosen*,
destined in accord with the *purpose* of the *One*
who accomplishes *all things* according to the *intention*
of his *will*,
so that we might *exist* for the *praise* of his *glory*,
we who *first hoped* in Christ.

There is not so much a contrast between the "we" here and the "you" below; emphasize instead that in Christ all are chosen. However, the "you" can be properly addressed to your assembly.

In him you *also*, who have heard the *word* of *truth*,
the *gospel* of your *salvation*, and have *believed* in him,
were *sealed* with the promised *holy Spirit*,
which is the *first installment* of our *inheritance*
toward *redemption* as God's *possession*, to the *praise*
of his *glory*.

Proclaim the final lines as a promise from God.

[Shorter: Ephesians 1:3–10]

In some ways, your ministry is similar to that of Amos; you too are called to proclaim God's word. It is a weighty responsibility. Reflect on the prophet's response to God's calling. Let it be your response as well.

READING II

The prayer that is today's second reading is found at the beginning of the letter to the Ephesians, which lacks the customary thanksgiving that usually appears in ancient letters. The author uses this prayer to claim that God's supreme will is fulfilled in Christ, and that Christians have been redeemed through the saving action of Christ as a result.

After praising God, the author quickly turns to a repeated theme in this passage: God has chosen us to be adopted children, a reality made possible through the saving blood of Christ. God's "mystery," God's cosmic plan of salvation, is made known to the first believers so that they might glorify God. The recipients of the letter are then reminded of their own experience of initiation; they heard the word of truth, believed and were therefore sealed with the Spirit. As adopted children, Christians are to receive their rightful inheritance (redemption), of which the Spirit is the first installment.

Remember as you read this selection that it is a prayer. It also outlines the purpose that God has for the world; ultimately, all things give glory to God. As you proclaim it, let your voice join in the praise as you recount the wondrous deeds of God.

GOSPEL Mark 6:7–13

A reading from the holy gospel according to Mark.

Emphasize the simple provisions for the journey.

Jesus summoned the *Twelve* and began to send them out *two*
by *two*
and gave them *authority* over *unclean spirits.*
He *instructed* them to take *nothing* for the *journey*
but a *walking stick*—
no *food*, no *sack*, no *money* in their *belts.*
They *were*, however, to wear *sandals*
but *not* a second *tunic.*

Lift your voice, perhaps with some distress in it, to draw attention to the rejection that awaits.

The last two lines summarize the success of the Twelve; the last line is particularly triumphant.

He said to them,
"*Wherever* you *enter* a house, *stay* there until you *leave.*
Whatever place does *not welcome* you or *listen* to you,
leave there and *shake* the *dust* off your feet
in *testimony against* them."
So they went off and *preached repentance.*
The *Twelve* drove out many *demons,*
and they *anointed* with *oil* many who were *sick* and
cured them.

GOSPEL Jesus chose twelve close followers. After a period of learning from him and witnessing his power over demons, illness and death, his intimate followers are here sent out as his representatives. They are to take nothing but the bare essentials, relying instead on the hospitality of those they will visit.

But it is clear that not everyone would accept them. Jesus instructs the Twelve to remove themselves from places where they are rejected, even to shake the dust from their feet. The inhospitable community is left to face God's judgment alone. Where they are heard, however, the Twelve are to preach repentance and perform signs of power, just as Jesus had.

It is not easy to trust that God will always care for us. We know too well the dangers of being without a "backup plan," without insurance against the vicissitudes of life. But Jesus says that in order to be his missionaries, to allow God's power to work through us, we must trust in God and depend on one another. It is not an easy task. Proclaim this gospel as a challenge to trust God's constant care.

16TH SUNDAY IN ORDINARY TIME

Lectionary #107

READING I Jeremiah 23:1–6

A reading from the book of the prophet Jeremiah.

Let this message thunder from your lips.

Woe to the *shepherds*
who *mislead* and *scatter* the *flock* of my *pasture*,
says the LORD.

Speak God's judgment slowly and solemnly.

Therefore, thus says the *LORD*, the *God* of *Israel*,
against the *shepherds* who *shepherd* my *people:*
You have *scattered* my sheep and *driven* them *away.*
You have *not cared* for them,
but *I* will take care to *punish* your *evil deeds.*

The tone changes here; God promises to take care of the people. Speak with increasing tenderness in your voice.

I myself will gather the *remnant* of my *flock*
from *all* the *lands* to which I have *driven* them
and *bring* them *back* to their *meadow*;
there they shall *increase* and *multiply.*
I will appoint *shepherds* for them who will *shepherd* them
so that they need *no longer fear* and *tremble*;
and *none* shall be *missing*, says the LORD.

This is a bold promise. Proclaim it strongly and with hope.

Behold, the *days* are *coming*, says the LORD,
when I will *raise up* a *righteous shoot* to *David*;
as *king* he shall *reign* and govern *wisely*,
he shall do what is *just* and *right* in the land.
In his days *Judah* shall be *saved*,
Israel shall dwell in *security.*
This is the *name* they give him:
"The *LORD* our *justice.*"

READING I In the decades preceding the fall of Jerusalem to the Babylonians, the kingdom of Judah was a vassal state, subject alternately to Egypt and Babylon. Kings ruled in quick succession, often installed by the foreign nation in power at the time. At one point, there were even two kings, one in exile and one in Jerusalem. In this chaotic situation Jeremiah proclaims the oracle we read today. The "shepherds" are those rulers who are responsible for the scattering of the people in the exile.

Beginning as an oracle of judgment, today's passage quickly turns to provide hope for those exiled in Babylon. God promises to take care of a remnant of the people who remain faithful, bringing them back home again. The prophet further predicts that God will raise up one from the lineage of David who will rule with justice.

The phenomenon of prophecy can be applied to many different ages and situations. The rebukes of today's reading can be addressed to any leader today who fails to exercise authority with faithfulness to God. Yet we can always have hope, believing that God has raised up in the person of Jesus one who can truly rule with divine justice.

Proclaim this reading knowing that God's rebukes might apply to members of your congregation. But speak comfortingly in the final sections, knowing that God will never abandon us, but continues to rule in righteousness.

READING II Ephesians 2:13–18

A reading from the letter of Saint Paul to the Ephesians.

The "you" here is the Gentile community to which this letter is addressed, but it can apply to any Christian.

Emphasize "peace" with gentleness in your voice. The unity described in this sentence is central to this reading.

Brothers and sisters:
In *Christ Jesus you* who once were *far off*
have become *near* by the *blood* of *Christ.*

For he is our *peace,* he who made *both one*
and *broke down* the *dividing* wall of *enmity,* through his *flesh,*
abolishing the law with its *commandments* and *legal claims,*
that he might *create* in himself *one new person* in place
of the *two,*
thus establishing *peace,*
and might *reconcile both* with God,
in *one body,* through the *cross,*
putting that *enmity* to *death* by it.

Those "far off" are the Gentiles; those "near" are the Jews. But the author's purpose is not to distinguish between groups, but to bring disparate peoples together as one.

He came and *preached peace* to you who were *far off*
and *peace* to those who were *near,*
for *through* him we *both* have access in *one Spirit* to
the *Father.*

READING II **Paul's central message is that those once far from God—the Gentiles (non-Jews)—are able to inherit with the Jews the promises of God to the Jewish people. Jesus provides a means for drawing together all people in unity. All divisions are gone as we all turn together to the one God through the Spirit.**

Surely this passage speaks volumes to our contemporary situation. Proclaim these words as both a promise of hope and a challenge to make them a reality. Christ has brought us peace; now we have the responsibility to live it.

GOSPEL **After having been sent out (the meaning of the word "apostle" is "one who is sent") in last week's gospel to travel and preach, to cure and cast out demons, the Twelve return and are eager to tell Jesus everything that has happened. It is easy to imagine their excitement and the need for them all to retreat from the crowds and talk in private, which is what they attempt to do.**

But, as a statement of Jesus' popularity and the needs of the people who listen to his words, Jesus and his small group of chosen followers are not left alone. Yet Jesus does not rebuke the crowds or insist on privacy. Instead, he is filled with compassion. Just

GOSPEL Mark 6:30–34

A reading from the holy gospel according to Mark.

The early lines are simply introductory and require no special emphasis.

The *apostles* gathered together with Jesus
and *reported* all they had *done* and *taught.*

He said to them,
"*Come away* by yourselves to a *deserted place* and *rest* a while."
People were *coming* and *going* in *great* numbers,
and they had *no opportunity* even to eat.
So they *went off* in the boat by *themselves* to a *deserted place.*

Here the pace picks up a bit.

People saw them *leaving* and *many* came to know about it.
They *hastened* there on foot from all the towns
and *arrived* at the place *before* them.

Slow your words and allow compassion to enter into your voice. This final line is the key to the gospel.

When he *disembarked* and saw the *vast crowd,*
his *heart* was moved with *pity* for them,
for they were like *sheep* without a shepherd;
and he began to *teach* them *many things.*

as Jeremiah knew that the people needed a true shepherd, Jesus also recognizes this need and provides the people with leadership by teaching them.

This passage allows us to see that the prediction in Jeremiah is ultimately fulfilled in Jesus. He is truly the righteous ruler, who lovingly guides his people. But the passage also provides a challenge to those of us involved in ministry — and all Christians are challenged to minister, whether to one another or to those outside the immediate flock. When we are sorely in need of some privacy and quiet time, how do we respond to the pressing crowds? It is difficult to follow Jesus' example and take pity on those in need when we ourselves are in need of care and attention.

Read this gospel as a call to compassion. Even when we least want to give of ourselves, we are asked to open our hearts and to love as Jesus loved.

17TH SUNDAY IN ORDINARY TIME

Lectionary #110

READING I 2 Kings 4:42–44

A reading from the second book of Kings.

Baal-shalishah = BAH-ahl shahl-ih-SHAH
Elisha = ee-LĪ-shuh

A man came from *Baal-shalishah* bringing to *Elisha,* the man of God,
twenty barley loaves made from the *firstfruits,*
and *fresh grain* in the ear.
Elisha said, "*Give* it to the *people* to *eat.*"

The servant's question is not unreasonable. Perhaps there is also a bit of panic in the servant's voice.

Proclaim this more slowly and forcefully than the first time it was said.

But his servant *objected,*
"*How* can I set this before a *hundred people?*"
Elisha insisted, "*Give* it to the *people* to *eat.*"
For *thus* says the *LORD,*
'They shall *eat* and there shall be *some* left *over.*'"

Recount the conclusion of the episode with a sense of wonder in your voice.

And *when* they had *eaten,* there was *some* left over,
as the *LORD* had *said.*

READING II Ephesians 4:1–6

A reading from the letter of Saint Paul to the Ephesians.

Speak with urgency in your voice.

Brothers and sisters:
I, a *prisoner* for the *Lord,*
urge you to live in a manner *worthy* of the *call* you have received,

READING I The story of Elisha is familiar, since it is echoed in the account of Jesus' actions told in today's gospel. Jesus acted in the tradition of the prophets before him.

Although familiar, the idea of a small amount of food being able to feed many is still amazing. The point of the story is not how it could be possible for such a thing to occur, but rather the importance of trusting God's word and following it. When that is done, all will be well.

As you proclaim this passage, allow the understandable doubt of Elisha's servant to be expressed, but respond with the firmness of Elisha's words. Inspire your assembly to imitate Elisha and trust in God's promises.

READING II In a beautiful exhortation to unity, the author of the letter to the Ephesians turns to moral instruction. All Christians have been "called" by God and are to live according to that call. The author proclaims that Christians are to seek to build up the community rather than draw attention to themselves. Christians are thus able to live humble, peaceful lives, always united in the one Spirit.

With a poetic flourish, the author underscores the source of Christian unity: There is but one Spirit, one Lord, one God who has united all Christians together in one body, sealed in a common baptism.

Read slowly so that each quality can stand on its own.

with *all humility* and *gentleness*, with *patience*,
bearing with one another through *love*,
striving to preserve the *unity* of the *spirit* through the *bond* of *peace:*

Pause before beginning this final section, proclaiming it with joy and emphasizing throughout the term "one." Proclaim each phrase slowly and with great emphasis, ending with a note of God's triumph.

one body and one *Spirit*,
as you were also called to the *one hope* of your *call*;
one Lord, one faith, one baptism;
one God and *Father* of *all*,
who is *over* all and *through* all and *in* all.

GOSPEL John 6:1–15

A reading from the holy gospel according to John.

This introductory material needs no special emphasis.

Jesus went *across* the Sea of *Galilee.*
A *large crowd* followed him,
because they saw the signs he was performing on the *sick.*
Jesus went up on the *mountain,*
and there he *sat down* with his *disciples.*
The Jewish feast of *Passover* was *near.*

Although Jesus was "testing" Philip, his question can be asked innocently. Philip's response is one of incredulity, while that of Andrew begins with hope, but ends in doubt.

When Jesus *raised* his *eyes*
and saw that a *large crowd* was coming to him,
he said to *Philip*,
"*Where* can we buy *enough food* for them to *eat?*"
He said this to *test* him,
because he *himself* knew what he was *going* to *do.*

Today you are a vehicle through whom God delivers this message of love and unity to a community that may be fractured and to people who may be filled with anxiety. Proclaim this message to your congregation as both a challenge to live in unity and as a promise of God-given strength to do so.

GOSPEL Although the account of the Last Supper in the gospel of John does not record Jesus' sharing of his body and blood with his friends, the gospel as a whole has numerous eucharistic allusions. Beginning today (but with the exception of next Sunday), we leave the gospel of Mark and turn to those eucharistic passages in John.

Today's story echoes that of Elisha in the first reading. A prophetic figure is able to feed the crowds, even with food to spare, from meager bits of bread and fish. The emphasis in the story is on the miraculous nature of the event. Even the statements of Philip and Andrew serve only to heighten the suspense and emphasize the impossibility of feeding so many.

Jesus acts as the head of the family, offering thanks for the food before distributing it. He gives an order similar to that of Elisha, but without the urgency of command.

Although similar feeding stories appear in the synoptic gospels (Matthew, Mark and Luke), the Johannine account gives Jesus a more central role. He notices the need, blesses the bread and even distributes it. What is strikingly unique in this account is the reaction of the people to the feeding.

Philip *answered* him,
"*Two hundred* days' *wages* worth of *food* would *not* be *enough*
for *each* of them to have a *little.*"

One of his *disciples,*
Andrew, the brother of Simon Peter, said to him,
"There is a *boy* here who has *five barley* loaves and *two fish;*
but *what good* are these for so *many?*"
Jesus said, "Have the people *recline.*"
Now there was a *great* deal of *grass* in that place.
So the men *reclined,* about *five thousand* in number.

Jesus is clearly in charge here. This sentence is central to this passage; proclaim it slowly and with care.

Then Jesus *took* the *loaves, gave thanks,*
and *distributed* them to those who were *reclining,*
and *also* as much of the *fish* as they wanted.

When they had had their *fill,* he said to his disciples,
"*Gather* the *fragments* left over,
so that *nothing* will be *wasted.*"
So they *collected* them,
and *filled twelve* wicker *baskets* with fragments
from the *five barley* loaves
that had been *more* than they could *eat.*

Allow some wonder to enter your voice as you recount the response of the people. Then lower your voice to indicate Jesus' withdrawal to the mountain.

When the people saw the *sign* he had *done,* they said,
"*This* is *truly* the *Prophet,* the one who is to *come* into the *world.*"
Since Jesus *knew* that they were going to come and *carry* him *off*
to make him *king,*
he *withdrew* again to the *mountain alone.*

Jesus perceives that they want to make him a king, so he withdraws to be alone. Although they see what Jesus has done, they simply do not understand. A little further on in the gospel of John, the reader will learn that Jesus is the bread from heaven, a revelation that forever changes one's outlook on food and meals. The point is not so much the power Jesus has to perform miracles, but the way he nourishes his people, even giving his body for others.

This is an exciting story. Communicate some of the suspense and doubt that must have existed in the hearts of Jesus' hearers, and give Jesus the centrality due him. Allow Jesus' retreat in the last line to provide your listeners with a necessary respite.

TRANSFIGURATION OF THE LORD

Lectionary #614

READING I Daniel 7:9–10, 13–14

A reading from the book of the prophet Daniel.

Read with wonder the description of the heavenly throne.

As I *watched:*
Thrones were set up
and the *Ancient One* took his *throne.*
His *clothing* was *snow bright,*
and the *hair* on his *head* as *white* as *wool;*
his *throne* was *flames* of fire,
with *wheels* of *burning* fire.
A *surging* stream of *fire*
flowed out from where he *sat;*
thousands upon *thousands* were *ministering* to him,
and *myriads* upon *myriads attended* him.

This is a solemn declaration of the expected judgment.

The court was *convened* and the *books* were *opened.*

Both wonder and hope accompany the description of this promised figure.

As the *visions* during the night *continued,* I saw
one like a *Son* of *man* coming,
on the *clouds* of *heaven;*
when he *reached* the *Ancient One*
and was *presented* before him,

Give emphasis to these terms.

the one like a *Son* of *man* received *dominion, glory,*
and *kingship;*
all *peoples, nations,* and *languages serve* him.

His *dominion* is an *everlasting* dominion
that shall *not* be taken *away,*
his *kingship* shall not be *destroyed.*

READING I Daniel's account of his vision of God's throne provides a spectacular glimpse into a type of biblical writing and expectation for the future commonly called "apocalyptic." Today's reading provides a revelation both of some aspects of the identity of God and of the hope for salvation embodied in a single figure.

The book of Daniel was written during a difficult time for the Hebrew people. Under Syrian domination, they longed to be independent. A revolt led by a family called the Maccabees eventually led to the establishment of an independent kingdom, but the period of revolution was frightening and costly. The book of Daniel provides another type of hope during this struggle, a hope that relies less on human abilities and more on divine intervention.

Daniel's bizarre vision of the "Ancient One" is the basis for the traditional portrait of God as an old man, enthroned in heaven. The elements are clearly not intended to be taken literally (a burning throne and streams of fire, a God who has hair!), but the image evoked is that of a majestic being, seated in judgment of those on earth and worshiped by a heavenly court.

The second part of Daniel's vision is of a being in human form who approaches the throne of God and is given universal authority and power. Although the author may have been referring to an angelic being, this passage came to represent hope in a messianic figure who would bring freedom to the Hebrew people and justice to the earth. Christians have held that it is Jesus who ultimately fulfills the expectations presented here.

This is a strange but beautiful passage to proclaim. Speak throughout with a strong voice of the wonders beheld by Daniel.

READING II 2 Peter 1:16–19

A reading from the second letter of Saint Peter.

Emphasize "power" and the phrase about Christ's coming. Proclaim this entire reading slowly and solemnly.

Beloved:
We did *not* follow *cleverly* devised *myths*
when we made *known* to you
the *power* and *coming* of our *Lord Jesus Christ,*
but we had been *eyewitnesses* of his *majesty.*
For he received *honor* and *glory* from *God* the *Father*
when that *unique declaration* came to him from the
majestic *glory,*
"*This* is my *Son,* my *beloved,* with whom I am *well pleased.*"

Proclaim the words of God with even greater solemnity, but resist the temptation to speak in a deep, booming voice. Allow God to use you as the messenger of these words.

We ourselves heard this voice come from heaven
while we were *with* him on the *holy mountain.*
Moreover, we possess the *prophetic message*
that is altogether *reliable.*
You will do *well* to be *attentive* to it,
as to a *lamp* shining in a *dark place,*
until *day dawns* and the *morning star rises* in your *hearts.*

Slow down for these final lines.

Proclaim for all your listeners the glories of God and the promise of one who will make all things right. Read slowly and solemnly so that your words might echo in the hearts of your listeners.

READING II The author of Second Peter prepares for an attack on false teachers (later in the epistle) by speaking now about his own reliability. In defense of what he has preached regarding the future coming of the Lord, the author appeals to the memory of Jesus' glorification, as well as his own prophetic gift.

What is of most interest on today's feast is the author's recollection of the transfiguration and his claims to have been an "eyewitness" to the event. The author recalls the event itself at which Peter, James and John saw Jesus transfigured in glory and heard God's declaration about Jesus as the one with whom God is well pleased. It is primarily this claim that gives the author the authority to instruct the community.

Although in its original context this passage was used to win an argument, it is a beautiful account of the same event recounted in today's gospel. We catch a glimpse today of the heavenly glory given to Jesus. Proclaim the splendor of God's chosen one and the favor bestowed on him. Read with solemnity and allow the praise of God to ring in your voice.

GOSPEL The account of the transfiguration is an awe-inspiring indication of the resplendent glory that belongs to Jesus as God's unique Son. It points forward to Jesus' role as coming judge and recalls the visions of Daniel.

GOSPEL Mark 9:2–10

A reading from the holy gospel according to Mark.

Jesus took *Peter*, *James* and *John*
and led them up a *high mountain* apart by *themselves.*
And he was *transfigured* before them,
and his *clothes* became *dazzling white*,
such as *no* fuller on *earth* could bleach them.

Emphasize the wonder of this sight.

Then *Elijah* appeared to them along with *Moses*,
and they were *conversing* with Jesus.
Then *Peter* said to Jesus in reply,
"*Rabbi*, it is *good* that we are *here!*
Let us make *three* tents:
one for *you*, one for *Moses*, and one for *Elijah.*"
He hardly knew *what* to say, they were so *terrified.*

Peter's comment is impulsive and illustrates his lack of understanding. Allow his words to sound eager and perhaps a bit confused. Pause before continuing.

Then a *cloud* came, casting a *shadow* over them;
from the cloud came a *voice*,
"*This* is my *beloved Son. Listen* to him."
Suddenly, looking around, they *no longer* saw *anyone*
but *Jesus* alone with them.

Resist the temptation to speak God's words in a deep, booming voice.

As they were coming *down* from the *mountain*,
he *charged* them *not* to relate what they had *seen*
to *anyone*,
except when the *Son* of *Man* had *risen* from the *dead.*
So they kept the matter to *themselves*,
questioning what *rising* from the *dead* meant.

The tenor of the story changes here and continues to the end. Instead of majesty, convey the uncertainty and confusion that must have filled the disciples.

The two figures who appear with the transfigured Jesus — Moses and Elijah — are the representatives of the Jewish Law and the prophets. This may also be a reference to the expected return of Jesus, since it was also hoped that Elijah and Moses would return as well. It is clear that Jesus is given authority at least equal to that of these two historic figures. In fact, his authority exceeds theirs, as the voice from heaven makes clear: Jesus is the beloved Son of God, to whom all are to listen.

This story of the glorification of Jesus is used in the gospel of Mark to emphasize one of the author's favorite themes — the need for suffering. The account of the transfiguration follows shortly after Peter's declaration that Jesus is the Messiah, and Jesus' first teachings concerning his own death. Peter had tried to argue with Jesus regarding suffering, but was rebuked by Jesus. Here Peter is again anticipating only a glorious reign for Jesus, as his impetuous comment about erecting booths (places to commune with God) suggests. But Jesus' emphasis lies elsewhere: He downplays the glory by charging his friends to be silent about it, again discussing his death. The author of this gospel does not allow the community to linger on the mountaintop but immediately points to the suffering and death that awaits Jesus and all those who follow him. From this point on in the gospel, Jesus moves steadily toward his death.

Your task today is to allow the splendor of the transfiguration to inspire your community and to proclaim the uniqueness of the one we call "Lord." At the same time, do not lose sight of the broader message of the gospel: Whoever follows Jesus must be willing to do what he did, renouncing glory in exchange for suffering.

19TH SUNDAY IN ORDINARY TIME

Lectionary #116

READING I 1 Kings 19:4–8

A reading from the first book of Kings.

Elijah = ee-LĪ-juh

Elijah went a day's *journey* into the *desert*,
until he came to a *broom* tree and sat *beneath* it.

Express Elijah's despair.

He prayed for *death* saying:
"This is *enough*, O LORD!
Take my *life*, for I am *no better* than my *fathers*."

Pause before recounting with wonder the appearance of the angel.

He lay down and fell asleep under the broom tree,
but then an *angel* touched him and *ordered* him
to *get up* and *eat*.
Elijah *looked* and there at his *head* was a *hearth* cake
and a jug of *water*.

After he *ate* and *drank*, he lay down again,
but the *angel* of the LORD came *back* a *second* time,
touched him, and ordered,
"*Get up* and *eat*, else the *journey* will be too *long* for you!"

There is a bit of urgency in the angel's words here.
Slowly proclaim the final sentence, especially the last phrase ("the mountain of God, Horeb").
Horeb = HOHR-eb

He got up, ate, and drank;
then *strengthened* by that food,
he walked *forty* days and *forty* nights to the *mountain*
of God, *Horeb*.

READING I Elijah is clearly discouraged, tired and depressed. Although he had defeated the prophets of the pagan god Baal earlier in the text, his victory was short-lived. Queen Jezebel was a follower of Baal and had threatened Elijah's life, so he fled. We find him wandering in the desert, tired, hungry and praying for death.

But God has other things in mind for Elijah, who had remained faithful when all others had turned away from God. Rather than allow him to die, God sends an angel to take care of Elijah. Twice Elijah is fed before continuing his long journey to the mountain of God, Horeb (or Sinai), where he will have an intimate encounter with God.

Today's story reminds us that God always cares for and provides for those who love God, although it may not be in ways that are anticipated. When it seems that prayer goes unanswered, it may be that God has another plan for us. Trusting in God's goodness can remove a tremendous burden from our shoulders.

As you proclaim this message today, keep in mind someone you know who may be close to despair. Speak as if to that person, encouraging trust in a God who provides what we really need.

READING II Ephesians 4:30 — 5:2

A reading from the letter of Saint Paul to the Ephesians.

Brothers and sisters:
Do *not grieve* the *Holy Spirit* of God,
with which you were *sealed* for the day of *redemption.*
All *bitterness, fury, anger, shouting* and *reviling*
must be *removed* from you, along with all *malice.*
And be *kind* to one another, *compassionate,*
forgiving one another as *God* has forgiven *you* in *Christ.*

So be *imitators* of God, as beloved *children*, and live in *love,*
as *Christ loved* us and *handed* himself *over* for us
as a *sacrificial* offering to God for a *fragrant* aroma.

Give due emphasis to each term.

Pause, then proceed by changing to a lighter, more compassionate tone. Again, give each term emphasis.

Pause again, then begin anew, reading thankfully of the love of God.

GOSPEL John 6:41–51

A reading from the holy gospel according to John.

The Jews *murmured* about Jesus because he said,
"*I* am the *bread* that came down from *heaven,*"
and they said,
"Is this not *Jesus,* the son of *Joseph?*
Do we not *know* his *father* and *mother?*
Then *how* can he say,
'*I* have come down from *heaven*'?"

Jesus answered and said to them,
"*Stop murmuring* among yourselves.

This is spoken in a spirit of controversy.

Jesus' response is strong. From here on, read slowly and allow Jesus to teach.

READING II In exhorting the Ephesians to live a holy life, the author begins with a catalog of behaviors to avoid, then turns to positive actions. Today's passage begins with an appeal to experience. The "sealing" (here clearly conveying protection) is that of baptism, when the Holy Spirit is bestowed on the believer to give strength and guidance. Negative attitudes are to be shunned, while kindness and forgiveness are to be adopted.

The inspiration for all this is the action of God. It is God who has forgiven "you" (the Ephesians and every member of your assembly), and so believers are to forgive one another in imitation of God. In a beautiful image of incense rising to God, Christ's death is seen as an offering, a demonstration of his love for us.

As you proclaim this reading, inspire your listeners to hear the words addressed directly to them, so that they might follow the precepts outlined there. The author gives both specific instructions on daily life and a general principle: love.

GOSPEL The question about Jesus claiming to be the "bread from heaven" follows an earlier discussion Jesus had about the gift of manna that God had supplied to the people of Israel as they wandered in the desert. The story of the manna is a story of the need to trust divine providence, and of God's commitment to provide for the people whenever they are in need.

God gives faith.

No one can come to me unless the *Father* who sent me *draw* him,
and I will *raise* him on the *last* day.
It is *written* in the *prophets:*
'They shall all be *taught* by God.'
Everyone who *listens* to my Father and *learns* from him *comes*
to me.
Not that *anyone* has seen the Father
except the *one* who is from *God;*
he has *seen* the *Father.*

Only the Son has seen the Father.

Amen, amen, I say to you,
whoever *believes* has *eternal life.*

Pause before beginning this central thought. Give each word in the "I" statements due emphasis, and read the final line with solemnity.

"*I* am the *bread* of *life.*
Your *ancestors* ate the *manna* in the desert, but they *died;*
this is the *bread* that comes down from *heaven*
so that one may *eat* it and *not die.*
I am the *living bread* that came down from *heaven;*
whoever *eats* this bread will *live forever;*
and the *bread* that I will *give* is my *flesh* for the *life*
of the *world.*"

Jesus says that he is truly the "bread of life," reminding the people that the manna in the desert provided nourishment only for a day, not for eternity. But the bread of Jesus, who obliquely claims that he alone is from God and has seen the Father, gives life forever.

This passage reminds us of the eucharist. Sharing in the bread that is Christ unites believers with him and brings them to God, conferring eternal life. In the closing line of this passage, Jesus links the life he gives with the sacrifice he will make on the cross. By dying, he offers his followers life.

Read the controversy in the first part of today's gospel for what it is: grumbling. Jesus' long discourse is more difficult; the subject shifts from the Father's initiative in calling followers, to Jesus' claim that only one person has seen the Father, to a discussion about Jesus as the bread of life. Give appropriate emphasis to these final few lines, and solemnly declare Jesus' words in the last sentence.

ASSUMPTION VIGIL

Lectionary #621

READING I 1 Chronicles 15:3–4, 15–16; 16:1–2

A reading from the first book of Chronicles.

A central concern of the author is to indicate how all of Israel serves God in Jerusalem. Emphasize the inclusion of "all Israel."
Levites = LEE-vīts
The descendants of Aaron were priests who offered sacrifice, while the Levites served as their assistants.

David assembled *all Israel* in *Jerusalem* to bring the *ark*
of the *LORD*
to the *place* that he had *prepared* for it.
David *also* called together the *sons* of *Aaron* and the *Levites.*

The *Levites* bore the *ark* of *God* on their *shoulders* with poles,
as *Moses* had *ordained* according to the *word* of the LORD.

Allow the excitement of the celebration to be heard here.

David commanded the *chiefs* of the *Levites*
to appoint their *kinsmen* as *chanters,*
to play on musical *instruments, harps, lyres,* and *cymbals,*
to make a *loud* sound of *rejoicing.*

Here the tone changes a bit; David makes a solemn offering to God. Allow your voice to become a bit more serious.

They *brought* in the *ark* of *God* and set it *within* the tent
which David had *pitched* for it.
Then they offered up *burnt offerings* and *peace offerings* to God.
When David had *finished* offering up the *burnt offerings*
and *peace offerings,*
he *blessed* the people in the *name* of the *LORD.*

READING I First and Second Chronicles retell the history of the monarchy in Israel, with emphasis on the importance of the Temple in Jerusalem. Today's passage details how the ark of the covenant, the container for the tablets of the Law given to Moses, was brought into Jerusalem with great fanfare.

The ark, containing the direct communication of God to the people of Israel, symbolized the presence of God in the midst of the people. Today's reading tells how it was brought into Jerusalem by David. Before the Temple was built by David's son Solomon, the ark of the covenant alone was the center of Israelite worship in Jerusalem.

This reading is chosen for today's feast because Mary, like the ark, is the bearer of the presence of God. The occasion described is one of great joy as well as reverence toward God. Convey in your voice the festive atmosphere and the importance that this event had for uniting Israel.

READING II In his first letter to the Corinthians, Paul discusses the resurrection of the dead, which some Corinthians were questioning. After insisting on its reality, he describes the need for a different body, one suited to the resurrected life. It would be a body that is not subject to decay but is imperishable, a body that will not die but is immortal. In this way, the words of the prophets quoted here are fulfilled. Death has been conquered; it can no longer claim victory.

Paul goes on to link death to the reality of sin. Death came about only because of sin; it is not part of the divine plan. According to Paul, adherence to the Jewish Law suggests, and even brings about, sin, since the Law is so demanding it cannot be met in full.

READING II 1 Corinthians 15:54b – 57

A reading from the first letter of Saint Paul to the Corinthians.

immortality = im-ohr-TAL-ih-tee (not immorality)

Read the quote triumphantly and slowly.

Brothers and sisters:
When *that* which is *mortal* clothes itself with *immortality*,
then the *word* that is *written* shall come *about:*
"Death is *swallowed* up in *victory.*
Where, O death, is your *victory?*
Where, O death, is your *sting?"*

Continue a sedate pace, but conclude with a joyous prayer of praise.

The *sting* of death is *sin,*
and the *power* of *sin* is the *law.*
But *thanks* be to *God* who gives us the *victory*
through our *Lord Jesus Christ.*

GOSPEL Luke 11:27 – 28

A reading from the holy gospel according to Luke.

Pause before beginning to make sure your listeners are attentive. This reading is so short that you don't want anyone to miss any of it!

Read the words of the woman and those of Jesus with great solemnity and sincerity.

While *Jesus* was *speaking,*
a *woman* from the crowd *called* out and *said* to him,
"Blessed is the *womb* that *carried* you
and the *breasts* at which you *nursed."*

He replied,
"Rather, blessed are those
who *hear* the *word* of *God* and *observe* it."

But none of this matters now since God has conquered death in Jesus Christ.

This text is used for today's feast because of the belief that Mary's body was not subject to decay after her death. Mary is seen as an example of what Paul describes: Her perishable body has put on imperishability, her mortal body has become immortal. Read slowly and carefully, conveying the hope that Paul expresses for a future life and his conviction that death, powerful though it may be, is not the final victor.

GOSPEL **After Jesus was accused of bearing demonic power, the woman in today's reading speaks in support of him and his contention that he acts as God's agent. She offers a word of praise for Mary in terms that recall how central bearing and rearing children were to women in this culture.**

Jesus' response does not negate the woman's claim but indicates that biological connections are of secondary importance. Instead of celebrating earthly relationships, Jesus calls attention to those whose goal is to listen to God's word and put it into action.

Mary is remembered as the first disciple of Jesus, the first to "ponder in her heart" the significance of his life and teachings. This reading is an appropriate way to honor her today, both for her role as mother of Jesus and for her willingness to recognize his significance and be his disciple.

Because this reading is so short, be especially careful to read slowly and to savor it.

ASSUMPTION

Lectionary #622

READING I Revelation 11:19a; 12:1–6a, 10ab

Note that it is not "Revelations" but "Revelation" (singular).

A reading from the book of Revelation.

God's *temple* in *heaven* was opened,
and the *ark* of his *covenant* could be *seen* in the temple.

A *great sign* appeared in the *sky*, a *woman* clothed with the *sun*,
with the *moon* beneath her *feet*,
and on her *head* a crown of *twelve stars*.
She was *with child* and *wailed* aloud in pain as she *labored*
to give *birth*.

The dragon is diabolical; speed up the tempo here in order to indicate the tensions inherent in the scene.
diadems = DĪ-uh-demz

Then *another* sign appeared in the sky;
it was a *huge* red *dragon*, with *seven heads* and *ten horns*,
and on its *heads* were *seven diadems*.
Its *tail* swept away a *third* of the *stars* in the *sky*
and *hurled* them down to the *earth*.
Then the *dragon* stood before the *woman* about to give *birth*,
to *devour* her child when she gave *birth*.

This is the Messiah promised by the prophets.

Although there is still urgency in the "catching up" of the child and the flight of the woman, begin to calm your voice.

She gave *birth* to a *son*, a *male child*,
destined to *rule all* the *nations* with an *iron rod*.
Her child was *caught up* to *God* and his *throne*.
The woman herself *fled* into the *desert*
where she had a place *prepared* by God.

READING I The heavenly vision that the author of Revelation describes in this passage is one of a great battle between forces of good and evil. The descriptions of the participants in the drama and the combat itself are drawn from both Greco-Roman and Jewish myths. The woman who gives birth appears to be Mary (or Israel) and the child is clearly the Messiah; elsewhere the woman seems to represent the church as her many offspring continue to be pursued by the dragon.

The apocalyptic imagery of this passage can be confusing. First, heaven is pictured as a great temple which contains the ark of the covenant, the ancient container that held the tablets of the Mosaic Law. Then, as in a dream, the scene changes and the focus shifts to a woman about to give birth. She is beautifully clothed with the sun, moon and stars; she is the queen of heaven.

The dragon who earlier tried to grasp heavenly authority (by sweeping the stars out of heaven) now enters the scene, seeking to harm the woman's child. The appearance of the dragon (seven heads and ten horns) comes from the depiction of the enemies of the righteous in the book of Daniel; the seven heads recall imperial Rome, the city on seven hills, which is here seen as the enemy of Christianity.

The child is born and taken to be with God. The woman now represents the church, cared for by God for a limited time (1260 days) until the dragon is defeated. During this time the Messiah already reigns, however, as the voice from heaven proclaims.

Proclaim this triumphant statement of divine rule with clarity and authority.

Then I heard a *loud voice* in heaven say:
"*Now* have *salvation* and *power* come,
and the *kingdom* of our *God*
and the *authority* of his *Anointed* One."

READING II 1 Corinthians 15:20–27

A reading from the first letter of Saint Paul to the Corinthians.

Pause briefly at the end of this line.

Pause.

Pause after "die."

Take a deep breath and change your tone as you begin the next line. "Then" all things will be different and God will reign supreme. Celebrate this proclamation with joyful expectation in your voice.

Your voice should be a bit more subdued for this final line; pause after "destroyed."

Brothers and sisters:
Christ has been *raised* from the *dead*,
the *firstfruits* of those who have *fallen asleep.*
For since *death* came through *man*,
the *resurrection* of the dead came *also* through *man.*
For just as in *Adam all* die,
so too in *Christ* shall *all* be brought to *life*,
but *each* one in proper *order:*
Christ the *firstfruits*;
then, at his coming, those who *belong* to Christ;
then comes the *end*,
when he hands over the *kingdom* to his *God* and *Father*,
when he has *destroyed every sovereignty*
and every *authority* and *power.*

For *he* must *reign* until he has put all his *enemies* under his *feet.*
The *last* enemy to be destroyed is *death*,
for "he subjected *everything* under his *feet.*"

This is a difficult but beautiful passage, chosen because of the imagery of the woman. Mary has often been depicted as ruling the cosmos, and her Son is the one enthroned with God in heaven. Read the selection with awe at the heavenly vision and the beauty of the woman, and with compassion for her pain. Convey also the danger of the dragon's threat. Finally, close with the triumphant realization that all will be kept safe by God, who reigns in majesty.

READING II After rejecting the claim of some Christians that there is no resurrection of the dead, Paul develops in this section the meaning of Christ's resurrection. In Jewish liturgical language, Christ is the "first fruits" of those who have died, the one who represents the whole. What he experienced in rising from the dead is available to all who die with faith in him.

Paul then alludes to his belief that death entered the world because of the sin of Adam. Christ—the second Adam—makes life possible both for Christians who have already died and for those who remain alive at Christ's second coming (as Paul expected himself and his contemporaries to be). Finally, after overcoming death and all other hostile powers, Christ will turn over all rule to God.

This reading is chosen for the feast of the Assumption because of the belief that Mary has already followed her Son and resides in heavenly glory. The tradition that she was taken into heaven after her death is a way of indicating that death was not the final word for her. Instead, she has already

GOSPEL Luke 1:39–56

A reading from the holy gospel according to Luke.

Mary set *out*
and traveled to the *hill* country in *haste*
to a town of *Judah*,
where she entered the *house* of *Zechariah*
and greeted *Elizabeth.*

Zechariah = zek-uh-RĪ-uh

When Elizabeth heard Mary's *greeting*,
the *infant* leaped in her *womb*,
and *Elizabeth*, *filled* with the *Holy Spirit*,
cried out in a *loud voice* and said,
"*Blessed* are you among *women*,
and *blessed* is the *fruit* of your *womb.*
And *how* does this happen to *me*,
that the *mother* of my *Lord* should *come* to me?
For at the moment the sound of your *greeting* reached my *ears*,
the *infant* in my womb *leaped* for joy.
Blessed are *you* who *believed*
that what was *spoken* to you by the *Lord*
would be *fulfilled.*"

Proclaim Elizabeth's words with sincerity and wonder. In order to avoid rattling through the familiar words, consciously try to slow down your diction, dwelling on every phrase.

And *Mary* said:
"My *soul proclaims* the *greatness* of the *Lord*;
my *spirit rejoices* in *God* my *Savior*
for he has *looked* upon his *lowly servant.*
From this day all *generations* will call me *blessed:*
the *Almighty* has done *great things* for me,
and *holy* is his *Name.*
He has *mercy* on those who *fear* him
in every *generation.*

Mary picks up the tone of praise.

Speak this and the following lines with a bit of disbelief in your voice; Mary must surely have been amazed at God's favor to her.

experienced a share in the resurrection promised to all who follow Jesus.

The beginning of the passage is difficult. Proclaim it slowly, emphasizing the contrasts between death and resurrection, between Adam and Christ. The second half of the reading is a proclamation of God's reign and can be read as a word of praise.

GOSPEL The gospel of Luke is known for the hymns it contains, and the Magnificat, spoken by Mary in today's gospel, is one of the most beautiful. Although the hymn itself clearly draws on material from the Hebrew tradition, it is the longest passage attributed to Mary in any gospel. It is not difficult to imagine a poor, unwed pregnant girl proclaiming these words, a celebration of God's compassion for the lowly and ability to humble the proud.

The context of the hymn is Mary's visit to Elizabeth. The mothers of two future itinerant preachers are brought together as friends and relatives. Since there was some tension between the followers of John and those of Jesus during their ministries and afterward, the author here makes it clear that Jesus is the greater, and the unborn John and his mother rejoice at and are humbled by Mary's visit. Elizabeth utters a cry honoring Mary for her trust in God's promise to her.

Mary's response is a joyful, trusting song of reversal that celebrates God's activity in her life and in Israel's. While the hymn is a song of praise to God, it is fitting for a Marian feast since it illustrates Mary's humility and faith, including her belief in a righteous God who acts on behalf of the lowly.

With this line, let your voice become firmer and more insistent. The words Mary proclaims are those of upheaval; nothing is at it seems.

"He has shown the *strength* of his *arm*,
and has *scattered* the *proud* in their *conceit.*
He has *cast down* the *mighty* from their *thrones*,
and has *lifted up* the *lowly.*
He has filled the *hungry* with *good things*,
and the *rich* he has sent away *empty.*
He has come to the *help* of his *servant* Israel
for he has *remembered* his promise of *mercy*,
the *promise* he made to our *fathers*,
to *Abraham* and his *children* for ever."

Pause before continuing in a subdued but clear voice.

Mary remained with her about *three* months
and then *returned* to her home.

The first half of the hymn discusses the favor God has bestowed on Mary. Although she proclaims herself a handmaid or servant, one of the lowly ones, she will be called blessed because of the great things God has done for her and through her. In this way, the first half of the hymn foreshadows what follows: God deals with the individual servant Mary in much the same way as God deals with servant Israel. Both are blessed beyond measure, recipients of God's protection, compassion and lavish graciousness.

Not only is there divine favor for the lowly, but God acts decisively to eliminate systems of power and inequity. The haughty and proud, who have placed themselves on a level with God as they scorn the less fortunate, are shown their rightful place. The images are of political leaders; the message is that the land of Israel, occupied by a foreign power, will be vindicated. But Israel has within it also the individual poor, the hungry; they too shall be cared for.

Sing with Mary this song of praise and thanksgiving. Read the passage as a way of honoring her, especially easy to do when quoting the words of Elizabeth. But read it also as a celebration of God's righteousness, the triumph of the poor and humble over the proud and strong. Then work to make the words a reality in your own community wherever there are discrepancies — whether ecclesiastical, political, social or economic in nature — between the proud and the lowly, the hungry and the rich.

20TH SUNDAY IN ORDINARY TIME

Lectionary #119

READING I Proverbs 9:1–6

A reading from the book of Proverbs.

Wisdom has built her *house*,
she has *set* up her seven *columns*;
she has *dressed* her meat, *mixed* her wine,
yes, she has *spread* her table.
She has sent out her *maidens*; she *calls*
from the heights out over the city:
"Let whoever is *simple turn* in *here*";
to the one who lacks *understanding*, she says,
"*Come*, *eat* of my food,
and *drink* of the wine I have mixed!
Forsake foolishness that you may *live*;
advance in the way of *understanding*."

This is a summons to join in a splendid banquet; make it sound inviting.

Emphasize with a bit more seriousness the rewards of sharing in this banquet: life and understanding.

READING II Ephesians 5:15–20

A reading from the letter of Saint Paul to the Ephesians.

Brothers and sisters:
Watch *carefully* how you *live*,
not as *foolish* persons but as *wise*,
making the *most* of the opportunity,
because the *days* are *evil*.

The early part of the reading encourages caution.

READING I **Wisdom, personified in the Hebrew Scriptures as a feminine consort of God, here tries to entice the wayward to partake of her food and drink. As a temptress she beckons those lacking in understanding to share in her table, to drink of her wine. But she does not seek to lead the foolish into the depths of debauchery; rather she is attempting to ensnare them in order to teach, that they may grow in knowledge.**

The Hebrew word for "wisdom" is grammatically feminine, and Lady Wisdom became personified as a quasi-divine being. She is presented as a woman who "hits the streets" in order to draw people to herself. Just as it is often necessary to join people on their own "turf" in order to teach them, minister to them, and encourage them to listen, so also Lady Wisdom does whatever she can to get attention, especially of young men, in order to help them learn.

Wisdom is something more than simple knowledge. Reflect on someone you know who is truly wise, and then read this passage as an invitation for all to share in that wisdom. The experience promises to be pleasant as well as profitable. Make it sound inviting to your listeners as well.

READING II **The author of Ephesians continues the reflection on wisdom begun in the first reading today. Here, wisdom and folly are contrasted and the recipients of the letter are given moral instruction. In fact, this is the central point of this passage: Wisdom is not simply intellectual or reflective, but is made known by action.**

Therefore, do *not* continue in *ignorance*,
but try to *understand* what is the *will* of the *Lord*.

With this line, begin to slow down and lighten your voice. The rest of the passage is to be spoken with a joyful and thankful spirit. Proclaim each item ("psalms," "hymns") or each phrase individually.

And do *not* get drunk on *wine*, in which lies *debauchery*,
but be *filled* with the *Spirit*,
addressing one another in *psalms* and *hymns* and
spiritual songs,
singing and *playing* to the Lord in your *hearts*,
giving *thanks always* and for *everything*

Pause. Read this closing line with special emphasis.

in the *name* of our *Lord Jesus Christ* to *God* the *Father*.

GOSPEL John 6:51–58

A reading from the holy gospel according to John.

Jesus said to the crowds:
"*I* am the *living bread* that came down from *heaven*;

The emphasis here is on the contrast between this bread and the manna from heaven.

whoever eats *this* bread will live *forever*;
and the *bread* that I will *give*
is my *flesh* for the *life* of the *world*."

The Jews *quarreled* among themselves, saying,

A reasonable question; speak it with incredulity.

"*How* can this man give us his *flesh* to eat?"
Jesus said to them,
"*Amen, amen*, I *say* to you,
unless you *eat* the *flesh* of the Son of Man and *drink* his *blood*,
you do *not* have *life* within you.
Whoever *eats* my *flesh* and *drinks* my *blood*
has *eternal life*,
and I will *raise* him on the *last day*.

Exhort your assembly to leave aside foolish ways and adopt behavior proper to the Christian life. When one is filled with the Holy Spirit, the joy of knowing God will be evident. Encourage your listeners to join with the Ephesians in praising God constantly, and in giving thanks always. Recognizing God's goodness and love is a sign of wisdom.

GOSPEL Today's gospel reading picks up where last Sunday's left off. There is a shift, however, from discussion of the "bread of life" to talk of Jesus' "flesh."

The emphasis on eating Jesus' flesh and drinking his blood is as striking to us as to those who question his words in this passage. We are accustomed to viewing the eucharist as the body and blood of Christ, but the mention of "flesh" is a little too literal and suggests cannibalism. This was precisely the charge leveled against early Christians by their detractors. Yet other early Christian writers use this term as well, perhaps in response to those Christians who attempted to deny the reality of Jesus' suffering by suggesting that his visible body was not real flesh and blood, and thus incapable of suffering.

While the idea of eating Jesus' flesh is startling and drew attacks from non-Christians, the suggestion of drinking his blood would have been even more of an

For my *flesh* is *true food,*
and my *blood* is *true drink.*
Whoever *eats* my *flesh* and *drinks* my *blood*
remains in me and *I* in him.

Pause briefly after "blood."

Emphasize here the indwelling of Jesus in the believer, a relationship that reflects the relationship between the Father and Son.

"Just as the *living Father* sent me
and I have *life* because of the *Father,*
so also the one who *feeds* on *me*
will have *life* because of me.
This is the bread that came down from *heaven.*
Unlike your *ancestors* who *ate* and still *died,*
whoever eats *this bread* will *live forever."*

Here the contrast with the manna in the desert is made explicit.

Slow down considerably at the end of this line.

abomination for Jews, who were prohibited from drinking the blood of animals. This gospel was written by Christian Jews at odds with the larger Jewish community, perhaps over issues such as this.

But the author is clear: The command to eat Jesus' flesh and drink his blood comes from his lips. Participation in this ritual celebration unites the believer with Christ and leads to life eternal, a life that is Christ's to offer just as he received life from the Father. The references to flesh and blood — the two components of the human person according to the ancients — bring to mind the reality of the cross: flesh pierced and blood shed for the sake of others.

Finally, a contrast is made with manna, received by the Israelites during their wandering in the desert and mentioned in last week's gospel. Precisely because he came from the Father, Jesus can say that this bread — his flesh — came from heaven. But it is unlike the heavenly manna that offers sustenance for a day. What this bread offers is the life of the living Father, made available through Jesus.

Your task in proclaiming this gospel is multifaceted. The bulk of the reading consists of a teaching by Jesus that refers to his impending death (his flesh given for the life of the world), his origin with the Father, and the importance of his followers dwelling in him by eating of the "bread from heaven." While the teaching can be understood as eucharistic, encourage your assembly to see the centrality of the crucifixion here as well, the event that makes real the possibility of eternal life.

21ST SUNDAY IN ORDINARY TIME

Lectionary #122

READING I Joshua 24:1–2a, 15–17, 18b

A reading from the book of Joshua.

Shechem = SHEK-uhm

Joshua gathered together *all* the tribes of *Israel* at *Shechem*,
summoning their *elders*, their *leaders*,
their *judges*, and their *officers*.
When they stood in *ranks* before *God*,
Joshua addressed *all* the *people:*

This is a bold attempt to provoke Israel into a positive response to God by pushing them in the opposite direction. From the people's response, we can see that it worked.
Amorites = AM-er-rīts

"If it does *not* please you to serve the *LORD*,
decide today whom you *will* serve,
the gods your *fathers served* beyond the *River*
or the gods of the *Amorites* in whose country you are
now dwelling.

Pause before beginning this line and then read it with solemn conviction.

As for *me* and *my* household, *we* will serve the *LORD."*

But the people answered,
"*Far* be it from *us* to *forsake* the LORD
for the service of *other* gods.
For it was the *LORD, our God,*
who brought *us* and our *fathers* up out of the *land* of *Egypt*,
out of a state of *slavery.*
He performed those *great miracles* before our very eyes
and *protected* us along our *entire journey*
and among the *peoples* through whom we *passed.*

Speak this line slowly and with great emphasis.

Therefore we *also* will serve the *LORD*, for *he* is our *God."*

READING I **Joshua reminds the leaders of Israel of all God's deeds on their behalf. He also reveals that many of the Hebrew people continue to revere other deities. Joshua challenges them, even taunts them, in an effort to make their response to God heartfelt and complete. The statement that he and his family will serve the God of Israel is a classic affirmation of Israel's covenant commitment.**

The response of the people provides a brief summary of God's activity in their lives. It ends with a proclamation that the God of action, the God who has guided them and saved them, the God who has chosen them personally, is the God Israel will worship. The text does not claim that there are no other gods — that will come later — but contains the Israelites' pledge to remain faithful to the one who has been ever faithful to them.

Today's passage provides a wonderful opportunity for a communal celebration of covenant renewal. Allow the response of the people to Joshua to ring in the ears of your hearers and inspire them to make a similar pledge.

READING II **The immediate concern of the author is to instruct the community in right action, and the letter is filled with ethical admonitions. The author includes a theological conviction regarding the relationship between the church and Christ. But all of this can be lost because of the language — so strange to our ears — regarding relationships within the family.**

The letter to the Ephesians borrows its language from the culture of its time in order to instruct people in proper behavior. The author of this letter uses general principles that clearly reflect the mores of an era quite

READING II Ephesians 5:21–32

A reading from the letter of Saint Paul to the Ephesians.

Brothers and sisters:
Be *subordinate* to one *another* out of *reverence* for Christ.
Wives should be subordinate to their *husbands* as to the *Lord.*
For the *husband* is head of his *wife*
just as *Christ* is head of the *church,*
he himself the *savior* of the body.
As the *church* is subordinate to *Christ,*
so *wives* should be subordinate to their *husbands*
in everything.

This passage is not easy to read. Avoid inserting your own opinion; there is no room for either triumphalism or apology.

Husbands, love your wives,
even as *Christ* loved the *church*
and handed himself *over* for her to *sanctify* her,
cleansing her by the bath of *water* with the *word,*
that he might *present* to himself the church in *splendor,*
without *spot* or *wrinkle* or any such thing,
that she might be *holy* and without *blemish.*

The admonition to husbands follows quickly upon that to wives. It is demanding. Truly loving one's spouse includes the desire to help that person be pure and holy; emphasize these terms in the reading.

So also *husbands* should *love* their *wives* as their own *bodies.*
He who *loves* his *wife loves* himself.
For *no* one hates his *own* flesh
but rather *nourishes* and *cherishes* it,
even as *Christ* does the *church,*
because we are *members* of his *body.*
"For *this reason* a man shall leave his *father* and his *mother*
and be *joined* to his *wife,*
and the *two* shall become *one flesh.*"

To love one's spouse completely is the same as loving oneself.
Pause briefly after "himself."

This is a great *mystery,*
but I speak in reference to *Christ* and the *church.*

[Shorter: Ephesians 5:2a, 25–32]

different from our own. The inclusion of the household code in works judged to be "scriptural" has led to the abuse of this passage, directly contradicting the passage's main point—the Christian responsibility to behave lovingly toward others. Scripture should never be used as a tool to dominate others.

What the passage actually says is that Christians are to treat one another with care and reverence. In the first century, women showed respect to their husbands by deferring to their them in everything. Husbands were to be responsible providers and were not to be abusive, but the extensive instruction given here regarding the proper treatment of wives is a unique contribution by this author. It becomes clear that the author's primary concern is to comment on the relationship between the community of Christians and Christ. The willingness of Christ to give himself up for the sake of the church is the model for Christian behavior. The intimate relationship between a husband and wife reflects the closeness between Christ and those who follow him.

Because of the difficulty inherent in these verses, some communities may choose to use the shorter reading, which begins with "Husbands, love your wives . . ." Be sure to check with the liturgy coordinator or the preacher to determine where you are to begin the reading. Whether you read the longer or the shorter reading, be sure to emphasize what is important here: the mutual respect enjoined on family members and the tremendous love Christ showers on his beloved church.

GOSPEL This passage is the conclusion of Jesus' teaching on the bread of life (see the discussions of the

GOSPEL John 6:60–69

A reading from the holy gospel according to John.

Many of Jesus'disciples who were listening said,
"This saying is *hard*; who can *accept* it?"

Since these are followers of Jesus, they would presumably want to believe what Jesus is teaching them, but cannot. Perhaps there is sadness in their voices.

Since Jesus *knew* that his disciples were *murmuring* about this,
he said to them, "Does this *shock* you?
What if you were to see the Son of Man *ascending*
to where he was *before?*
It is the *spirit* that gives life,
while the *flesh* is of *no avail.*
The words I have spoken to you are *Spirit* and *life.*
But there are *some* of you who do *not* believe."
Jesus knew from the *beginning* the ones who would *not* believe
and the one *who* would *betray* him.

As always in this gospel, Jesus has complete knowledge. This is a parenthetical statement; speak it in a slightly lower voice.

And he said,
"For this reason I have told you that *no one* can *come* to me
unless it is *granted* him by my *Father.*"

As a result of this,
many of his disciples returned to their *former* way of life
and no longer *accompanied* him.
Jesus then said to the *Twelve,* "Do *you also* want to *leave?*"

Simon Peter answered him, "Master, to *whom* shall we *go?*
You have the words of *eternal life.*
We have come to *believe*
and are *convinced* that *you* are the *Holy One* of *God.*"

Slow down as you read Peter's words. Peter's response is deeper than what this question alone might suggest. Not only is there nowhere else to turn, but in fact he and the others would never want to follow anyone else. In essence, there is no alternative because they have chosen the path Jesus himself walks.

last two weeks). Jesus' teaching here turns radically from that presented before. "Flesh" is no longer that which Jesus gives his followers to eat, but is instead "useless."

This blatant contradiction cannot be explained away, but it is possible to understand the message more fully. "Flesh" here does not have the same meaning that it had earlier, but instead refers to the mortal human person in contrast to the divine Spirit. Jesus says that his words, including those regarding eating his flesh and drinking his blood, give witness to the life-giving Spirit of God. In fact, Jesus says that his words do more than simply bear witness: They bear that Spirit within them. Once again, Jesus is presented as the ultimate revelation of God. He does not simply point to something beyond the world; he himself is what is revealed, he himself is that to which he points.

The departure of some of Jesus' followers from him may reflect the experience of the community from which this gospel arose. Non-Christian Jews may have been willing to accept the teachings of Jesus on many subjects, but probably could not tolerate the claim that Jesus was himself the revelation of God. Peter speaks for the Twelve and for all Christians, expressing the belief in Jesus as the "Holy One of God": "You have the words of eternal life."

Inspire your listeners to share in the conviction of Peter. Jesus' words are difficult, but the follower of Jesus asserts that there is really nowhere else to turn. For the Christian, it is only through Jesus that there can be life.

22ND SUNDAY IN ORDINARY TIME

Lectionary #125

READING I Deuteronomy 4:1–2, 6–8

A reading from the book of Deuteronomy.

Moses said to the people:
"*Now,* Israel, hear the *statutes* and *decrees*
which I am *teaching* you to *observe,*
that you may *live,* and may *enter* in and take *possession* of the land
which the LORD, the God of your *fathers,* is *giving* you.
In your *observance* of the *commandments* of the LORD, your *God,*
which I *enjoin* upon you,
you shall *not add* to what I command you *nor subtract* from it.

Announce this to your congregation just as Moses did to Israel.

"Observe them *carefully,*
for thus will you give evidence
of your *wisdom* and *intelligence* to the *nations,*
who will hear of all these statutes and say,
'This *great* nation is truly a *wise* and *intelligent* people.'
For what *great nation* is there
that has gods *so close* to it as the LORD, *our God,* is to *us*
whenever we call upon him?
Or what *great nation* has *statutes* and *decrees*
that are as *just* as this whole *law*
which I am setting *before* you today?"

If the commandments are obeyed, their results will be clear to all.

Proclaim this with a bit of wonder in your voice.

These are rhetorical questions. Stress "so close" with awe; it is amazing that the transcendent God has chosen to be so present to Israel and to us.

READING I After the Exodus from Egypt, as Israel approaches the Promised Land from the east, Moses delivers speeches concerning the Law of God. Moses begins by reviewing the history of Israel. He then exhorts the people to cherish the Law. Rather than being burdensome, it is precious and good, guiding its followers and instilling wisdom within them.

There are practical consequences to following the Law; observing the Law will allow Israel to enter the land that awaits it. But its primary purpose is not simply to secure the land for Israel. The Law serves to teach Israel, and what Israel learns from it is not lost on other nations. Moses describes the Gentiles envying Israel and its Law, and noting the intimacy shared between Israel and its God. Proclaim with Moses how beautiful and precious are the commands of God, so that your assembly may embrace them as did Israel.

READING II Central to the message of the letter of James is the proclamation that human action must accompany conviction: Be doers of the God's word, not merely hearers.

Time and again the letter lists the responsibilities of the community to those less fortunate. The letter is unequivocal in stating that having wealth and advantage on earth can be detrimental to one's standing before God. There is a clear call for social

READING II James 1:17–18, 21b–22, 27

A reading from the letter of Saint James.

Dearest brothers and sisters:

The first section of the passage can be read joyfully and smoothly.

All good giving and *every perfect gift* is from *above*,
coming down from the *Father* of *lights*,
with whom there is no *alteration* or *shadow* caused by change.
He willed to give us *birth* by the word of *truth*
that we may be a kind of *firstfruits* of his creatures.

This is a transition sentence; begin to slow down.

Humbly *welcome* the word that has been *planted* in you
and is able to *save* your *souls*.

Read this slowly and forcefully; pause here.

Be *doers* of the word and *not hearers* only, *deluding* yourselves.

Pause here before solemnly stressing the command of God to care for those in need.

Religion that is *pure* and *undefiled* before God and the Father
is this:
to care for *orphans* and *widows* in their *affliction*
and to keep oneself *unstained* by the world.

GOSPEL Mark 7:1–8, 14–15, 21–23

A reading from the holy gospel according to Mark.

When the *Pharisees* with some *scribes* who had
come from *Jerusalem*
gathered around Jesus,
they *observed* that some of his disciples ate their meals
with *unclean*, that is, *unwashed*, hands.

justice, for a righteousness lived out in concrete deeds for the benefit of "orphans and widows," a stock phrase for those in need. This is not simply nice behavior but actually makes one pure before God.

We need to hear this message today more than ever; it has been entrusted to you. Proclaim it forcefully.

GOSPEL The Law of Moses recorded in the Pentateuch (the first five books of the Bible) was supplemented by oral traditions regarding diet, ritual purity and other matters of Jewish piety. Although it was not recorded until after the time of Jesus, the core of the oral tradition is ancient and has long been revered by the Hebrew people. Here such traditions come under attack by none other than Jesus himself.

The author's parenthetical statement explaining the Jewish practice of purification indicates this early community's lack of familiarity with Jewish tradition. Jesus' disciples had not been observing these practices, and the religious leaders challenged him regarding their behavior. Jesus does not respond to the question directly, but looks beyond it to what he sees lying at the heart of the issue.

In verses that have been removed from our reading, Jesus points out that the oral tradition is sometimes used as a means of avoiding the intent of the commandments of God. One can make an excuse not to care for

The author writes for a non-Jewish audience and explains Jewish customs. Lower your voice a bit as you read this explanatory statement.

(For the *Pharisees* and, in fact, *all* Jews,
do not *eat* without carefully *washing* their hands,
keeping the *tradition* of the *elders.*
And on coming from the *marketplace*
they do not eat without *purifying* themselves.
And there are many *other* things that they have traditionally observed,
the purification of *cups* and *jugs* and *kettles* and *beds.*)
So the Pharisees and scribes *questioned* him,
"*Why* do your disciples *not follow* the tradition of the *elders*
but *instead* eat a meal with *unclean hands?*"

Jesus' words are harsh; speak them as such.

He responded,
"*Well* did Isaiah *prophesy* about you *hypocrites*, as it is written:
'This people honors me with their *lips*,
but their *hearts* are *far* from me;
in *vain* do they worship me,
teaching as *doctrines human* precepts.'
You *disregard God's* commandment but cling to *human* tradition."

This is what Jesus considers important. Slow your delivery to concentrate on his words regarding the human heart.

He summoned the crowd again and said to them,
"*Hear* me, all of you, and *understand.*
Nothing that *enters* one from outside can *defile* that person;
but the things that come out from *within* are what defile.

Read the list slowly and deliberately.

"From *within* people, from their *hearts*,
come *evil thoughts, unchastity, theft, murder,*
adultery, greed, malice, deceit,
licentiousness, envy, blasphemy, arrogance, folly.
All these evils come from *within* and *they* defile."

Emphasize the word "they." The contrast is between the ritual washings stressed by the Pharisees and the deeds and attitudes residing in the heart which Jesus has just listed.

one's parents ("Honor thy father and thy mother") by claiming that one's resources are being offered to God. Jesus castigates the religious leaders for allowing such hypocrisy. He goes on to point out that what really matters is what is inside a person's heart; outward behavior stems from what is within.

Although the author of the gospel suggests that Jesus nullified Jewish dietary regulations, it is important to note that Jesus' own words do not challenge the validity of the Law itself, but rather what he perceived as hypocrisy on the part of the religious leaders. Jesus concentrates first on the human heart as the source of activity.

It is not difficult to think of bureaucratic regulations that can take on a life of their own at the expense of the persons they are supposed to serve. Jesus criticizes this tendency of rules and regulations to become more important than the human person. It is especially important for those in leadership positions within the church — whether as parish council members, teachers or pastors — to reflect on ways in which we are hypocritical, upholding the law while ignoring the real needs of those we are called upon to serve.

23RD SUNDAY IN ORDINARY TIME

Lectionary #128

READING I Isaiah 35:4–7a

A reading from the book of the prophet Isaiah.

Thus says the LORD:
Say to those whose hearts are *frightened:*
Be *strong,* fear *not!*
Here is your God,
he comes with *vindication;*
with *divine recompense*
he comes to *save* you.

Speak with encouragement.

Then will the *eyes* of the *blind* be *opened,*
the *ears* of the *deaf* be *cleared;*
then will the *lame leap* like a stag,
then the *tongue* of the *mute* will *sing.*

With this line your voice can change slightly. Now you are proclaiming the wondrous things that will happen when God comes to save. Speak with certitude.

Streams will *burst forth* in the *desert,*
and *rivers* in the *steppe.*
The *burning sands* will become *pools,*
and the *thirsty* ground, *springs* of *water.*

Allow your voice to rise with this phrase, then gently soften to the end of the reading. steppe = step

READING I The beautiful images in today's first reading arise from the prophet Isaiah's undying hope that the Assyrian threat to the kingdom of Judah (a threat that resulted in the fall of the northern kingdom of Israel) will end and the Hebrew people will have cause to rejoice. Isaiah gives encouragement even in darkness. The themes in today's reading reflect the expectation of divine blessing in the political affairs of the eighth century BCE, but have long been taken to refer as well to the promises of God for a day in the future when righteousness will reign and paradise will be restored.

There are many in your congregation whose hearts are frightened and who have little hope. Proclaim God's words of encouragement with joy, but also with sensitivity to the pain in people's hearts. By your strength of voice and conviction, offer real hope that God is able to make all things right, correcting wrongs, bringing healing and life, and providing refreshment for those who struggle.

READING II "Show no partiality." This was a central precept in the Hebrew tradition when one member of the community brought a charge against another in a legal setting. It is the insistence that "justice is blind," that one's appearance or social position ought not determine how one is treated.

It is not clear if this section of the letter of James envisions a liturgical assembly or a judicial setting. In either situation the command to look beyond appearance

READING II James 2:1–5

A reading from the letter of Saint James.

Stress this central precept.

My brothers and sisters, show *no partiality*
as you adhere to the *faith* in our *glorious* Lord Jesus Christ.

This sentence is long and difficult to read; it will require much practice. Read it slowly but without dragging it out. Pause often, beginning after "assembly," then after "also comes in," "please," "Stand there" and "feet."

For if a man with *gold* rings and *fine* clothes
comes into your *assembly*,
and a *poor* person in *shabby* clothes *also* comes in,
and *you* pay *attention* to the one wearing the *fine* clothes
and say, "Sit *here*, please,"
while you say to the *poor* one, "Stand *there*," or
"Sit at my *feet*,"
have you *not* made *distinctions* among yourselves
and become *judges* with *evil designs*?

Take a deep breath before continuing with urgency in your voice.

Listen, my beloved brothers and sisters.

Pause briefly after "faith."

This is a rhetorical question; your voice need not rise at the end. Instead, speak with conviction.

Did not God choose those who are *poor* in the world
to be *rich* in faith and *heirs* of the *kingdom*
that he *promised* to those who *love* him?

is appropriate, but the image evoked is especially striking if we imagine a group of people gathered for prayer. How vile it is if those who have much are given honor while those in need are further insulted and excluded! The author points out that God has chosen those who are poor in the world and given them great faith. We could add that Jesus himself was a poor itinerant preacher.

The situation in this passage is so similar to our own that it is embarrassing. How often do we revere as "role models" those who have wealth, fame, prestige? How often do we give our time and attention to those who dress nicely, who have important positions or jobs, or who are educated and articulate? Your task today is to challenge attitudes that are deeply ingrained in your listeners. Offer your hearers the possibility of approaching others not with eyes that see only what is external but with God's own vision, which sees the dignity and honor of the poor and less fortunate.

GOSPEL **Christians have long held that Jesus is the fulfillment of the prophecies spoken by Isaiah. This passage, especially when proclaimed together with today's first reading, presents Jesus as the one who restores sight to the blind, makes the lame walk, and helps the deaf hear and the mute speak. According to the evangelist, Jesus brings about the promised day when God will truly reign over all forces of evil and illness, so that all people can enjoy fullness of life.**

GOSPEL Mark 7:31–37

Tyre = tīr
Sidon = SĪ-duhn
Galilee = GAL-ih-lee
Decapolis = dih-KAP-uh-lis
The Gentile author of this gospel presents Jesus accomplishing several miracles in Gentile territory.

A reading from the holy gospel according to Mark.

Again Jesus left the district of *Tyre*
and went by way of *Sidon* to the *Sea* of *Galilee*,
into the district of the *Decapolis*.

And people brought to him a *deaf* man who had a
speech impediment
and *begged* him to lay his *hand* on him.
He took him off by *himself away* from the crowd.
He put his *finger* into the man's *ears*
and, spitting, *touched* his *tongue*;
then he *looked up* to heaven and *groaned*, and said to him,
"Ephphatha!"—that is, "Be *opened!"*
And immediately the man's ears were opened,
his *speech* impediment was *removed*,
and he spoke *plainly*.

ephphatha = EF-fah-thah
Speak the word with authority, then pause.
With this line, allow the wonder of the event to inform your reading.

He ordered them *not* to tell anyone.
But the *more* he ordered them *not* to,
the *more* they *proclaimed* it.
They were *exceedingly astonished* and they said,
"He has done *all* things *well*.
He makes the *deaf hear* and the *mute speak*."

Convey the astonishment of the crowd.

The miracles of Jesus in the gospel of Mark serve to designate him as the manifestation of God's power. The amazement of those who witnessed the miracle indicates Jesus' power. The irony of this story is that Jesus, while displaying his power and receiving positive comments from those present, insists that the witnesses are to keep the deed secret. This "messianic secret," so prominent in the gospel of Mark, is the author's way of de-emphasizing the spectacular and concentrating instead on the difficulties of ministry—Jesus' ministry and that of all his followers. Although Jesus is the embodiment of God's power, Jesus does not rely on that power to avoid suffering.

Allow the members of your congregation to hear the wonder in your voice as you recount this healing miracle of Jesus. Let them see, as did the crowd in the story, that God's promises are fulfilled through this event. Encourage your listeners to be part of the crowd, to feel the excitement, to wonder at Jesus' command to keep silent.

24TH SUNDAY IN ORDINARY TIME

Lectionary #131

READING I Isaiah 50:5–9a

A reading from the book of the prophet Isaiah.

The *Lord* GOD opens my *ear* that I may *hear;*
and I have *not rebelled,*
have *not* turned *back.*

Speak solemnly, but without bitterness, of the servant's sufferings.

I gave my *back* to those who *beat* me,
my *cheeks* to those who *plucked* my *beard;*
my *face* I did *not shield*
from *buffets* and *spitting.*

Lift your voice with hope and conviction.

The *Lord* GOD is my help,
therefore I am *not disgraced;*
I have set my *face* like *flint,*
knowing that I shall *not* be put to *shame.*
He is *near* who upholds my *right;*

Here is a confrontation with an imaginary adversary.

if anyone wishes to *oppose* me,
let us appear *together.*

Who disputes my *right?*
Let that man *confront* me.

End slowly and with certitude.

See, the *Lord* GOD is my *help;*
who will prove me *wrong?*

READING I The last half of the book of Isaiah includes "servant songs"—poetic reflections on suffering in the service of God. At times it appears that the servant is Israel and at other times an individual who will soon come to inaugurate a new age. In this passage, however, the servant of God seems to be identified as the speaker. The servant is one who is faithful to God's commands and relies on God for strength and vindication, unflinching despite tremendous human opposition and persecution.

The servant songs of Isaiah have long been understood by Christians to provide particularly appropriate interpretations of the suffering of Jesus. It was Jesus who remained true to his mission despite opposition. It was Jesus who suffered cruel torture without cowering. Abandoned, he relied solely on God for his strength.

While the servant songs can certainly be read meaningfully in reference to Jesus, they also reflect the experience of anyone who stands for a principle against all odds. Any servant of God will know suffering, but reliance on God's support provides comfort.

READING II The importance of taking action to live out one's faith is a central theme of the letter of James. The author is insistent that one cannot claim to be a Christian without working for the benefit of others. In this passage, the author treats with scorn the idea of being able to wish another

READING II James 2:14–18

A reading from the letter of Saint James.

The passage begins at once with the main theme, spoken as a challenge.

What good is it, my brothers and sisters,
if someone says he has *faith* but does not have *works?*

Utter this second question with disbelief.

Can that *faith save* him?

Break up this long sentence by pausing after "day."

If a brother or sister has *nothing* to wear
and has *no food* for the day,
and one of you *says* to them,

Pause after "well."

"Go in *peace,* keep *warm,* and eat *well,"*
but you do *not give* them the necessities of the *body,*

Speak this as a real question.

what *good* is it?
So also *faith* of *itself,*
if it does not have *works,* is *dead.*

Indeed someone might say,
"You have *faith* and *I* have *works."*

Let your voice resound with this concluding declaration.

Demonstrate your faith to me *without* works,
and *I* will demonstrate *my faith* to you *from* my works.

well or speak pleasant words without ensuring that one's words can become a reality.

In our lives as well it is not enough to wish someone a good day unless we are willing to change the social and economic systems that allow children to go to bed hungry, adults to lack shelter and live on the street, and the many blessings of wealth to be enjoyed by only a select few. Allow God to speak this challenge through you: If we claim to have faith in God, we must demonstrate it in our actions toward others.

GOSPEL **Peter's declaration of faith ("You are the Messiah") and the subsequent teaching of Jesus marks a turning point in the gospel of Mark. Earlier in the gospel Jesus was traveling from city to town, teaching, healing and discussing God's reign. After this event, although he continues to teach and heal, Jesus turns decisively toward Jerusalem and death.**

Although Jesus' question regarding his identity is innocent enough, it is clear that many have misunderstood his mission and identity. It is left to Peter to identify Jesus as the one for whom Israel had been waiting, the one in whom the people could place their hope. Jesus seems to accept this designation, but not without serious misgivings. He must correct the mistaken assumption that the Messiah would be a political leader,

GOSPEL Mark 8:27–35

A reading from the holy gospel according to Mark.

Caesarea Philippi = sez-uh-REE-uh fih-LIP-pī
The story begins as a fairly simple conversation between Jesus and his disciples.
Elijah = ee-LĪ-juh

Jesus and his disciples *set out*
for the villages of *Caesarea* Philippi.
Along the way he *asked* his disciples,
"*Who* do people say that *I am?*"
They said in reply,
"*John* the *Baptist*, others *Elijah*,
still *others* one of the *prophets.*"

Here the tone becomes more serious.

Speak this with conviction.

And he asked them,
"But *who* do *you* say that I *am?*"
Peter said to him in reply,
"*You* are the *Christ.*"
Then he *warned* them *not* to tell *anyone* about him.

This is a hard teaching, but important. Do not rush through it.

He began to teach them
that the *Son* of *Man* must *suffer greatly*
and be *rejected* by the *elders*, the *chief priests*, and the *scribes*,
and be *killed*, and *rise* after *three days.*
He spoke this *openly.*

Allow your tone to convey Jesus' anger.

Then *Peter* took him aside and began to *rebuke* him.
At this he *turned* around and, *looking* at his disciples,
rebuked Peter and said, "Get *behind* me, *Satan.*
You are thinking *not* as *God* does, but as *human beings* do."

He *summoned* the crowd with his disciples and *said* to them,
"*Whoever* wishes to come *after* me must *deny himself,*
take up his *cross*, and *follow me.*
For *whoever* wishes to *save* his life will *lose* it,
but *whoever loses* his life for *my sake*
and that of the *gospel* will *save* it."

perhaps a revolutionary, or a priestly figure, or a prophet, or an eschatological judge, or at least a respected and revered teacher. Instead, Jesus teaches that he will be rejected, even to death.

Peter's discomfort with such a Messiah is understandable (what glory would there be in death?), and he disputes Jesus' teaching. Jesus' response is harsh; he has no patience for anyone who attempts to weaken his resolve or sacrifice principle for comfort. Today's passage ends with Jesus' teaching about discipleship; following Jesus involves suffering. There is no alternative. Just as Jesus had to travel the long road to Jerusalem and death in order to experience the glory of the resurrection, so also those who believe in him must be willing to walk the path he trod.

It is so much more inviting to bask in the warmth of the Christian faith and to triumph in the glory of Easter. This must have been the attitude of the first readers of this gospel, an attitude that the author repeatedly seeks to correct. Read this gospel as a declaration from Jesus to your community that suffering is integral to Christian faith.

25TH SUNDAY IN ORDINARY TIME

Lectionary #134

READING I Wisdom 2:12, 17–20

A reading from the book of Wisdom.

Be sure to make it clear that these are the words of the wicked and not something the author is advocating. Proclaim this opening phrase strongly and clearly, then change your voice to a mocking tone as you continue reading.

The *wicked* say:
Let us beset the *just* one, because he is *obnoxious* to us;
he sets himself *against* our *doings,*
reproaches us for transgressions of the *law*
and *charges* us with *violations* of our *training.*

Let us *see* whether his *words* be *true;*
let us *find out* what will *happen* to him.
For if the *just* one be the *son* of *God,* God will *defend* him
and *deliver* him from the *hand* of his *foes.*

The claim that God will defend the just one might be sarcastic, or it could be spoken sincerely, but with the expectation that this one is not truly God's child. Either way, the "wicked" clearly do not expect God to care for their victim. Decide which interpretation seems best to you, and reflect that in your voice.

With *revilement* and *torture* let us put the just one to the *test*
that we may have *proof* of his *gentleness*
and *try* his *patience.*
Let us *condemn* him to a *shameful death;*
for according to his *own* words, *God* will take *care* of him.

READING I The author of the Wisdom of Solomon does not simply criticize opponents, but lets them speak for themselves in this passage. The "wicked" are those who have given in to the pressures of the broader society and, especially in view of this selection, attempt to demonstrate their power over others. They are particularly caustic, even violent, in their treatment of the servant of the Lord, who was featured in last Sunday's first reading. The self-control of the just one is treated with sarcasm and a plan is made to test him, with the clear expectation that he will fail. The wicked are bitter because they have been criticized for violations of Jewish Law, and they react with violence against the law-abiding servant.

This passage has been understood as a prediction of the passion of Jesus. Although it was probably intended as a commentary on the author's own treatment at the hands of the wicked, the example of the just one who patiently withstands insult and torture, even to the point of death, appropriately describes Jesus.

The good person who is mocked for choosing what is right, for working hard and doing well, whether in school, at home or in the workplace, is part of our culture as well. We are all prone at times, whether out of resentment or envy, to slight or even revile these "goody two-shoes." Imagine that you are involved in such behavior and

READING II James 3:16—4:3

A reading from the letter of Saint James.

Beloved:
Where *jealousy* and *selfish ambition* exist,
there is *disorder* and every *foul* practice.

Make clear the contrast between the "wisdom from above" and the envy and selfishness of the earlier lines. Speak this list of blessings slowly and invitingly.

But the *wisdom* from *above* is first of all *pure,*
then *peaceable, gentle, compliant,*
full of *mercy* and *good fruits,*
without *inconstancy* or *insincerity.*
And the fruit of *righteousness* is sown in *peace*
for those who *cultivate* peace.

Change your tone again; ask this as a real and urgent question. Then answer it in the following lines.

Where do the *wars*
and *where* do the *conflicts* among you *come* from?
Is it *not* from your *passions*
that make *war* within your *members?*

Make clear the contrast between the beginning and ending phrases in each sentence.

You *covet* but do not *possess.*
You *kill* and *envy* but you cannot *obtain;*
you *fight* and wage *war.*

You do *not possess* because you do *not ask.*
You *ask* but do not *receive,*
because you ask *wrongly,* to spend it on your *passions.*

speak these words with a bit of a sarcastic sneer. Help the members of your community to identify their own attitudes in your words, that they may be challenged to leave aside such "wicked" ways and to treat others with respect.

READING II This admonition from the letter of James serves as a follow-up to the first reading. Here, true wisdom with its many positive attributes is contrasted with the selfishness and lack of discipline that so often dominate human behavior. The vice of envy appears as the source of many of the conflicts of human life. But envy cannot bring about anything that really satisfies. One who is envious and undisciplined does not ask correctly, does not ask for what is truly healthful and good.

There is a choice offered in this reading: One can choose the path of wisdom with its many "good fruits," or one can choose the path of selfishness with its violence and resulting unhappiness. Read the attributes of the "wisdom from above" with a gentle voice; then stress the conflict of the alternative, especially the contrasting ideas in the last several lines. Make the options clear for your listeners to choose.

GOSPEL Predictions of Jesus' anticipated passion come frequently after Peter's confession of Jesus as Messiah (last week's gospel). This second announcement of the death Jesus would

GOSPEL Mark 9:30–37

A reading from the holy gospel according to Mark.

Galilee = GAL-ih-lee

Jesus and his *disciples* left from there and began a *journey*
through *Galilee,*
but he did *not* wish *anyone* to *know* about it.
He was *teaching* his disciples and *telling* them,
"The *Son* of *Man* is to be *handed over* to *men*
and they will *kill* him,
and *three* days after his *death* the *Son* of *Man* will *rise."*
But they did not *understand* the saying,
and they were *afraid* to *question* him.

Capernaum = kuh-PER-n*m

They came to *Capernaum* and, once inside the *house,*
he began to *ask* them,
"*What* were you *arguing* about on the *way?"*
But they remained *silent.*
They had been *discussing* among themselves on the way
who was the *greatest.*

Allow a pregnant pause before stressing what follows.

Then he sat *down,* called the *Twelve,* and *said* to them,
"If *anyone* wishes to be *first,*
he shall be the *last* of all and the *servant* of all."

Jesus gently instructs his wayward disciples by offering a concrete example — his warm embrace — of how to treat the powerless.

Taking a *child,* he placed it in the their *midst,*
and putting his *arms* around *it,* he *said* to them,
"Whoever *receives* one *child* such as *this* in *my name,*
receives *me;*
and whoever *receives me,*
receives *not me* but the *One* who *sent* me."

undergo is completely lost on his disciples. The gospel explicitly claims that the disciples did not understand Jesus and were afraid to ask him what he meant.

Even more telling is the incident in Capernaum that demonstrates the depth of the disciples' misunderstanding. As Jesus contemplates where his mission is leading him, as he perhaps reflects on the treatment of the just by the wicked (described in the first reading) or the plight of the suffering servant of Isaiah. As he embraces vulnerability and the expectation of pain, his friends and followers are competing for greatness.

Rather than rebuke them, Jesus seeks to instruct. True honor is not found in lording it over others, but rather by serving. To illustrate, Jesus chooses a child, a symbol of vulnerability and dependency, to serve as a symbol of Jesus himself and of God who sent him. Such unassuming persons are those who truly represent what Jesus stands for. There is no room for competition, no time for seeking greatness, no need for lording it over another. The attitude of the servant and child (the same Greek word is used for both "slave" and "child") is to be the attitude of the follower of Jesus.

26TH SUNDAY ON ORDINARY TIME

Lectionary #137

READING I Numbers 11:25–29

A reading from the book of Numbers.

The LORD came down in the *cloud* and *spoke* to Moses.
Taking some of the *spirit* that was on *Moses*,
the Lord *bestowed* it on the seventy *elders*;
and as the spirit came to *rest* on them, they *prophesied.*

This begins a new aspect of the story; allow your voice to begin again with vigor. Eldad = EL-dad Medad = MEE-dad

Now *two men*, one named *Eldad* and the other *Medad*,
were *not* in the gathering but had been *left* in the *camp.*
They too had been on the *list*, but had *not* gone out to the *tent*;
yet the *spirit* came to *rest* on them *also*,
and they *prophesied* in the *camp.*

Joshua = JOSH-oo-uh Nun = nuhn

So, when a young man quickly told *Moses*,
"*Eldad* and *Medad* are *prophesying* in the *camp*,"
Joshua, son of Nun, who from his *youth* had been Moses' *aide*, said,
"*Moses*, my lord, *stop* them."

The phrase "would that" (meaning "if only" or "I wish") can trip up even the best readers. Practice it until you are comfortable with it.

But Moses *answered* him,
"Are you *jealous* for *my* sake?
Would that *all* the people of the LORD were *prophets!*
Would that the LORD might *bestow* his *spirit* on them *all!*"

READING I **Today's first reading is a wonderful statement of the inclusiveness of the spirit of God! During the wandering of the Israelites in the desert, Moses had been complaining that the burden of leadership was too much for him to bear alone. So God told him to choose seventy people (a coded way of saying "a lot"!) to help him. When two of those chosen, Eldad and Medad, did not join Moses and the others in a special tent set up outside the camp, they were still invested with the same prophetic spirit as the others, the spirit that had previously resided only with Moses.**

The earliest form of prophecy in Israel was that of ecstatic singing, dancing and chanting. That is surely what is envisioned here, rather than the prediction of future events. Being imbued with the spirit of God results in a spontaneous, spirited rejoicing.

Moses, who had previously been the only prophet of God among the Israelites, shows no resentment toward the new prophets, nor is he jealous of God's gift. In a hope that the early Christians saw fulfilled in the experience of Pentecost, Moses insists that the spirit of God cannot be contained in one place or within certain people alone. He looks forward to a day when God will inspire all to sing praises and to proclaim God's name.

Your task today is to challenge your community to recognize God's prophetic spirit in its midst, acting not only through official channels and chosen individuals, but wherever it might manifest itself.

READING II **The biting condemnation of wealth in today's second reading concludes our series of readings from the letter of James. Throughout the**

READING II James 5:1–6

A reading from the letter of Saint James.

Read the early part of the reading slowly and with great solemnity.

Come now, you *rich*, *weep* and *wail* over your impending *miseries*.
Your *wealth* has *rotted* away, your *clothes* have become *moth-eaten*,
your *gold* and *silver* have *corroded*,
and that *corrosion* will be a testimony *against* you;
it will *devour* your *flesh* like a *fire*.

Pause after this line.

You have stored up *treasure* for the *last days*.

Emphasize "Behold!" and pause slightly before continuing. Read the rest of the passage with great urgency.

Behold, the *wages* you withheld from the *workers*
who *harvested* your *fields* are *crying aloud*;
and the *cries* of the *harvesters*
have reached the *ears* of the LORD of *hosts*.

You have lived on earth in *luxury* and *pleasure*;
you have *fattened* your hearts for the day of *slaughter*.
You have *condemned*;
you have *murdered* the *righteous* one;
he offers you *no resistance*.

work, the author is concerned about right behavior, about acting justly in accord with the Mosaic Law given by God to Israel.

Wealth provides comfort and security; the wealthy need not fear adversity in the future since their resources are sufficient to protect them. But, says the author, the treasure they have stored away for the future is in reality a treasure of judgment. All their gold will be a sign of their unfairness and greed when God judges their deeds. The assumption is that great wealth can be obtained solely through racticing injustice toward others. But God listens to the cry of the oppressed; even the falsified wages themselves will cry out against the rich employer.

The suffering caused by poverty is the same as murder in the author's eyes. The author holds the wealthy accountable for this, but also turns the tables by indicating that the impending judgment will be appropriate: The rich "fatten" themselves only to be "slaughtered" on the day of judgment, as livestock are fattened for the slaughterhouse. All that the wealthy have and do for pleasure now will bring doom upon them in the future.

This is not an easy reading; it is caustic, accusing, condemning. Read it firmly, but with humility.

GOSPEL The first part of this gospel selection sounds like the story of Moses in the first reading. Following this story is a collection of independent sayings, each connected to the one before it by some catchword rather than by content.

The disciples in the gospel take the role claimed by Joshua in the first reading: John speaks, offended that someone not of

GOSPEL Mark 9:38–43, 45, 47–48

A reading from the holy gospel according to Mark.

At that time, *John* said to *Jesus*,
"*Teacher*, we saw someone *driving* out *demons* in *your name*,
and we *tried* to prevent him because he does not *follow* us."
Jesus replied, "Do *not prevent* him.
There is *no* one who performs a *mighty* deed in *my name*
who can at the *same* time speak *ill* of me.

Pause before continuing.

For whoever is not *against* us is *for* us.
Anyone who gives you a *cup* of *water* to drink
because you belong to *Christ*,
amen, I say to you, will surely *not lose* his *reward*.

Pause again. The stories that follow are exaggerated accounts of how to avoid sin. Read them as such.

"*Whoever* causes one of these *little* ones
who *believe* in me to *sin*,
it would be *better* for him if a great *millstone*
were put around his *neck*
and he were *thrown* into the *sea*.

Gehenna = geh-HEN-nah
At one time Gehenna was a real valley near Jerusalem. By the time of Jesus it was probably understood solely as the place of eternal punishment.

If your *hand* causes you to sin, *cut* it *off*.
It is *better* for you to enter into life *maimed*
than with *two* hands to go into *Gehenna*,
into the *unquenchable fire*.
And if your *foot* causes you to sin, *cut* if *off*.
It is *better* for you to enter into life *crippled*
than with *two* feet to be *thrown* into *Gehenna*.
And if your *eye* causes you to sin, *pluck* it *out*.
Better for you to enter into the *kingdom* of *God* with *one* eye
than with *two* eyes to be *thrown* into *Gehenna*,
where 'their *worm* does not *die*, and the *fire* is not *quenched*.'"

the intimate group following Jesus has been given power by God. It is ironic that just a short time earlier in this gospel the disciples of Jesus were themselves unable to cast out demons. Now they want Jesus to rebuke someone else who was exorcising in Jesus' name. Jesus responds, as did Moses, by affirming that the power of God is not given only to those officially designated to receive it, but can be conferred on anyone God desires. Indeed, Jesus' name has such power that invoking it changes a person; anyone who uses it to perform a sign of power cannot be abusing it.

Jesus had earlier spoken about receiving "little ones," the humblest members of the community, and the subject is again visited here from a negative perspective. Now Jesus speaks to those who impede the progress of those little ones who follow Jesus; even death by drowning would be better than suffering the consequences of such an action. Being a "bad example" is not an insignificant trifle but a serious offense.

The theme of stumbling or sinning concludes the passage. In graphic language Jesus suggests that anything that becomes a cause of sin should be removed. The demands of discipleship, of being united with the name of the Lord, are great. The body parts mentioned are indications of types of sin; the point is not self-mutilation but total commitment and dedication to God.

Allow each section of this passage to stand separately; pause between each section before continuing. Do not be afraid of the use of hyperbole in this reading, but use it to proclaim to your assembly how the power of God is not limited to certain groups or individuals, and to illustrate the demands of being a disciple of Jesus.

27TH SUNDAY ON ORDINARY TIME

Lectionary #140

READING I Genesis 2:18 – 24

A reading from the book of Genesis.

It is in the nature of the human being to be in relationship with others, to live interdependently.

The *Lord God said:* "It is not *good* for the man to be *alone.*
I will make a *suitable partner* for him."
So the *Lord God formed* out of the *ground*
various wild *animals* and various *birds* of the *air,*
and he *brought* them to the man to *see* what he would *call* them;
whatever the man *called* each of them would be its *name.*
The man gave *names* to all the *cattle,*
all the *birds* of the *air,* and *all* wild *animals;*
but *none* proved to be the *suitable partner* for the man.

This story creatively conveys the intimacy between men and women; they are formed from the very same substance.

So the *Lord God* cast a *deep sleep* on the man,
and while he was *asleep,*
he took out one of his *ribs* and *closed* up its place with *flesh.*
The *Lord God* then *built up* into a *woman* the *rib*
that he had taken from the man.

Speak the man's words with joy, relief and contentment.

Pause before proclaiming the central message of this second creation account.

When he *brought* her to the *man,* the man said:
"*This* one, at *last,* is *bone* of my *bones*
and *flesh* of my *flesh;*
this one shall be called '*woman,*'
for out of 'her *man*' this one has been *taken.*"
That is why a man *leaves* his *father* and *mother*
and *clings* to his *wife,*
and the *two* of them become *one flesh.*

READING I Of the two creation stories at the beginning of Genesis, the second is told today. In the first story, humanity is created male and female. Only in this second story are the sexes differentiated in a beautiful passage about the importance of the woman and the unity of husband and wife. There is a play on words in the Hebrew: Adam *(adam)* is the one formed from the earth or ground *(adamah).* Only when the concern becomes the creation of the female companion does Adam become the name of the male person.

After God creates all the creatures of the earth and gives them to the man to name, the man is left without an equal companion. So God forms a woman directly from the man, rather than from the ground as the animals were created. The woman is not subject to the man as were the animals, but is a mirror of the man's very being.

The man's response is informative: Three times he describes the woman as "this one," proclaiming a direct contrast to the other creatures, which were inadequate partners for him. His claim that she is "bone of my bones and flesh of my flesh" is a statement of her intimate relationship with him. Often, a commitment between individuals or peoples is phrased in these terms; for example, David said to the elders of Judah, "You are my bone and my flesh." The line in Genesis brings a smile since God had just used a bone of the man to create the woman. Anyone who suggests that this somehow subjugates the woman to the man does not understand what is intended here. In fact, the woman and the man are continually affirmed as equal and suitable partners for one another.

READING II Hebrews 2:9–11

A reading from the letter to the Hebrews.

In other words, he became human.

The death of Jesus is of universal consequence. It is through it that he is glorified and we are as well.

Brothers and sisters:
He "for a *little while*" was made "*lower* than the *angels*,"
that by the *grace* of God he might taste *death* for *everyone.*

For it was *fitting* that he,
for whom and *through* whom all things *exist*,
in bringing *many children* to *glory*,
should make the *leader* to their salvation *perfect*
through *suffering.*

Jesus is the sanctifier, the one who makes us holy; but we are all united as children of God.

He who *consecrates* and those who are being *consecrated*
all have *one origin.*
Therefore, he is not *ashamed* to call them "*brothers.*"

GOSPEL Mark 10:2–16

A reading from the holy gospel according to Mark.

The Pharisees approached Jesus and asked,
"Is it *lawful* for a husband to *divorce* his *wife?*"
They were *testing* him.
He said to them in reply, "What did *Moses* command you?"
They replied,
"*Moses permitted* a husband to write a *bill* of divorce
and *dismiss* her."

Finally, there is another wordplay as the woman *(ishsha)* is given her name because she was formed from the man *(ish)*. This is the first time that the Hebrew uses words that differentiate between man and woman. Because of their origin as one creature, the man and the woman are forever united as one flesh.

Your listeners will surely not understand all the nuances of this selection. Proclaim it as a poetic tale about the unity of men and women, and the dignity of each person created by God. The last line serves to celebrate the holiness of that most intimate of relationships, marriage.

READING II The letter to the Hebrews here expresses an understanding of Jesus that recognizes his humiliation — his willingness to share fully in our humanity, even to the point of death — and his glorification. Throughout Hebrews, it is precisely through his death that Jesus is said to be glorified.

Because Jesus' sufferings have a salvific function, it was "fitting" for God to allow them. Jesus is the first to be glorified, but by his suffering he makes it possible for all the children of God to be glorified as well. This is confirmed by the fact that all those made holy by Jesus' actions, and Jesus himself, are children of the one God, united as brothers and sisters.

This is indeed good news: God's magnanimity and generosity are evident in God's willingness to accord to us the same honor properly due Jesus. With gratitude and joy sing of Jesus' exaltation that exalts us too, the brothers and sisters of Christ.

But Jesus told them,
"Because of the *hardness* of your *hearts*
he wrote you this *commandment.*

What follows here is the central teaching of Jesus in this passage; proclaim it with certitude. It is contrasted with the concessions that are naturally made for those unable to live up to its high ideal.

But from the *beginning* of *creation,* 'God made them *male*
and *female.*
For *this reason* a man shall *leave* his *father* and *mother*
and be *joined* to his *wife,*
and the *two* shall become *one flesh.*
So they are no longer *two* but *one flesh.'*
Therefore what *God* has joined *together,*
no human being must *separate."*

Pause. Jesus then continues his demanding teaching with the disciples in private.

In the house the disciples *again* questioned Jesus about this.
He said to them,
"Whoever *divorces* his wife and *marries another*
commits *adultery* against her;
and if *she* divorces her *husband* and marries another,
she commits adultery."

The scene shifts dramatically; pause and begin anew.

And people were bringing *children* to him
that he might *touch* them,
but the disciples *rebuked* them.
When Jesus *saw* this he became *indignant* and said to them,
"*Let* the children *come* to me;
do *not prevent* them, for the *kingdom* of God *belongs*
to such as *these.*
Amen, I say to you,
whoever does *not* accept the *kingdom* of God like a *child*
will not *enter* it."

Try to picture this scene in your own mind and convey it to your listeners.

Then he *embraced* them and *blessed* them,
placing his *hands* on them.

[Shorter: Mark 10:2–12]

GOSPEL Jesus' teaching on marriage and divorce in Mark differs from that in Matthew and from Paul's treatment of the subject. Elsewhere, reasons are provided for dissolution of marriage. In this gospel there is no concession made for divorce. Jesus says that such concessions were made because of people's obstinacy. God intended complete unity and equality in drawing men and women together in marriage.

Although Jewish Law allows the husband only to divorce his wife, not vice versa, this passage allows for the possibility of a woman divorcing her husband. The idea that a man commits adultery against his first wife by marrying again also goes beyond the Jewish Law, which understood adultery to be an offense against a man but not against a woman.

What Jesus does in responding to a hostile question is to raise marriage to a level above the fractious issue of divorce. His quote from Genesis proclaims that husbands and wives are united so intimately that they actually become one, indivisible. Unfortunately, Jesus' words are often understood in the opposite way, as providing regulations and placing blame. Know that many of your listeners will be uncomfortable with this selection. Read it with sensitivity to their pain, while striving to proclaim the holiness of marriage as taught by Jesus.

The concluding story in today's gospel pictures Jesus welcoming young children as they approach him. Apparently, the disciples of Jesus try to dismiss them, but Jesus indignantly defends their right to approach. His statements about the kingdom of God allude to the wide-eyed receptivity of children. He enjoins just such openness on all his followers.

28TH SUNDAY IN ORDINARY TIME

Lectionary #143

READING I Wisdom 7:7–11

A reading from the book of Wisdom.

Read this passage slowly and deliberately, stressing the priceless value of wisdom and the utter worthlessness of all riches.

I *prayed*, and *prudence* was given me;
I *pleaded*, and the *spirit* of *wisdom* came to me.

I *preferred* her to *scepter* and *throne*,
and deemed *riches nothing* in comparison with *her*,
nor did I liken any *priceless gem* to her;
because *all gold*, in view of her, is a little *sand*,
and before her, *silver* is to be accounted *mire*.

Beyond *health* and *comeliness* I *loved* her,
and I chose to have *her* rather than the *light*,
because the *splendor* of *her* never yields to *sleep*.

Close with a slow and steady proclamation of the untold wealth true wisdom brings.

Yet *all good things* together came to me in her *company*,
and countless *riches* at her *hands*.

READING II Hebrews 4:12–13

A reading from the letter to the Hebrews.

This short reading deserves a strong proclamation. Read slowly, giving careful balance to each phrase. The images are strong, even violent; don't shrink away from them.

Brothers and sisters:
Indeed the *word* of God is *living* and *effective*,
sharper than any two-edged *sword*,
penetrating even between *soul* and *spirit*, *joints* and *marrow*,
and able to discern *reflections* and *thoughts* of the *heart*.

READING I True understanding is of more value than any amount of gold or silver. The author loves wisdom above all else and prays to receive it.

Wisdom here is both an attribute of God and something more: a quasi-divine being enthroned with God. Wisdom is that ability to comprehend what is truly important, to reflect deeply, to recognize proper thought and behavior; and it is the source of all happiness. Personified as a woman (the Hebrew and Greek words for "wisdom" are feminine), it is a priceless gift.

The book of Wisdom has been attributed to King Solomon, and this section upholds that pretense, as the author claims royal lineage. But, as the text notes, wisdom is of more value than any of the splendors of the royal palace.

It is not common in our culture to value learning for its own sake. We often see education as providing a means for earning a living, as a necessary hurdle to jump before practicing a profession. This passage challenges any line of thought that does not uphold learning as its own reward. Spend some time meditating on the reading before sharing it with your assembly. Such reflection is, according to the author, the source of all good things and the path to God.

READING II God's word is powerful. However long ago it was spoken, it remains relevant for those who hear it. It can penetrate deep within a person, judging heartfelt thoughts, for God sees everything, and God's word is precisely the active communication of God.

This is an apt message for anyone who proclaims the word of God in the assembly

This is the key line; God, to whom we are all accountable, sees completely.

No creature is *concealed* from him,
but everything is *naked* and *exposed* to the *eyes* of him
to whom we must *render* an *account.*

GOSPEL Mark 10:17–30

A reading from the holy gospel according to Mark.

As Jesus was setting out on a *journey*, a man *ran* up,
knelt down before him, and *asked* him,
"*Good teacher*, what must I do to inherit eternal *life?*"

Note the man's reverence and sincerity.

Jesus answered him, "*Why* do you call me good?
No one is good but *God alone.*
You know the commandments: 'You shall not *kill*;
you shall not commit *adultery*;
you shall not *steal*;
you shall not bear false *witness*;
you shall not *defraud*;
honor your father and your mother.'"

Jesus' response is not meant to insult the man but to point to the goodness of God.

Read these commandments as though you have just received them from Moses: with solemnity and awe.

He replied and said to him,
"*Teacher*, *all* of these I have observed from my *youth.*"
Jesus, looking at him, *loved* him and said to him,
"You are lacking in *one* thing.
Go, *sell* what you have, and give to the *poor*
and you will have *treasure* in *heaven*; then *come*, follow *me.*"

Emphasize Jesus' tenderness toward one who so clearly seeks to do God's will.

At *that* statement his face *fell*,
and he went away *sad*, for he had many *possessions.*

The man's dejection is palpable. Let your voice echo his sadness.

to consider seriously. The words you read are more than simply marks on a page. They are living, and they bear within them the ability to bring judgment. Your task is a crucial one: You are to proclaim every reading faithfully and instill in your listeners a respect for God's message. Thus, when all is exposed and God looks into our hearts, truthfulness and integrity will be evident.

Take time to reflect on your role as a lector, then read this selection forcefully, confident that you are a vehicle through which God's word penetrates hearts.

GOSPEL The evangelist here touches on a number of interesting topics: the nature of God, Jesus' relationship to the Jewish Law, Jesus' teaching techniques, and the central gospel theme of the kingdom of God.

The story itself conveys the man's eagerness and the honor he gives to Jesus by running up to him, kneeling and addressing him with sincerity and high esteem. Jesus uses the honorary title ("good teacher") to teach something about God, upholding the traditional view that only God, as the source and fullness of all that is good, could be so addressed. Coupled with the later proclamation that all things are possible for God, Jesus' clarification serves to point the hearers' attention away from himself and toward the God whom he proclaims.

It is interesting that Jesus directs someone seeking eternal life straight to the Jewish Law. Jesus himself did not repudiate the Law, although Christians later questioned its necessity. But he also did not see the Law as the source of life in and of itself. Instead, Jesus' further advice is twofold: Sell everything and give to the poor; then "follow me."

Jesus, too, must have been disappointed; perhaps he said these words with a sigh in his voice.

Jesus looked around and said to his disciples,
"How *hard* it is for those who have *wealth*
to enter the *kingdom* of God!"
The disciples were *amazed* at his words.
So Jesus again said to them in reply,
"*Children*, how *hard* it is to enter the *kingdom* of God!
It is easier for a *camel* to pass through the eye of a *needle*
than for one who is *rich* to enter the *kingdom* of *God*."

A rabbinic form of this saying has an elephant attempting to go through the eye of a needle. It is impossible. Jesus exaggerates here to make his bold claims even more startling.

They were *exceedingly* astonished and said among themselves,
"Then *who* can be *saved*?"
Jesus *looked* at them and said,
"For *human beings* it is *impossible*, but *not* for *God*.
All things are possible for *God*."

The promise of suffering changes everything. The exaggerated blessings are no simple benefits, but carry a price. Close slowly and deliberately.

Peter began to say to him,
"We have given up *everything* and followed you."
Jesus said, "*Amen*, I say to you,
there is *no* one who has given up *house* or *brothers* or *sisters*
or *mother* or *father* or *children* or *lands*
for *my* sake and for the sake of the *gospel*
who will not receive a *hundred* times more *now* in this
present age:
houses and brothers and sisters
and mothers and children and lands,
with *persecutions*, and eternal *life* in the age to *come*."

[Shorter: Mark 10:17–27]

Perhaps Jesus' answer to the wealthy young man falls in the realm of exaggeration, similar to his later comment regarding a camel passing through the eye of a needle (another impossibility), or the suggestion that one who gives up everything will receive a hundredfold in this life. But the second part of the response — to follow Jesus — is ignored. Was it easier to follow Jesus than to live in abject poverty? Indeed, Peter's statement indicates the disciples' view that they, in following Jesus, had already done everything he was asking. Although we are told that the man's disappointment centered on the idea of giving up his riches, Jesus hints that it might be the easier task of the two: The one who gives up everything for Jesus' sake will have great wealth — including an abundance of persecution. Immediately following today's selection is the third teaching on Jesus' passion and death. Following Jesus entails suffering.

Today we learn that it is not easy to enter the kingdom of God. But God is the one who can accomplish it; all that we can do is be open to receiving God's gracious gift.

The vivid imagery of this story makes it great for storytelling. Use all your talents to convey the various emotions evident in the characters throughout the story, as well as the firmness of Jesus' teachings and the demands of his words. Do not be tempted to dismiss the difficulties as fanciful or unnecessary extremes. However uncomfortable Jesus' words make us, let us read them for what they really say.

29TH SUNDAY ON ORDINARY TIME

Lectionary #146

READING I Isaiah 53:10–11

A reading from the book of the prophet Isaiah.

The LORD was pleased
to *crush* him in *infirmity.*

It is difficult to think of God wanting someone to suffer. The following line suggests that the servant as well as others will benefit.

If he gives his life as an *offering* for *sin,*
he shall see his *descendants* in a *long* life,
and the *will* of the LORD shall be *accomplished* through him.

Because of his *affliction*
he shall see the *light* in *fullness*
of days;

Here is the promise picked up in the gospel and so meaningful to Christians.

through his *suffering,* my servant shall *justify many,*
and *their* guilt *he* shall bear.

READING I Of the several servant songs in the book of Isaiah, this differs from the others in that the servant seems to be an individual within Israel rather than the entire community. The sentiments expressed — that one could be righteous and still suffer — are fairly novel in Israel. Previously, the belief was strong that those who acted rightly would be blessed, while those who did what was wrong would be punished on earth. But the experience of the exile in Babylon, which gave rise to this section of the book, seems to have altered that conception.

A central thought of this passage is that the servant of God has suffered, but has done so for the sake of others. It is not clear how that suffering is redemptive, but there is no doubt that it benefits others. Through the undeserved pain experienced by this righteous one, many shall be made righteous.

This idea has made this passage a beloved one for Christians, who see Jesus as the righteous one who suffered for the sake of the unrighteous. The author did not intend to predict what happened to Jesus, but the description of the redemptive value of suffering — especially by one who is innocent — fits the experience of Jesus. It is true as well of those in our day who suffer wrongly, whether victims of crime or those languishing on death row, whether victims of genocide or those who live on the streets. Their pain can be redemptive only if we learn from it, if we resolve to bring an end to suffering so that theirs will not have been in vain.

READING II Hebrews 4:14–16

A reading from the letter to the Hebrews.

Brothers and sisters:
Since we have a great *high priest* who has passed
through the *heavens,*
Jesus, the *Son* of *God,*
let us hold *fast* to our *confession.*
For we do not have a high priest
who is *unable* to sympathize with our *weaknesses,*
but one who has *similarly* been tested in *every* way,
yet *without sin.*

Speak with awe this promise that we can enter the divine presence with confidence.

So let us *confidently* approach the *throne* of *grace*
to receive *mercy* and to find *grace* for timely *help.*

GOSPEL Mark 10:35–45

A reading from the holy gospel according to Mark.

Zebedee = ZEB-uh-dee

James and *John,* the sons of *Zebedee,* came to Jesus and said
to him,
"*Teacher,* we want you to do for us whatever we ask of you."
He replied, "What do you wish me to *do* for you?"
They answered him, "*Grant* that in your *glory*
we may sit one at your *right* and the other at your *left.*"

In this, the earliest gospel, the disciples are not always portrayed in a flattering light. Here they appear quite demanding.

As so often, the disciples desire glory, ignoring the need to suffer.

Jesus said to them, "You do not *know* what you are *asking.*
Can *you* drink the cup that *I* drink
or be *baptized* with the baptism with which *I* am baptized?"

As you read this passage, keep in mind those who have suffered for others. Proclaim with sadness the anguish of such pain, but at the same time proclaim the hope that such a life can, in fact, be an "offering for sin," an inspiration to others to live their lives for justice.

READING II The central proclamation of the letter to the Hebrews is that the earthly Temple and its activity are reflective of a heavenly reality. Jesus is the true high priest, like the Temple high priests who entered the Holy of Holies in the Jerusalem Temple only once a year. This high priest enters God's presence by being exalted in heaven, making it possible for us, with whom he shared the reality of temptation but not sin, to come into the divine presence and approach the "throne of grace."

Proclaim this passage as a word of praise for Jesus, the one who both shares human frailty with us and who yet is exalted with God. You are encouraging your listeners to "hold fast" to their faith and to be willing to stand up for it when challenged. The tone is one of confidence (let your voice reflect this) and also one reflecting the sympathy Christ has for our plight.

GOSPEL In characteristic Markan fashion, today's gospel highlights the importance of suffering and the folly of seeking glory. Essential to being a follower of Jesus is the willingness to go

Jesus' followers innocently and ignorantly assure him that they can join him in his experiences. Jesus solemnly replies that they are correct — although they do not yet understand the significance of his words.

They said to him, "We *can.*"

Jesus said to them, "The *cup* that I drink, you *will* drink,
and with the *baptism* with which I am *baptized*, you *will*
be baptized;
but to sit at my *right* or at my *left* is not *mine* to give
but is for *those* for whom it has been *prepared.*"
When the *ten* heard this, they became *indignant*
at James and John.

Jesus summoned them and said to them,
"*You* know that those who are recognized as *rulers* over
the Gentiles
lord it *over* them,
and their *great* ones make their *authority* over them *felt.*
But it shall *not* be so among *you.*
Rather, whoever wishes to be *great* among you will be
your *servant*;
whoever wishes to be *first* among you will be the *slave* of *all.*
For the *Son of Man* did not come to be *served*
but to *serve* and to give his *life* as a ransom for *many.*"

[Shorter: Mark 10:42–45]

Given the pain and humiliation of actual slavery, this line is difficult to read. Proclaim it for the paradox inherent in Jesus' words: The slave need not be ashamed, but suffers for the sake of others.

where he goes and to undergo what he experiences. In this gospel, that means pain and death, without thought of vindication. Treatment of the resurrection in the gospel of Mark was added only later; the gospel originally ended with the account of the passion.

James and John were convinced that Jesus would be glorified and hoped they would benefit. They rashly affirm that they can share in what awaits him. This appears foolish from our perspective, but Jesus agrees that indeed they will participate in the pain of his passion.

The cup that Jesus says he will drink is a reference not only to the fate that awaits him (a common metaphor) but also contains a reference to judgment. The prophets spoke of the enemies of God drinking the cup of God's punishment. Jesus proclaims that he will partake of that judgment. The gospel agrees with the first reading in its proclamation that a guiltless one can suffer for the sake of others.

The central thrust of the gospel is the teaching on greatness. Those who want to be great must be willing to serve. Your task is to strive to apply Jesus' words in your own life and to challenge the members of your assembly to see how to serve others as well.

30TH SUNDAY IN ORDINARY TIME

Lectionary #149

READING I Jeremiah 31:7–9

A reading from the book of the prophet Jeremiah.

Thus says the *LORD:*
Shout with *joy* for Jacob,
exult at the *head* of the nations;
proclaim your *praise* and say:
The *LORD* has delivered his *people,*
the *remnant* of *Israel.*

Lift up your voice and sing God's praise! Note that God instructs the people to ask to be saved; this can be read with trust that it will happen.

Behold, I will bring them *back*
from the *land* of the *north;*
I will *gather* them from the *ends* of the *world,*
with the *blind* and the *lame* in their *midst,*
the *mothers* and those with *child;*
they shall *return* as an immense *throng.*

They departed in *tears,*
but I will *console* them and *guide* them;
I will *lead* them to brooks of *water,*
on a *level* road, so that *none* shall stumble.
For I am a *father* to Israel,
Ephraim is my *first-born.*

This line is difficult; "in tears" does not indicate tears of joy. Perhaps it refers to a penitential attitude that needs to characterize wayward Israel, even as it rejoices to return home.

Ephraim = EE-fray-im

READING I For the most part, Jeremiah was a prophet of gloom, condemning Judah's lack of faithfulness and predicting defeat at the hands of the Babylonians unless the people changed their ways. But as defeat actually grew closer, he changed his message to one of hope—that God would not forever abandon Judah, and that after a period of chastisement the people would return to their land.

Today's passage is from a section within the book of Jeremiah called the Book of Consolation. The Book of Consolation speaks joyfully and hopefully of the restoration of Judah and, in the passage we read today, even of the restoration of the northern kingdom of Israel, which had fallen to the Assyrians 150 years before Judah fell to Babylon.

God will bring back a faithful remnant of the people, including those with physical limitations. On that joyful day, the people of God will return to their homes and their worship, centered around the holy city of Jerusalem. Their journey will not involve great hardship, for God will provide for them on the way. In a beautiful familial image, the prophet proclaims the intimate relationship between God and the chosen people.

This selection is joyful, triumphant and full of praise. Let your voice reflect the excitement of refugees returning to their beloved homeland, of people in love with their generous God. When God speaks (in the "I" passages) proclaim with warmth the love and care that is expressed.

READING II The letter to the Hebrews continues to discuss Jesus' role as high priest (see the discussion from

READING II Hebrews 5:1–6

A reading from the letter to the Hebrews.

Brothers and sisters:
Every high priest is taken from among *men*
and made their *representative* before God,
to offer *gifts* and *sacrifices* for sins.
He is able to deal *patiently* with the ignorant and erring,
for he *himself* is beset by *weakness*
and so, for *this* reason, must make *sin* offerings for *himself*
as well as for the *people.*
No one takes this honor upon *himself*
but only when *called* by *God,*
just as *Aaron* was.
In the *same* way,
it was not *Christ* who glorified *himself* in becoming high priest,
but rather the one who *said* to him:
"*You* are *my* son:
this day I have *begotten* you";
just as he says in *another* place:
"*You* are a *priest forever*
according to the *order* of *Melchizedek.*"

A contrast will later be made between the high priests described here, who sacrificed many times for their own sake and for the people, and Jesus, who offered himself as a perfect sacrifice once for all.

Psalm 2:7

Psalm 110:4
Melchizedek = mel-KEEZ-ih-dek

last week). The Jewish high priest, although chosen by God, offered sacrifices for his own sins as well as for those of the people. Although Jesus is superior to the earthly high priests, he does share with them his appointment by God to his role.

Jesus was not from a priestly family but was chosen directly by God, according to the author, as the words of the psalms indicate. In fact, Jesus' priesthood is based on that of the priest-king Melchizedek; it is far more ancient than and superior to the priesthood given to the children of Moses' brother Aaron. Melchizedek met and blessed Abraham in Genesis 14, but the passage quoted here comes from Psalm 110.

Because this material is somewhat unfamiliar to most modern listeners, read this passage slowly and carefully. Proclaim the psalm passages with a bit of triumph in your voice; you are being asked to share the special role that Jesus has in the history of salvation.

GOSPEL It is not difficult to imagine a person who causes a disruption when someone famous comes near. The reaction of the people to Bartimaeus and their attempts to hush him are understandable. But he was persistent and cried out even more loudly.

Jesus' conversation with the blind man is reminiscent of the talk Jesus had with James and John, proclaimed last Sunday. Jesus asks the same question, and the blind man makes a demand. But Jesus' subsequent response is quite different. The man asked for healing rather than glory, and Jesus claims that his trust and faith have healed him. His sight restored, the man becomes a disciple of Jesus.

GOSPEL Mark 10:46–52

A reading from the holy gospel according to Mark.

As Jesus was leaving *Jericho* with his disciples and
a sizable *crowd,*
Bartimaeus, a *blind* man, the son of *Timaeus,*
sat by the *roadside begging.*

Bartimaeus = bahr-tih-MAY-uhs
Timaeus = tim-AY-uhs

On hearing that it was *Jesus* of *Nazareth,*
he began to *cry out* and say,
"*Jesus,* son of *David,* have *pity* on me."

The persistence of the blind man is unmistakable. Do not be afraid to make Bartimaeus sound like a nuisance, or to make the people sound exasperated with him.

And many *rebuked* him, telling him to be *silent.*
But he kept calling *out* all the *more,*
"Son of *David,* have *pity* on me."
Jesus stopped and said, "*Call* him."

Jesus' words are quiet; he is in control.

So they *called* the *blind* man, saying to him,
"Take *courage;* get *up,* Jesus is *calling* you."

Now the crowd supports the blind man.

He *threw* aside his cloak, *sprang* up,
and *came* to Jesus.

Jesus *said* to him in reply, "What do you want me to *do* for you?"
The blind man replied to him, "*Master,* I want to *see.*"
Jesus told him, "*Go* your way; your *faith* has *saved* you."
Immediately he *received* his sight
and *followed* him on the way.

Speak this quietly but forcefully. It is fulfilled in the following line, a line that should convey some awe in Jesus' power, both to heal and to inspire faith.

In the gospel of Mark, proclamations of Jesus as a royal Messiah are dismissed by Jesus (a phenomenon called the "messianic secret" in Mark). However, the claim of Bartimaeus that Jesus is "Son of David" is allowed to stand. Jesus is drawing closer to Jerusalem, the royal city of David, the place from which Jesus too will rule—on the cross.

Inspire your listeners to join with Bartimaeus in obstinately demanding mercy and then trusting that healing will follow. The story is fairly straightforward, but there is a great deal of emotion expressed. Read the words of Bartimaeus with feeling, and convey the harsh rebukes of the crowd. Jesus' own words are subdued, but the statement of healing is central; proclaim it firmly.

ALL SAINTS

Lectionary #667

READING I Revelation 7:2–4, 9–14

Note that it is "Revelation" (singular), not "Revelations."

A reading from the book of Revelation.

I, John, saw another *angel* come up from the *East,*
holding the *seal* of the living *God.*
He *cried out* in a loud voice to the *four angels*
who were given *power* to damage the *land* and the *sea,*
"Do *not* damage the *land* or the *sea* or the *trees*
until we put the *seal* on the foreheads of the *servants* of our *God."*
I heard the number of those who had been *marked* with the *seal,*
one *hundred* and forty-four *thousand* marked
from every *tribe* of the *Israelites.*

After this I had a vision of a great *multitude,*
which no one could *count,*
from every *nation, race, people,* and *tongue.*
They *stood* before the *throne* and before the *Lamb,*
wearing *white robes* and holding *palm* branches in their hands.
They *cried out* in a loud voice:
"*Salvation* comes from our *God,*
who is *seated* on the *throne,*
and from the *Lamb."*

Pause before reading the words of the crowd, then proclaim them loudly and clearly.

All the *angels* stood around the *throne*
and around the *elders* and the four living *creatures.*
They *prostrated* themselves before the *throne,*
worshiped God, and *exclaimed:*

READING I The visionary John tells of his experience in being taken before the throne of God, where he sees angels and a lamb (Christ) who has been slain. After the lamb opens a sealed scroll, an angel bears the instrument for the final seal, the seal of God. In antiquity, seals were used to close documents and to mark possessions. Here the divine seal, a sign of ultimate authority, is used to mark those faithful to God.

Those eligible for marking with the seal are a vast number. The number 144,000 is intended to signify the complete nation of Israel. Not only the Israelites, but Gentiles of every race and nation are included among the chosen ones of God. The number of Gentiles is so great that it cannot be determined. Although these numbers are sometimes used to justify exclusion and the superiority of a few, the idea is really one of inclusion: Anyone faithful to God is worthy to be counted as one of God's servants.

The faithfulness of this crowd becomes evident as the vision continues. The white robes and palm branches indicate those martyred for their faith. This is confirmed by the elder, who tells John that these faithful have "washed their robes . . . in the blood of the Lamb." They cry out with the angels before the throne of God.

The purpose of apocalyptic writing is to encourage those who are struggling and who might even face persecution for the faith. Just as those dressed in white have been vindicated and now bask in God's presence, so also anyone who faithfully endures trial now will be justified by God and made to share in the heavenly glory.

Today's feast is a feast of memories, family stories and inspiring saints. As we remember today all the saints—those widely

Read this quotation slowly and with great emphasis on each term of honor. Pause slightly after "God" and be sure not to swallow the final "Amen."

"Amen. Blessing and *glory*, wisdom and *thanksgiving*,
honor, *power*, and *might*
be to our *God forever* and *ever. Amen."*

Then one of the elders spoke up and said to me,
"Who are these wearing *white robes*, and where did they
come from?"
I said to him, "My *lord*, *you* are the one who knows."
He said to me,

Speak this as the message of comfort it was intended to be.

"These are the ones who have *survived* the time
of great *distress*;
they have washed their robes
and made them *white* in the *blood* of the *Lamb."*

READING II 1 John 3:1–3

A reading from the first letter of Saint John.

Speak tenderly and lovingly throughout this selection. Read slowly.

Beloved:
See what *love* the Father has *bestowed* on us
that we may be called the *children* of *God.*

Pause briefly before and after this line. Read it with conviction.

Yet *so* we *are.*
The reason the world does not *know* us
is that it did not know *him.*

Beloved, we are God's *children* now;
what we shall be has not yet been *revealed.*
We *do* know that when it *is* revealed we shall be *like him*,
for we shall *see* him as he *is.*

This is both a statement of reality and an exhortation to your listeners to be pure.

Everyone who has this *hope* based on *him* makes himself *pure*,
as *he* is pure.

recognized for their holiness and those known only to a few — we realize that we belong to a community of faith. We recall those who have instilled faith in us, and who have gone ahead to experience the full revelation of God. We would not be here, would not be joining our voices in praise of God, were it not for them. And so we take comfort in knowing that they are part of that multitude standing before the throne of God, free of all pain and anxiety.

READING II **Building on the promise of the first reading is a passage from the Johannine correspondence, addressed both to the recipients of the letter and to us as well. This passage affirms the tremendous love bestowed by God on us. We are not simply God's creatures, nor are we recipients from afar of God's goodness. Rather, we are part of the family of God, heirs to all of the blessings God can give. The great chasm that divides imperfect mortals from the magnificent, immortal God is bridged, and we are called children of God.**

The author offers this message, just as the mystic John did in the first reading, to encourage those who are facing adversity. "The world" does not recognize the identity of these children of God, but that does not change the reality. But there is still more: The final outcome for our lives is still shrouded in mystery. The author makes two claims about that future reality: On that day we shall be like God; and we shall share in the beatific vision of a God fully revealed.

This is a message of hope for the future and encouragement for the present. The final line makes it clear that those who hope to become like God and to see God must now live lives of purity worthy of God.

GOSPEL Matthew 5:1–12a

A reading from the holy gospel according to Matthew.

When *Jesus* saw the *crowds,* he went up the *mountain,*
and after he had sat *down,* his disciples *came* to him.
He began to teach them, saying:
"*Blessed* are the *poor* in *spirit,*
for *theirs* is the kingdom of *heaven.*
Blessed are they who *mourn,*
for they will be *comforted.*

Do not try to rush through the Beatitudes. Speak each one as a distinct unit before moving on to the next. If it seems right to you to emphasize "blessed" more than is indicated here, feel free to do so. But be careful not to make each line sound exactly the same.

"Blessed are the *meek,*
for they will *inherit* the *land.*
Blessed are they who *hunger* and *thirst* for *righteousness,*
for they will be *satisfied.*

"Blessed are the *merciful,*
for they will be *shown* mercy.
Blessed are the *clean* of *heart,*
for they will *see God.*

"Blessed are the *peacemakers,*
for they will be called *children* of *God.*
Blessed are they who are *persecuted* for the sake
of *righteousness,*
for *theirs* is the kingdom of *heaven.*

Direct this line to your listeners.

"Blessed are *you* when they *insult* you and *persecute* you
and utter every kind of *evil* against you *falsely* because of *me.*
Rejoice and be *glad,*
for your *reward* will be *great* in *heaven.*"

The final line indicates the attitude that is to greet adversity; there is a promise of good things yet to come.

This selection requires a slow, sincere and thoughtful rendering. Although the term "child of God" might be familiar, meditate on its significance. Share some of your joy with the members of your assembly as your address these words to them.

GOSPEL The Beatitudes in Matthew "spiritualize" the concerns expressed also in the Beatitudes in Luke. In Luke the needs are concrete: the poor are really poor, the hungry are really starving. Here, however, the ones who are blessed are not only those struggling to survive or those mistreated by the powerful but anyone who loves righteousness and is willing to suffer for it. Each beatitude tells of a present reality and offers a promise for the future that turns the present experience upside down or bestows a reward of heavenly magnitude. What we know now is not all that there is to know.

The Beatitudes offer an assurance that the faith-filled pilgrims who have preceded us on this journey, having steadfastly endured the trials of their age, now enjoy peace and happiness in the presence of God. They are also a promise to us, living in a world filled with sorrow and slander, that there is more to come. The Beatitudes in the gospel of Matthew in particular are a challenge to us who live in comfort to share in the struggle to create a just, compassionate world.

The natural rhythm of this passage makes it easy to proclaim but also offers pitfalls to the inattentive. Each blessing must be spoken sincerely and simply, with a pause before reading the "reward." Listen to your own words as though you are hearing the passage for the first time, so that it can truly provide comfort and challenge to your listeners.

31st SUNDAY IN ORDINARY TIME

Lectionary #152

READING I Deuteronomy 6:2–6

Proclaim this passage slowly and forcefully.

A reading from the book of Deuteronomy.

Moses spoke to the *people*, saying:
"*Fear* the LORD, *your God*,
and *keep*, throughout the *days* of your lives,
all his *statutes* and *commandments* which I enjoin on you,
and thus have *long life*.

"*Hear* then, Israel, and be careful to *observe* them,
that you may *grow* and *prosper* the *more*,
in keeping with the *promise* of the LORD, the God
of your *fathers*,
to give you a land *flowing* with *milk* and *honey*.

There is a note of joy as well as solemnity in this proclamation. Read each line slowly and pause briefly between lines. This is the text that forms the core of Jesus' teaching in today's gospel.

"*Hear*, O Israel! The LORD is our *God*, the LORD *alone!*
Therefore, you shall *love* the LORD, *your God*,
with *all* your *heart*,
and with *all* your *soul*,
and with *all* your *strength*.
Take to *heart* these words which I *enjoin* on you today."

READING I The book of Deuteronomy ("second law") is purported to be an account of God's Law given by Moses to a second generation of Israelites, those who had not been present to receive it at Sinai. As such, it is addressed to all subsequent generations and is a reminder to be faithful to God's great gift.

The present selection, following shortly after a list of the Ten Commandments, presents Moses exhorting the people to be faithful to God's commands. The traditional understanding of prosperity is presented: By keeping the commandments of God the people ensure themselves a "land flowing with milk and honey." We know that blessings do not always follow right behavior, but we can still proclaim this passage as a promise of God to care for us and guide us.

The final paragraph contains the famous Shema prayer (*shema* is the Hebrew word for "hear"), the declaration of Israel's monotheism. This is what makes Israel a nation, what distinguishes it from its contemporaries: belief in one God and complete devotion to and love for that God.

READING II The comparison and contrast between the Jewish high priests and Jesus as high priest continues as we progress through the letter to the Hebrews (see also the discussions in previous weeks). Last week's reading introduced the comparison of Jesus with Melchizedek, who appears so suddenly in Genesis that he was believed to have no beginning and no end. This is behind today's claim that the priesthood of Jesus does not pass away. The intercessions of the Temple priests in Jerusalem were temporary, but those of

READING II Hebrews 7:23–28

A reading from the letter to the Hebrews.

Brothers and sisters:
The *levitical priests* were *many*
because they were prevented by *death* from *remaining* in office,
but *Jesus*, because he remains *forever*,
has a *priesthood* that does *not* pass *away*.
Therefore, he is *always* able to save those who approach God
through him,
since he lives *forever* to make *intercession* for them.

It was *fitting* that we should have such a high priest:
holy, *innocent*, *undefiled*, *separated* from sinners,
higher than the heavens.
He has *no need*, as did the high *priests*,
to offer sacrifice *day* after *day*,
first for his *own* sins and *then* for those of the *people*;
he did that *once* for all when he *offered himself*.

For the *law* appoints men subject to *weakness* to be high priests,
but the word of the *oath*, which was taken *after* the law,
appoints a *son*,
who has been made *perfect forever*.

Read each term separately in order to give each due emphasis.

Christ the high priest is unlike any other. He is the perfect Son, exalted with God.

Jesus go on forever, as long as people continue to call on his name.

Jesus is unlike the Jewish high priests in other ways as well. They were sinful; he is not. They repeated their sacrifices; his sacrifice of himself on the cross was made once and cannot be repeated. Again today, Jesus is proclaimed as "Son." This one is not like any other who has served in the high priestly office before, but is the chosen one, the intimate of God, who gave up his exalted state to humble himself for us.

Because the tradition of the high priest is somewhat unfamiliar to most Christians, this can be a confusing reading. Speak slowly and clearly. Emphasize the appropriateness of Jesus as the true high priest and his attributes—holiness and innocence—as well as the uniqueness of his sacrifice.

GOSPEL **The prayer from Deuteronomy quoted by Jesus in today's gospel, the Shema, is a community-forming recognition of the uniqueness of Israel's God and the special role of God's chosen people. It is part of Jewish daily prayer. Although the form of the prayer in the gospel of Mark differs slightly from that in Deuteronomy in its addition of a fourth category of devotion to God, the purpose of the various terms is not to differentiate aspects of the human person but to indicate that the entire person is to be devoted completely to God.**

The second commandment offered by Jesus is taken from the "holiness code" in

GOSPEL Mark 12:28b – 34

A reading from the holy gospel according to Mark.

One of the *scribes* came to Jesus and *asked* him,
"Which is the *first* of all the *commandments?*"

Jesus repeats Deuteronomy 6:4, but includes "with all your mind."

Jesus replied, "The *first* is *this:*
'Hear, O Israel!
The *LORD our God* is *LORD alone!*
You shall *love* the *LORD* your *God* with *all* your *heart,*
with *all* your *soul,*
with *all* your *mind,*
and with *all* your *strength.'*
The *second* is *this:*
'You shall love your *neighbor* as *yourself.'*
There is *no* other commandment *greater* than these."

Avoid the temptation to read the list in a sing-song manner.

The scribe said to him, *"Well said,* teacher.
You are *right* in saying,
'He is *One* and there is no *other* than he.'
And 'to *love* him with *all* your *heart,*
with *all* your *understanding,*
with *all* your *strength,*
and to *love* your *neighbor* as *yourself'*
is worth *more* than *all* burnt offerings and *sacrifices."*

The scribe zeroes in on the relative unimportance of worship to moral conduct. This does not make worship unimportant, but it remains secondary to love of God and neighbor.

And when Jesus saw that he answered with *understanding,*
he said to him,
"You are *not far* from the *kingdom* of *God."*
And no one *dared* to ask him any more *questions.*

The conversation resulted in an awed silence.

Leviticus, a compendium of general principles on how to be holy. The first and primary commandment involves relationship with God; the second looks toward others in the human community. This twofold emphasis is important for any age: Devotion to God is not genuine unless it involves love for neighbor. At the same time, commitment to others is incomplete without recognition of God as the source of all love. Note finally that the command from Leviticus asks that one love one's neighbor "as yourself." A genuine self-respect and regard for oneself gives rise to healthy relationships with others.

No teaching of Jesus could carry greater weight than that given today. Jesus' answer to the scribe indicates his love for the Law of Moses, as well as his ability to see the essentials of its regulations. But Jesus insists that all of the individual regulations must give way to the command to love. The scribe wisely recognizes the truth of Jesus' words, especially with regard to the Temple cult, and Jesus even compliments the scribe for his insight.

The challenge of Jesus' words is always with us. Proclaim to your community the centrality of the twofold command to love, and consider as well its fulfillment in your midst.

32ND SUNDAY IN ORDINARY TIME

Lectionary #155

READING I 1 Kings 17:10–16

A reading from the first book of Kings.

Elijah = ee-LĪ-juh
Zarephath = ZAYR-uh-fath

In those days, *Elijah* the *prophet* went to *Zarephath.*
As he arrived at the *entrance* of the city,
a *widow* was gathering *sticks* there; he *called* out to her,
"Please bring me a *small* cupful of *water* to drink."
She left to *get* it, and he called out *after* her,
"Please bring along a bit of *bread.*"

Elijah sounds demanding. Perhaps the woman recognizes him as a holy man as she seeks to provide for him. Allow the woman's exasperation, and then fear, to be heard.

She answered, "As the *LORD*, your God, *lives,*
I have *nothing baked*; there is only a *handful* of flour in my *jar*
and a little *oil* in my *jug.*
Just *now* I was collecting a couple of *sticks*,
to go in and *prepare* something for *myself* and my *son*;
when we have *eaten* it, we shall *die.*"

Elijah seeks to comfort the woman.

Elijah said to her, "Do *not* be *afraid.*
Go and do as you *propose.*
But *first* make me a little *cake* and *bring* it to me.
Then you can prepare something for yourself and your son.
For the *LORD*, the God of *Israel*, says,
'The jar of *flour* shall not go *empty*,
nor the jug of *oil* run *dry*,
until the *day* when the LORD sends *rain* upon the *earth.*'"

Again Elijah seems to think of himself first. This requires great faith and trust on the part of the woman, and she is rewarded in the end.

READING I The prophet Elijah stood up to King Ahab during a severe drought. Ahab had married the foreign Jezebel and introduced the worship of the god Baal, believed to control rain. Elijah asserted that the God of Israel was the only one in control of the world, including the weather. Although Elijah would eventually prove the superiority of the God of Israel, he first had to flee from Ahab, apparently for fear of his life. In the course of his flight, he met the widow of Zarephath, the story proclaimed today.

As it stands, the story is fairly straightforward: The man of God seeks assistance from a poor woman whose aid is rewarded. But the personalities are interesting. Elijah, apparently knowing that God will provide, is quite insistent, even demanding. The widow, crushed first by poverty and then by drought, tries to assist him but knows her limits. She believes that death is imminent. But by trusting Elijah's words and extending her generosity, she finds that her needs are met.

Read the dialogue between the widow and Elijah with plenty of expression in order to convey Elijah's initial insistence, the widow's fear and hesitation, and Elijah's words of comfort. Close with a tone of wonder at the fulfillment of Elijah's prediction.

READING II Here, in a nutshell, is the meaning of much of what we have heard from Hebrews over the last several weeks (see earlier weeks' discussions). What Christ did is compared with the action of the high priest at the Temple in

She *left* and *did* as Elijah had said.
She was able to eat for a *year*, and *he* and her *son* as well;
the jar of *flour* did *not* go *empty*,
nor the jug of *oil* run *dry*,
as the LORD had *foretold* through *Elijah*.

READING II Hebrews 9:24–28

A reading from the letter to the Hebrews.

This passage, building as it does on arguments already presented in Hebrews, is a difficult one to understand. Do not rush, but give your listeners plenty of time to grasp the points being made.

Christ did not enter into a sanctuary made by *hands*,
a *copy* of the true one, but *heaven itself*,
that he might now appear *before* God on *our behalf*.

The high priest offered the sacrifice of animals to atone for human sins. Christ offered his own body and shed his own blood on the cross.

Not that he might offer himself *repeatedly*,
as the high priest enters *each* year into the *sanctuary*
with *blood* that is not his *own*;
if *that* were so, he would have had to suffer *repeatedly*
from the *foundation* of the *world*.

But *now once* for *all* he has appeared at the *end* of the *ages*
to take away *sin* by his *sacrifice*.
Just as it is appointed that human *beings* die *once*,
and *after* this the *judgment*, so also *Christ*,
offered *once* to take away the sins of *many*,
will appear a *second* time, not to take away *sin*
but to bring *salvation* to those who eagerly *await* him.

The author held an active hope that Jesus would return soon in glory.

Jerusalem, but Christ's actions are considered far superior. The Temple itself is a copy of the true Temple in heaven, into which Christ has entered. The high priest entered the Holy of Holies annually on the Day of Atonement, but Jesus' sacrifice — his very life offered on the cross — was made once. That sacrifice is completely effective in atoning for sin and need not be repeated.

The final lines capitalize on the singular character of Christ's death, as well as those of all human beings. The idea of an immediate judgment after death is present. Christ, the passage concludes, has already taken away sin, but will return again to consummate the salvation already begun. It is both "already" and "not yet" — his singular death cannot be repeated, but there is more that awaits those who trust in him.

Your task today is to help your listeners understand the uniqueness of Christ's action. Reflect on the passage privately, then read it slowly and clearly, trusting that God speaks through you.

GOSPEL Today's gospel selection provides us with two challenges: humility and generosity. In the first section, Jesus criticizes the religious leaders for their pride and ostentation. How natural it is to seek recognition for one's accomplishments and honors! But such pride is to be condemned, insists Jesus. The scribes' high opinion of themselves may have been a contributing factor in their abuse of power and their willingness to take advantage of the widows — women without family members to provide for them who were therefore dependent on public

GOSPEL Mark 12:38–44

A reading from the holy gospel according to Mark.

In the course of his *teaching* Jesus said to the crowds,
"*Beware* of the *scribes,* who like to go around in *long robes*
and accept *greetings* in the marketplaces,
seats of *honor* in synagogues,
and places of *honor* at banquets.
They *devour* the houses of *widows* and, as a *pretext*
recite *lengthy* prayers.
They will receive a very *severe condemnation.*"

The scribes were entrusted with copying the scrolls of the Law. They were educated and respected for their knowledge of God's commands. Jesus suggests that some not only relished the attention and honor they received but even used their knowledge to take advantage of others.

He sat down *opposite* the treasury
and observed how the crowd put *money* into the treasury.
Many *rich* people put in *large* sums.
A poor *widow* also came and put in two *small coins* worth a few *cents.*
Calling his disciples to himself, he said to them,
"*Amen,* I *say* to you, this *poor widow* put in *more*
than *all* the *other* contributors to the treasury.
For *they* have all contributed from their *surplus* wealth,
but *she,* from her *poverty,* has contributed all she had,
her *whole livelihood.*"

The scene shifts, and this story recalls the generosity of the poor woman toward Elijah in the first reading.

Recall the words of Pope Paul VI: "Give not from your excess, but from your need."

[Shorter: Mark 12:41–44]

charity. The scribes' injustice is not only reprehensible behavior but is also a violation of the spirit of Mosaic Law.

It is not entirely clear how closely related the second account is to the first. It is possible that the widow's offering of two small coins to the Temple treasury illustrates precisely the point Jesus was trying to make in his criticism of the scribes. But Jesus does not actually praise the woman's action and might have considered encouragement of such an action one of the ways by which widows were robbed by the Temple establishment. The Greek indicates that the woman was destitute, and her offering was literally "her life." There may be an indication that her needs were so great that her simple offering would in fact result in her death.

Your task today is to challenge the members of your community to recognize their gifts and yet accept them with humility. Inspire them to be willing to give even when it hurts and, even more importantly, to strive to change unjust systems that allow the destitute to be further mistreated. Finally, be aware that you may be challenged as being like one of the "scribes." Strive to listen without defensiveness, so as to instruct.

33RD SUNDAY IN ORDINARY TIME

Lectionary #158

READING I Daniel 12:1–3

A reading from the book of the prophet Daniel.

In *those* days, *I Daniel,*
heard this *word* of the *LORD:*
"At *that* time there shall arise
Michael, the great *prince,*
guardian of your people;
it shall be a time *unsurpassed* in *distress*
since nations *began* until that time.
At *that* time your people shall *escape,*
everyone who is found written in the *book.*

"*Many* of those who *sleep* in the dust of the *earth* shall *awake;*
some shall *live forever,*
others shall be an everlasting *horror* and *disgrace.*

"But the *wise* shall shine *brightly*
like the *splendor* of the *firmament,*
and those who lead the *many* to *justice*
shall be like the *stars forever.*"

The archangel Michael has the dual roles of representing the people of Israel and protecting them.

The presence of a heavenly book of judgment is an ancient tradition.

Raise your voice in giving this promise, then lower it for the final phrase of this sentence.

The wise are those who agree with the author's view of resistance to the Syrians. Read these lines with joyful hope.

READING I In this passage from the book of Daniel there is an innovation in the belief system of the Hebrew people. Earlier thought held that death was a final life-extinguishing event, and that rewards or punishments occurred during one's lifetime or were visited upon one's children. As time passed, it became evident that such was not always the case: The good were not always rewarded and the wicked were not uniformly condemned. As a result, the idea of an afterlife developed. This passage is the first clear reference to an afterlife in the Hebrew tradition. Interestingly, it incorporates the idea of astral immortality: The stars in the sky are the spirits of the righteous dead.

Here, the end of the age is thought to be near, occasioned by the great persecution of the Jewish people under the Syrian ruler Antiochus IV Epiphanes. But the author asserts that those who trust in God will be protected and those who die will live. In fact, the tribulation described in the book of Daniel came to an end and resulted in a period of political independence and the restoration of Temple worship.

Offer this reading to your community as a proclamation of hope. Although our contemporary situation is different from that in Daniel, the words have a timeless quality. Remind your listeners that God cares for them, especially in times of trial, and that God's justice will indeed prevail.

READING II Hebrews 10:11–14, 18

A reading from the letter to the Hebrews.

Brothers and sisters:
Every priest stands *daily* at his *ministry*,
offering *frequently* those *same* sacrifices
that can *never* take away *sins.*

But *this* one offered *one* sacrifice for sins,
and *took* his seat *forever* at the *right* hand of *God*;
now he *waits* until his *enemies* are made his *footstool.*
For by *one* offering
he has made *perfect forever* those who are being *consecrated.*

Where there is *forgiveness* of these,
there is *no longer offering* for *sin.*

This is the language of exaltation. In being lifted up on the cross, Jesus was also raised to his rightful place at God's right hand, where he now reigns.

Pause before continuing. The final sentence indicates the result of Jesus' action, which makes the Temple cult unnecessary.

READING II Christ stands in the tradition of the priests of the Jerusalem Temple who offered sacrifices for the people of Israel. But the perfection of his sacrifice of himself on the cross eliminated guilt for sin, such that the sacrifice need never be repeated. As a result, he was exalted to the right hand of God and, in the words of Psalm 110, his enemies made a footstool for his feet.

For the author of Hebrews, the old cultic system is no longer in force because of the actions of Christ. The perfection brought about by his sacrifice lasts forever, thus making continued practice of the Jewish cult unnecessary. In its place is Christ's offering, an offering of his own body to atone for sins, an offering made once and resulting in his exaltation in heaven.

Read this selection as a statement of the uniqueness of Christ and a proclamation of the wondrous effects of his actions. As a result of his atoning sacrifice, humans need no longer be bound by sin or by human efforts to make amends for it. Reflect on this reality and your gratitude for his generous gift. Then convey your appreciation to your listeners.

GOSPEL The dire predictions given by Jesus in today's gospel, in a scene that immediately precedes the Last Supper and the account of Jesus' passion and death, are part of the so-called "Little Apocalypse" in Mark. Like other apocalyptic literature, it seeks to comfort a persecuted community by illustrating how God will judge the community's enemies

GOSPEL Mark 13:24–32

A reading from the holy gospel according to Mark.

Jesus said to his disciples:
"In *those* days after that *tribulation*
the *sun* will be *darkened*,
and the *moon* will not give its *light*,
and the *stars* will be *falling* from the sky,
and the *powers* in the heavens will be *shaken*.

Such cosmic disturbances are not unusual in descriptions of "end times."

"And then they will see 'the *Son* of *Man coming* in the clouds'
with great *power* and *glory*,
and then he will *send* out the *angels*
and *gather* his *elect* from the four winds,
from the *end* of the earth to the *end* of the sky.

The tone is a bit lighter here; speak in a calm voice. This is Jesus' lesson about the implications of current events.

"Learn a *lesson* from the *fig* tree.
When its branch becomes *tender* and sprouts *leaves*,
you know that *summer* is near.
In the *same* way, when you see *these things* happening,
know that he is *near*, at the *gates*.

"*Amen*, I say to you,
this *generation* will not *pass away*
until *all* these things have taken *place*.
Heaven and *earth* will pass away,
but *my words* will *not* pass away.

The message changes here. Pause, then read this final sentence slowly and clearly.

"But of *that* day or hour, *no* one *knows*,
neither the *angels* in heaven, nor the *Son*, but *only*
the *Father*."

and eventually reign victorious, despite the calamities of the present moment.

As such, it is written especially for the first recipients of this gospel, who were experiencing upheaval, both externally and within the community. The Jewish uprising against Roman occupation is in mind here. In addition, there were some who had entered the community of Jesus' followers who used the events of the war to claim that the second coming of Jesus was imminent. These words are thus attributed to Jesus, and he claims that such signs indeed indicate the beginning of the end. But no one can predict when the Messiah will appear to draw the present age to a close.

Despite the speculation that has accompanied the end of a millennium, such imagery is foreign to our everyday lives. At the same time, the lessons included in today's reading are timeless. Current events can indeed serve to "predict" the future, if only people would be attentive to their implications. This is precisely what characterized the classical prophets: They were people who looked closely at present conditions with an eye toward their future ramifications. At the same time, false teachers are those who seem too confident in their predictions. Only God knows what will really happen in the future. The original community that received this gospel is instructed not to speculate too confidently about what is to come, nor to be passive and ignore the lessons of today.

Offer this reading to your community as a call to be truly prophetic: to reflect on events of today without attempting to usurp God's role in governing the future. Today's gospel calls us to be both knowledgeable and willing to trust in the providence of God.

NOVEMBER 26, 2000

CHRIST THE KING

Lectionary #161

READING I Daniel 7:13–14

A reading from the book of the prophet Daniel.

The human figure, representing Israel, is presented before God and given great honor and authority. Proclaim from here until the end with rising intensity and excitement in your voice.

As the *visions* during the night *continued*,
I saw *one* like a *son* of *man coming*,
on the *clouds* of *heaven*;
when he reached the *Ancient One*
and was presented *before* him,
the *one* like a *son* of *man* received *dominion*,
glory, and *kingship*;
all *peoples*, *nations*, and *languages serve* him.
His *dominion* is an *everlasting* dominion
that shall *not* be taken *away*,
his *kingship* shall *not* be *destroyed*.

READING II Revelation 1:5–8

Note that it is "Revelation" (singular), not "Revelations."

A reading from the book of Revelation.

Jesus Christ is the *faithful witness*,
the *firstborn* of the dead and *ruler* of the *kings* of the *earth*.
To him who *loves* us and has *freed* us from our *sins* by his *blood*,
who has made us into a *kingdom*,
priests for his *God* and *Father*,
to *him* be *glory* and *power forever* and *ever*. *Amen*.

Build up to and then pause after "Amen."

READING I Daniel's vision offers comfort to Israel as it is persecuted by the Syrians, whose king desecrated the Temple in Jerusalem. The figure of the human one enthroned in glory represents faithful Israel. It came to be applied to the expected Messiah, who would bring about God's judgment. Christians see this as fulfilled in the person of Jesus.

This is a message of triumph and praise. Read it with joy and confidence.

READING II The book of Revelation, like the book of Daniel, is apocalyptic literature, written to comfort a people struggling with oppression. This difficult reading opens with a word of praise and honor to Jesus. His death, which demonstrates his love for us, also results in the formation of a community of dual significance: a royal people deserving of honor, and a priestly people active in worship. Next, the vision from Daniel 7 is applied to his return in glory, a return that will reveal his authority and his power to all people.

Finally, God speaks, claiming dominion. Alpha and omega are the first and last letters of the Greek alphabet; the point is that God is the beginning and the end of everything, the source and summation of all that is.

Read this passage several times until you are comfortable with it. Proclaim it as a word of triumph and praise, but with all due gravity and majesty as well, especially in the last line.

GOSPEL On this feast of Christ the King, the readings celebrate the authority of God and the Messiah enthroned with him. But the words of Jesus himself seem to refute the claim that he has

Speak this a bit breathlessly, as if pointing out a spectacular phenomenon to others.

Behold, he is *coming* amid the *clouds,*
and *every* eye will *see* him,
even those who *pierced* him.
All the peoples of the *earth* will *lament* him.
Yes. Amen.

Pause again after "Amen," then continue with great solemnity, pausing briefly after "is," "was," and "come."

"I am the *Alpha* and the *Omega,*" says the *Lord God,*
"the one who *is* and who *was* and who is to *come,* the *almighty.*"

GOSPEL John 18:33b – 37

A reading from the holy gospel according to John.

Pilate said to *Jesus,*
"Are you the *King* of the *Jews?*"
Jesus answered, "Do you say this on your *own*
or have *others* told you about me?"
Pilate answered, "*I* am not a Jew, *am* I?

Pilate confirms that Jesus' own people have accused him, failing to recognize his significance.

Your *own* nation and the *chief priests* handed you *over* to me.
What have you *done?*"

The author reinterprets the "kingdom." Christianity is not political or military. Stress the negatives.

Jesus answered, "*My kingdom* does not belong to *this world.*
If my *kingdom did* belong to this world,
my *attendants* would be *fighting*
to *keep* me from being handed *over* to the *Jews.*
But as it *is,* my kingdom is *not* here."

Strongly emphasize "are."

So Pilate said to him, "Then you *are* a king?"

Jesus proclaims something by avoiding a question. His kingdom is one in which truth reigns supreme.

Jesus answered, "*You* say I am a *king.*
For *this* I was born and for *this* I came into the world,
to *testify* to the *truth.*
Everyone who *belongs* to the truth *listens* to my voice."

royal authority. Jesus does not deny the title "King of the Jews"; indeed he seems to claim it. But he denies its political force: "My kingdom is not of this world." His followers, he says, do not exercise violent means to free him, as they would if he were an earthly king. Instead his purpose is to bear witness to the truth.

The story as told in the Fourth Gospel places responsibility for Jesus' condemnation squarely on the shoulders of the Jewish authorities. They have reported the claim to Pilate, pressing for a punishment of death that they themselves could not impose. They have completely misunderstood Jesus, his significance and the meaning of the title when applied to him.

Behind this portrayal of "the Jews" is the community for which this gospel was written, which was apparently expelled from the synagogue by the Jewish authorities, who did not accept Christian claims about Jesus. The harsh portrayal of "the Jews" does not include all Jews (the author and the community were themselves Jewish), but only those who rejected the Christian interpretation of Jesus' significance.

As so often in the gospel of John, Jesus responds by pointing to himself as the one who reveals something about God. He directs attention *beyond* himself by calling attention *to* himself. His very person and life are the revelation of God.

Today's gospel provides us with a wonderful opportunity to reflect on what it means to claim that Christ is king. Read it as high drama, and challenge your community to be among those who listen to his voice and therefore belong to the truth.